Saskatchewan Writers
LIVES PAST AND PRESENT

Saskatchewan Writers

LIVES PAST AND PRESENT

Series Editor
Brian Mlazgar

Volume Editor
Heather Hodgson

2004

Copyright © 2004 Canadian Plains Research Center, University of Regina

Copyright Notice
All rights reserved. No part of this work covered by the copyrights hereon may be reproduced or used in any form or by any means—graphic, electronic, or mechanical—without the prior written permission of the publisher. Any request for photocopying, recording, taping or placement in information storage and retrieval systems of any part of this book shall be directed in writing to the Canadian Reprography Collective.

Canadian Plains Research Center
University of Regina
Regina, Saskatchewan S4S 0A2
Canada
Tel: (306) 585-4758
Fax: (306) 585-4699
e-mail: canadian.plains@uregina.ca
http://www.cprc.uregina.ca

Library and Archives Canada Cataloguing in Publication

Saskatchewan writers : lives past and present / editor, Heather Hodgson.

(TBS ; 13)
ISBN 0-88977-163-4

1. Authors, Canadian (English)—Saskatchewan—Biography. 2. Canadian literature (English)—Saskatchewan—History and criticism. 3. Saskatchewan—Intellectual life. I. Hodgson, Heather, 1957- II. University of Regina. Canadian Plains Research Center. III. Series.

PS8081.1.S27 2004   C810.9'97124   C2004-905256-X

Cover design: Brian Danchuk Design
Printed and bound in Canada by Houghton Boston, Saskatoon
Printed on acid-free paper

We gratefully acknowledge the financial support of the following:
• The Government of Canada through the Book Publishing Industry Development Program (BPIDP)
• The Cultural Industries Development Fund, Government of Saskatchewan

—TABLE OF CONTENTS—

Preface vi
   Series Editor, Brian Mlazgar

Preface viii
   Volume Editor, Heather Hodgson

Introduction: Lives of the Writers of Saskatchewan...........................xii
   David Carpenter

Saskatchewan's Writers...1
   listed alphabetically

Appendix A: Contributors 245

Appendix B: Instructors who fostered writing in Saskatchewan 247

—PREFACE—

Series Editor, Brian Mlazgar

Saskatchewan's provincial motto, *Multis E Gentibus Vires/From Many Peoples, Strength*, is very much in keeping with the philosophy that lies behind the development of the "Saskatchewan Lives Past and Present" book series, to which the present volume belongs.

Over the course of nearly two decades of publishing books about the prairie region, and more specifically Saskatchewan, I have become increasingly concerned about the paucity of information available about the people who helped to build this province. To be sure, almost everyone has heard of Tommy Douglas and John Diefenbaker, and biographies of prominent (mainly political) figures have occasionally been published over the years. Such biographies, however, fail to recognize the countless, lesser-known individuals who often laboured their entire lives in semi-anonymity, tirelessly contributing to the development and enrichment of their communities.

With this in mind, I decided that it would be appropriate for the Canadian Plains Research Center to launch the "Saskatchewan Lives" book series. Inaugurating the series, however, proved to be far easier than actually deciding what—and who—would be included. Our original list included eighteen possible books. Due to a variety of budgetary, editorial and temporal constraints, we were obliged to focus on five titles that will be published in 2004–2005:

- *Saskatchewan Agriculture: Lives Past and Present*, edited by Lisa Dale-Burnett, focuses on Saskatchewan men and women over the past century who were dedicated to building agricultural communities as well as agriculture itself.
- *Saskatchewan First Nations: Lives Past and Present*, edited by Christian Thompson, recognizes and celebrates the vital and ever-growing contributions of First Nations people to this province and its cultural mosaic.
- *Saskatchewan Politicians: Lives Past and Present*, edited by Brett Quiring, includes, by necessity, only a fraction of the many men and women—some quite famous, some infamous—who have held political office in the province over the past one hundred years.
- *Saskatchewan Sports: Lives Past and Present*, edited by Tim Switzer, applauds the sports figures who have consistently allowed this province to achieve successes on the "playing field" far beyond what would be expected from our small population.
- *Saskatchewan Writers: Lives Past and Present*, edited by Heather Hodgson, features many men and women whose writing has at some point been nurtured by the richness of the Saskatchewan landscape and by the vibrant writing community in the province.

Books of this nature must, by necessity, be developed using some sort of selection process. The editor's preface in each volume outlines the criteria used for that particular book, as well as any factors which prevented inclusion of some individuals who would otherwise have "qualified." Readers are invited to contact the publisher directly with suggestions for future, supplementary volumes.

Because we wanted to include in these volumes not only those who are already well-known in their field, but also many who are lesser-known but who have nonetheless contributed much to the province, the individual biographies are relatively brief and ought not, therefore, to be considered as definitive biographies. Rather, they are designed to increase awareness, stimulate interest, and promote further research.

I would like to extend my appreciation to the editors who helped to compile these books, to the CPRC staff who checked facts where necessary, and did the copy-editing, layout, and design. I also want to acknowledge the funding agencies (listed on the copyright page) without whose support the development of these books would not have been possible. Finally, I want to extend my deepest thanks to the hundreds of individuals who voluntarily wrote entries for this book series. Through their collective efforts they have demonstrated, yet again, the wisdom of our provincial motto: *Multis E Gentibus Vires/From Many Peoples, Strength*. Quite simply, in Saskatchewan, this is how things are done.

As Saskatchewan approaches the 100th anniversary of its formation as a province in 2005, it is fitting that its citizens reflect on those whose contributions and accomplishments have created and nurtured the culture and society of this place we call home. It is hoped that this series of books will help, in some small measure, to accomplish that.

—PREFACE—

Volume Editor, Heather Hodgson

This volume collects biographies of Saskatchewan's creative writers and poets, which in turn contributes to the province's literary history. While our extremes in climate, our vast spaces, and our small population might be thought to hinder creativity, they seem, in fact, to nourish it in Saskatchewan's writers. In the same way that adversity sweetens the grape elsewhere, it nourishes the muse here.

David Carpenter, who for decades has been actively involved in Saskatchewan's literary scene, introduces this volume. An award-winning author and poet, with many books to his credit, "Carp" has taught and mentored writers all across the country. The two of us developed the "criteria for inclusion" for the biographies in this book and agreed that writers had to have published at least one book of a certain length in one of the genres of poetry, fiction, or creative non-fiction, by an established publisher. An invitation was then sent out to those who qualified and when the mail began to arrive (by post and electronically), I worked with the authors to prepare their biographies for the book. I also sent batches of biographies to David while he was writing his Introduction.

By and large the entries herein are first-person narratives in that most of the biographies were written by the authors themselves. So in fact they are *auto*biographical which makes for a unique and distinctive book in itself. Herein we witness as we read the diversity of the lives centred in writing, and we also hear the distinctive voice of each writer. Some entries, of course, had to be written by others. Contributing writers are acknowledged at the end of the biography and information about each contributor can be found in Appendix A on pages 245 and 246.

The photographs that accompany the biographies are the result of my request to authors to "send a photo of the quintessential you." What arrived varied from the serious to the ironic, to the comical, and even the surreal. Unfortunately, I could not get photographs for every writer. In the case of Sarah Binks (for obvious reasons) I was grateful for the artistry of Paul Denham who sketched the "Sweet Songstress of Saskatchewan" especially for this book. While most of the writers chose the photos they sent to me, some were obtained from publishers and the Internet.

At an early stage of compiling and editing this book, I hoped to include each writer's complete bibliography but the lists proved somewhat cumbersome. Instead, titles of major works are integrated directly into the narratives.

My work with the writers reacquainted me with many I first met at Fort San in 1982 when I was a student of poetry there. It was a memorable summer and for that reason, a short note about my *own* experience—if only as a prism to refract some shared memories with others in this book—does not seem out of place here.

I was once a student in a grade ten English class taught by Gary Hyland, in Moose Jaw. Gary taught us to experience the hard-won satisfaction to be achieved through honing our writing skills. We wrote weekly creative journals in his classes and that, for many students, opened up a whole new world of possibility for expression. His enthusiasm for literature and poetry and especially for creative writing was both contagious and unforgettable, so he left a lasting impression on all of us.

More than a decade later, I ran into Gary again—this time as an aspiring poet in one of his writing workshops at Fort San. By then I had met Anne Szumagalski. She was the Writer-in-Residence at the Public Library in Saskatoon where I was a third-year English major at the University of Saskatchewan. After we talked about my writing she was adamant that I "*must* go to Fort San!" and before I knew it, she was on the phone to someone on my behalf. That was the day I was *smuggled* into the Summer School of the Arts (the deadline for admission had passed), and after Anne hung up I learned it was Gary Hyland who had answered her call. My first creative writing workshop at Fort San was an Introduction to Creative Writing; after completing it, I registered in Joe Rosenblatt's Advanced Poetry workshop.

Fort San was part school of the arts and part myth. In the rooms of the former sanitarium where we slept and dreamed, and where we struggled alone with our notepads and pens and typewriters, there were rumours of ghosts. It was also the place where many of us began seriously to hone our skills as writers—the place where many now-established Canadian writers and poets spent summers as students or instructors. Many friendships began at Fort San; hence the collective affection for the place. But the luxury of a writing retreat like it or Sage Hill or St. Peter's Colony is found in the fact that such sanctuaries guarantee long, relatively empty hours to devote to nothing but writing. They are days that end, invariably, with good food (Spike's Pizza was one of the rites of passage at Fort San), good company, and conversation. There are magical evenings too: readings, storytelling, music, and often, much laughter. I won't forget the night a dozen or so of us climbed a hill to lie on our backs and watch a lunar eclipse.

Alas, good things come to an end, but what is worthwhile is sometimes renewed. Fort San closed but other sanctuaries keep the tradition of fostering writing in this province alive: St. Peter's, the Sage Hill Writing Experience, the Kenderdine Emma Lake Campus, Riverhurst on Lake Diefenbaker, and "The Quest" at Christopher Lake. "Urban retreats" were also founded so that writers in Saskatoon and Regina could apply for and have access to offices to use as individual retreats.

The writing instructors, too, are to be credited for the renewal of the tradition of fostering writing in Saskatchewan. Without their mentoring, guidance, and support of writers and the arts, this might be a much colder place to live and write. With gratitude to their efforts, the names of those instructors are listed in Appendix B on page 247.

Writers and poets know first-hand what inspires them and what they must do to get their stories, novels, and poems written. For that reason, I asked all of those in this book to include some words of wisdom *about writing* in their biographies. Their responses range from the philosophical to the practical, and from the instructive to the humorous, but *all* of them are about some aspect of the *craft* or *work* or *joy* or *hell* of writing, and they are words that do indeed inspire!

On the wall beside my desk at home are the words of John Sheffield, from his 1682 *Essay on Poetry*. They are words which inspire me:

Of all those arts
in which the wise excel,
Nature's chief masterpiece
is writing well.

Elegant, poetic, true. Beautifully ordered words can make one forget, for a few moments, that *writing well* is also difficult, lonely, and more often than not, extremely frustrating! Thankfully, the rewards of such a struggle are many: the camaraderie provided through membership in writing groups, the public readings and public affirmation provided to writers at book awards. All deliver the comfort of being part of a community of like-minded people: writers, poets and readers!

Quite apart from reading the literature they produce, I also simply love the company of writers. Their keen sense of the need to transgress and extend boundaries—not the least of which is language itself—and their creative ways in doing so, make writers some of the most vital and interesting people I know. And I concur with Brenda Niskala who in her biography in this book says: "Hanging out with writers keeps you young!"

It has been my pleasure to get to know some of the writers in this book for the first time, and I have been grateful to encounter old friends, too—especially a few I've not seen since I was at Fort San in 1982. For that reason, editing this book has been something of a homecoming for me. *And those who edit also serve!*

—ACKNOWLEDGEMENTS—

My special thanks to my old friend and partner in this venture, David Carpenter. I'm also grateful to to Byrna Barclay, Marion Beck, Nik Burton, Ven Begamudré, Lorna Crozier, Paul Denham, Craig Grant, Gary Hyland, Don Kerr, Bill Klebeck, Pat Krause, Amy Nelson-Mile, Brenda Niskala, Dolores Reimer, Steven Ross Smith, Shelley Sopher, Paul Wilson, Joyce Wells, and others who wrote biographies, or tracked down information, addresses, and phone numbers for writers and poets I had trouble finding on my own.

Brian Mlazgar of the Canadian Plains Research Center asked me to take on this project. Fiona Stevenson, also of the CPRC, provided all kinds of support. This book owes its aesthetic appeal to the talents and good taste of Donna Achtzehner of the CPRC, whose sharp eye in her role of copy editor improved the text in many ways. Thank you, Donna!

—THANKS TO THE WRITERS AND POETS—

For all of the pitfalls of and complaints about electronic mail, without it, this book would not have been completed in the time it was. Although busy with their own lives and writing projects, the writers included in this book did their best to be prompt in responding to the call for biographies.

Despite the efforts of many, some writers and poets are missing from this book and while initial deadlines were g-e-n-e-r-o-u-s-l-y s-t-r-e-t-c-h-e-d, a few potential contributors could not meet them. Regarding the short biographies written by me, Nik Burton, Paul Wilson, and others, we did our best to find the most current information we could about the authors we wrote about. I hope those missing in this volume might be included in a future edition should there be one.

Heather Hodgson

—LIVES OF THE WRITERS OF SASKATCHEWAN—

This volume of biographies was commissioned by the Canadian Plains Research Center, who handed the job to Heather Hodgson, who has ridden herd on hundreds of maverick authors and me to complete the project. Most of these bios are autobiographical, even the ones written in the third person, but there are some obvious exceptions. The bios of deceased writers have been farmed out or written by Heather. There were also a number of writers whom we tried without success to contact, and these too were written by other writers.

We have gone a long way to be inclusive in this book in order to document the vibrant and engaging literature this province has nurtured; and the many ways in which this province has, in turn, been heralded (mythicized, satirized, memorialized, recreated, reinvented, reflected, cursed, and blessed) by its writers. If writers lived here, if their books were published, we did our best to include them.

Wallace Stegner, to my knowledge, never was a Canadian citizen, but growing up in southwestern Saskatchewan was the central informing experience of his life as a writer. So he's in here. Robert Kroetsch never actually resided in Saskatchewan for more than a month at a time. But his experiences here at Sage Hill and the Saskatchewan School of the Arts have given birth to quite a range of poems and stories. As well, his many residencies here have stretched over three decades. As I write this, he is at Sage Hill reading a big stack of novel manuscripts.

We have tried to include as many writers as we could account for whose books have reached some level of professional standing. This includes former Saskatchewan writers like John Newlove, T(Ed) Dyck, Lorna Crozier, and Ian Adam, who left the province to live elsewhere. It includes writers born and raised in other countries (Ven Begamudré, Dave Margoshes or Anne Szumigalski, for instance) who came here to live and write.

Excluded from here are writers whose books haven't (yet) hit the shelves, writers from disciplines outside of literature, and writers resident in Saskatchewan whose experience has not (yet) entered into their work.

Even so, there will be many arguments about what sort of work should be included. For example, what constitutes literary writing? Anything in book form that has to do with literature? I would say no, but we've tried to keep this category as broad as possible without losing all sense of what literature has been to us throughout our lives. We've gone beyond the usual genres (poetry, prose fiction, drama) to include quite a variety of writers of literary nonfiction. This broad category includes writers of creative nonfiction (Anne Campbell, for example, or Kristjana Gunnars), but perhaps a larger number of nonfiction writers who fall outside this distinctive category.

Robert Calder's books would not be classified as works of creative nonfiction, but because he writes engaging narratives, they certainly qualify as literary writing. (The Governor General's committee for nonfiction seemed to think so.) Calder is included here, then, not because he was an academic writing about literature, but because he has distinguished himself as a writer, and because some of his best writing arises out of his Saskatchewan experience. One could advance similar arguments for the narratives of Maggie Siggins and Trevor Herriot.

I am very impressed with the work Heather has devoted to this book in my small role as her literary adviser. Her labours have given us a valuable tool of reference for anyone who wants to know about our writers. But most of all, this volume constitutes a sort of proclamation of our existence as a cultural community. Saskatchewan has become well known for its wheat and canola, its hockey players, its potash mines, its appalling gift of uranium to the world, its curlers, and most recently for its amateur football teams and diamond deposits. The time has come to chronicle Saskatchewan's books and the people who made them.

The writers whose lives are told in these pages are part of an extraordinary cultural community that has touched and been touched by the people and landscape of this province. There was a time in Saskatchewan when our writers could not conceive of actually living here for very long. Our best and brightest (W.O. Mitchell, Eli Mandel, Sinclair Ross, for example) got out as soon as they could, and hauled the memory of their birthplace along with them to more hospitable lands.

In the late sixties and early seventies, however, everything changed when some scribes all over the province began to organize themselves into a community of writers. Ken Mitchell, Pat Krause, Lois Simmie, Geoffrey Ursell, Barbara Sapergia, Anne Szumigalski, Bob Currie, Caroline Heath, and Gary Hyland are the names most frequently mentioned. These writers realized that with the help of the Saskatchewan Arts Board and the Canada Council, and with their own sometimes heroic efforts, they could not only afford to live as writers in Saskatchewan, but they could create a vibrant and supportive literary society that flourishes to this day.

In the thirties, forties, and fifties, this province, in all its drought-stricken glory, inspired some pretty memorable literature. It was blessed with the first arts board in North America. But it wasn't until Ken Mitchell and company mobilized that we had a genuine literary community. What followed from their efforts, in no particular order, was: 1) our country's first system of writers' retreats; 2) the Saskatchewan Writers' Guild; 3) the Saskatchewan School of the Arts (which has morphed into the Sage Hill Writing Experience); 4) several literary publishers (Coteau Books and Thistledown Press, for example); 5) several venerable literary magazines (*Grain* is the best example); 6) the Saskatchewan Playwright's Centre; and 7) a rich assortment of writers' groups across the province with such names as The Poets' Coterie, The Bombay Bicycle Club, and The Moose Jaw Movement.

When my father was a boy, Saskatchewan had just about one million people. Almost a century later, it still has about a million people. In years like this one, the year of the Mad Cow Scare, we export more people than cattle. Economically and politically, we are

Alberta's opposite. We have a grain and cattle economy, a resource economy that in most years is so uncertain that breaking even is equated with success. How do you nurture a literary culture in this fragile ecology?

The same way you build a co-op, I suppose. Too much isolation spells doom for farmers, ranchers, rural communities, and artists. Inclusion of writers in this list may seem at odds with the popular notion of the writer as rugged individualist. After all, we work alone; writing is not a team sport. But we write in (not aloof from) a community, a place that nurtures and inspires us. When we need an intelligent opinion on a manuscript that is troubling us, we now have people to go to. When our agents and publishers are giving us grief, we have friends to phone up. When we're trying to improve our lot or learn more about the trade, there are people further along than we are to consult with, university creative writing courses and workshops to go to (Sage Hill is a shining example). When we need long uninterrupted stretches of writing time free of other responsibilities, there are group retreats for us in various peaceful rural settings (St. Peter's Abbey is my favourite). Even now, in much of Saskatchewan, if the enterprise is going to flourish, the crop is going to get planted or go to market, the job is going to get done, you need to organize your community, and everyone seems to benefit from this arrangement. When a writer in the community is in trouble, you answer the call.

If this sounds a bit like Saskatchewan chauvinism, it's because I'm writing this from Moose Jaw. Blame it on Moose Jaw. I am participating in their annual literary festival, which is organized by Gary Hyland and his army of 150 volunteers. There will be dancing, exotic suppers at Nit's, challenging questions from one writer to another that begin with phrases like *Where do you get off sayin' somethin' like*.... There will be flirtations, squabbling, egos soaring and deflating like circus tents, songs by Nancy White, eloquent dialogues with Yann Martel, Phil Hall, Tom Wayman, Guy Vanderhaeghe, Dennis Lee, Sue Goyette and dozens of other luminaries; there will be deals made, memorable readings, exchanges of books with inscriptions like *For _____, who was there for me when the shit hit the fan*; there will be political spats, films to view and their makers present to talk about the making of them, a tribute to Peter Gzowski with anecdotes from his daughter Alison and from Shelagh Rogers, debates over the limits of agnosticism, and a whole lot of belly laughter. Whether as a presenter or a literary tourist, I never fail to have a great time down here.

It seems appropriate to be writing these words in Moose Jaw, where so many of our writers began their careers and in some cases continue to write. With each reading, with each round of applause from the audience, the festival re-enacts and re-affirms Saskatchewan literary history. The people in this book put on quite a party.

David Carpenter, July 2003

Saskatchewan's Writers

MARK ABLEY was born in England and has lived for many years in Montreal, but he still prefers to say he's "from Saskatchewan." He wonders now if that's wishful thinking on his part.

It was 1967 when his parents moved to Saskatoon. He was a rootless boy of twelve who had lived in the English Midlands, northern Ontario, and southern Alberta. Almost from the start, he felt at home in Saskatoon. At City Park Collegiate he was lucky enough to come under the influence of Frank Roy, a truly great English teacher— Frank had a passion for birds as well as words, and each spring he would drive a few students along the riverbank and out to the sloughs north of town in search of dowitchers, godwits, longspurs, and the like. Under his tutelage Abley grew to love the prairies.

In 1971 he began to study Honours English at the University of Saskatchewan. There too he encountered some excellent teachers (along with a few duds). More important, he joined the Saskatoon Poetry Group—not that they thought of themselves in capital letters— learning his craft in the company of writers like Anne Szumigalski, Terry Heath, Caroline Heath, Lois Simmie, Nancy Senior and S. Padmanabh. Abley's first prose publication was in *Blue Jay*, the magazine of the Saskatchewan Natural History Society; his first poems saw the light of day in *Saskatoon Poetry Now*, *Salt*, and *Grain*. Some of Abley's friends were actors, others painters; his own father was a musician. It never occurred to him to doubt what a previous generation had struggled so hard to believe: that art of the highest quality could emerge from Saskatchewan.

MARK ABLEY

But Abley was young and hungry, and he wanted to see more of the world. He won a scholarship to study in England, and when he came back to Canada he began to earn a living as a freelance writer. That meant being close to editors and publishers; it meant living in the east; or, he asks himself now, did it just mean that he had grown intoxicated by the cultural and other pleasures of big cities? Whatever the reason, his home after 1977 was always somewhere else. He became a contributing editor of *Maclean's* and *Saturday Night*; he wrote and narrated several programs for CBC Radio's *Ideas*; eventually he joined the *Montreal Gazette*, first as a feature writer, later as book-review editor and literary columnist. In 1996 he won a National Newspaper Award for critical writing.

Abley has written or edited nine books, some of which have no direct or obvious connection with Saskatchewan; but if you look for them, the links are there. The central figure in his children's picture book, *Ghost Cat*, is an elderly lady of socialist convictions whose beloved cat has the name of Saskatchewan's greatest premier, Tommy Douglas. A poem in his first collection, *Blue Sand, Blue Moon*, was dedicated to Anne Szumigalski; a poem in his second collection, *Glasburyon*, is in memory of Caroline Heath; more recently, his poem "The Ruff" served as a frontispiece for that long awaited and much needed volume, *The Birds of Saskatoon*.

Abley's need to make a kind of peace with the prairies—to understand, retroactively, why he felt he had to leave—provided the psychological underpinning for his first book of prose, *Beyond Forget: Rediscovering the Prairies* (1986). In it he revisited a few places he had known, and also explored towns and landscapes he'd never seen when he lived in Saskatchewan and Alberta. Abley tried to cast a cool, unsentimental eye on things but now feels that he was probably unfair to the region—Frank Roy, his first mentor, certainly thought so. There was, perhaps, too much of Abley in the book, his own anxieties and insecurities, and too little of the people he was ostensibly describing. By 1989, when he wrote a text to accompany a book of photographs by Ottmar Bierwagen—it was published under the title *Heartland: Prairie Portraits and Landscapes*—he was already trying to make amends.

Fast forward a decade. In 2000 Abley began work on a major prose work about the disappearance of minority languages in many countries. The book, which involved travel as far afield as Baffin Island and the Isle of Man, northern Australia and southern France, would be published three years later under the title *Spoken Here: Travels Among Threatened Languages*. (Of Saskatchewan's aboriginal languages, Cree and Michif make brief appearances.) Just before *Spoken Here* saw the light of day, Abley quit the *Montreal Gazette* and returned to a freelance life.

His most direct connection with Saskatchewan today arises from his work as Anne Szumigalski's literary executor. Anne adored the province, and her love shines through in many of her poems. From time to time Abley returns to her adopted city. Though he may not feel entirely at home there, he doesn't feel a stranger, either. "How could I?" he asks: "Saskatoon made me."

About Writing... *There's a sense in which it scarcely matters whether you're writing fiction or nonfiction, prose or poetry, adult or children's literature. Some of the most urgent qualities in any good book transcend all those divisions. To write with both control and passion; to use the most vivid, evocative details and images; to make the reader see and feel the world anew—these are, or should be, constant goals.*—MARK ABLEY

IAN ADAM was born in Cabri in 1932, where his parents met and courted in the 1920s. His father, Stuart, a then recently arrived dentist, was the son of a Presbyterian minister who had emigrated from Scotland; his mother, Damienne, was a registered nurse and the daughter of an unfrocked Catholic priest from a francophone community in Quebec. Perhaps not surprisingly, Ian and his brother Kenneth were raised as free-thinkers, independent of religious creed. The history of his mother's family is given in rich detail in *As I Remember Them* (2002), written by her sister Jeanne Olsen and edited by Adam and a cousin for the University of Calgary Press.

After his first twelve years under the

IAN ADAM...ON A BEACH AT POINT NO POINT, ON THE JUAN DE FUCA STRAIT, SOUTHWESTERN VANCOUVER ISLAND.

stupendous Saskatchewan skies, Adam's family moved to Ponoka, Alberta. The striking contrast between the grand austerities of the first landscape and the parkland fecundities of the second imprinted itself on Adam's imagination and has persistently haunted him. In both Saskatchewan and Alberta, the influence of his parents was also striking: from his father he absorbed an interest in the outdoors, which found expression in hunting, in wanderings in the countryside, and in investigations of flora and fauna. Through his mother he was exposed to a well-stocked library, musical training, and the rigours of debate.

In the summers Adam was engaged variously as labourer for the CPR, gravel checker in Menaik, Alberta, and paving inspector out of Pincher Creek. Those who travel the highway from Pincher Creek to Waterton move along a route he trudged. Summer employment continued during university in the early 1950s. His experience with gravel and asphalt earned him enough *cachet* to move onward and upward to concrete as he was deemed qualified to inspect the curbs and gutters of roads in the booming city of Edmonton. This employ was followed by work as a journalist, a manual labourer, and attendant at the psychiatric hospital in Ponoka.

Adam attended the University of Alberta majoring in Honours English with a minor in French. Throughout he was engaged in creative projects but in a fairly haphazard fashion. Briefly auditing one of F.M. Salter's pioneering classes in creative writing, he never applied to be one of Salter's students. Adam graduated in 1955, spent a year as a sessional lecturer, and then left for the University of London supported by an I.O.D.E. scholarship. He received his M.A. at London in 1960.

At this time he was married and had a child, so he felt an urgent need for paid employment. The University of Calgary, newly established, provided the position where Adam became an Assistant Professor of English. The small size of the department in those early years necessitated teaching in several areas, so Adam enjoyed the opportunity to range widely over the canon. He eventually focused on Commonwealth and Western Canadian literature, and poetry.

Adam continued to write poetry. He had never previously sought its publication, but in the mid-1960s, when he was an editor with *Edge* magazine (which ran from 1964 to 1969, and was Western Canada's first "little magazine"), he began to send out material in a tentative manner. Louis Dudek at *Delta* and Dorothy Livesay at *Prism International* were first to publish his poems. Since then he has published some 150 poems in journals and anthologies including *Dandelion, Grain, Prairie Fire, Mattoid, Textual Studies in Canada*, and *The Wascana Poetry Anthology*. His work has been broadcast on CBC Alberta, CBC Saskatchewan, and CBC Radio 1. His book, *Encounter*, was published in 1973, and a second, *Songs from the Star Motel*, appeared in 1987. A third, tentatively titled *Nomadic*, is due in autumn of 2003. Adam writes in lyrical and in longer modes, the latter often narrative; much of his work draws on his experiences in the west. He retired from the university in 1997 to work full-time as a writer and literary consultant. His current projects include an autobiographical manuscript and a further gathering of long poems.

Adam finds it difficult to speak of "influences" on writing when he contemplates the many figures he has known both personally and through reading that have contributed to an awareness of form and language. Yet, two senior poets have had considerable impact: Al Purdy and Earle Birney. The former used the resources of a working-class vernacular to bring readers close to the rawness of pure experience, and the latter provided a model of moral engagement through which to explore the relations between the environment and its human predators. Like many western poets, Adam has considerable admiration for the poetry of Robert Kroetsch, witty and full of linguistic adventure.

Adam is engaged with environmental issues, and tries to curb a perhaps genetically induced tendency to preach. Keenly observant of the odd and quirky in human behaviour, he makes humour a major part of his aesthetic. Part of his education was philosophical and he tries to base his poetics and poetic practice on considered theoretical principle. Such principle leads him to the belief that the world is not a mere linguistic construct, no matter what it might seem to be. He has a soft spot for the post-modern as play, and for the pun, "A man's speech should exceed its gasp, or what's a metaphor?"

From 1980 to 1990 he edited *Ariel*, and *Glass Canyons* (1985), Canada's first urban anthology, about Calgary. He has also authored numerous essays and has served on the boards of *Dandelion* and *Prairie Forum* as well as on the executives of the Writers Guild of Alberta and the League of Canadian Poets. He and his wife live in Calgary.

About Writing... *There are two sides to a poetic awareness of language. One consists in the assiduous pursuit of precision, in finding the exact match in sound, meaning, and association for the words in context. The other consists in play, in turning the language loose and letting it uncover new combinations, possibilities, and energies. The site of the poem is the meeting point of these two contrary impulses. I sometimes call this interface; more often I think of it as plot.*—IAN ADAM

EDNA ALFORD was the recipient of the Marian Engel Award for Fiction and co-winner of the Gerald Lampert Award. She was co-founder and co-editor of *Dandelion* magazine, and is co-editor of *Kitchen Talk*, an anthology. Alford is on the editorial board of Coteau Books and is a past fiction editor of *Grain* magazine.

PHOTO BY CHARLES LAMB, 1992

EDNA ALFORD

Alford has edited short-fiction collections by writers such as Geoffrey Ursell, Bonnie Burnard, Fred Stenson, Diane Warren, Jennifer Wynne Weber, and Marlis Wessler. She also edited *Meltwater: Fiction and Poetry from The Banff Centre for the Arts* (1998), *Rip-Rap: Fiction and Poetry from the Banff Centre for the Arts* (1999), and *Intersections: Fiction and Poetry from the Banff Centre for the Arts* (2000).

Alford's own work appears in many anthologies at home and abroad, including *The Oxford Collection of Canadian Short Stories*, *Short Stories: An Anthology for Canadian Students*; *Alberta Bound, Saskatchewan Gold* (1982); *Kanadisch Erkrunger*; *Celebrating Canadian Women*; *Best Canadian Short Stories*; *Stories by Canadian Women*; *La Reina Negra Y Otras Historias*; *Kolumbus und die Riesendame*; and others.

Her books include *The Garden of Eloise Loon* (1986), and *A Sleep Full of Dreams* (1981).

Alford was raised and educated in Saskatoon, and now lives in Livelong.

HEATHER HODGSON

ELIZABETH ALLEN was born in 1945 in Whakatane, New Zealand. She grew up on a dairy farm near Leigh in the North Auckland district. After graduating from high school, she worked at a number of jobs in Auckland, from waitressing to accounts clerk in a bank. In 1975, Allen came to Canada with her husband, living on a mixed farm near Lemberg for many years and raising two sons.

Allen began writing seriously in 1976 after attending a creative writing workshop with Anne Szumigalski at the Saskatchewan School of the Arts Fort San. Later she taught at the school herself. She was an active member of the Saskatchewan Writers Guild and the Saskatchewan Writers and Artists Colony Committee.

Her first book of poetry, *A Shored Up House* (1980), won the Gerald Lampert Memorial Award for best first book in Canada. Her second book, *Territories*, was published in 1984. She has had poetry published in a number of magazines in Canada and broadcast on CBC radio. Allen has also published work in *Draft: Essays on Canadian Writing* (1980) and in *Number One Northern* (1977).

Liz Allen returned to New Zealand in the mid-1980s. She currently serves as executive director of the New Zealand writers association.

NIK BURTON

SUSAN ANDREWS GRACE was born Susan Mary Grace to Thomas Joseph and Mary Elizabeth Grace (nee Cavanagh) in Tisdale on February 26, 1949. Joseph Grace grew up in the Muenster area and Mary, who was born in Montana, was raised in the Powell River area of British Columbia. Susan is the eldest of eight siblings: Michael, Melanie, Thomas, James, Maureen, Robert and Peter. The family moved often—from Tisdale, to Saskatoon, Brandon, Burnaby, and then back to Saskatoon. On August 29, 1970, at 4 p.m., Susan married Gordon James Andrews at St. Philips Church in Saskatoon. In 1974 they moved back to Saskatoon after traveling in Europe and living in Toronto for three years. In 1975 Katherine Mary was born, followed by Thomas Gordon in 1977 and Patrick Daniel in 1979. The institution of the family is the crucible of influence in the work of Susan Andrews Grace.

Andrews Grace worked as a registered nurse in Saskatoon and Toronto in the early 1970s. She began a B.A. in philosophy at the University of Saskatchewan in 1969 and continued studies at the University of Toronto, Wordsworth College, graduating finally in 1998 with a B.A. in Philosophy (she also won a Philosophy Prize from St. Thomas More College at the University of Saskatchewan). Andrews Grace studied at Fort San's Saskatchewan School of the Arts with Lorna Crozier and Lois Simmie in 1979, and with Patrick Lane in 1980. She studied with Paulette Jiles and Margaret Gibson (of the USA) in 1987.

Andrews Grace also studied with Don Coles at the Banff Centre in 1986 and 1988. She published her first poems in *Grain* in 1980 and has since published poems in periodicals in Canada, the United Kingdom, and the United States, as well as in several anthologies. Her radio play *Mairead, Moira, Molly* was produced by CBC Radio.

Andrews Grace received a Canada Council Explorations Grant in 1987 to work on both poems and quilts, as she had been exhibiting and selling textile works since 1978. This grant period marked the beginning of a more political approach to the state of feminine consciousness in her work. In 1987 she received, along with Judith Fretz and Jennifer Neal, a Messenger of Peace Award from the United Nations in New York on behalf of a community peace quilt project. She also received a Saskatchewan Arts Board grant in 1992 to write the first draft of *Ferry Woman* and then in 1996 to begin *Love and Tribal Baseball*, another serial poem. She has published one chapbook entitled *Wearing My Father* in 1990, and *Water is the First World* in 1991. Her *Ferry Woman's History of the World*, was published in 1998 and it was shortlisted for four Saskatchewan Book Awards and won Book of the Year award.

The Saskatchewan tradition of workshop groups and attendance of colonies ensured that Susan wrote at all while raising children. In the early 1980s Andrews Grace joined the Poet's Coterie, which included Brenda Niskala, Kim Morrisey, Alan Barr, Bill Klebeck, Lorne Kulak, and Craig Grant. In 1989, Anne Szumigalski called the Connaught Group to order: Ron John Clark, Martha Gould, Steven Ross Smith, S. Padmanab, and Elyse Yates St. George. The workshop group continued for three years and marked the beginning of Grace's interest in the serial poem, the concept of an extensive poem defined by Jack Spicer, Robert Duncan, and Robin Blaser and introduced to Andrews Grace by Ronald John Clark. Anne Szumigalski was a constant influence and source of encouragement. Elizabeth Philips became a lifelong friend.

In 1996 Gord was offered and accepted a position in a software design company in Las Vegas, Nevada. Their children experienced what teenagers always wish for, that their parents would leave town. Andrews Grace followed her husband to the United States in 1997, leaving her arts administration job at CARFAC Saskatchewan, which had been her employer for eight years. All three children had finished high school.

She returned in May of 1998 for the launch of *Ferry Woman's History of the World*, and for the convocation ceremonies at the University of Saskatchewan where she and her daughter Katie received baccalaureate degrees.

Andrews Grace sold the house at 419 10th Street and upon return to Las Vegas began an M.F.A. in Creative Writing at University of Nevada, Las Vegas, as a Graduate Teaching Assistant. She taught English, Creative Writing, and Literature for the English and Honors Departments. As part of her M.F.A. studies she combined visual work with writing and made work for the exhibition "The Narrow Good: A Serial Poem," which was exhibited at McCarran International Airport in 1999. This exhibition was in "conversation" with a critical essay written in requirement for the degree on the serial poem and Jack Spicer. She attended graduate visual art seminars by Dave Hickey, not for credit, during her time at the University of Nevada. He loosely supervised the visual work she had done during her M.F.A. Andrews Grace defended her thesis, "Flesh, A Naked Dress" in April 2001. Her graduate committee was comprised of Richard Wiley, Douglas

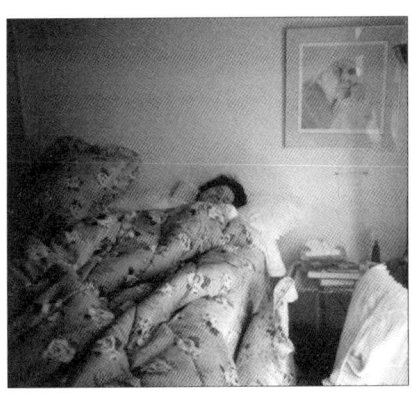

SUSAN ANDREWS GRACE... BED: WHERE SOME OF THE BEST IDEAS COME FROM. MORNING AFTER M.F.A. DEFENSE AND PARTY IN LAS VEGAS.

Unger, Claudia Keelan, and Dave Hickey. After graduating in May of 2001, she settled with her husband in Nelson, British Columbia, to teach at the Kootenay School of the Arts during the year 2001-2. Shortly after, the Creative Writing Studio was discontinued as a result of a cut in government funding. The following year Andrews Grace began teaching at the Nelson Fine Art Centre, founded by former writing and fine art KSA faculty.

Andrews Grace continues as publisher of Hag Papers, limited-edition chapbooks, in Nelson, having published eight titles since 1992, seven of them Saskatchewan writers. Her work as the hag of publishing is emblematic of her desire to bring feminine consciousness to expression in the interest of the survival of the planet for succeeding generations of all species.

About Writing... *People who waste their lives writing might as well write what they please.* —SUSAN ANDREWS GRACE

BRENDA BAKER's story began in 1958 in Ithaca, New York, where her father, Harold, had his nose to the Cornell University grindstone completing a Ph.D. in Rural Education. At the same time, his new wife Phyllis (née Kipps), a graduate of Ryerson's fashion program, was self-employed as a dress designer. Despite their busy lives, they managed to conceive their first child. They moved to Saskatoon where Harold took a one year position at the University of Saskatchewan Extension Division, and on April 6, 1959, Brenda Lee was born.

Although their original intention was to return home to Ontario, the "one year in Saskatoon" stretched, happily, into a lifetime. They built a home in Greystone Heights, where they still reside. They were active in numerous community groups, including Grosvenor Park United Church, where Brenda is still a member. She soon had a brother, Brian, and several years later, a sister, Diane (Phillips). The children were musically inclined, and from an early age often produced concerts for any adults who cared to listen.

During her high school years at Evan Hardy, her father took a sabbatical to pursue research overseas which meant that Brenda started grade ten in Geneva and finished it in Edinburgh. The fourteen months they spent travelling through Europe was one of the great blessings of her life. So, too, was spending a summer in Mexico City, when at the age of sixteen she worked as a nanny for a Saskatoon family.

During her last two years at high school, Brenda taught herself to play the guitar by writing songs. She was a closet songwriter during the early years of university. Inspired by her mother, who had been completing a B.F.A. in visual art, Brenda entered the same program at the University of Saskatchewan. She earned her B.F.A. (with distinction) in 1981, and continued to take university acting classes until 1983.

In 1982 Baker initiated Saskatoon's first artist-in-residence program for the public schools. She received a studio space at Nutana Collegiate in exchange for giving art-related presentations to the students. She was fortunate to have a half-time position as Educator for the Mendel Art Gallery from 1980 to 1983, which allowed her the time and finances to continue painting, but also to pursue her burgeoning interests in theatre and songwriting. During the same years she discovered the existence of Café Domingo and the Regina Folk Festival, places where songwriters from all over the country shared their original music on a regular basis. As a songwriter, she attended her first writers' colony at Fort San, sponsored by the Saskatchewan Writers Guild. The folk club, music festival, and colonies would have a huge impact on her future.

After a stint in Estevan (1984 to 1985) working as the Visual Arts Coordinator for the Organization of Saskatchewan Arts Councils, Brenda toured Europe for four months. Her travels included art education studies in Austria, The Netherlands, Sweden, England, and Scotland. She then moved to Regina where she'd already made connections with the folk music and literary communities. From 1986 to 1991, life in Regina was exciting. At the tail end of the "golden age" of CBC Radio, she became a summer replacement host for the weekend arts shows. She also freelanced for provincial and national arts programs. This part-time work provided the flexibility needed to launch a songwriting career, which began with satirical songs about provincial politics aired on CBC Saskatchewan's morning show. When people heard her on the airwaves, the bookings began to come in.

By the end of her time in Regina Brenda had played numerous folk festivals and clubs across Canada, becoming known for her socially conscious lyrics and strong melodies. She was a guest on national CBC radio shows such as *Swinging on a Star*, *Musical Friends*, *Gabereau*, and *Morningside*. She had also become established as a children's entertainer, and that part of her life ultimately became her "bread and butter." In Regina she released two recordings—a self-titled CD for adults (which won a Saskatchewan Music Award) and one for kids called *Megamunch*. She became heavily involved in the Saskatchewan Writers Guild, serving two years as President (1987 to 1989) after numerous years as a director. She was inspired by the many committed writers she met, and for a while she tried her hand at poetry through Extension classes with Brenda MacDonald Riches. As a member of The Correction Line, she learned much about writing from Bruce Rice, Anne Campbell, Victor Jerrett Enns, and Paul Wilson. Ultimately, fiction won out over poetry, and in 1989 she received an SWG Literary Award for her first short story, which was subsequently published in *Event*. Two short prose pieces were also published in *Malahat Review*.

By 1991 Brenda had moved back to Saskatoon and she was now able to work full-time as a writer and performer. In the early nineties her one-woman show, *Busking on Mars*, was produced for the Saskatoon and Edmonton Fringe Theatre Festivals, and a segment was aired on CBC Radio's *Morningside*. She began negotiations to star in a children's television series created by Geoffrey Ursell and Barbara Sapergia, and she continued to plug away at her short stories. Baker also released two more CDs: *Daughter of Double-Dare* was a critically acclaimed "feminist odyssey" created largely for a female audience, and *Looking for Grandma's Teeth* featured more great singalong songs for kids. More of her writing appeared in a few anthologies and journals, and she was a musical guest

BRENDA BAKER... WITH TWO OF HER GREATEST LOVES: HER GARDEN AND TORI.

on CBC radio's *Off In All Directions* and *Basic Black*. In 1999 the children's TV series *Prairie Berry Pie with Brenda Baker* became a reality, and she won the Saskatchewan Book Award for her story collection *The Maleness of God*. In editing the book she had the great privilege of working with Bonnie Burnard, and learned much from their discussions.

Brenda now performs almost exclusively for children, mostly in Saskatchewan and Alberta. Recently she released a story-song CD called *The Old Elephant's Christmas* and she performs the show annually. In 2001 she received a YWCA Women of Distinction Award for her contribution to the arts. In 2003 she became the first Artist-in-Residence for the historical Marr Residence. While she continues to juggle several writing projects at once, home, garden, and community life have taken on greater importance. In 1997 she married writer Arthur Slade and in 2003 they welcomed their first child, Tori Lorranne.

About Writing... *There are lots of people who would like to believe there are absolutes in music or writing, and that they are capable of making those absolute judgements. What you come to learn is that there are few, if any, absolutes, and that those people who believe there are often suffer from delusions of grandeur.* [From a 1990 music industry conference presentation]—BRENDA BAKER

MARIE ANNHARTE BAKER was born in Winnipeg, Manitoba, in 1942 and currently lives on the west coast prairie by the sea, in Vancouver, British Columbia. She publishes under the name Annharte.

Baker has worked extensively as a cultural arts worker on community projects that required a knowledge of First Nations families and also the understanding of the complexity of community development issues. Since the early days when she was a founding member (1960s) in the Canadian Indian Youth Council and worked at the Friendship Centre in Winnipeg, Manitoba, she has come full circle in her life and writing career. She is so grateful for the programs and projects which provided her with work experience and information about how to better serve First Nations people.

While she is not a "rez sister" and lives in a city where she does not get that many opportunities to indulge herself in the creative arts as an Ojibwe woman within an Anishinabeg community, Baker's current book, *Exercises in Lip Pointing*, does address the various ways she had been silenced. She had thought that after she had written and published *Being on the Moon* and *Coyote Columbus Café*, she had exhausted the privilege of having a literary voice. Baker is a member of Little Saskatchewan First Nations in the Interlake but presently "don't have the soonias [money]" to visit very often.

Baker's most immediate accomplishments and interests have included literature, performance, and the visual and media arts. In a dedication to personal healing through art therapy and journal writing, she has been able to offer more as an instructor than the required "basics" of literacy. She has participated in popular theatre and popular education programs which attempt to help First Nations people better narrate stories such as oral history and personal accounts of struggle. Baker found that her freedom of expression was at times limited because of a party line where everyone was speaking about colonization but hardly anything was said about "decolonizing" one's mind as stated by Ngugi Wa Thiongo.

Baker is sensitive and aware of the age

discrimination issues in the First Nations community but strongly upholds the rights of older women to express their voices about community betterment. She sometimes refers to this visioning as establishing more recognition of the geriatric gynocentric model that Paul Gunn Allen, a Pueblo author, has written about. She seriously wants to start a Granny Boot Camp where First Nations women can gather and teach the essentials.

Baker has taught workshops on writing in both Saskatchewan and Manitoba for what is called Writers in the Schools. She wants to create curriculum that goes beyond the "medicine wheel teachings" approach and actually develop curriculum that is based on oral history and the experience of Indigenous Peoples. She thinks that the "new age" has had a detrimental effect on the sharing of cultural stories and people have become confused. She watches it ("the secondhand ignorance of the elites") broadcasted every night on Aboriginal Peoples Television Network. Baker presumes that when she spoke as a *dud ndn*, she got the laughs in most places because she was considered to be such a freak.

Having been the butt of a jillion jokes, Baker has had to embrace the "ludens" aspect of what she does in performance. Chrystos has praised her sense of humour and her transgressive nature. Recent performances had Baker dressed in a duck outfit (duct-taped) to read her *Duck Tape* poem at a *Poets vs War* event in the Vancouver library. Fooling around was always an *ndn* priority but since our recent economic adventures (for the few who get jobs) she thinks of what she does as an isolated venture. Lucky for her, she was gifted with a son whose last name is Funmaker (derived from Hochunk expression Bear Cubs Playing—his first name is Forrest). She says she is always outstaged by his bottomless abyss of humour, as he is a writer, educator, and great comedian. He is, in fact, a great inspiration to other *ndn*s. For some, Baker is just Forrest's mother. She is not Annharte nor Marie Annharte Baker. Not even Rakuna Kahuna, Ezbunkwe, Shining Wing or any complex combo of monikers. In her writing Baker is usually just Annharte.

About Writing... *Might as well pretend to be humble.*—MARIE ANNHARTE BAKER

MARY BALOGH grew up in post-war Wales as Mary Jenkins. She had an idyllic childhood even though Swansea, her home-town, had been heavily bombed during the war, rationing was still on, and material possessions were few. If anyone knew how to stretch a penny to do the work of two, it was Mary's mother.

Her sister, Moira, who was two years older, was a constant playmate. Their few dolls became their family and the girls created names, personalities, and histories for each of them. They would lie awake in bed at night—until their mother would call up, promising dire consequences if they did not stop talking—inventing stories about the dolls' antics. On summer days their mother would construct a tent out of blankets, string, and clothes pegs attached to the clothesline and the garden fence, and the girls would play "house" all day. Mary and her sister filled notebooks with stories. They read voraciously, mainly books by Enid Blyton when they were children, and the classics when they were a little older.

MARY BALOGH

Both wanted to be authors when they grew up, though the word they used then was authoress. In the end, they fulfilled their dreams, and both financed those dreams with careers as high school English teachers.

Mary had a very good education thanks to parents who emphasized the importance of school and career at a time when many people were still saying that education was wasted on girls. She was fortunate to be young at a time when there was employment in almost any field she might have chosen. She wanted to teach and travel, and came to Kipling, Saskatchewan, Canada, on a two-year teaching contract. At the end of the first year she had a blind date with a man named Robert Balogh. He was standing in her landlady's kitchen when she came down from her room on the fateful evening. They were married a little over a year later.

Balogh and her husband have three adult children: Jacqueline, who lives in Regina, Saskatchewan, Chris, who lives in St. Louis, Missouri, and Siân, who lives in Valencia, California. Wanting to be an author is a dream; wanting to be a teacher is a practical goal. Marriage and motherhood intervened to take time off Balogh's hands and her daughter Siân was six years old before she felt she had enough time to take up an evening hobby— writing! Balogh was addicted to the novels of Georgette Heyer, whom she discovered while working her way through a Grade XI reading list during a maternity leave. Heyer's books enchanted her and transported her into a world she had experienced before only through Jane Austen. Balogh knew that if she ever wrote, it would be in that romantic world of Regency England. And so *A Masked Deception* got written in longhand at the kitchen table while home and family functioned around her after the supper dishes were done. Finally, at the end of 1983, three months after she had started it, her manuscript was ready to be submitted. But where? And how? She knew nothing about the publishing world and nothing about any writers' organizations. So she picked out the publisher she thought did the best job of Regencies, found a Canadian address inside the cover of one of the Signet books, and sent her manuscript there with a brief covering letter. Although the Mississauga address was a mere distribution centre, someone there read the manuscript, liked it, wrote to tell Balogh so, and sent it on to New York. Two weeks later she had a call from Hilary Ross, offering her a two-book contract.

And so the dream became reality. *A Masked Deception* was published in 1985 and Balogh won the Romantic Times Award for best new Regency writer that year. Since then there have been numerous Regencies, historicals, and novellas, and more awards too, culminating with a place on the New York Times bestselling list with *Slightly Scandalous*, published in June 2003.

Balogh's first five books were written in longhand and typed into an ancient typewriter. *The First Snowdrop* was the first book to be written on a computer—an all-in-one dinosaur of a machine that delighted her because she could actually go back and correct typing errors! Best of all—and Balogh has still not quite recovered from the novelty of it—when she was finished, she could press a key (no mouse in those days!) and the printer would do the typing for her while she put her feet up and relaxed—or washed another load of dishes, or marked another set of essays.

Finally, in 1988, Balogh was able to retire from teaching after twenty years in order to devote herself to her writing. And as the children grew up and left home and empty bedrooms behind them, she was able to set up her own study and surround herself with her books and finest treasures. When she is not writing, Balogh is a voracious reader of fiction, non-fiction, classics, and blockbusters. Her favourite reading-associated activity is the monthly meeting with her book club. She also loves music and attributes this to having grown up in Wales, which is very famous for its music. Listening to a Welsh male voice choir, according to Balogh, is one of the most emotionally satisfying experiences of this life. Balogh in fact wrote about Welsh music in *Longing*, which is often quoted by her readers as their favourite of her books.

About Writing... *Being able to spend my days immersed in my imagination and harnessing it through the power of language and writing—and actually to make a living from it all!—is so much my idea of bliss that I consider myself one of the most blessed of mortals.* —MARY BALOGH

BYRNA BARCLAY was conceived in a tent on a Swedish homestead near Livelong, born under a Marcel machine at the Marvel Beauty School in Saskatoon, then incubated for a month. (She is one year older than David Carpenter.) Her father died the day before her third birthday, which may explain why the theme of loss and recovery pervades her fiction. When she was five years old her mother gave her a yellow pencil and a scribbler, then sent her across the road to the castle school so she could learn how to put words on paper. A chronic daydreamer who was always in trouble with her teachers, she always sat by the wall of windows so she could look out and make up stories she saw drifting in clouds. There were no sheets and towels in the linen closet, just storybooks, and Barclay was allowed to read herself to sleep every night. By grade five she was reading her father's books. She still remembers vividly her first lesson in grammar, her excitement when she learned how to parse a sentence.

At university, Barclay was heavily influenced by the Naturalist School when she took a class in the English novel and one in Creative Writing taught by Edward McCourt. One of her first overly long short stories was inspired by her great-grandfather's life as a judge in India during the Mutiny, and McCourt told her she was a "cockeyed romantic" who needed to temper her worldview with prairie realism. But it was the parkland, her Livelong stomping grounds, and her family myths, that shaped her worldview evoked in the Quartet of novels: *Summer of the Hungry Pup* (which won the Saskatchewan Culture & Youth First Novel Contest), *The Last Echo* (which explores all the reasons why our ancestors left Europe for the new world), *Winter of the White Wolf* (a revelation of the reversal of the immigrant experience through the retelling of Nordic myths), and *The House of the White Elephant* (a soon-to-be-published epic that sweeps from Saskatoon to India to London in an exposé of what it means to be Canadian).

A young mother up to her armpits in diaper pails, a reformed social worker and children's librarian who wrote and performed puppet plays, and a research-writer for the Federation of Saskatchewan Indians' Council on Indian Rights and Treaties, Barclay served a twelve-year apprenticeship as a novelist, researching the aftermath of the Riel Rebellion and studying Cree during the winter, while attending the now defunct Saskatchewan School of the Arts for two weeks each summer. Her mentors were Robert Kroetsch and Rudy Wiebe. In 1982, the year *Summer of the Hungry Pup* was published, she became a legend at the University of Alberta, flying in once each month for one day to attend Wiebe's English 584 under the M.F.A. program; that year she wrote the first draft of *The Last Echo* and was President of the Saskatchewan Writers Guild.

In 1984, Barclay returned to the Summer School of the Arts to study the short story with Leon Rooke. Her first collection, *From the Belly of a Flying Whale*, evokes the dark side of humanity and the passions of people living on the edge of madness. One story, "Speak Under Covers," was listed as one of the hundred most distinguished stories of 1988 by Best American Short Stories. Her second collection, *Crosswinds*, won the Best Fiction category of the Saskatchewan Book Awards in 1995. Because the boundaries among genres have collapsed for Barclay, "searching for the nude in the landscape" reads like a novel, yet contains layers of stories and poetry; she calls her first complete departure from parkland realism, her hybrid. Through the years, her short fiction has appeared in many literary anthologies and magazines, including *Grain*, *Event*, *Prism International*, *Descant*, and *Fiddlehead*. "Where My Mother Goes," a story in *Crosswinds*, won the 1995 Geography of Gender Fiction Contest sponsored by *Room of One's Own*. "To the Nth Degree," a story from her stories-in-progress *Women from Snow* won *Prairie Fire*'s Long Short Story Contest in 1999.

Barclay's first stint as an editor occurred in 1977 when she was editor of *FreeLance*. As well as editing books of poetry for Thistledown Press in the '70s, she was Fiction Editor of *Grain* from 1988 to 1990, Editor-in-chief of *Transition* from from 1983 to 2002, and founding editor of *Spring* magazine for emerging writers in 2000. In addition to teaching creative writing classes and workshops and acting as a mentor for the Saskatchewan Writers Guild, she has been a guest lecturer at the universities of Wisconsin, Idaho, and Calgary, and also the Government of the Northwest Territories.

Through the years, Barclay worked as hard for the arts as she did at her craft. She served as vice-chair of the Saskatchewan Arts Board for seven years, at which time she was Chair of the Saskatchewan School of the Arts Committee and Literary Arts Committee. She has been president of the Saskatchewan Writers Guild twice, served for another seven years on the Saskatchewan Arts School board, and currently is a member of the Saskatchewan Book Awards Board of Directors and the Saskatchewan Playwrights Centre Board of Directors.

A fierce advocate for those suffering from mental illnesses, Barclay was the President of the Canadian Mental Health Association from 1984 to 1994, the founding Chair of the first Family Advisory Committee in Canada, the founding Chair of the Minister's Advisory Committee on Mental Health, the Director/Co-ordinator of submissions to the Saskatchewan Commission on Directions in Health Care from 1989 to 1990, and the Co-ordinator of the Hands-Across-Saskatchewan Rally in 1993. These volunteer positions won her many community awards, including Woman of the Year 1989 YMCA Humanitarian Service Award; Canadian

STORY CHASES BYRNA BARCLAY, THIS TIME IN TUSCANY.

Mental Health Association National Distinguished Service Award in 1992; Saskatchewan Writers Guild Member Achievement Award 1992; the Commemorative Medal for the 125th Anniversary of the Confederation of Canada; and the Saskatchewan Council of Cultural Organizations Volunteer Award 1997.

Barclay's interest in dramatic performance began with *Tabloid Love*. The Poets Combine performed it at the Saskatchewan Writers Guild International Writing Conference in 1993; at a benefit for Persephone Theatre in 1994; at various teachers and librarians conferences; and for the League of Canadian Poets in 1994. With the turn of the century, her work took an artistic double-leap with *Room with Five Walls: the Trials of Victor Hoffman*, a poetic drama performed at the Saskatchewan Playwrights Center Festival of New Plays in 2002, and produced by Curtain Razors in partnership with the University of Regina in 2004.

Barclay has lived in Regina since 1962, but has traveled widely in Europe where stories always chase her down, culminating in her forthcoming collection, *The Girl at the Window*. She has raised an actor daughter, Julianna, a musician/artist son Bruce, and husband Justice Ronald Barclay.

About Writing... *My advice to young or emerging writers is always the same. It doesn't matter what other life choices you make, whether or not you go to university, marry, or have children, or even what work you do; those experiences will inform your worldview, and if you are a serious writer willing to work hard and take all the rejection that goes with artistic pursuit, you will have no choice in the matter, but will be compelled to clamp words on the page. Anyone can learn the craft of writing, but not everyone has the creative drive, which is sometimes stronger than the need for sleep, food, or sex.* —BYRNA BARCLAY

MARION BECK was born in Rossendale, a valley on the Lancashire–Yorkshire border in northern England. After winning a major scholarship she went directly from grammar school to Leeds University to read geography. Here her first attempts at poetry were roundly rejected by *Gryphon*, the university's literary magazine, with the terse comment to try again when she was more mature. This was to take some time.

After a short teaching career during which she married fellow Leeds student, Les Beck, she emigrated to Canada, living first in Regina and then in Uranium City, where her husband had been sent to be resident geologist. Three sons and four years later, the Becks returned to Leeds for academic reasons and finally, in 1966, returned permanently to Regina.

On finding their second son was autistic, any literary aspirations for Beck were put on hold and she became involved in advocacy work, writing numerous articles on the syndrome and a book, *The Exorcism of an Albatross*. The book is an account of coming to terms with an autistic child and was self-published for use at a conference in Vancouver in 1978. It was also the subject of an interview by Don Harron on *Morningside* and an article by Fredelle Maynard in *Chatelaine* a year later in 1980. Maynard commented it cried out for editing; a cautionary warning for all self-publishers.

By now, suffering from burn-out, Beck was persuaded by her husband to do something for herself so she joined a creative writing class led by Mick Burrs (Steven Michael Berzensky) who, in turn, persuaded her to write poetry again. Tongue in cheek, she sent a poem to the *Malahat Review*, whose editor at that time had also been at Leeds. This time she was successful!

By 1991, Beck had poems published in a

number of literary magazines, such as *Wascana Review* and *Grain*, and she had others read on CBC's *Ambience*. Beck also won the Short *Grain* Prose Poem Competition.

She had worked for a short time for the Saskatchewan Writers Guild, learning useful skills such as cleaning an offset press, edited poetry for *Green's Magazine* from 1980 to 1986, and served on the City of Regina's Arts Commission. In 1981, Beck was president of the Wascana Writer's Group. She had also taken an advanced poetry class at Fort San in 1984 from Robin Skelton, who became a firm friend and had a lasting influence on her poetry.

In 1989 Beck had surgery for breast cancer and the experience became the theme underlying a chapbook, *Poems for Amazons*, published in 1995. The chapbook also formed part of the opening programme for the exhibition "Survivors in Search of a Voice," which was installed at the Norman Mackenzie Art Gallery in Regina.

These years saw her becoming interested in people's poetry and especially in the work of the late Ted Plantos in Toronto. Beck wrote articles for *People's Poetry Magazine*, of which Plantos was editor, and she was twice asked to judge the Milton Acorn People's Poetry Book Award. She was also a member of the Literary Networks Poetry Panel, and was twice a winner in the Political Poetry Contest, a competition run by the magazine.

Beck's writing was not confined to poetry. In the early 1990s, she completed a history booklet for the Regina Council of Women's centenary entitled, *Some of Ishbel's Ladies, the founding of the Regina cottage hospital*.

MARION BECK... BLUE DOG CAFE, INVERMERE, BRITISH COLUMBIA

One of the strangest events regarding her writing occurred in 1995 after *NeWest Review* published her article on the last days of Uranium City. She was contacted early one morning by phone from Barcelona asking her to write a sidebar for the Encyclopedia Catalan on settlements in Canada's boreal forests. A United Nations publication, it involved a great deal of red tape, many faxes, and precious little remuneration.

Since then Beck has published two more chapbooks. *Trench in the Rockies*, published in 2000, is a sequence of poems relating to the Columbia River valley in British Columbia, which was also a holiday destination for Beck for over thirty years. The second of these two is *Dry: is the long term forecast*, published on the first wet summer day of 2002, a sequel to *Notebook of an Immigrant*, published in 1984.

Beck is working on a full-length manuscript about heredity. Much of her writing is related to her own experiences and has often been a way of coping with the various crises in her life, but there is humour too and she can write a fine limerick such as those she had published in *100% Cracked Wheat* in 1983.

About Writing... *Write about what you know and be honest, no matter if this can be unflattering. Learn to accept rejections and don't take years to write again.*—MARION BECK

VEN BEGAMUDRÉ has led a somewhat magical life. He was born in 1956 in Bangalore, South India, into a family of engineers. He emigrated to Canada in 1962. These events, including an interlude on the island of Mauritius, led to his autobiographical first novel, *Van de Graaff Days* (1993), which includes a cameo appearance by his family god. Ven lived in various North American locations—in Ontario, Pennsylvania, and British Columbia—before settling in Regina in 1978. He has also travelled in Europe and India.

Many of these places provide settings for the stories in his two collections, *A Planet of Eccentrics* (1990) and *Laterna Magika* (1997). Both books contain realistic and speculative fiction, and he delights in recalling that the first two books he owned as a boy were a collection of tales from *The Arabian Nights* and a history of mathematics. (Both were gifts. Ah, but from whom?)

Not that Begamudré planned to become a writer. In childhood and youth his interests ranged so widely that he thought he was good for nothing, and certain people told him so, too. As a teenager, while serving in two reserve regiments, the Seaforth Highlanders of Canada, and later the Governor General's Foot Guards, he considered a career in the Canadian Armed Forces. He decided to become a civil servant instead and studied at Carleton University in Ottawa and at Schiller College in Paris. He graduated from Carleton in 1977 with a Bachelor of Arts with Honours in Public Administration.

Begamudré specialized in budgetary theory, and his honours essay included a hand-drawn diagram that tried to illustrate what he called N-dimensional budgeting. Many years later, while writing his family history—*Extended Families*, a still unpublished lifetime-work-in-progress—he learned that one of his grandfathers, who had studied at Trinity College, Cambridge, had been an expert in N-dimensional geometry. (These things happen.)

Over the next decade, Begamudré divided his time between working for the Saskatchewan Government and learning to write. In 1988, he took the risky step of becoming a full-time writer—this, in a society that romanticizes intellectual and artistic pursuits but which places little value on such nonsense unless it results in dollars, not cents.

Learning to write included taking workshops and tutorials at the Saskatchewan School of the Arts, and at The Banff Centre for the Arts. It also meant joining a writing group called The Bombay Bicycle Club, and trying to read all the books Begamudré should have read in high school when he hadn't realized there was such a thing as Canadian Literature. Finally, in his early forties, and against the advice of most of his friends, he attended graduate school. In 1999 he earned his M.F.A. in Creative Writing from Warren Wilson College in Asheville, North Carolina. This pleased his extended family to no end because most of his relatives earned their doctorates in their twenties and sometimes earned a fourth degree later on. (You can see why that old Indian proverb, "Live far from relatives and near water" drove him to Saskatchewan, of all places.)

But why did most of his friends try to discourage Begamudré from earning his M.F.A.? Because they thought he was too qualified to go back to school. For by now he was holding

PHOTO BY DON HALL

VEN BEGAMUDRÉ...WITH HIS FIGMENT CAP FROM EPCOT® AT WALT DISNEY WORLD®.

posts as a writer-in-residence, teaching other writers, and editing their work. Slowly, but surely, Begamudré was influencing Canadian Literature.

He has been a writer-in-residence for the University of Calgary's Markin-Flanagan Distinguished Writers Programme, the University of Alberta's Department of English, the Canada-Scotland Exchange, Regina Public Library, McMaster University's Department of English, and the Yukon Public Libraries. He has taught at the Saskatchewan School of the Arts and the Sage Hill Writing Experience. He has co-edited, with the poet Judith Krause, *Out of Place: Stories and Poems* (1991) and edited *Lodestone: Stories by Regina Writers* (1993).

Begamudré has worked on manuscripts that have gone on to win major awards—though his only book award to date is the F.G. Bressani Literary Prize for Prose—and he offers a mentorship program for selected, mainly South Asian, writers. He sees his teaching, editing, and mentoring as a way of thanking those who have taught him, and who continue to teach him, so much about writing and about life.

As for Begamudré's influence on Canadian Literature, this is harder to pin down because of his wide-ranging interests (though now no one tells him that he's good for nothing) and because he is something of an anomaly. He's a Saskatchewan writer who rarely writes about Saskatchewan. He writes devastatingly funny works about race, politics, and religion without using words like race, politics, or religion. He is equally at home writing about both men and women—perhaps because he spent the first six years of his life surrounded by women. He likes to play with numbers and with words.

In his fiction, non-fiction, and poetry, he can be realistic and/or speculative. (Why not, given that one of his ancestors is a saint who was born some four centuries ago and still has not died?) Recently, Begamudré published work that can be enjoyed by young adults and adults alike: a postmodern biography, *Isaac Brock: Larger than Life* (2000), and an historical fantasy novel, *The Phantom Queen* (2002).

Let's finish on an appropriately magical note. Shortly after he turned seventeen, Begamudré decided to become a civil servant; shortly after he turned eighteen, he decided to become a writer. A month before he turned twenty-two, shortly after his mother died, he was sorting through her personal effects in India and found his horoscope, which had been cast just after he had been born. The horoscope said something like—"This boy can only become two things. He will become either a writer or an administrator."

About Writing... *[The secret of creation is] the ability to hold an entire work in the mind while devoting all the energy of a moment to a single detail. And, as important, the ability to understand what each detail contributes to the whole.*—VEN BEGAMUDRÉ

SHERI BENNING was born in Humboldt on December 14, 1977. She was baptized on Christmas Eve in a small country church, St. Scholastica, seven miles south of Humboldt and she grew up on a farm a mile north of that church. Her father, Larry Benning, was born and raised on a farm southwest of Muenster. Like a lot of young men in the area of St. Peter's Colony, Larry and his six brothers attended St. Peter's College and Abbey in Muenster for high school.

Benning feels strongly connected to St. Peter's. Prior to meeting her grandmother, her paternal grandfather, Anthony Benning, was a monk at the abbey, and three of his brothers were priests: Father Xavier, who was the dean of the college, Edward, who was a parish priest, and Leonard, who ran the farm. Benning's mother, Rosalie Tobin, grew up on a farm outside of St. Benedict and attended the Ursuline Convent in Bruno for high school. Her maternal grandmother, Mina Klein, was a teacher and painter. Her family homesteaded in Ponteix, Saskatchewan, and was of Dutch descent. Upon arriving in Canada, Mina's father died, and her family—five sisters and her mother—successfully managed a small farm on their own.

Upon working hard at a variety of jobs (road construction secretary high-school teacher road-grader bank clerk store clerk) Benning's parents were able to scrape enough money together for a down payment on their own farm. They moved there in 1977, the year she was born. Her brother Kurt was born in 1979 and her sister Heather was born in 1980. Kurt is now a dentist and Heather will graduate with a B.F.A from the Nova Scotia College of Art and Design in Spring 2004. The three remain deep friends and they share many strong memories of farm life. Because of the impending farm crisis, in 1997 the family chose to sell their farm. This is a loss the family will always collectively grieve.

After finishing high school, Benning attended St. Peter's College, Muenster, for her first two years of Arts and Science. These were extremely important years for Sheri; it was at St. Peter's that she first realized her vocation to study literature and to write. She believes the philosophy and creative writing courses that she took with Tim Lilburn and the spirit of monasticism that she witnessed at St. Peter's are crucial to her continuing development as a writer. Sheri proceeded with her studies at the University of Saskatchewan and earned an Honours B.A. in English with great distinction in 2001. While at the university, the generous mentorship of John Livingstone Clark, Hilary Clark, William Slights, and William Bartley contributed to her ongoing love of writing and academics.

After graduating, Sheri taught literacy for a semester with Northland's College in LaRonge while living near Nemeiben Lake at the fishing camp her parents currently operate. She was also the recipient of the Hannon travel scholarship through the University of Saskatchewan which funded travel to St. Petersburg, Russia, where Sheri studied Russian for a semester at St. Petersburg State University. Upon returning to Canada, she embarked on an M.A. in English and Creative Writing at the University of New Brunswick in Fredericton. She will complete her M.A. in the spring of 2004.

Benning has participated in a number of writing workshops and seminars. In 1997 she won the W.O. Mitchell Bursary to attend the Sage Hill Writing Experience, where she had the good fortune to work with Elizabeth Philips and Lee Gowan. She was also accepted to participate in the Saskatchewan Writers Guild's mentorship program during which time she worked with Barbara Klar. In the

PHOTO BY YI-MEI TSIANG

SHERI BENNING... WALKING ALONG THE EMBANKMENT OF THE NEVA IN ST. PETERSBURG, RUSSIA.

summer of 2001, she was invited to participate in a nature writing colloquium facilitated by Don McKay and Tim Lilburn at St. Peter's Abbey. She also won a scholarship through U.N.B. to attend the Maritime Writer's Workshop where she learned much from the Nova Scotian poet and novelist Anne Simpson.

Benning has also been the grateful recipient of Saskatchewan Arts Board literary grants that have afforded her the blessing of time to study and write. As a result, her poetry has been published in literary journals across Canada including *Grain*, *Arc*, *Malahat Review*, *New Quarterly*, *Event*, *Fiddlehead*, *Other Voices*, *CV2*, *Qwerty*, *NeWest Review*, and *Wascana Review*. Two suites of her poems were broadcast on CBC's *Gallery*. Her first poetry publication was in the first volume of the Saskatchewan Writers Guild's magazine, *Spring*, and her poetry appeared in *Spring* again in 2003. Benning's first book of poetry, *Earth After Rain*, was published in 2001 and was the recipient of two Saskatchewan Book Awards: the Anne Szumigalski Prize for Poetry and the Best First Book Award. In 2001, along with Heather Benning, Rosalie Benning, Tim Lilburn and Jennifer Still, she started a publishing collective, Jackpine Press. Jackpine seeks to feature chapbooks by emerging writers alongside more established artists. They launched their first series of chapbooks in the winter of 2002.

About Writing... *I don't know if I have much to say about writing—maybe, if I'm lucky, one day I'll be a wise old woman with something to share. In the meantime, I know that it's important for me to nest myself in the wisdom of others. My walls are cluttered with taped up bits of paper that are scribbled with the words of poets, philosophers, friends, and strangers. Whenever I look up from my desk (often in tired defeat), there's something inspiring for me to briefly meditate on.*—SHERI BENNING

STEVEN MICHAEL BERZENSKY, also known as Mick Burrs, became a poet soon after moving to Canada. Albert Arthur Burrs, born in Kiev, Ukraine, and Shirley Levi, born in Indianapolis, Indiana, celebrated the birth of their son on April 10, 1940. He moved with his family to the San Fernando Valley in January 1950, and later chronicled his early years in the poetry sequence *The Fabled Blue Pools of Paradise*. Initially trained as a journalist at Birmingham Senior High in Van Nuys, California, he served as his student newspaper's sports and features editor. After high school graduation in 1958, he attended Butler University in Indianapolis, then San Fernando Valley State College at Northridge, where he edited the college's first literary magazine and earned a Bachelor's degree in English and Art in 1962.

When he was twenty-one, he sought conscientious objector status with the Selective Service through his local draft board in North Hollywood. He lost his final appeal in 1962. No longer desiring to become a high school teacher, he pursued a second career in "creative reading" in 1964, working toward a Master's degree in Interdisciplinary Studies in Reading Improvement and Programmed Instruction at San Francisco State College. But when the war in Vietnam began escalating, Berzensky left the United States as a "moral draft dodger" in November 1965.

He became a teaching assistant for the Reading and Study Service at newly opened Simon Fraser University in Burnaby. Immersed in Vancouver's burgeoning poetry scene, Berzensky was himself surprised when he wrote his first serious poems in the spring of 1966. Less than a year after moving to Canada, the 26-year-old landed immigrant's first two poems were published in Vancouver's *Talon* magazine. In 1967, he gave his initial solo public reading in Simon Fraser's University Theatre—the same place where he had been inspired by observing the wondrous diversity of Canadian and American poets, including Lionel Kearns, John Newlove, Al Purdy, Dorothy Livesay, Robert Creeley, and William Stafford, among others.

Berzensky chose to commit his life to "the precarious profession of poetry." He moved to Edmonton in October 1969, where he taught himself rudimentary guitar and composed original songs, soon performing them at local coffeehouses. He worked as a freelance broadcaster at CKUA AM-FM, producing 39 half-hour shows over a two-year span. He became a Canadian citizen in May 1971, and a few months later published the first of 26 poetry chapbooks, *In the Dark the Journeyman Landed*.

In October 1973, he moved to Saskatchewan. He worked as an oral history annotator at the Provincial Archives on the University of Regina campus in 1974–75. Inspired by the Métis interviews he had annotated, he wrote his ten-poem sequence "Under the White Hood" about the life and death of Louis Riel. He also edited the first "found poetry" book in the province's history, published in 1975. *Poems in Their Own Voices: Going to War* (Métis Series) was distributed free to northern schools and libraries throughout Saskatchewan.

While he occasionally performed his songs at the Regina Folk Guild, his main source of income became the creative writing courses he taught for Regina Plains Community College and University of Regina Extension. In summer 1975, he began selling his poetry chapbooks for "99 cents a bag" at the Regina Farmer's Market. For the next ten years his book table also displayed and sold books of the province's new publishers, Coteau, Thistledown, and Fifth House, as well as self-published books by other local poets and authors. Building up a clientele for Saskatchewan literature at the ground roots level, he maintained that it was "another kind of produce: food for the soul."

In 1975, Berzensky inaugurated Regina's first local poetry reading series. He promoted and hosted "Warm Poets for Cold Nights" at the Norman Mackenzie Art Gallery on the old college campus. The premiere reading, featuring H.C. Dillow, Peter Huston, Mildred Rose, and John G. Trehas, was enthusiastically attended by an unprecedented 80 people on a wintry February night. For the next three years, forty "warm poets" reached their first public audience in Regina, including Catherine Buckaway, Lorna Crozier, Kristjana Gunnars, Gary Hyland, Judith Krause, Garry Radison, and Andrew Suknaski. In 1978, the Saskatchewan Writers Guild took over the series.

His first poetry collection, *Moving in from Paradise*, was published in 1976. His writings also

PHOTO BY SHARON SINGER

STEVEN MICHAEL BERZENSKY...
IN WINTER WITH GLOVES.

appeared in the literary anthologies *Number One Northern: Poems of Saskatchewan* (1977) and *Sundogs: Stories from Saskatchewan* (1980). In 1977, his second poetry book, *Children on the Edge of Space*, appeared.

In 1983, Berzensky was named a co-winner of the Saskatchewan Writers Guild's Long Poetry Manuscript competition, judged by Eli Mandel and Daphne Marlatt. A few months later his prize-winning manuscript, *The Blue Pools of Paradise*, was published. He dedicated the book to poet Andrew Suknaski, who had inspired him to explore and write about his own Jewish family roots.

Berzensky moved to Yorkton in 1985 as its first writer-in-residence. In 1988, he succeeded Brenda Riches as editor of *Grain*. He was the first editor whose editorial office was located outside the Regina–Saskatoon axis—on the mezzanine floor of Yorkton's public library. He founded the popular and influential Annual Short *Grain* Contest to increase subscriptions and further the development of the prose poem and postcard story.

His fourth book, *Dark Halo*, was published in 1993. Featuring his longest poetry sequence, "Veil," about the mother of a murdered girl whose body was never found, and poems on the lives of Hitler and Stalin, this book made the official short list for the Milton Acorn Memorial People's Poetry Award in 1994. *Dark Halo* was cited by the judges as "a victory for poetry over tyranny."

In 1995, he changed his literary name to Steven Michael Berzensky. He won the 1998 Saskatchewan Book Award for Poetry with his fifth collection, *Variations on the Birth of Jacob* (1997). His sixth book, *The Names Leave the Stones: Poems New and Selected*, edited by Catherine Hunter, covers 30-plus years of his published poetry. It was a finalist for the 2002 Saskatchewan Book of the Year.

Berzensky currently resides in Yorkton, where a major writing grant from the Saskatchewan Arts Board helped him complete a manuscript of over 180 "liberated sonnets" in 2001-02.

About Writing... *Poetry is soundfulness. No poem is written on stone, all poems are written on water. First vision, then re-visionings. I enjoy going beyond brevity into a state of imaginative amplitude. I believe complexity and clarity can co-exist. I'm a dreamer, a poetic trespasser, marking my own paths, discovering unfamiliar voices. In my poems wordplay and seriousness dance together. I learn some conventions, then break them heartily.*—STEVEN MICHAEL BERZENSKY

SARAH BINKS, often known as "the Sweet Songstress of Saskatchewan," was born near Willows, Saskatchewan, in 1905, to a family of homesteaders who probably came from South Dakota around 1900. Educated rather sketchily at the local school, she nevertheless took a keen interest in geology as a result of the efforts of one of her early teachers, William Greenglow, who had failed his introductory course in geology at university and engaged the whole school in his studies for the supplemental examination.

Friendship with a neighbouring German-speaking family, the Schwantzhackers, led to an interest in German poetry. Early poems appeared in *The Horsebreeder's Gazette, the Piecemeal Excelsior, Swine and Kine*, and other local publications, and won her a small but significant readership. These poems were mostly lyrics about farm and community life written in conventional verse forms—modernism had not yet penetrated rural Saskatchewan —but there were also poems on historical subjects and translations from German. She won the McCohen and Meyers

Stock Conditioner Company Prize at the Quagmire Agricultural Fair for a poem entitled "The Farm Skunk."

In 1926 Binks ran away to Regina with a travelling salesman, Henry Welkin, and spent two blissful weeks (estimates of the time vary) with him, dazzled by the lights of the big city. Regina (population 34,400 in 1921) was a much bigger and more glamorous city during this period than it later became. Although Binks's biographer Paul Hiebert (*Sarah Binks*, Oxford University Press, 1947) does his best to be discreet about this rather sensational episode, it appears that it ended with the arrest and detention of Welkin for earlier unspecified offenses and Sarah's despairing return to the family farm at Willows. Fortunately, the reputation she might have acquired as a fallen woman and sexual adventuress did not develop, and nobody in Willows seems to have thought the worse of her.

In the following winter she wrote her great epic, *Up From the Magma and Back Again*, based on what she had learned from Greenglow's geology lessons, using the blank sides of bills and other farm documents which her father had turned over to her. The result was a "full cubic foot of closely written manuscript" (Hiebert 130) which is usually regarded as her major work, and which, like many major works, no-one has ever read in its entirety. It has, indeed, never been published except in fragments, and the fate of the manuscript is at present unknown. It won her the Wheat Pool Medal, however, in a year of general crop failure in which Binks's poem was

SKETCH BY PAUL DENHAM
SARAH BINKS... WINNER OF THE WHEAT POOL MEDAL.

the biggest thing produced on a Saskatchewan farm. Although its subject may seem unpromising, we should note that poems about rocks constitute a significant tradition in Canadian poetry (see, for example, poems by E.J. Pratt, F.R. Scott, and Christopher Dewdney's *A Palaeozoic Geology of London*, Ontario, 1973), and Binks would seem to be squarely in this tradition.

In 1929 she died of mercury poisoning brought on by accidentally swallowing the contents of a horse thermometer with which she was attempting to take her own temperature orally—an episode possibly best left to the imagination. A civic monument to her was unveiled at her place of burial in Willows in 1931.

Binks is, with one or two exceptions, virtually the only significant poetic figure in Saskatchewan between Henry Kelsey (1693) and Eli Mandel, who began writing in the 1950s. She is largely responsible for fixing in the public mind the idea that there is something essentially unpoetic about Saskatchewan, that the prospect of such a region producing great poetry is in itself laughable. In Canada, and perhaps particularly in Saskatchewan, we laugh at ourselves first in order to anticipate and forestall the laughter of others, those who might be more sophisticated or more powerful. The work of the generation of Saskatchewan poets that emerged in the 1960s and later is in part a reaction to Binks's work—this place can produce good poetry—and in part a response to it—this place has wit, humour, and an awareness of its own marginal position.

Certainly she continues to be a much-loved figure. Two examples of her continuing role in Canadian life take the form of stage productions; one is *The Wonderful World of Sarah Binks*, produced in 1979 by the National Arts Centre in Ottawa, and starring Eric Donkin as narrator Miss Rosalind Drool. The other is *Sarah Binks, the Sweet Songstress of Saskatchewan*, a musical by Ken Mitchell and Doug Hicton, presented at the Saskatoon Fringe in 2002. We haven't outgrown her; we've assimilated her.

PAUL DENHAM

SANDRA BIRDSELL is the daughter of a Russian-born Mennonite and a Métis father who met in Morris, Manitoba, at the Scratching Chicken hotel. Her mother worked at the hotel as an upstairs maid, and her father worked downstairs apprenticing as a pool shark and barber. Five children later, Sandra was born but there were five more Bartlette children yet to come. Sandra's mother is reputed to have held a low opinion of poets, saying that liars and poets will wind up in hell. At the age of ten, the author embarked on a career as a poet and wrote a poem about dying and being denied entry into heaven. She was awarded first prize in the Most Serious Poem category, by the student council of Morris MacDonald Collegiate. The prize was five dollars' worth of free dry cleaning.

Thus, the writer, Birdsell, was born. But not before she married, had three children, two dogs, several cats and a collection of ill-fated goldfish, turtles and hamsters. She also toiled at various other professions, such as reading income tax forms for Revenue Canada, a stint as a cocktail waitress in a knock-off Playboy Bunny club, an Avon Lady, communications writer, seamstress and hapless secretary in her first husband's manufacturing business. Although she always desired to be a dancer, actor and clown, writing became her first love. That was twenty years ago. Since then she has published seven books and has been fortunate to receive accolades and nominations for awards.

Birdsell discovered the short stories of Alice Munro while working as a stringer for the Canadian Book Information Centre. She swears that Munro's *Who Do You Think You Are* was the only book she ever stole from a book display. She began writing short fiction when she attended a workshop and heard a young man read a story about growing up in small town Manitoba.

Her first creative writing instructor was James Walker at the University of Winnipeg. This was a university-at-noon course, and Birdsell had enrolled as a mature student. When Professor Walker came into the room, he was aghast to find nearly twenty-five would-be writers crammed around the table. He said, "I want you to know that there are likely only two people in this room who are writers." Birdsell remembers looking around the table and asking herself, "I wonder who the other one is?"

She then studied with Robert Kroetsch at the University of Manitoba. He was instrumental in coaxing the people at Turnstone Press to have a look at her stories. In a review of those first stories, *Night Travellers*, William French of the *Globe and Mail* said, "Birdsell has us well and truly hooked." By this time, Birdsell herself was well and truly hooked, and couldn't think of anything she would rather do than write.

When Birdsell's three children grew old enough to find the refrigerator and fill their own bottles, writing began to take up more and more of her time—writing and attending readings and discovering South American, British and American authors. She especially was enchanted by the work of Flannery O'Connor, and then later by Anton Chekhov.

Since the publication of her first book, which contains stories that came together in Robert Kroetsch's Creative Writing 301 class, Birdsell has written three collections of short fiction, three novels, a novel for children, radio and theatre plays, as well as television and film scripts. Her first two volumes of short stories, *Night Travellers* and *Ladies of the House*, were published to critical acclaim in 1982 and 1984 and were subsequently published in a single volume, *Agassiz Stories*. Birdsell's short stories have appeared in many anthologies, including *The Oxford Book of Canadian Stories*, *From Ink Lake*, and *Stories by Canadian Women*. Many of the stories have been translated and published in Spanish, Polish, Italian, French and German.

Her first novel, *The Missing Child*, received the WH Smith/Books in Canada first novel award in 1989. Her second novel, *The Chrome Suite*, was awarded the McNally Robinson prize for best book of the year, and was nominated for a Governor General's Award in 1992. A third short story collection, *The Two Headed Calf*, was a Governor General Award nominee in 1997 and was also the Saskatchewan Book of the Year. It was followed by a children's novel, *The Town That Floated Away*, which caught the attention of young readers, who nominated it for both a Silver Birch Award and Red Cedar Award.

PHOTO BY DEBRA MOSER, WINNIPEG

SANDRA BIRDSELL... AND HER DOG, SHEP, AT OMAN'S CREEK IN WINNIPEG.

Birdsell has letters from readers who attest that the book is as good as Rowling's *Harry Potter and the Philosopher's Stone*.

Sandra Birdsell has been writer-in-residence at the universities of Waterloo, Alberta, British Columbia, Prince Edward Island, and McMaster, where she completed work on a novel, *The Russländer*. *The Russländer* was published in September 2001, and was a bestseller and finalist for the prestigious Giller Prize. *The Russländer* was also awarded Book of the Year, Best Fiction, and the City of Regina awards by the Saskatchewan Book Awards in 2001.

Birdsell was awarded the Marion Engel Award in 1993, Canada's most prestigious prize given to a woman in mid-career, and the Joseph B. Stauffer Prize in 1992 by the Canada Council for the Arts for meritorious achievement.

"The further west I come, the better I feel in my skin," Birdsell is quoted as saying. She moved to Regina in 1996 and since then has written three books in a room the size of a postage stamp, while listening to the cars whiz by on the TransCanada highway. But the prairie landscape is only a twenty-minute walk from her back door, and she goes out into it early in the morning, in spring, winter and fall. That landscape and its people continue to influence and inspire her work.

Birdsell is presently writing another novel. She continues to give up on various hobbies such as sketching, T'ai Chi, dog training, physical fitness and improvisation. She now concentrates on gardening, taking vitamins, and in being what her grandson calls "silly."

About Writing... *Writing a novel can be like having an illicit love affair. You may find yourself sneaking away from the family to be with it. Calling it up in the wee hours of the mornings just to hear its voice. You want to talk about the novel to everyone and anyone, but you're wise, and so you remain silent, knowing that talking will steal from the pleasure of being in its presence. The novel and you share secrets, which makes you inseparable, and self-sufficient; you don't need anyone, only each other. You turn to one another in the early morning, your minds perfectly connected, understanding one another perfectly without needing to speak, while all around you everyone else is asleep.*—SANDRA BIRDSELL

DOREEN M. BLEICH was born May 9, 1951, in Denzil, the eldest daughter of Joseph and Rose (Lessmeister) Reiniger. She has three sisters and two brothers. In 1971, she married Howard Bleich and they have two sons, Todd and Troy.

She grew up in the Denzil area, and graduated from Denzil High School in 1969. She attended the College of Education at the University of Saskatchewan in Saskatoon. After moving to Nipawin, various jobs followed—clerk, school bus driver, receptionist, bookkeeper, and bank teller.

In 1996, Bleich graduated from a three-year creative writing program that she completed by correspondence. In 1998 she quit her job with a local bank and began to write full-time.

Bleich's first published work was a cookbook entitled *Cooking Country Style*. It was released in 1989 and reprinted in 1998. Her work has also been published in several magazines and newspapers, including *Folklore*, *Dugout*, *Briarpatch*, and *Parent Care*, as well as in the Saskatoon *Star Phoenix*.

In December 2002, Bleich's first work of fiction, a novel titled *Ready Or Not*, was published. Her most recent works appear in the *Tisdale Writers 15th Anniversary Anthology*, published in June 2003. At present, she is dabbling in playwrighting and finishing a second novel.

DOREEN M. BLEICH

About Writing... *Writing is the most challenging, frustrating, lonely work I've ever done. It's also the most thrilling, personally satisfying and rewarding experience. And I expect the best is yet to come!*—DOREEN M. BLEICH

MARTHA BLUM was born in Czernowitz, Austria, in 1913. Her parents were Abraham and Susanne (Hershmann) Guttmann. In 1914, at the outbreak of WWI, Blum's mother fled with her children to Vienna, where they stayed until the end of the war. Her father, a pharmacist and an Austrian officer, was at the front. In 1918, the Austrian Hungarian Empire fell apart and this part of the world was incorporated into Romania. In consequence, Blum's high school years and some of her studies were in Romanian and in Romania.

Blum's studies then took her to Prague, Strasbourg, and Paris for pharmaceutical chemistry, music, and languages. At the outbreak of the Second World War, she returned to her hometown and was, because of her

Jewish ancestry, employed as a slave-labourer by the German-Romanian forces from 1941 to 1945.

1950 saw her in Israel for a year. She immigrated to Canada in 1951, landing in Halifax, Nova Scotia, with her husband and child. In 1954, she followed her husband (a professor of mathematics) to Saskatoon, where he had obtained a position at the University of Saskatchewan.

Blum had always been a writer, albeit in French, Romanian, and German and, at the age of forty-one, started her new career to perfect her English and to work as a pharmacist in the city of Saskatoon.

Being a musician, a pianist, and a singer, she taught text and voice to aspiring classical singers. She also participated actively in theatre and is a co-founder of the Opera Association of Saskatoon, and also of the 'Alliance Française' of which she was the treasurer for four years.

Blum also was a translator and is the recipient of the Universal Declaration of Human Rights Award from the Human Rights of Canada, along with 49 other Holocaust survivors in 1998. The award recognized the recipients' having contributed to the cultural development of Canada.

Her first English novel, *The Walnut Tree*, was published in 1999. Blum received two book awards for it: the Brenda Macdonald-Riches Book Award for best first book and the Saskatoon Library Book Award, both in 1999.

Blum's second novel appeared in 2002. Called *Children of Paper*, it is a collection of short stories depicting a small town (a *shtetl*) at the beginning of the twentieth century. The collection finishes in 1941 with the start of the Russian campaign.

Blum is working on two more novels—one with a Canadian theme and the other one as a probable continuation of the post-war life in Europe to complete the trilogy. She is also often asked to contribute to art magazines and anthologies. Her article, "Reflections on Ethics and Art," appeared in *The Structurist*, which is the University of Saskatchewan's art magazine, in 2002, and her short story, *Romeo and Juliet in Suczorno*, appeared in *Tapestry of Hope, Holocaust Writing for Young People*, in 2003.

Blum has lived in Saskatoon with her husband Richard since 1954, when the couple began to contribute to the artistic and scientific life of the community. She has enjoyed the influence of local literacy, art, and music. She and her husband are very fond of the prairie landscape, the riverscape, and they are eager hikers and swimmers. They both have always been lovers of nature—the mountains in their hometown and the prairie sky in their adopted homeland.

MARTHA BLUM... SMILING FOR THE ART OF WRITING (2003).

About Writing...

For me writing is an absolute necessity. I did it all my life even under the most wrenching historical circumstances. I would make notes and I would think "as if" I was writing. I do this constantly and in many languages. I don't translate but rather, I use the nature of the tongue itself to express the thought.—MARTHA BLUM

ALEATA E. BLYTHE was born to Charles and Ruth Robinson at Dodsland on October 6, 1931. At a very young age, she with her parents and siblings came north to the Loon Lake area where she grew up during the depression and war years. Her parents eked out a scant living from a hard rock farm, and although poverty was the rage in pre-war years, there was never a shortage of love. Aleata has many fond memories of her childhood and her stories and poems reflect much of this.

Blythe got only a grade eight education and she spent her teenage years working in hotels and as a hired person for households until her marriage at age eighteen. It was not until she had school age children that she decided to finish her schooling by correspondence and actually wrote high school exams with her children. Her dream of being a teacher never came about, but she did get her grade twelve.

She cannot remember a time when she did not write stories and poems. The first piece she sold was at the age of twenty-four and was hand-written as she was a farm wife and could not afford a typewriter. As time went by a typewriter was a must and eventually she was given an old style Remington. She found that farm and Christian magazines willingly bought her stories. The pay was low but enough to cover ribbons and stamps. She was always interested in history, and with the help of those who knew the district stories she was able to put together two local histories. Being in the country she never had the opportunity to take writing courses but kept in touch with other writers and got encouragement from them.

Blythe has been published in papers and magazines from coast to coast. She has two local history books which are on the data page of the University of Calgary and are also in libraries across Canada. She has a book of fiction, *A Bit of Yesterday*, and a book of poems, *The Ballad of Alice Moonchild and Others*. Her work has also been published in anthologies. She is presently working on a tongue-in-cheek bit of trivia called, *Things You Might or Might Not Want to Know*. This is a dozen pages of bits and pieces gathered over the years that tickled her fancy and it goes on with funny facts about things that have happened as the years passed by.

About Writing... *If you like to write, just keep doing it, whether you're published or not!*—ALEATA E. BLYTHE

ALEATA BLYTHE... IF YOU GO TO DRY ISLAND BUFFALO JUMP, ALBERTA, TAKE A 4X4 OR YOU WILL HAVE TO CRAWL OUT ON YOUR OWN (SUMMER 2000).

RITA BOUVIER was born and raised in Île à la Crosse (a Métis settlement and site of an historic trading post) by her late grandparents, Flora (Gardiner) and Joseph Bouvier, and her extended family on her mother's side. Her first memory of place is an island known to the local people as Île Bouleau or Birch Island. The space was shared by five family members of the Bouvier clan. Here, she tended gardens, cleaned fish nets, hauled water and did other daily chores such as milking and feeding the cows, and feeding and watering the horses and dogs which served as the main means of transportation in the winter from the island to the mainland.

Bouvier was often her grandfather's helper. She remembers that her grandmother spent a significant period of time in the sanitorium in Prince Albert. Surrounded by her aunts (a special aunt, Albertine), uncles and cousins, she did not feel the loss that one might experience when a family member is gone for a long time. In the evenings, she loved to listen to the radio or play cards with her grandfather and sometimes her cousins.

Once her grandmother returned home for good, Rita remembers tagging along with her on her afternoon visit with friends. She remembers the afternoons as lazy days filled with storytelling, canning, making birch syrup, beading, rug braiding, and embroidery. Occasionally, she and other girls who had tagged along with their Kokums were included, but more often they just spent the whole time playing games away from the adults.

Rita met both her parents early in her life (her mother, Annie Opikokew, who had married into the Canoe Lake Band and her father, Emile Lavoie, who had moved to Vancouver from Ile a la Crosse to continue his mink business) and developed a special bond with both families. Her grandfather's perspective on this matter was constantly reminding her she was rich. She agrees.

Rita always did well in school. She learned to read and speak English very quickly (Michif was her first language) and often acted as translator for her grandfather when strangers came to the house. She attended high school away from home (Prince Albert), as did all other young people who wished to pursue a higher education. Schooling beyond grade eight was not available in the community. After completing high school, she attended the University of Saskatchewan and graduated with a B.Ed. (1973) and later an M.Ed. (1984). Since her family could not afford the costs associated with attending university full-time, this period was a combination of work and school, and so she did not graduate at the same time as many of her classmates.

Her interest in writing poetry was kindled in high school. English was not her strength; nonetheless, she loved reading and reciting poetry, especially Shakespeare, although she did not share this love openly. It was about this time that she began what she calls her shoe box, closet collection of poetry. Bouvier did not pursue the idea of getting her writing published until her sabbatical in 1994. She was too busy paying back student loans, making a living, and fulfilling her calling in education—not just participating in it but transforming it, making it more meaningful to the people she loved/loves.

Rita is married to Paul Jacoby, who teaches English at Nutana High School. They live in Saskatoon with their son, Matthew Joseph Jacoby.

Bouvier is currently serving as an executive assistant with the Saskatchewan Teachers' Federation. She describes herself as a teacher with a special interest in social justice. Through her work at the Federation she has had the opportunity to serve on the provincial advisory committee on Aboriginal education, to serve in India, and to address educational issues affecting Indigenous peoples by participating in sessions of the Working Group on Indigenous Peoples in Geneva through Education International—the international body representing teachers. She has also been a regular attendee at the World Conferences of Indigenous Peoples on Education (New Zealand, Australia, the United States—Hawaii and New Mexico—and Canada—Morely Reserve) held every three years.

Other roles and responsibilities Bouvier has assumed in the education system include teacher, curriculum developer, administrator in the Saskatchewan Urban Native Teacher Education Program, and sessional lecturer in cross-cultural studies at the university.

Beyond work, to stay connected to her own community and the broader community, she has made time to serve on various boards, commissions, and committees. Recently, the focus of her volunteer work has been on her creative interest in writing—serving on the creative writing team initially, and then as a board member with the Batoche Theatre Company, Inc. The company has produced a successful musical that has captured the hearts and minds of the people who attend the Back to Batoche Festival annually.

Bouvier's first book of poetry, *Blueberry Clouds*, was published in 1999; "Medicine Man" was selected from it for the anthology *Sundog Highway—Writing From Saskatchewan*. Her other publications include a selection of two pieces, "Annie's Caw Caw" and "Why Geese" in *Prairie Fire*'s *First Voices, First Words* (2001) which was edited by Thomas King, a piece entitled, "The Portrait" in *The Women of Glenairley*, a chapbook with her 'Booming Ground' poetry pals and with Lorna Crozier as master-teacher (2001), and an excerpt from Kitatawi ekwa ("one of these days now") which was selected by the Saskatchewan Arts Board and the City of Saskatoon as part of the "Poetry in Motion Project" in 2002. Two poems, "Gabriel Dumont Overture" and "A Ritual for Goodbye" were recently selected for *Spring*, volume 111.

On writing of a different kind, Bouvier has written various papers and essays, and keynote addresses; she has participated in research studies, prepared workshops and presentations which address the systemic issues of race, class, and gender. Recently, she co-edited *Resting Lightly on Mother Earth, Urban Experiences in Education of Indigenous People* with Angela Ward (2002) which included her essay, "Good Community Schools Are Sites of Educational Activism." A second book of poetry, *papîyâhtak*, was released in the spring of 2004.

RITA BOUVIER... CONTEMPLATING.

About Writing... *Language is music, trees sing and history/memory leaps and lingers just around the corner. Listen. Observe. Through speaking and writing, movement, and dreaming, words come to give expression to ordinary and not so ordinary moments of consciousness. Run, listen to the rhythmic sound of your breathing, read, reflect, dream, dance, recite, and then write, and write again!*—RITA BOUVIER

GAIL BOWEN, daughter of Bert and Doris (Miller) Bartholomew, was born in Toronto on September 22, 1942. She learned to read by the age of three, her primary reading material being found on the tombstones in Prospect Cemetery. This ability was extremely useful when she was struck by polio two years later and had much time to read. Bowen earned a B.A. in English from the University of Toronto and an M.A. in English from the University of Waterloo. She completed everything but the dissertation in her doctoral program at the University of Saskatchewan.

For ten years Bowen taught extension classes throughout the province for the Saskatchewan Indian Federated College (now First Nations University of Canada). Since 1986 she has held a full-time appointment there and is currently Associate Professor and Head of the English Department.

Her writing career began in 1987 with the publication of *1919: the love letters of George and Adelaide*, which she wrote in collaboration with Ron Marken.

Bowen has had four plays produced at Regina's Globe Theatre—*Dancing in Poppies* (in 1993), an adaptation of *1919: the love letters of George and Adelaide*; *Beauty and the Beast* (in 1993); *The Tree* (in 1994); and an adaptation of *Peter Pan* (in 1997). Manitoba Theatre for Young People chose her *Peter Pan* as its 2000 Christmas production. The Grand Theatre in London, Ontario, presented *Dancing in Poppies* in October 2002 and *Peter Pan* as its Christmas production in 2003. Bowen's latest play, *The White Bear*, premiered at Manitoba Theatre for Young People in 2004.

Bowen has received widespread acclaim for her detective series featuring Joanne Kilbourn, a fictional character who has much in common with her creator. Both Kilbourn and Bowen teach at Saskatchewan universities and both are occasional TV panelists. As well, each has a politically connected husband and several children. Bowen's husband is Ted and their children are Hildy (30), Max (28), and Nat (23). They also have two "miraculous grandchildren": Madeleine and Alejandra.

The nine books in the detective series are *Deadly Appearances*, 1990; *Murder at the Mendel*, 1991; *The Wandering Soul Murders*, 1992; *A Colder Kind of Death*, 1994, winner

PHOTO BY TED BOWEN

GAIL BOWEN... RELISHING ROYALTIES AT TRANQUILITY BAY, BRITISH COLUMBIA.

of the Crime Writers of Canada Arthur Ellis Award; *A Killing Spring*, 1996; *Verdict in Blood*, 1998; *Burying Ariel*, 2000; *The Glass Coffin*, 2002; and *Murder at Lawyer's Bay*, 2004.

Deadly Appearances, Murder at the Mendel, The Wandering Soul Murders, A Colder Kind of Death, A Killing Spring, and *Verdict in Blood* have been adapted to the screen and broadcast as made-for-television movies. Readers of Bowen's novels tend to be attracted to the tightly constructed plots, the credible characters, and the strong sense of time and place.

BERNARD SELINGER

About Writing... *Write every day. Never leave your writing in a bad place.*—GAIL BOWEN

BEVERLEY BRENNA was born in Saskatoon in 1962 and spent the first few years of her life stuck between the lilac hedge and the back fence, communicating with God. This oral language practise became the underpinnings for storytelling, and Brenna remembers concocting all sorts of tales to pacify her elementary teachers regarding skipped assignments, as well as to support her early graded book reviews of material by imaginary authors and illustrators.

Eventually, Brenna turned her muse toward writing, and has published three books for children, *Daddy Longlegs at Birch Lane* (a Smithsonian Picture Book), *Spider Summer* (a Nelson junior novel), *The Keeper of the Trees* (a Ronsdale Press junior novel), and numerous short stories and poems for children and adults. One of her Young Adult stories—"Toe Jam" (in the anthology *Takes*)—is about a young man who gets his big toe stuck in the power head of the family vacuum. Brenna often writes from real experiences, and in this case, it was she who had the stuck toe. After her children and the neighbors couldn't solve the problem, a good samaritan phoned the Fire Department, which came with great fanfare to release her.

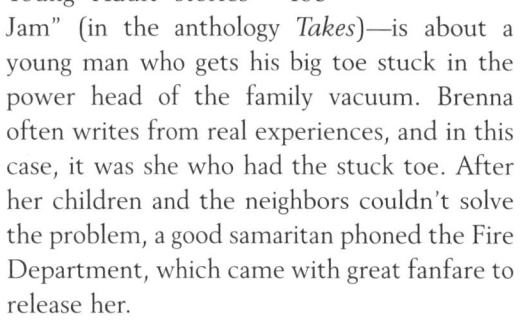

Her work for adults includes various short stories and poetry collections showcased on CBC's *Gallery*, as well as work published in magazines such as *Grain*, *Dandelion*, and *Contemporary Verse*, and British journals such as *The Auteur*. Since 1994, she has written monthly book reviews of children's literature for Saskatoon's *Star Phoenix*, and she also writes family humour for magazines such as *Western People* and *Canadian Living*.

Brenna has a Master's degree in Education (1991) and her thesis involved ethnographic research regarding the metacognitive reading strategies of preschool readers. She received her B.Ed. in 1984, also from the University of Saskatchewan, and has taught in elementary classrooms in rural Saskatchewan communities as well as in Saskatoon (where she has been a special education teacher since 1998). Most recently, she completed a B.A. in English, and has been pursuing various correspondence options to study early British literature. She continues to reflect as a teacher-researcher and her articles have been published in a variety of journals including the United Kingdom Reading Assocation's *Journal of Research in Reading*.

Brenna lives with husband Dwayne, children Wilson, Eric, and Connor, and various pets on an acreage south of Saskatoon. She enjoys sleeping in the children's treehouse in the summer and skating on the family rink in the winter. The family boasted a pet tarantula for fifteen years, and still keeps a shed skin and other memorabilia in the kitchen. This pet was a great influence in the writing of *Spider Summer*, a story about a boy with a pet tarantula. The family spent two years in London, England, while Brenna's husband completed a Ph.D., and this setting influenced the above novel as well as *The Keeper of the Trees*, also set in London. Brenna began working as a freelance storyteller in London, performing original as well as traditional tales with puppets and props, a practise she has continued back on the prairies, performing in schools and libraries as well as at the Northern Saskatchewn International Children's Festival.

BEVERLEY BRENNA

ELIZABETH BREWSTER was born in Chipman, New Brunswick, in 1922, the youngest of five children of Frederick John and Ethel May (Day) Brewster. Her earliest education was in a one-room country school in Hammtown, New Brunswick. A meeting with P.K. Page while Brewster was in her teens and Page was in her early twenties, was an important influence on Brewster's later writing. She graduated from Sussex High School and the University of New Brunswick (1946) where she was one of the founders of the little magazine *Fiddlehead*. During her first two years at the University of New Brunswick, her English teacher was Edward McCourt, who later taught at the University of Saskatchewan for many years. It was McCourt who introduced her to the work of George Crabbe, on whom she later did her doctoral dissertation.

She earned her M.A. degree in English Literature from Radcliffe College (Harvard) in 1947, her B.L.S. from the University of Toronto in 1953, and her Ph.D. from Indiana University in 1962. She also spent a year at King's College, the University of London, and attended a class with the fiction writer Norman Levine.

Brewster published three small chapbooks of poetry entitled *East Coast* (1951), *Lillooet* (1954), and *Roads* (1957). A substantial collection, *Passage of Summer*, was published in 1969 and *Sunrise North* in 1972. These were published while she was living in Edmonton, Alberta, where she worked in the university library and taught Creative Writing in the English department. She received her first Senior Artists Award from the Canada Council for 1971-72.

Edward McCourt, her old professor, had died in January 1972, and in the spring of 1972 she was invited to apply for a position in the English Department at the University of Saskatchewan. She moved to Saskatoon on September 1, 1972, and has lived there ever since. She taught in the department until 1990, and is still Professor Emeritus.

During these thirty years she has had many more books published. Among her books of poetry are *In Search of Eros* (1974), *Sometimes I Think of Moving* (1977), *The Way Home* and *Digging In* (1982), *selected poems, 1944-1984* (1985), *Entertaining Angels* (1988), *Spring Again* (1990), *Wheel of Change* (1993), *Footnotes to the Book of Job* (1995), *Garden of Sculpture* (1998), *Burning Bush* (2000), and *Jacob's Dream* (2002). She has published two novels, *Sisters* (1974) and *Junction* (1982); three collections of stories, *It's Easy to Fall on the Ice* (1977), *A House Full of Women* (1983), and *Visitations* (1987); and two autobiographical volumes, *The Invention of Truth* (1991) and *Away from Home* (1995).

ELIZABETH BREWSTER...
IN THE COMPANY OF FRIENDS.

She received additional Senior Artists Awards for poetry from the Canada Council in 1976, 1978-79, and 1985-86; the University of Western Ontario's President's medal for best magazine poem in 1980; CBC award for poetry, 1991; Saskatchewan Arts Board's Lifetime Award for Excellence in the Arts, 1995. She is a life member of the League of Canadian Poets. She was shortlisted for the Pat Lowther Award in 1991 (for *Spring Again*) and for the Governor General's Award in 1996 (for *Footnotes to the Book of Job*). She was made a Member of the Order of Canada in 2001. *Jacob's Dream* won the award for Poetry at the 2003 Saskatchewan Book Awards.

Her work has been included in many anthologies through the years, from *Canadian Poems, 1850–1952*, edited by Louis Dudek and Irving Layton (1953) through A.J.M. Smith's *Oxford Book of Canadian Verse* (1960) and Margaret Atwood's *New Oxford Book of Canadian Verse* (1982); also regional anthologies both east and west, such as *A Sudden Radiance* (1987) *Bridge City Anthology* (1991), and *Poetic Voices of the Maritimes* (1996).

She has published poetry and stories in many little magazines through the years: from *Fiddlehead*, *Poetry* (Chicago), *Canadian Forum*, *Contemporary Verse*, *Northern Review*, *Dalhousie Review*, *Queen's Quarterly*, *Quarry*, *Ontario Review*, *Saturday Night*, *Malahat Review*, including prairie magazines such as *Grain*, *NeWest Review*, *Prairie Fire*, and *Wascana Review*. She was briefly fiction editor for *NeWest Review*.

She tends to agree with Frank Scott in saying, "The world is my country." She has been treated with kindness by people in London, Dublin, Auckland, and Bloomington, Indiana, and has felt a sense of spiritual kinship in Delphi and Jerusalem. Nevertheless, most of her writing is firmly rooted in Canada. She is fond of both the Atlantic and Pacific coasts of Canada, but is as much at home in Saskatoon as anywhere. (We are all exiles.)

She has not been a passionately active member of literary groups (though she is a life member of the League of Canadian Poets and belongs to the Writers' Union, the Saskatchewan Writers' Guild, and Pen International). She has, however, been friendly with a number of poets through the years: P.K. Page, Dorothy Livesay, George Johnston, Alden Nowlan, Miriam Waddington, Jay Macpherson, and (in Saskatoon) Anne Szumigalski. She has inherited one of Anne's groups of poets, who still meet sometimes at her home, and who oblige her to write on occasion.

As the poems for *Jacob's Dream* were collected only recently, she has not written many new poems since. As usual, she thinks this is her best collection. Many of these poems are connected with the prayers of the Jewish liturgy and the Jewish year, though the winter poems could probably have been written only in Saskatoon (or maybe Winnipeg or Edmonton).

Perhaps it's time for more prose. She has a few scattered essays that might be gathered together.

About Writing... *I don't have any regular routine for writing poems. I wait around for them, and hope that an idea or a line will come. Sometimes keeping a dream notebook helps, or going on a journey to a new or an old place, or reading a good book or two, or calling up memories of the past. Just doodling helps sometimes—drawing pictures of stars or flowers. I've never fished, but I imagine it's a bit like fishing: sitting on the river bank with a baited line waiting for a nibble. Maybe a splendid poem may bite, but if not the day passes pleasantly enough. This wouldn't be good advice for everyone, but I've written quite a few books.—* ELIZABETH BREWSTER

VERONICA EDDY BROCK (1926–2002) grew up in southern Saskatchewan, the eighth of ten children, and attended Sacred Heart Academy in Regina. In 1944, she was diagnosed with tuberculosis and was forced to live the next five years of her life at the Fort San Sanitorium in the Qu'Appelle Valley, northeast of Regina.

During these five years at Fort San, Veronica's life changed drastically. She underwent surgeries that included the removal of one of her lungs as well as seven ribs. Her determination and strong will helped her to survive the ordeal and she was eventually free of her ailment.

She then worked in purchasing for the government of famed politician and fellow Weyburn-ite, Tommy Douglas.

In 1955 she married Russell Brock, a farmer from McTaggart, Saskatchewan. Despite the obvious risks, the couple had five children, two of which were twins—Anna and Ava, Duncan, Warren, and Sarah.

Brock recounted her experiences at Fort San in her first book, *Valley of the Flowers* (1987), an autobiographical novel set in the beautiful Qu'Appelle Valley. In the book, she describes the good times amidst the despair of the T.B. sanitorium. A sequel, *Beyond the Valley of the Flowers*, was self-published in 2001.

Along with her writing, Veronica Eddy Brock was an accomplished painter. Many of her works became part of the city of Weyburn's permanent collection. She received awards for her art from Saskatchewan Culture, Youth and Recreation.

NIK BURTON

CATHERINE M. BUCKAWAY (1919–1996)

was born in North Battleford, lived for many years on a farm at Janzen, and eventually moved to Saskatoon. She first began writing when she was 48 years old, and published five books of poetry. Her work appeared in many Canadian and American poetry magazines. At the time of her death in 1996, Buckaway had published nearly 4,000 haiku in books and periodicals. She had been published in 136 magazines and 21 anthologies in Canada, the United States, Italy, and Puerto Rico. She gave numerous readings of her work and was the recipient of writing grants from the Canada Council, Saskatchewan Arts Board, and the Carling Community Arts Foundation.

Buckaway was widely known as a master of miniature Japanese poetic forms such as haiku, tanka, and senryu, and was one of the world's most recognized writers of these forms. She was elected to Japan's exclusive society of haiku poets.

Her books include the new-and-selected collection *Blue Window*, published in 1985. Other publications include her haiku books *The Silver Cuckoo* (1974), *AIR 17* (1973), and *Tanka: The Lavender Nightingale*.

Catherine Buckaway also wrote and published lyric poetry, books for children and even an historical work. These titles include: *Strangely The Birds Have Come* (1973), *Charlotte* (1975), *Alfred, The Dragon Who Lost His Flame* (1982), and *Waiting For George* (1985). Her history book is *The Prairie Rose Story* (1960).

NIK BURTON

KELLEY JO BURKE

was born on a gladiola farm—nobody believes this. One of the problems, as the wolf explained to the shepherd boy—talking with his mouth full but still anxious to leap on a teachable moment—one of the problems with continually tightening and refining the truth is that when you actually deliver a pearl like "She was born on a gladiola farm"—no one believes it ever saw the inside of an oyster.

But Burke really was born on a small gentleman's farm, which had been planted with a variety of specialty crops, in Westminster, Massachusetts. Her ancestors' bones have held the better spots in the town graveyard for nine generations. Her house, which had been her great-great aunt's, stood between her grandfather's and her great-grandfather's on a short gravel road just off Main Street—and the road carried her mother's family's name.

She came to Canada when she was a little kid, in the late sixties. Her dad was a university professor. Bobby Kennedy was dead. Martin Luther King was dead. The black body bags just kept coming off the planes, special D from Vietnam—and besides, they were giving tenure away for box tops in Canada back then—they were so desperate for faculty. So it was northward ho.

Her first winter in Canada, it went to minus 50, and she almost died wearing her "winter" coat from Massachusetts, which was barely a fall coat in Winnipeg. She glared at her folks for pretty much the next seven years, and said "Take me home" in answer to almost any comment that came her way.

Then a funny thing happened. The summer she was fifteen, she fell in love with Canada. Not the winters. And not, to be perfectly honest, the summers. Not the place at all, really. She fell in love with this country the way you fall in love with the late-blooming guy at the back of the party with greasy hair, and a cigarette shoved up each nostril, laughing too hard at his own joke. You fall for the genuine intelligence hiding behind the butts up his nose. The compassion in his eyes. The dispassionate, self-deprecating, funny, sad, wide-awakeness of him. You fall, finally, for his decency. That's how Burke fell for Canada.

So she stopped sulking and got into the game. She joined the Manitoba Theatre Workshop, and began to act and write for their young company. She went to the University of Winnipeg, and wrote more for the school paper. She went home with the guy with the greasy hair—he'd quit the cigarette trick by the time she got to him—and made children and a life in Regina, that always seemed to include some sort of writing. She started to become who she was going to be.

She wrote for a living, and for herself, and in 1989, soon after the birth of her first child, a set of poems she'd been working on appeared in *Grain*. She still has the letter from Lorna Crozier, accepting her writing. She plans to be buried with it.

In the same year, Michele Sereda of the *Curtain Razors* asked Burke if she'd write a skit for Paula Costain and herself, to take to the Edmonton Fringe.

That was Burke's first play, *Goddessness*. The experience of hearing people actually laugh at and understand stuff from the recesses of her mind was overwhelming, and intoxicating. And she's been at in some form ever since.

She writes plays, the best known of which is *Charming and Rose; True Love*. She writes poetry. She writes radio plays, one of which, *Big Ocean*, played in seven countries in 2000. She is a regular contributor to CBC Radio's *Ideas*, writing and producing documentaries. Her favourite is called *Mothers of Miscarriage*. She also writes for a show called *Gallery*, which she co-hosts. She directs radio

KELLEY JO BURKE

drama and readings. She's received some awards and a good number of publications and productions, but the only real measure of success she has is that she now gets to spend her working day writing, and creating, in the company of talented actors, producers, musicians, and writers.

When Burke was in university, people kept asking her what she was going to "be" with a degree in English and Philosophy. She always answered "Better educated" but that seemed to satisfy no one. So one day she said "a Renaissance woman." She had no idea what she meant—just someone who does all sorts of things, and follows her passions and curiosities, and even whims. Someone who brings not just the mind, but the heart, and the belly, and good strong dancing feet to everything she does. You know, somebody with doublets and hose. And servants.

It sounds, in retrospect, like a recipe for nervous collapse, and she should have known better. But she was very young, and she said it. And as sometimes happens to her, the words clanged out of her mouth like bells, ringing not of truth, but of contractual obligation. Burke's been trying to meet the terms of that contract ever since.

About Writing...

HH: So tell us something about writing.
KJ: No.
HH: What?
KJ: No. I'd rather not.
HH: Why not?
KJ: I'd rather not say.
HH: You're uncomfortable with the topic?
KJ: Me? Of course not. I'm a writer. Right? I'm a writer... there's no reason I should feel unworthy—I mean—ill equipped to discuss writing. No. Writing. Sure. Great. I love writing. I stopped vomiting in front of the keyboard years ago. I just don't want to.

HH: You've had some success.
KJ: You think? Really? What? What in particular? Tell me exactly what you liked. No. Don't. You won't like it enough. Peculiar weather we're having, huh?
HH: If you're this uncomfortable, why on earth do you keep writing?
KJ: It's not like that. It's not a matter of "Do I write?" or "Don't I write?" It's "I write." It the same thing as "I am."

BONNIE BURNARD was born in a small town in southern Ontario in 1945, a sister to four older brothers. The war and the depression that preceded it had a profound effect on her extended family. Her mother's beloved young brother Oliver, who is still remembered, in 2003, as funny, had been killed in France and two other brothers, farm boys, came home filled both with shrapnel and debilitating memories. Her mother's family were horse people, breeding prize Clydesdales which they showed at the Royal Winter Fair; there were buying trips to Scotland to improve bloodlines. Burnard's father, whose parents died when he was a boy, was raised by strict, apparently humourless relatives who needed a farm hand. In his twenties, after squeaking through the depression working at anything he could find, he started his own small wholesale business; as a young married couple Burnard's parents often loaded the trunk of an old car with eggs and drove through the night to be at the Toronto market at dawn. By the early forties, her father had been contracted by Ottawa to ship tens of thousands of cases of eggs to England and after the war he continued to sell to Toronto and Montreal. He made jobs for people. Privately, he provided financial support where it was needed, as did many men of his generation. Burnard's mother, secure now after years of risk and grief and hard work and making do, and well aware that good times can dry up, turned her attention to generosity and hospitality. A crowded house, exquisite food, gifts, music, the silent closing of ranks at funerals or around someone's 'private trouble', the beach, jokes, wit, stories: this was Burnard's first world. Her mother, entirely a woman of her time and having sent five kids off to school every day, year after year after year, was extremely proud of their usually moderate success and proud too that none of them had ever been late, because this reflected directly on her. If nothing else, she meant to teach her children that only fools take opportunity for granted. When Burnard, sneaking quickly through the halls of her high school during the playing of *God Save the Queen*, destroyed this long-standing family achievement, her mother phoned the principal to ask if the infraction might be stricken from the official record. Throughout her life, Burnard has had many such second chances.

Burnard graduated from the University of Western Ontario in 1967 with a B.A. in English. She then left southern Ontario, briefly taught high school, travelled to western Canada with a friend, worked for a lawyer (where she saw a filed 8" x 10" glossy of a murdered rancher), worked at several other jobs, travelled more, taught again. Shiftless, you could say, or curious. Certainly wanting something. She returned to southern Ontario and married in 1973, settling down it was called, and soon thereafter moved to Regina with her transferred husband. They bought a wonderful big old house near the legislature, had three children, D'Arcy, Melanie, and David, and made friends.

Living in Regina, Burnard stumbled on a strange, unexpected thing: the possibility of writing literary fiction. While attending classes at the University of Regina, she took the opportunity to attend a reading by Marian Engel, a middle-aged mother and fiction writer. From this short, anonymous hour, Burnard seized permission to try to write. Why on earth did she need permission? Because this was literary Canada in 1979. Because she was a young, standard-issue, middle-class Canadian mother who had been encouraged to believe that her place in the world of the mind was out there in the dark, mostly female, audience, sitting quietly and properly awed: not acting but reacting. Because her own time and place and thoughts, with no steppes or moors or beguiling accents or wars or bright lights and big cities, were, without doubt, negligible.

Through the year, she wrote on her dining room table, using her husband's secretary's cast-off typewriter. In the summers, initially at the suggestion of Ken Mitchell, she attended Fort San for a week or ten days of dreaming and from this dreaming she sometimes produced a first draft of a story to take home to the dining room table for the winter. At Fort San she learned what was meant by S.A.S.E. She met many writers, both aspiring and established; she learned to hug some of them. It would be foolish to try to describe exactly which writers affected her in what ways but the cumulative

PHOTO BY JUDITH KRAUSE

BONNIE BURNARD... AT THE FIRE AT FORT SAN, CIRCA 1981.

effects were profound and lasting. Early names include Ven Begamudré, Andreas Schroeder, Jack Hodgins, Pat Krause, Judith Krause, Byrna Barclay, Anne Szumigalski, David Carpenter, Lorna Crozier, Patrick Lane, David Helwig, Clarke Blaise, Liz Phillips, Geoffrey Ursell, Barbara Sapergia, Chris Fisher, Leon Rooke, Sandra Birdsell, Edna Alford. Slightly later important names include Connie Gault, Dianne Warren, Marlis Wesseler, and selected others from those early times: Don Kerr, Bob Currie, Rosemary Sullivan, Alberto Manguel, the late Carol Shields. And several friends to writing: Wenda MacArthur, Heather Wood, Nik Burton, and Gwen Currie.

Writers not then met but enthroned: Munro, Gallant, Atwood. This is a common list, for good reason. Dead writers: Shakespeare, for the sheer joy in his words; Hardy, for the ache.

First, almost simultaneous short story publications: *Saskatchewan Gold* and *NeWest Review*. Subsequently, stories have been widely anthologized and, occasionally, broadcast.

Early on, Burnard was the grateful recipient of time purchased through the support of both the Canada Council and The Saskatchewan Arts Board (where she worked as literary officer from 1988 to 1990). And she is grateful to Coteau Books for gainful employment as an editor (which she loved), to Sage Hill and The Humber School of Writing, for gigs, to the University of Western Ontario for a residency, and to the Writers Trust.

More recently she has taught at Booming Ground (the summer creative writing program at the University of British Columbia) and at Banff. She is currently adjunct professor in the writing department at the University of Windsor.

Burnard's fiction has been widely translated and thoroughly reviewed, receiving both astonishingly positive comments and a few good horse-whippings. It has won awards and for the usual reasons: a particular jury liked a book on a certain day. Sales have improved, including foreign sales. She has travelled extensively to read from her work, discovering an infatuation with both European and American cities. Distant readers have telephoned her at home to argue a point and she has enjoyed this, to a point.

She is a member of The Writers' Union of Canada, has served on the Public Lending Rights Commission, and the boards of Coteau Books and the Saskatchewan Writers Guild. She has been on the Giller jury panel and on other juries where the lesson learned was pretty much the same: after the initial, subjective cull, what on earth does the word *best* mean?

Burnard and her kids returned to southern Ontario in 1994, where she will stay, continuing to write. She is working on new stories and a new novel: *The Life I Want*. After family and friends, after life, she loves writing literary fiction. Importantly, she would not be a fiction writer at all had she not lived, for a time, in Saskatchewan.

Burnard's publications include her novel, *A Good House*, which was published in Canada, the United States, the United Kingdom, Germany and twelve other countries (1999, 2000, 2001, 2002). She has also published *Casino* (1994, 1995) and *Women of Influence* (1988, 1993), which was translated into *Femmes d'Influence* by S. Brault (1995). Her work has been anthologized in Oxford University's *Short Fiction* (2003), *Donde Es Aqui?* (2002), *Notes from Home* (2002), *Dropped Threads* (2001), *Oxford Stories by Canadian Women* (1999), *Turn of the Story* (1999), *Desire* (1999), *Mothers and Daughters* (1997), *Sunrise to Sunset* (1997), *Penguin Anthology of Stories by Canadian*

Women (1997), *Desde El Invierno* (1996), *Arnold Anthology of Post-Colonial Literature* (1996), *The Best of NeWest* (1996), *Spin on 2* (1995), *The Oxford Book of Canadian Short Stories* (1995), *The Second Gates of Paradise: Anthology of Erotic Short Fiction* (1994), *Writing from Canada* (1994), *Lodestone* (1993), *Kitchen Talk* (1992), *Best Canadian Stories* (1992), *Beyond Borders* (1992), *Canadian Short Stories* (1991), *Worlds Unrealized* (1991), *Soho Square 111: Bloomsbury* (1990), *Best Canadian Stories* (1989), *Last Map* (1989), *Sky High* (1988), *Best Canadian Stories* (1984), *Double Bond* (1984), *More Saskatchewan Gold* (1984), *Coming Attractions* (1983), and *Saskatchewan Gold* (1982).

Burnard has also published in a variety of magazines, including *Toronto Life, Imperial Review, House and Home, Chatelaine, Grain, NeWest Review, Dinosaur Review, Prism International, Kunapipi* (Denmark), and *Viva* (Amsterdam).

Her awards include The Giller Prize (1999) and the Canadian Booksellers Association People's Choice Award (2000) for *A Good House*. She also received the Marian Engel Award (1995) for a body of work. Her book *Casino* was a Giller prize finalist in 1994, and it won the Saskatchewan Book of the Year award that same year. Burnard has also received the CBC Literary Competition award (1992), the City of Regina Writing Award (1984), the W.O. Mitchell Bursury at Fort San (1983), and several other Saskatchewan Writers Guild awards.

Burnard has served as editor for a number of anthologies and books of fiction.

About Writing... *Advice? Be promiscuous in your living and in your reading and in any editorial response you might seek. Absorb so much that you are able to forget it all. In this way, there is the chance that you might come, pristine, to your own authentic voice.—*
BONNIE BURNARD

SHARON BUTALA was born on August 24, 1940, in Nipawin. She is the daughter of Achille Antoine LeBlanc and Margaret Amy Alexis Graham, and she has four sisters: Cynthia, Sheila (deceased), Deanna, and Kathleen. Butala writes of the land of Saskatchewan and the people who live there. Living in the province for all but five years of her life, she has been surrounded by the Saskatchewan landscape and lifestyle. She first had a sense of herself as a writer at the age of nine, but she lost the image of that possibility and didn't attempt writing again until she was 38.

Butala's first medium of expression was painting, and she received a B.A. in Fine Arts as well as a B.Ed. She worked in Saskatoon with teenagers who were, as they were then called, "educable mentally handicapped." Butala was about to finish her Master's degree in special education when she left the academic environment in 1976 to move with her second husband to his ranch near Eastend. There she was awakened by the power of the land and moved to express what she experienced. At the same time, she found that something in her heart had been lost to her, and her former medium was no longer accessible to her. So, Butala turned to writing.

Those familiar with Butala's works will know the name Eastend and the character of the ranch land that surrounds it because her books explore the personalities and issues of ranchers and small town people. She first honed her craft with short stories and after two dozen of them, tried the novel. Crafting the novel was a challenge. She had to determine the themes that she felt she could competently incorporate into her work, and came up with love. During twenty years of studying and deepening her craft, and accumulating more knowledge and insights about life, she felt increasingly better able to rely on her instincts so she gradually moved inward to more complex and deeper themes. Her insights and meditations were published in the beautifully sensitive award-winning *The Perfection of Morning* in 1994. Butala then explored the more internal and external terrains of human experience, incorporating issues surrounding drought-stricken Ethiopia in her novel *The Garden of Eden* (1998).

Butala's passions are not only printed words on paper but the evidence, both natural and man-made, of history on the land. Recognizing the distinct characteristics and delicate ecosystem of the original prairie grasslands of southwestern Saskatchewan, she together with her husband have been instrumental in having portions of the land designated as the Old Man On His Back Prairie and Heritage Conservation Area that will not be farmed. Recognizing the distinct literary accomplishments of Wallace Stegner, she has also been instrumental in having the Eastend house that he lived in declared a historical site and made into an artists' retreat.

Sharon Butala's books include *Country of the Heart* (1984), *Queen of the Headaches* (1985), *The Gates of the Sun* (1986), *Luna* (1988), *Fever* (1990), *Upstream* (1991), *Harvest* (1992), *The Fourth Archangel* (1992), *The Perfection of the Morning: An Apprenticeship in Nature* (1994), *Coyote's Morning Crying: Meditations and Dreams From a Life in Nature* (1995), *The Garden of Eden* (1998), *Wild Stone Heart* (2000), *Real Life* and *Old Man on His Back*, both released in 2002.

Butala's plays include *Sweet Time* (1989), *Natural Disasters* (1986), *A Killing Frost* (1988), *The Element of Fire* (1989), and *Rodeo Life* (1993). She has been interviewed on many occasions with the CBC, and she has been published abroad.

Butala has been awarded numerous times for her work. She received the Saskatchewan Writers Guild Member's Achievement Award, a Silver Award for Fiction from the National Magazine Awards (1991), a First for Paperback Fiction from the Foundation for the Advancement of Canadian Letters (1992), a Canada 125 Commemorative Medal (1992), the Non-Fiction Award and Spirit of Saskatchewan Award from the Saskatchewan Book Awards (1994), the Saskatchewan Gold Award from the Western Magazine Awards (1992, 1993, 1996), and the Marian Engel Prize (1998).

Butala was awarded the Queen's Jubilee Medal in 2002 and an honourary LL.D. in

PHOTO BY DUANE PRENTICE/NOMADIC VISIONS, VICTORIA, B.C.

SHARON BUTALA... IN THE FIELD IN HER BOOK *WILD STONE HEART*.

2000. In 2002 she became an Officer of the Order of Canada.

About Writing... *If I could do it over again— the last twenty-five years of hard labour—would I still be a writer? I suspect I would because it seems writing chooses you, rather than the other way around. It can be a frivolous career, but for most of us it is death-defying.*—SHARON BUTALA

GREG BUTTON was born and raised in Moose Jaw, where he has lived all his life. Astonishingly prolific, Button has composed over 2,000 poems since he started writing in 1976, many of which have been published in journals and magazines. His inspiration to write poetry has been his struggle with schizophrenia and his experiences at a welfare hotel for fourteen months. *Inside of Midnight* (1993) is Button's first book.

HEATHER HODGSON

ROBERT CALDER was born in Moose Jaw in 1941, the son of Earle Fenwick and Mildred Jane (nee Remey) Calder. In 1948, following her divorce, his mother took him and his younger brother, Kenneth, to Saskatoon, where they grew up and were educated. Living on College Drive, across the street from the University of Saskatchewan, it was inevitable that both boys would attend university. Kenneth graduated with Honours and Master's degrees in History, and went on to a career in the Department of National Defence, where he became Assistant Deputy Minister (Policy). Robert left with Honours and Master's degrees in English, writing his thesis on "Women in the Writing of Jonathan Swift."

Before he had completed his Master's work in 1965, Calder was hired as an instructor by the English Department at the university, and he has been a member of that department ever since. From 1967 to 1970, he took an educational leave and completed the requirements for his doctoral degree at the University of Leeds, in Great Britain. His dissertation was a critical examination of the writings of W. Somerset Maugham.

Back in the Department of English, he was promoted to assistant professor in 1971, associate professor in 1975, and full professor in 1981. In 1979, at the age of thirty-eight, he became one of the youngest heads in the department's history, and from 1981 to 1984 he served as the first associate dean (Fine Arts and Humanities) in the College of Arts and Science. In 1989-90, though he cannot sing, dance, or play a musical instrument, he was appointed acting head of the Department of Music.

Though his articles on such figures as George Orwell, Arthur Morrison, Elizabeth Bowen, Somerset Maugham, D.H. Lawrence, P.G. Wodehouse, and John Gardner are conventional scholarly pieces, Calder has always written his books with an eye on the general intelligent and educated reader both in and beyond academia. *W. Somerset Maugham and the Quest For Freedom*, a critical study based on his doctoral dissertation, was published in Great Britain and the Commonwealth by William Heinemann Ltd. in 1972, in the United States by Doubleday in 1973, and in Japanese translation by the Hokuseido Press, Tokyo, in 1980.

Calder established himself as one of the leading authorities on Maugham in the world when Heinemann published his full-scale biography of the British author, *Willie: The Life of W. Somerset Maugham*, in 1989. Written with the exclusive cooperation of

Maugham's private secretary and lover, *Willie* was widely praised by such critics as Anthony Burgess, Peter Ackroyd, Frederic Raphael and Anthony Curtis, and St. Martin's Press's publication of an American edition elicited a five-page review-essay by Gore Vidal in the New York Review of Books. In Canada, it won the 1989 Governor General's Literary Award for Non-Fiction. In 2000, a Moscow publisher, Interdialect, brought out a Russian translation, and in 1992 Calder was commissioned to write the Introduction, Explanatory Notes, and Selected Bibliography for its Twentieth-Century Classics edition of Maugham's novel *Of Human Bondage*.

In 1984, Calder astonished his academic colleagues by co-writing with Garry Andrews *Rider Pride: The Story of Canada's Best-Loved Football Team*. It is the history of the Saskatchewan Roughrider Football Club from its formation as the Regina Rugby club in 1910 to 1984, blending accounts of its struggles and achievements on the field with the evolving history of the province of which it is such an integral part. In addition to the 7,500 trade copies that were sold—a bestseller in Canadian terms—1,200 numbered deluxe box set copies were given out at the Roughriders' $200-a-plate Dinner in 1984.

Calder continues to balance his academic publication with more general writing. *Beware the British Serpent* (2004) is a full-scale examination of the role of British writers in propaganda in the United States during the Second World War. *A Richer Dust* (2004) is about Calder's uncle, who served for five and a half years in World War II, came home, and committed suicide three weeks later. More personal than anything he has written before, this book is an examination of battle fatigue, the war ethos, and the wide-ranging and long-lasting effects of one soldier's death on a number of families. *A Richer Dust* won the 2003 John V. Hicks Manuscript Award.

ROBERT CALDER... "HEMINGWAY OF THE NORTH"

About Writing... *Non-fiction writing, especially in Saskatchewan, is never given the respect accorded poetry and fiction, but I agree with Paul Fussell that books based on ideas are just as exciting as those written around characters.*—ROBERT CALDER

PHIL CAMPAGNA was born in Calgary, Alberta, in 1960, into a roaming lifestyle that involved moves every few months. An only child, he eventually became the adopted stepbrother to numerous younger children. As a result, he quickly learned the art of storytelling to ward off mutiny against the sitter—himself. During a stint of small-town living, this took the form of writing to ward off his own boredom. The wanderlust that resulted from living in a small town, combined with news reports of oppression in South America, sparked his interest in Chile. While still in his teens, he scribbled the first pages of what would eventually become his first young adult novel.

Campagna got the original idea from a TV documentary on teenage missionaries. Teens

PHIL CAMPAGNA... ON A HIKE IN THE ALBERTA BADLANDS.

were being sent everywhere, even to countries that weren't politically stable. What would happen, he wondered, if a Saskatchewan teen with a habit of getting into trouble went along? What if he got on the wrong side of the wrong kind of government? When Campagna read about political orphans, the children of the "disappeared ones," the book wanted to write itself before he could get to a keyboard.

The partially completed manuscript, however, sat for years on a shelf. Other duties had called that left no time to write—such as attending the University of Saskatchewan to study computer science. It wasn't until re-entering the workforce later that he finally found the time. As a young single writer in his early twenties, he would take vacations just to write. Endless days of introspection and wandering in the Rocky Mountains provided substance to *The Freedom Run*.

The eventual result was over 400 pages long—nearly twice the length it needed to be! The entire work had been produced on an Olympus manual typewriter, exactly two fingers at a time. It was here that Campagna learned the value of cutting and trimming. He proceeded to put the manuscript through not one or two but five revisions—each typed out the same way as the last. The finished copy of the manuscript took two typewriter ribbons and a bottle of whiteout.

After submitting the manuscript twice on his own, Campagna sought an agent "to peddle it." The book was first published in 1991, and became a Canadian Children's Book Centre Choice.

After publication of that work, Campagna found himself tending to matters closer to home. In addition to purchasing a house (and "renovating it endlessly"), he married in 1994—becoming an instant dad to a teen in the process. His stepson quickly became his "test reader."

In the 1990s, Campagna became fascinated with two separate, but not entirely dissimilar, social phenomena: racist groups and religious cults. What if the two merged, in the form of a charismatic leader? What if this leader tapped into the anger of disenfranchised urban youth and organized them for his own purposes? What if a teen got himself into such a group—would he be able to leave again? What if?

The next many months saw the plot for Campagna's second young adult novel form and reform many times over. The actual writing took nearly three years—on a computer this time.

Finally, in 2000, *The Liberty Circle* was published. Again touching on the subject of civil rights, this novel delved into the dark worlds of racist skinheads and cults. The book was a finalist for both a Saskatchewan Book Award and an Arthur Ellis Award.

Recently, Campagna returned to school, upgrading his education and acquiring Microsoft Certified Professional and Microsoft Certified Systems Engineer certifications. In addition to working as a computer consultant and technical trainer, he is still at work on the writing; more novels for young adults are in the works. He also has projects in mind for younger readers.

"It seems the window of opportunity for catching YA readers is exactly five minutes wide. That's the period between the time they set down Harry Potter and the time they pick up Stephen King. In between—as someone who writes at a plod—I've barely enough time to reach them with a single new book! Hopefully, I'll pick up speed as I go along."

About Writing... *A writer should write, daily, even if it's only a page or two. While it's true that perspiration should follow inspiration, it doesn't always work that way. Sometimes the only way to begin is to do just that—begin. Once the mind heats up, inspiration will follow. Usually!*—PHIL CAMPAGNA

ANNE CAMPBELL was born at Paddockwood in a Red Cross Outpost Hospital, the first to be built in the British Empire. Her father, Joseph King, born just after his parents arrived in Canada from England, grew up in Detroit. Returning to Canada as an adult he homesteaded with his parents at Paddockwood, later working summers "south," for Anne's mother's family (Paul Tomlenovich). Anne's father and his brother, Brother Ozwald King, a Benedictine monk from St. Peter's Abbey, were both somewhat eccentric mechanical geniuses.

The Tomlenovich family is pictured on the cover of the history *Croatians in Canada*, Paul having been one of three young men from the Adriatic coast to settle a Croatian community in Saskatchewan (near Kenaston) at the turn of the century. Anne's mother, Rose, was a gifted student and seamstress, not to mention mother of Anne and her six siblings.

Anne grew up in Saskatoon and Hanley, walking in the countryside, playing with cousins, drawing, and later singing and acting in high school chorus and theatre. She left Hanley as a teenager for Regina and summer work at the Saskatchewan Power Corporation, as it was then called, where she met and married Jock (JW) Campbell, one of four young engineers who in the mid-fifties had put in place Saskatchewan's natural gas system.

With three babies, Joseph, Jill and Jacqueline, quickly in tow, Anne resumed her studies, in drama, at the Conservatory of Music, receiving a scholarship award in her second year; she later studied at the University of Regina. In 1972 she began to write social commentary regularly for CBC Radio though, strangely, she didn't think of it as writing. Rather, she thought of it as a continuation of the work she was doing with others for recognition of the educational needs of children, work which led in Regina to the first Association for Children with Learning Disabilities. In 1975 Anne followed her early

PHOTO BY LEONA KING

ANNE CAMPBELL... AT THE SITE OF HER BIRTHPLACE, RED CROSS HOSPITAL, PADDOCKWOOD, SASKATCHEWAN.

love of visual art and, with communications experience, began work at the (Regina) Mackenzie Art Gallery, later moving to Calgary and the Glenbow and Heritage Park Museums.

In 1977 Anne took her first writing class at the historic Fort San Summer School of the Arts; her teachers were Lorna Crozier and Eli Mandel. She found her "family" there and never looked back. After another year at Fort San with Anne Szumigalski, and with regular Writers Colonies, Anne published much well-received poetry and stories in magazines and journals, as well as four books of poetry: *No Memory of a Move* (1983), *Death is an Anxious Mother* (1986), *Red Earth, Yellow Stone* (1989) and *Angel Wings All Over* (1994). As well, she published poems, stories, and non-fiction in various anthologies. Anne also worked with composer Tom Schudel on chamber and choral compositions, which continue to be performed worldwide. Her work has received Saskatchewan Writers Guild, City of Regina, Saskatchewan Arts Board, Canada Council, and other awards. Giving back to the writing community during this time, Anne served on local and national writing executives and, as did many others, regularly provided writing workshops.

In 2002 she received the George Bothwell Memorial Award for public service through public relations. During much of her writing career Anne worked at the Regina Public Library, in charge of Public Relations, Aboriginal and Literacy Service, and Public Programming, including the Writer-in-Residence Program which she defended regularly during budget review. In 1999 Anne took an early leave to work half-time as coordinator of the Office for Ecumenism ("inhabiting the earth together") at the Archdiocese of Regina and on writing projects. In 2002 Anne was named a Research Fellow of the Canadian Plains Research Center, University of Regina. Early in 2003 she took a second early leave, finally to work full-time on writing. Anne lives in Regina where her children and (five) grandchildren also live.

Anne's day jobs and her writing both reflect her passion for reconciliation, an undertaking not so much to be fully accomplished as worked towards. Her present work, a biography of the complex Canadian visual artist Arthur McKay, one of the "Regina Five," has taken her back to her beloved north where McKay too was born in a Red Cross Outpost Hospital.

About Writing... *I like to keep in mind the words of theologian Paul Tillich: "Be open, always be open." The gift of writing—access to the unknown—is too often shut down by an urge to judgement or premature closure; both can end work still needing to go into the unknown. Having said that, sometimes writers do keep writing long after an ending has presented itself. Writing is risk, best undertaken with a large heart.—* ANNE CAMPBELL

MARIA CAMPBELL is a Métis writer, playwright, filmmaker and teacher who was born and raised in the Treaty Six area of Saskatchewan. She is a widow, the mother of four children, and the grandmother of seven.

Campbell received an honourary doctorate in Laws in 1985 from the University of Regina, and an honourary doctorate in Letters from York University in 1992.

She has served as writer-in-residence all across western Canada, including at the universities of Alberta and Saskatchewan, at the Regina and Prince Albert Public Libraries, and as playwright-in-residence at Persephone Theatre in Saskatoon.

Campbell's teaching experience is extensive. She has taught and facilitated workshops and seminars on creative writing, film and video, and community organizing, all across Canada and the United States, including at the Banff School of Fine Arts, in the Departments of English and Native Studies, at the University of Saskatchewan, and for the Saskatchewan Indian Federated College in Saskatoon. Campbell taught drama at Saskatchewan Urban Native Teachers Education Program in Saskatoon as well.

Campbell has been guest speaker at numerous conferences on issues related to justice, women and youth in crisis, community development, literature, and the arts. She has presented papers and guest-lectured at universities around the world.

Her books include *Halfbreed* (1973), *People of the Buffalo* (1975), *Riel's People* (1976), *Little Badger and the Fire Spirit* (1977), *Achimoona* (1985), *The Book of Jessica* (1987), and *Stories of the Road Allowance People* (1995). Four of her books have been published in eight countries and four languages (German, Chinese, English, and Italian).

Campbell has also written a number of stage plays, including *Flight* (1979), *Jessica* (1982), *Uptown Circles* (1984) and *One More Time* (1995). *Jessica* was produced in Edmonton, Toronto, Ottawa, Montreal, Scotland, Denmark, and Italy, and *One More Time* played at both 25th Street Theatre and Globe Theatre, as well as touring the province.

Campbell's films include *Edmonton's Unwanted Women* (1968), *Red Dress* (1977), and her independent documentaries include *Road to Batoche* (1985), *Cumberland House* (1986), *A Centre for Buffalo Narrows* (1987), *Joseph's Justice* (1994), *La Beau Sha Sho* (1994), and *Journey to Healing* (1995).

Campbell has also been documenting Elders on video since 1980 with the goal of eventually producing a documentary series in Michif, Cree, and English. She has also been a writer and producer for radio and her thirteen part series *Kiskamimsoo* was broadcast in 1973 and 1974 by CKUA in Edmonton. She also hosted weekly interviews with historical people, entitled *Tea with Maria*, and broadcast a five-part radio series called *Batoche 85*.

She was named Honourary Chief by the Black Lake First Nation in 1978, and was the recipient of the Vanier Award by the Vanier Institute in 1979. That same year she was named National Hero by the Native Council of Canada. In 1986 Campbell was given a Dora Mavor Moore Award and a Chalmers Award, for playwrighting and for *Jessica*, respectively. In 1985 she was presented with the Order of the Sash by the Métis Nation of Saskatchewan, and in 1992, she was given the Gabriel Dumont Medal of Merit by Gabriel Dumont Institute. In 1994 Campbell received a Saskatchewan Achievement Award from the Government of Saskatchewan, and that same year she was awarded a Golden Wheel Award from the Rotary Club of Saskatchewan. Campbell was appointed Aboriginal Scholar in 1995 by the University of Saskatchewan and that year she was also presented with a National Aboriginal Achievement Award by the Canadian Aboriginal Arts Foundation. In 1996 the Department of Native Studies at the University of Calgary gave her a Chief Crowfoot Award.

Campbell has also been a volunteer community worker for most of her life. That work has been primarily focused on women and children in crisis. She has been a member of the Saskatchewan Indigenous Coalition and the Saskatoon Community Outreach and Education Centre.

Campbell is also co-founder of the Women's Halfway House and the Women and Children's Emergency Crisis Centre in Edmonton, Alberta. She has worked with other volunteers to organize and set up food cooperatives in the inner cities of Edmonton and Calgary, and she was also involved in the setting up of a housing co-op in Edmonton.

Her recent works in progress include a collection of poetry and prose, and a new play, as well as a one-hour video documentary on the Canoe Lake Elders.

Campbell has worked under the direction and guidance of traditional elders since 1964. She says she was fortunate to have had as teachers her father, John Campbell, Chief Robert Smallboy, Albert Lightning, Daisy Crowchild, Mariah Cardinal, Mariah Joachim, Adrian Hope, and Smith Atimoyoo. Other teachers to whom she is grateful include Peter O'chiese, Veronica Merasty, Leada Gaudry, Maruis and Cecelia Iron. Campbell's non-aboriginal teachers have been the late Saul Alinski, Rick Salter, Leora Proctor, and Elaine Husband.

HEATHER HODGSON

About Writing... *Storytellers have a big job. They must understand their sacred place and they must also understand the new language and use it to express their stories without losing the thoughts and images that are culturally unique to them. This new storyteller must also be a translator of the old way, so that it will not be lost to a new generation. And all of this must be done on paper, for that is the new way. (Achimoona, 1985)* — MARIA CAMPBELL

WARREN CARIOU, the first child of Ray and Melba Cariou, was born into an enormous extended family in Meadow Lake, and he lived in that town until the age of ten, when his family moved to a farm three miles away. Most of his writing draws upon his experiences of life in and around Meadow Lake, a place that is rich in wilderness, storytelling traditions, and history. His literary ambitions were awakened quite early by his father's storytelling abilities, and as a child he wrote fantasy, science fiction, and animal fables. In 1981, at the age of sixteen, he attended the Saskatchewan School of the Arts in Fort San where instructors Pat Krause, Gertrude Story, and David Carpenter did their best to convince him that it was possible—perhaps even desirable—to write more than one draft of a story or poem. His Fort San experience was also a revelation in other respects, connecting him to a community of writers and introducing him to the elements of craft in writing. From that point onward, he was determined to become a writer.

After high school, Cariou studied English at the University of Saskatchewan, taking creative writing courses from Patrick Lane and David Carpenter, and attending writing colonies at Fort San and St. Peter's Abbey. His first publications, a story and a poem, appeared in the University of Saskatchewan newspaper, *The Sheaf*. After receiving his B.A. he continued to work on short stories, regularly taking writing courses at the Saskatchewan School of the Arts and its later incarnation, the Sage Hill Writing Experience, working with Fred Stenson, Guy Vanderhaeghe, and David Arnason.

Before going on to graduate school at the University of Toronto, Cariou worked as a speechwriter for Saskatchewan's then-Health Minister, George McLeod, and this experience served as the inspiration for one of the novellas in his first book, *The Exalted Company of Roadside Martyrs* (1999). While trying to avoid work on his Ph.D. dissertation (on the

PHOTO BY ROBERT TINKER

WARREN CARIOU

poetry and art of William Blake), he wrote the second novella of the collection, which is narrated by an errant priest. As a whole, the book became an exploration of the place of belief in politics and religion.

In the summer of 1998 Cariou finished his Ph.D. and moved to Vancouver with his partner Alison Calder, a poet and critic of Canadian Literature. He taught in the English department of the University of British Columbia (UBC) for two years, and during this time he intensified his scholarly work on First Nations literature, some of which he had begun in his last years at the University of Toronto. His interest in this field was sparked in his late twenties when he learned of his grandmother's suppressed Métis heritage. Much of his critical writing on Aboriginal subjects has focused on the Métis and on issues of racial passing, hybridity, and stereotype.

While at UBC, Cariou began writing a memoir which examined some of the above-mentioned issues through a technique derived from oral storytelling. Hearkening back to his father's stories, Cariou sought to explore the idea of belonging and the meanings of home, as well as questions of racism and community identity. This book was published as *Lake of the Prairies: A Story of Belonging* (2002), and it went on to win the Writers' Trust Drainie-Taylor Prize for Biography.

In 2000, Cariou and Calder moved to Winnipeg, where she took up a position in the English Department at the University of Manitoba. Two years later, Cariou began teaching in the same department. From 2000 to 2002, he also taught creative writing at the Sage Hill Writing Experience. He is now continuing his research on First Nations literature and is working on a novel entitled *Exhaust*, which examines the oil industry and its relationship to Aboriginal people in the Americas.

About Writing... *While writing is a solitary activity, I don't think I would have become a writer without the support and stimulation that a literary community afforded me. Saskatchewan's writers not only gave me the idea that it was possible for Prairie people to write their own stories and histories; they also helped me to expand my notions of what literature is capable of. My advice to new writers would be: seek out a community, because the best writing arises from situations where we challenge ourselves by interacting with other practitioners of the craft.*—WARREN CARIOU

DAVID CARPENTER was conceived in Saskatoon but born in Edmonton in 1941. His parents (Paul Hamilton and Marjorie E. Parkin) met and courted in Saskatoon during the late 1920s and early 1930s. His father was born in Regina in 1905. Paul's father (Henry Stanley) was one of the first land surveyors in the province, and later the deputy minister of Highways, after whom the village of Carpenter was named. David's mother grew up in Saskatoon. Her family's eccentricities are the subject of "This Shot," a story in Carpenter's 1994 book of essays, *Writing Home*.

Carpenter spent his first 23 years in Edmonton, working in the mountains nearby during the summers as a car hop, a driver for Brewster Transport, a fish stocker, a trail guide, and a folksinger. He read French and German at the University of Alberta where he was an indifferent student. He graduated and taught high school in Edmonton until 1965, then went south to do an M.A. in English at the University of Oregon. He returned to Canada in 1967 and once again taught school until the summer of 1969, when he enrolled for his Ph.D. at the University of Alberta. Early in this program, he dropped out twice and re-instated himself twice, and after a period of prolonged grumbling, graduated in 1973. During this year, he was awarded a two-year post-doctorate at the University of Manitoba, where he also taught courses in American literature for the inmates of Stoney Mountain Penitentiary.

By the mid-1970s Carpenter had published a few poems and some translations (poetry and fiction) from the French. When he was appointed to his job at the University of Saskatchewan in 1975, he was still a hobby writer. This appointment was in Canadian literature with a specialty in regionalism, and included teaching English to Aboriginal students from the north.

The following summer (1976, Austin, Texas) he was caught in a heat wave and confined to quarters after his shifts each day at the University of Texas library. It was here (to avoid going crazy with boredom) that he began to write seriously. This new work eventually became a series of novellas and long stories, *Jokes for the Apocalypse*, *Jewels*, and *God's Bedfellows*, all of which appeared between 1985 and 1988. *Jokes* was runner up for the Gerald Lampert Award, and his novella "The Ketzer" won first prize in the *Descant* Novella Contest. A revised version of this story was published in book form in 2003.

PHOTO BY HONOR KEVER

DAVID CARPENTER... WITH FRIEND
(A BROWN TROUT, DECEASED).

While these stories were under way, he did a workshop in creative writing down at Fort San with Robert Kroetsch, on whom he had done research as a Ph.D. student. His other instructors were Matt Cohen and Jack Hodgins. He did only a few workshops with these writers, but the sessions proved to be a period of intense learning for him. Another influence at this time was the professor, poet, and playwright Don Kerr, for whom he worked as fiction editor of the *NeWest Review*.

The problem during this time was that the writing was taking over his life, and during the teaching year he was able to get very little work done. Around 1985, he split his appointment and job-shared with Pat Lane, Lorna Crozier, and Maria Campbell. This arrangement formalized what he had been doing since 1979, and it lasted until 1997 when Carpenter turned to writing full-time.

In the fall of 1988, Carpenter began work on his first full-length novel, entitled *Banjo Lessons*, which was published in 1997. This novel won the City of Edmonton Book Prize. During the early nineties he also finished the last of his personal and literary essays which make up *Writing Home*, his first book of nonfiction. The essays explore his engagements with such writers as Richard Ford, Mordecai Richler, the French writer/scientist Georges Bugnet, and the late Raymond Carver. Several of these pieces won prizes for literary journalism and for humour in the Western Magazine

Awards. Most had been published in such places as *Saturday Night, The Globe & Mail* and its affiliates, or in some equivalent American publications. One of these essays was featured in an expanded form on CBC Radio's *Ideas*. In 1996 he brought out a second book of essays all about life around home, a month-by-month salute to the seasons entitled *Courting Saskatchewan*. It won the Saskatchewan Book Award for non-fiction.

Virtually all of Carpenter's work is set in and inspired by the Canadian West. Since 1975, with the exception of three years in Toronto and on the west coast, he has lived and written in Saskatoon. He sees life and literature through the eyes of a woodsy neighbourhood intellectual and wants very much to believe that cities and industrial towns are not a grotesque ecological blunder. (Jury's out on this one.) Throughout the years he has always been a passionate outdoorsman and environmentalist. This abiding love of lakes, trails, streams and campsites translates into city life in Saskatoon as well, where he lives with his wife, artist Honor Kever, and their son Will.

His first book of poetry, *Trout Stream Creed*, was published in 2003. He is at work on his second novel, entitled *Whoever You Are*.

About Writing... *Most novelists must eventually learn to make a pact with dullness: not boredom or lack of imagination or passion, but dullness of routine. Keep your daily appointment with the computer screen and keep your ass on the chair until you've reached your daily quota. However rich your inner life may be, seek also the dullard within.*—DAVID CARPENTER

KEN CARRIERE is of Swampy Cree– Métis ancestry. He was born in 1951 at Cumberland House. His parents were Agnes Mackenzie and Pierre Carriere.

Carriere studied geology at Concordia in Montreal. His first career as a geologist, combined with the training he received as a child from his father and his uncles, make him a keen watcher. A teacher, Carriere has taught at both the primary and secondary levels. A fluent speaker of Swampy Cree, he has also developed Cree language curriculum.

Carriere is the author of *The Bulrush Helps the Pond*, written in both Cree and English. The Gabriel Dumont Institute, Saskatoon, won the First Peoples Publishing award at the Saskatchewan Book Awards for Carriere's book.

PHOTO BY BRENDA NISKALA

KEN CARRIERE... AT CHURCHILL RIVER PICTOGRAPHS, JUNE 1987.

Carriere currently resides in LaRonge, Saskatchewan.

HEATHER HODGSON

DONNA CARUSO's mother, a shepherdess in Italy, married the son of a shoemaker in northern New Jersey. Donna, far down the line in a large family, recalls that her mother dressed all her daughters alike, which meant that not only did Donna have to wear her older sisters' hand-me-downs, but her wardrobe didn't change for about fifteen years. As a result, Donna grew up with an affinity for nuns, Chinese peasants, and nudists, who, like her, seem unconcerned about fashion.

It also, perhaps, contributed to the development of Donna's quirky sense of humour, which has served her well in a career as a writer, filmmaker, singer and performer. Not to mention Boomba player extraordinaire!

Caruso, who lives in Fort Qu'Appelle, has made her living as a documentary filmmaker since 1993. She's also the author of *Under Her Skin*, a collection of short stories published by Thistledown Press in 1999, and is working on a new story collection. The book spawned the one-woman performance piece of the same name, a unique theatre experience, influenced by her Italian family background, in which she cooks onstage and feeds her audience. Delicious!

Caruso's Italian heritage has figured prominently in her work, including the one-hour narrative films, *Doll Hospital* and *Story Album*, one-woman stage plays entitled *Grace Before Meals* and *The Clothesline*, and a current video work in progress, *A Glass of Wine, a Sip of Sake*.

Noted for strange but gentle comedy in her stage performances, Caruso has graced stages throughout the province. Her film documentaries, broadcast nationally on several networks, are marked by a deep sense of intimacy and spirituality and have won awards internationally. Her stage plays include *A Celebration Of The Mess*, and the musical comedy for children, *Francis The Pig, A Hero For Our Time*; her films include *Doll Hospital*, *Twixt Heaven and Earth*, and *The Honey Children*.

Doll Hospital, a sensitive look at breast cancer, won a number of awards, including Best Doc at the 1999 CanPro competition, and best documentary at the 1998 Rhode Island Film Festival. It was nominated for best documentary at the 1999 Hot Docs festival in Toronto.

Caruso grew up near Jersey City and was educated at an all-girls' high school and an all-men's university. She and her husband and young son emigrated to Canada in 1974 directly to Fort Qu'Appelle, where she's lived ever since, raising her two sons, Jason and Elliot (now 34 and 27 years old, respectively). Donna is truly amazed that her children are so old, while she remains so young.

In the '70s, Caruso was a mainstay of the writing school at Fort San—but as neither student nor faculty member. She and her husband ran the Fort Qu'Appelle pizza place, Spike's, so popular with people from the School of the Arts, especially the writers.

In 1980, Caruso, newly separated from her husband and raising two children on minimum wage, needed some extra money to pay for fire insurance. She worried and worried. Happily, fate intervened when a newspaper ad caught her eye... a talent competition offered a cash prize. Caruso entered and won, paid her fire insurance, and launched a new career.

Caruso has worked as a stand-up comedian and a children's performer ever since, often making comic use of the Boomba, a musical instrument of her own design. She started writing for radio in 1983, and her comic skits, songs, and radio plays are heard on CBC locally and nationally. She began writing children's musical comedies in 1987, and wrote and toured a new original show yearly in the Regina area for ten years.

PHOTO BY ORMOND MCKAGUE

ROSES APPEAR SPONTANEOUSLY AS **DONNA CARUSO** RIDES BUS IN PERU.

She also began writing short stories, which have been read on CBC radio, and which have been published in numerous magazines and anthologies. Donna has won several awards for her writing, including an award for erotica from *Prairie Fire* magazine and first prize in 2001 for non-fiction writing in a contest sponsored by the Writers Federation of New Brunswick.

While her writing and performing is often comic, Caruso is never one to be pigeonholed, and she also produces very serious video documentaries. Working in film and video since 1988, Donna formed her company, Incandescent Films, in 1992. Since then she has produced numerous documentaries for broadcast on CBC, BBS, and STV, Vision TV, WTN, the Discovery Channel, and several educational channels across Canada.

Her television series, *Life Without Borders*, an idiosyncratic view of prairie life, premiered on SCN in 2003; *Story Album*, a series of shows on Saskatchewan poetry, is in production.

Her subject matter is usually people, although she has spent an inordinate amount of time doing shows about birds. But usually it's people... her work including *Chasing The Cure* (the story of Fort San as a tuberculosis sanitorium), and profiles of Saskatchewan seniors such as Alice Jenner and Sr. Yvonne Toucanne. Her 1998 documentary, *Top Brass*, about the Regina Lions Junior Band, won a national award at the Can-Pro festival in Toronto. Her profile of poet Anne Szumigalski, *Rapture of the Deep*, has thrilled audiences around the country.

In her spare time, Donna is working on a comic opera about menopause.

She never forgets that she's a short person, whose parents have had their picture taken with the Pope. Her goal is to be the Patron Saint of Something, hopefully something not too offensive, so as not to embarrass herself or her parents, much less the Pope.

All that's fine and dandy, but, what everyone really wants to know first and foremost about Donna Caruso, is that yes, Enrico *is* her uncle.

DAVE MARGOSHES

About Writing... *Writing requires a brave heart and a courageous spirit. Writers constantly deal with what the rest of the world is trying to avoid: the stuff that's in our subconscious, the stuff that makes life complex and delicious and awful. Writers spend half their lives dreaming some lovely lie, and the other half in a cold sweat. If you want a safe life, sell insurance, don't write.*—DONNA CARUSO

MARILYN CAY is the daughter of John and Ruth Unger who farmed southwest of Kinistino, Saskatchewan. She was born on April 23, 1945, in Prince Albert.

Cay's education began at the age of four at the kitchen table. She could read and write at grade three level when she started school in 1951. She attended a small country school until high school in Kinistino. Cay graduated from grade twelve in 1963 and was class valedictorian. English and literature had been her strong subjects and she was writing poetry that can still be found in the old yearbooks. She had several teachers who encouraged her in this interest.

She married Norman Cay shortly after finishing high school and they moved to a farm near Tisdale. Her daughter Karen was born in 1966 and her son Robert in 1971. Cay has always been a fully participating partner in the farm. She has maintained a herd of cattle, and after her children were older she did her share of every operation on the farm. Cay's love of

MARILYN CAY... WITH GRANDCHILDREN, RACHEL, JACK AND SARAH, 2003.

her family and farm have been the driving force behind her writing.

When Cay's children were becoming teenagers, she was still deeply interested in writing and she was armed with a subject. She had inspiration but few skills. In 1983 she journeyed to the Saskatchewan Writers Guild's Summer School of the Arts Program at Fort San. She took part in Joe Rosenblatt's intermediate poetry class and met many wonderful writers. Hungry for knowledge, she also made friends with the short fiction class and listened in on their classes when she had the chance. Her time spent at Fort San was life-changing. She went home and wrote the poems and stories of her own experience on a northeastern Saskatchewan farm in the 1980s. Her work started to be accepted in literary magazines across Canada, including in *Prism International*, *Grain*, *Cross Canada Writers Quarterly*, *Canadian Author and Bookman*, *NeWest Review*, and others. Her work was also broadcast on CBC's *Ambience*.

Cay returned to Fort San in 1987 with a manuscript for Paulette Giles' advanced poetry class. Again, she met many new writers and soaked up knowledge. Cay received the Jerry Rush Memorial Scholarship to attend the first Sage Hill Poetry Experience in 1990 where she was instructed by Sharon Thesen.

Cay won various Saskatchewan Writers Guild awards for short fiction (1986), poetry (1987), the long manuscript award for her manuscript *Farm* (1991), and again for poetry (1991).

Anthologies containing her work include *Heading Out* (1986), *200% Cracked Wheat* (1992), *Prairie Dreams* (1989), *In the Clear* (1998), *Waiting For You To Speak* (1999), and *2000% Cracked Wheat* (2000).

Cay published a chapbook entitled, *Pure and Startled Seconds* (1991) and *Farm* (1993). *Farm* was shortlisted for the Saskatchewan Award at the first Saskatchewan Books Awards in 1993.

Marilyn Cay has been influenced by her own experience, other writers she has met and admired, and her farm family. The poet Earle Birney and his stirring poem, "David," as well as the poems of Carl Sandburg, have also influenced Cay's writing. She continues to farm with her husband and son and family at the farm near Tisdale, Saskatchewan.

HILARY CLARK was born in Vancouver but now lives in Saskatoon, where she teaches English and Gender Studies at the University of Saskatchewan. In 1998 Clark emerged on the Canadian poetry scene with two books of poetry: her first, *Two Heavens*, was followed by *More Light* which won the attention of literary award juries, winning the Pat Lowther award and the Saskatchewan poetry prize.

Clark emerged as a mature artist who draws for inspiration on the images and insights of writers as diverse as Virginia Woolf and Gerard Manley Hopkins. Arising clearly from a rich and varied literary tradition, her work is both a worthy addition to that and a wholly new, peculiarly Canadian exploration of the mysteries that have exalted and bedeviled humankind for millennia.

Clark's deft and sensitive imagery opens the reader's experience to an exquisite interrogation of such mysteries as love, knowledge, and faith; and though we don't come away with simple solutions to life's great problems, the heartfelt fullness this poetry engenders clearly points the way to a journey that matters. Hilary Clark's newest volume is *The Dwelling of Weather*. The poems trace, through their web of reference, a life story of reading—the Bible, Shakespeare, Blake, Lewis Carroll, and Emily Bronte meet Michael Palmer, Fred Wah, and Robert Duncan—not just Clark's life story but any reader's who finds in words a way to lure the spirit homeward.

PAUL WILSON

JOHN LIVINGSTONE CLARK was born Ronald John Clark on Saltspring Island on August 6, 1950, to Robert Edgar and Helen Jean (Livingstone) Clark. His father, Bob, was an autodidact, who read extensively in literature and philosophy, and loved music. At one point he was the opera critic for the *Victoria Times*. His own family in Edinburgh had been middle class and well educated—leaning towards business, farming, manufacturing—and Lawrence and his twin brother had run away on a clipper to find adventure in the new world. He had a great deal of influence on his grandson, John, leaving the latter his extensive library.

As an only child on Saltspring Island, Clark was read to constantly and was never without a book or comic in hand. The radio was also a major stimulus, and Clark remembers how important the various dramatic and suspense serials were in developing his imagination: *The Shadow, The Whistler, The Lone Ranger*. By the time he was three-and-a-half he could read and had memorized dozens of works. The beauty of the island and sea, the love and attention of his parents, the words of books and radio programs, all contributed to his future life as a poet. Hence the numerous references to his family throughout Clark's poetry. He has an instinctive capacity for mythologizing the everyday elements of his life.

After Saltspring, the family finally settled in Abbotsford, British Columbia. Clark proceeded through grades one through twelve, and took two grade thirteen courses. He detested school, excelled only occasionally when he liked a teacher and/or the subject, and was generally a nuisance. He did, however, become an accomplished bagpiper—winning several awards. He played rugby, football, lifted weights, and finally became the hippy editor of the school newspaper.

Thanks to his English teacher, Ray Grigg, Clark was turned on to Leonard Cohen, and the intrinsic magic and mystery of poetry worked its spell. Cohen's first album, the writings of the "beats," the English Romantics, the lyrics of Bob Dylan, Paul Simon and others, made Clark certain by the time he was eighteen that poetry was the only quest that mattered on earth.

University was important for many reasons; it was where Clark discovered the delights of the mind. He ended up with a high cum laud degree and a Commonwealth Scholarship to study English at the graduate level. And what marvels along the way— Religious Studies, Anthropology, Psychology, English Literature—all part of his inner quest, for he had come to UBC with serious questions about the nature of Self, Spirit, God. It was all relevant but English was the one discipline where he could use all his reading in the required essays. He finished with a double major in English and Anthropology, and was soon off to Australia to the University of Sydney.

Clark had never stopped writing poetry. He had surrounded himself with lovers of the muse. Vancouver in the 1970s was an exciting place to be, including the poetry scene. Warren Tallman, an English professor at UBC, was bringing in the biggest names in American poetry, and Robin Blaser at SFU was doing the same thing: Charles Olson, Robert Duncan, Allan Ginsberg, Jack Spicer, Robert Creeley, WS Merwin, and Ed Dorn gave readings at the Western Front off Broadway. Hundreds packed in to hear poets lift their minds, spirits, bodies. Clark was there, too, with notebook and pen to hear his favourites.

The Vancouver scene turned out to be too doctrinaire. Clark had become a Christian while in Australia, making for endless trials and tribulations in radical old SFU, so he eventually followed a friend to Saskatoon where things soon brightened up. Clark now admits that if he had not left Vancouver for Saskatoon, he would not have emerged as a poet. In Saskatoon he met important allies and supporters like Don Kerr and Carolyn Heath. He also met Joe Rosenblatt who was writer-in-residence at the library. Rosenblatt was his first important mentor, and he credits him as being a key midwife for his poetic voice—the other key influence was Anne Szumigalski.

Clark says that if Providence led him to Saskatoon, meeting Anne was probably the reason. Rosenblatt connected Clark with Szumigalski and so began a great fifteen-year friendship. Clark fully emerged as a poet under Anne's quiet, understated direction. What she championed, Clark had in raw abundance: imagination, risk, passion, intellect. It was just a question of experience, judgement, discernment—developing the editorial maturity necessary to see what chaff to cut. Anne's poetry groups also provided Clark with some of his best friends, strong writers and thus influences upon his work: Martha Gould, Liz Phillips, Susan Andrews Grace, later Hilary Clark. Szumigalski and these writers worked from a strong sense of 'mythopoeisis;' the eternal questions provided an essential background in the works, the poems themselves often acting as spells or incantations to lift the reader to a higher or deeper apprehension of existence.

JOHN LIVINGSTONE CLARK

This was the environment Clark needed. Szumigalski was raised Anglican by her father (wiccan by her mother), so the two often talked about the beauty of the King James Bible and the Book of Common Prayer. They joked that as Anglicans they could believe almost anything and they shared a deep sense of humour and felt that you could be totally serious and uproariously funny at the same time. This is evident in Clark's work.

In 1990, needing a completed graduate degree to continue lecturing at the University of Saskatchewan, Clark returned to UBC to do a Master of Fine Arts degree in Creative Writing. He worked with George McWhirter in poetry and completed the degree in two years and he also won the CBC/UBC Drama Award (1990) and saw his first book of poetry appear: *Stepping Up to the Station* (1990). His friend David Carpenter had told him, before he left for UBC, "when you get back here after a solid year of work, you'll feel like a writer." That's how it turned out; Clark returned having no doubts about being a writer.

Although teaching for the University of Saskatchewan, the Saskatchewan Indian Federated College, or St. Peter's College, Clark published: *Breakfast of the Magi* (1994), *Prayers and Other Unfinished Letters* (1995), *Passage to Indigo* (1996), a novella entitled *Back to Bethany: 89 Paragraphs about Jesus and Lazarus in Abbotsford* (1997), *Stream Under Flight* (1999), and *Body and Soul: Poems New and Selected* (2002).

He continues to write in the Saskatoon area working on prose, drama and creative non-fiction as well as poetry. He was also one of the partners running Hagios Press, dedicated to the spiritual vision of poet Anne Szumigalski. Literature, especially poetry, has been his greatest passion—alongside his kids of course—and he shall always be grateful that he's been able to live so close to the bones of the great bards.

About writing... *the only writing I would want to comment on is poetry, and it is a wierd, wonderful practise and craft that plays with words for the sole purpose of going beyond words. At its best it is "awe-full" (one of Szumigalski's favorite words), and should leave the reader/listener open mouthed, dumbfounded and drooling: an infinite horizon of light and possibility dancing before his mind.*—JOHN LIVINGSTONE CLARK

EILEEN ELNA COMSTOCK

(1926–2001) was born May 7, 1926, to Carl and Elna Kopperud of the Cadillac district in Saskatchewan. The eldest of five Kopperud children, Eileen's official "birthplace" is Section 27, Township 8, Range 14, West of the 3rd Meridian. Eileen spent her early years in the Boule Creek/Cadillac district, acquiring an abiding love of family and learning, along with a strong faith that would serve her throughout the rest of her life.

Early in her teaching career, Eileen met Evert Comstock, a young farmer from the Mitchellton district. They married on January 14, 1949, at Eileen's home country church in Cadillac. At the time of her passing, Eileen and Evert had been married for over 52 years… a true testament to both their love and devotion to each other, as well as their endurance!

Eileen and Evert had four children: Lyle (Carol Strykiwsky, Battleford), Anne (died at birth), Keith (Janet Harder, Regina) and Karen (Jim Burke, Calgary). Her family was a source of great pride for Eileen, as was she for them. Her strength, patience, ingenuity and penchant for delivering good advice while acknowledging it might well be ignored, made Eileen a wonderful wife, mother, mother-in-law, and grandmother.

Eileen went to a little white schoolhouse in Boule Creek. The community was noted for good softball teams, great Christmas concerts, and a new teacher almost every year because the locals (including her dad, uncles and other young farmers) kept marrying them.

Toward the end of World War II, Eileen borrowed a small sum from her father and enrolled in a two-month teacher-training summer course that had been set up to, as she said, "recruit warm bodies to fill teaching positions." Upon successful completion of that course, Eileen began her teaching career, eventually ending up in Mitchellton where she met her husband-to-be, and then serving as vice-principal at Limerick and Spring Valley.

Eileen loved learning and was a voracious reader. As a teacher, one of her favorite sayings was "there is NO such thing as a dumb kid… there is only a teacher who hasn't figured out how to get through to them yet." Eileen believed that a good teacher had to have at least five methods for teaching any lesson and anyone who knew her well will remember the joyful look on her face when a student finally "got it"... she truly loved the challenge of helping others.

Eileen's writing career developed in good measure out of her skill as a storyteller. Although she didn't wear it on her sleeve, Eileen related very strongly to the sort of oral history tradition that is commonly seen in Scandinavian and Aboriginal cultures. Depending on the situation, her stories amused, soothed, entertained, inspired and taught the listener in a way that was sincere and meaningful but not overly preachy. Although her stories often had a moral or a message, the listener never felt like that was the most important part... they just liked to hear the words.

In the descriptions that Eileen gave of how to be a storyteller, her advice was to start at the beginning and continue on to the end, without getting lost in the middle. Basic, but sage, advice... advice she took to heart in her own writing. She also tried very hard to be a good technical writer. That is to say she worked at it, studied it, went to workshops and classes, and was an active member of several writing groups over the years.

Perhaps most important, though, was the subject matter she wrote about. Eileen wrote from her own experience, partly because, as she said, she had "almost no creative imagination, but a very good memory," but also because that was what she knew best and felt most strongly about. Eileen saw both the amusing and the ironic in everyday things, and

EILEEN COMSTOCK... 40TH WEDDING ANNIVERSARY.

used these viewpoints effectively to get her message across.

Humour, in fact, was a very big part of Eileen's writing style. While her stories are not all necessarily laugh-out-loud hilarious, most of them will certainly give the reader a chuckle or two as well as the opportunity to reflect on how funny and strange life really is. Eileen's humour has been described by those who know the craft well as "pithy," "tongue-in-cheek," "dry," "wise-cracking" and even occasionally "acerbic."

As Eileen told it, when she turned 55 she decided she had best get busy and start doing some of those things she had always wanted to do. In addition to taking up oil painting and watercolours, she started doing ceramics, and became an active "on the tractor" farmer, which as she said, was a lot more fun than housekeeping. She was very proud of this part of her career and in many descriptions of her station in life, proclaimed herself as a farmer. As has been mentioned, Eileen was always a great storyteller and that naturally led to a second (third??... fourth??) career as an author. In the late 1990s her stories were a regular feature on CBC radio and she also recorded two audio tapes.

In addition to writing her own stories, Eileen completed her family's history, a cookbook for teens, some children's stories, and a travel book, but, as she noted, the only writing she made any money out of were the humorous pieces that told about how things were in the old days. After receiving the requisite number of polite rejection letters for her first real manuscript, in 1999 a publisher decided that Eileen's writing was worthy of some investment and a deal was struck for *Aunt*

Mary in the Granary and Other Prairie Stories.

Aunt Mary turned out to be a best-seller and by that time Eileen was working on a second book, *Sunny Side Up: Fond Memories of Prairie Life in the 1930s*. Unfortunately, in the fall of 2000 her health began to fail and the last real writing work Eileen was able to complete before her death was to finish the final edits on *Sunny Side Up* and to assemble the stories for a proposed third book.

Sunny Side Up was published in 2001 and also became both a commercial and critical success. Since then, in cooperation with Eileen's family, a CD of her stories has been completed, and a third book entitled *No Spring Chicken... Thoughts on a Life Well Lived* was published in 2002.

In addition to receiving some critical acclaim, Eileen has received feedback from all over North America and even the U.K. As just one example, The Canadian Museum of Civilization has used excerpts from her work in a display on the role the "mail-order" business had in opening up the west. Her stories seem to resonate in some way with everyone who reads them... for some people it is the humour and for others it is feeling the same way about life and family. And for many it seems that the most powerful feeling is that of having shared similar experiences... one person even wrote that it seemed Eileen had "lived her life."

KEITH COMSTOCK

WILLIAM CONKLIN was born in 1906, on a farm near Fort Carlton, Saskatchewan. He received his early education in country schools and his formal education at Regina College (now the University of Regina).

Conklin's first job, at the age of thirteen, was as a farm labourer. He tried many other types of employment, accepting any kind of job that would cover living expenses. He moved to Prince Albert in the mid-1920s, working for the federal civil service there for much of his life. He retired to Victoria, British Columbia, and died there in the late 1980s.

Conklin's writing career began while he was still in public school. His publications include: *Wind-Blown Leaves* (1951), *For the Infinite* (1960), and *Selected Poems of William Conklin* (1978).

NIK BURTON

DENNIS COOLEY was born on August 27, 1944, on a farm near Estevan. He was the third child and only son of Orin and June (Wilson) Cooley. He has three sisters, Sharon Irene (Thompson), Beverley Lynn (Kindopp), and Laurel Louise (Duczek). Cooley married Diane Sanderson, with whom he has two daughters, Dana and Megan. Cooley is the author of *Leaving* (1980), *Fielding* (1983), *Bloody Jack* (1984), *Soul Searching* (1987), *Dedications* (1988), *Perishable Light* (1988), *Burglar of Blood* (1992), *This Only Home* (1992), *Goldfinger* (1995), *Passwords* (1996), *Sunfall* (1996), a second edition of *Passwords* (1999), *the bentley poems* (2000), *Irene* (2000), a second edition of *Bloody Jack* (2002), *seeing red* (2003), and *translations* (2003). Some of his early essays are collected in *The Vernacular Muse: The Eye and Ear in Contemporary Literature* (1987). His poetry has been published in numerous journals and has been widely anthologized.

Cooley edited essays about Prairies writers (*RePlacing* [1980]) as well as collections of Prairie poets: *Draft: An Anthology of Prairie Poetry* (1981) and *Inscriptions: A Prairie Poetry Anthology* (1992). He has also written studies of writers such as Dorothy Livesay, Sinclair Ross, Eli Mandel, Margaret Laurence, Robert Kroetsch, as well as the American poet Robert Duncan. He has edited the work of many writers (roughly 50 book-length manuscripts) and has been the editor of Saskatchewan poet Andrew Suknaski (*In the Name of Narid* [1981]). Cooley's south Saskatchewan roots are featured regularly in his verse, based as it is in local and family lore, including most dramatically his two elegies, *Fielding* (for his father) and *Irene* (for his mother). Those beginnings can be heard also in his criticism, where he has theorized vernacular and lineation into a complex regional poetics. His creative writing, often concerned with outsiders or modest figures, is open-ended, mixing verse and prose forms, and mingling a range of voices—lyrical, comic, satirical, meditative, oral, documentary, playful. The writing is both referential and reflexive as it mingles a love for form and language with a respect for the things of this world.

Cooley's family moved from the farm into Estevan when he was fourteen. He graduated from Estevan Collegiate in 1962, then entered the University of Saskatchewan, earning a B.Ed. in 1966, a B.A. in English in 1967, and an M.A. degree in 1968 (his thesis was on Stephen Crane).

Cooley's interest in American literature led him to the University of Rochester, New York, where he completed a Ph.D. in 1971 (writing his dissertation on Robert Duncan). When he returned to Canada, he taught upgrading for one year in Estevan and then served in Regina as executive assistant for the Blakeney government in Saskatchewan. In 1973 he moved to the University of Manitoba, where he was caught up in a swirl of literary activity with Ken Hughes, Robert Enright, Wayne Tefs, David Arnason, Birk Sproxton, and Robert Kroetsch, and where he has taught ever since in Canadian literature, American literature, literary theory, and creative writing. Cooley co-founded (with Robert Enright and John Beaver) Turnstone Press in 1975. He was also involved in the beginnings of the Manitoba Writers' Guild, and several years later served for a number of years on the MWG executive. In the 1970s and 1980s Cooley was central to the establishing of a series of literary conferences at St. John's College where he holds an office, and where he has since contributed as a major organizer for conferences on the prairies. He and David Arnason run one of the first websites to be established in the world, the Canadian Literature Archives, out of St. John's. He was involved in the decision of the Elizabeth Dafoe archives at the University of Manitoba to collect prairie literature. He has taught, lectured, read, done readings and workshops at dozens of places in Canada, Germany, France, Spain, Portugal, Hungary, Poland, and Scotland. He has been poetry editor of and contributed regular columns to the journal *Border Crossings*, which began at St. John's College as *Arts Manitoba*. He has won a teaching award at the University of Manitoba.

PHOTO BY DANA COOLEY

DENNIS COOLEY... AT A PUB IN EDINBURGH, MARCH 2003.

About writing... *#1 I've often argued that all poems are love poems. If that's true, and I convince myself again and again that it is, then all writing is done out of love. It's not always 'nice' and it's not necessarily pleasing to readers, and it may not even be a happy experience to writers, always. But we write, I think, because we care. We care a lot about something or someone. And we care about writing. We take care with it because it matters to us—sometimes more than anything. The empty page is not frightening, we get to fill it every chance we get. In a crazy way we are called to the poem, it happens to us. We do everything we can to be ready for it: we read and we study and we practise. We work hard at writing, practising up to write. We bring all of our intelligence and knowledge and imagination to the page. And then it flares up again. Malarial. We do it because it takes us over, and because we love it. We are amused—deeply, easily, always amused. Always ready to be ravished, hoping to be chosen. Prepared to revise when the words are not good enough.*

#2 The crazy thing about poetry is it swings in a world of words—everybody's words, almost. Except they get put to odd use, hung like a suspension bridge between how they look and how they sound. There they are—an eye on one side and an ear on the other, the words slung meaningfully between. On one end the poem leaks into graphic art and poets fiddle with the way they lay ink on the page. Sometimes they break down words and even letters. You've seen the way ink can skitter and jerk, flow and roll, across the page—that's what I'm talking about. Doodle. Concrete poetry.

On the other end, running to sound, the poem begins to think it's music. Words, infatuated with their own voices, start to forget the dictionary. When this happens the poem kicks off "meaning," moves around in bare-foot and audible abandon, turns to babble on the air. The lure of music, the ear's siren call. Sound poetry. The poem with words that hold it up, evidently, in the "real" world, wants to doodle and babble too. Somewhere out there on the bridge it wants to have it both ways. It gets tired having to mean all the time, wants to have some fun. "When you speak, you become a little deaf to the world," someone has said. That's why poets are honoured when their words are brought to the special ear which music is, to a sounding they have never themselves quite known. More than a few of them, I think, are touched to hear the sounds let out of their words. [Mon, Mar 15, 1993 in Groundswell: the best of above/ground press *(2003)]*—DENNIS COOLEY

VIOLET COPELAND (1917–1999) was born in 1917 on a homestead near Freemont, Saskatchewan, and except for six years in New York and seven in Alberta, made Saskatchewan her home. Copeland's "traditional" poetry has been published in many Canadian and American periodicals and anthologies, and has been read on CBC Radio in Saskatchewan and Alberta. Copeland's publications include *A Circle of Willows* (1970), *Of Many Colours* (1970), *Tarpaper and Wild Roses* (1979), *The Beautiful Friendship* (1980), *Shorty* (1985) and *The Black and White Christmas: a book of short stories* (1985).

Violet Copeland resided in Maidstone, where she grew a fruit orchard, until her death in January 1999.

NIK BURTON

SAROS COWASJEE was born in Secundrabad, India, in 1931. He received his Cambridge School Certificate from Scindia Public School, Gwalior, in 1947, and his B.A. (1951) and M.A. (1955) from Agra University, Agra. After teaching at Agra College, Agra, for two years, Cowasjee joined the University of Leeds (U.K.) where he completed his Ph.D. on the Irish dramatist Sean O'Casey in 1960.

Cowasjee returned to India and worked as Assistant Editor with the *Times of India* Press

(Bombay) for two years. In 1963 he was offered an Instructorship at the University of Regina (then called Regina College), and at the same time he was awarded a Woodrow Wilson Fellowship to study journalism at Columbia University, New York. Cowasjee accepted the teaching appointment, and became full professor of English in 1971. During his long teaching career in Regina, he spent a semester at Darwin College, Cambridge, a sabbatical as Research Associate at the University of Berkeley, California, and another sabbatical as Professor of Commonwealth Literature at the University of Aarhus in Denmark.

Cowasjee has travelled widely, and given scholarly papers and readings from his own fiction in England, France, Denmark, Fiji, Singapore, India, and Australia. Some of these have been published in magazines and journals such as *A Review of English Literature*, *Journal of Commonwealth Literature*, *The Literary Criterion*, *Literature East and West*, *World Literature Written in English*, *Encounter*, *The Toronto South Asian Review*, and *Journal of Canadian Fiction*. Others have found a place in anthologies of fiction and of critical writings.

Cowasjee's first significant publication was a short story called "His Father's Medals" in *The Illustrated Weekly of India*. It remains his most anthologized piece, and shows strong influence of the Indian novelist Mulk Raj Anand on whom he wrote two books for Oxford University Press: *Coolie: An Assessment* (1976) and *So Many Freedoms* (1979). He also adapted Anand's novel *Private Life of an Indian Prince* into a screenplay called *The Last of the Maharajas* (1980). Prior to this, Cowasjee had published two critical studies, *Sean O'Casey: the Man Behind the Plays* (1963) and *O'Casey* (1966), both based on his doctoral dissertation at Leeds.

Though Cowasjee made his debut as a critic, his interest in fiction never wavered. He kept working on short stories, and before he came to writing his first novel *Goodbye to Elsa* (1974) he had published a collection titled *Stories and Sketches* (1970). But it was his novel that won him attention. The novelist Henry Miller described it as "a crazy book—not a novel at all, but just a book, a damn good one too." And George Woodcock, the dean of Canadian literature, praised the book unstintingly, calling it "the most acid portrait of the chicaneries and pretenses of Canadian campus life I have yet read."

Cowasjee followed up *Goodbye to Elsa* with a book of short stories called *Nude Therapy and Other Stories* (1979) and a novel titled *Suffer Little Children* (1982). A sequel to *Goodbye to Elsa*, the novel was revised and published as *The Assistant Professor* in 1996. Despite some enthusiastic reviews, the book failed to capture the public imagination and it dampened the author's hopes of becoming a popular novelist. Like most fiction writers, Cowasjee too had dreamed of writing a bestseller. These dreams he transmuted into bringing fiction of merit, either long forgotten or out of print, to the attention of readers. While doing his study on Mulk Raj Anand, he had

SAROS COWASJEE'S SCHOLARLY PET TO WHOM HE DEDICATED HIS *WOMEN WRITERS OF THE RAJ*.

persuaded The Bodley Head (London) to reprint *Untouchable* (1934), *Coolie* (1935) and *Private Life of An Indian Prince* (1952). These titles, to which he supplied the Introductions, did much to rekindle interest in this Indian novelist. In 1984 he got himself appointed General Editor of Arnold-Heinemann's "Literature of the Raj" series and saw to the reprint of outstanding novels by Meadows Taylor, Flora Annie Steel, Edmund Candler, Dennis Kincaid, Christine Weston, J.R. Ackerley and others. Some of the Introductions he wrote are included in his volume *Studies in Indian and Anglo-Indian Fiction* (1993).

Cowasjee's most significant contribution to English studies lies in resurrecting fiction of merit by Raj writers (British writers on India from Kipling to Indian independence) either long forgotten or ignored. He has edited five volumes of Raj short stories. The first of these was *Stories from the Raj* (1982), and the last to-date is *The Oxford Anthology of Raj Stories* (1998). In his Preface to the former, Paul Theroux wrote: "Saros Cowasjee has rendered us a great service by disinterring these stories and bringing so many of these writers from an undeserved obscurity." Cowasjee's latest effort is an omnibus called *Four Raj Novels* (2004); he is also putting together a selection of his own short fiction (with some new additions) for publication.

Cowasjee took early retirement in 1995 as Professor Emeritus.

About Writing... *It is an addiction. But with some determination, faith, good sense, and help from advancing age, you can overcome it.*—SAROS COWASJEE

ARCHIE CRAIL is the author of one book of fiction and numerous plays for theatre and radio. *The Bonus Deal*, published in 1992, was a finalist for the Governor General's Award for Fiction. Five stories from it aired on the CBC Radio One program *Ambience*. Crail has also published works in the anthologies *Out of Place* (1990) and *Short Grass* (1989). His play *Exile* (1990) was originally produced by 25th Street Theatre of Saskatoon, and later toured, in a one-act version, in South Africa.

Archie Crail was born in Paarl, South Africa. Educated through the University of South Africa, he also spent two years at a theological college in Alice, Cape Province, where Bishop Desmond Tutu was his lecturer in doctrine.

During his writing career, Archie Crail was the only active African National Congress (ANC) member writing in Canada. His political involvement during the seventies in South Africa—with both labour struggles and the South West Africa People's Organization (SWAPO)—forced his move to Namibia (formerly South West Africa) and his flight to Botswana. He came to Canada with his wife and four children in 1980. When they arrived in Regina in 1984, he studied journalism at the University of Regina and began writing seriously.

In July 1991, after the ban on ANC members returning to South Africa was lifted, he attended the ANC conference in Durban even though he was never granted the amnesty pass officially necessary to avoid arrest.

NIK BURTON

LORNA CROZIER. Show me a person's landscape and I'll show you his character, someone famous once wrote. I wonder what he'd make of me? I come from a vast, sky-filled place where the wind never stops blowing. The small city I was born in, Swift

Current, is named after a creek, though that creek winds through town with its beautiful name as slowly as a dazed snake dragging the burden of its skin. In summer the city glimmers with the green of trees and watered lawns, but the surrounding countryside is dry and treeless. The only tall vegetation is what the farmers planted years ago in long strips across the land to break the wind. It is, one could say, a place for poetry, a place where a person needs to make sense of the silences and openness that seem to define the land and its inhabitants. What grows, what moves, can be seen only by an alert and discerning eye that knows there is no such thing as emptiness. What lives is subtle, tough, close to the earth but sky-struck. This kind of place can't help but give birth to poets. Small in the vastness that rolls into the thunderheads of hot July, write a word that insists you are here; write a word that speaks what the land is saying.

From the start, the landscape, the weather, and the creatures of this place have been a part of my poetry. You can hear it in the titles, from my first book *Inside Is the Sky* (1978) to my most recent *Apocrypha of Light* (2002). In between were seven others, including *The Weather* (1983), *The Garden Going On Without Us* (1985), *Inventing the Hawk* (1992), *Everything Arrives at the Light* (1995), and *A Saving Grace* (1996).

The last book followed the characters in Sinclair Ross's great novel *As for Me and My House*. Set in the dismal decade that prairie people call The Dirty Thirties, the novel tells the kind of stories I heard from my parents, especially when I'd whine about having to wear someone else's skates that pinched my toes, or when I'd complain about having to walk ten blocks to school. "You should have been kids when we were in The Thirties," they'd say. "There was one pair of shoes for seven kids, we got pajamas made out of flour sacks and a single orange to share for Christmas, we had to quit school two winters in a row because there was no feed for the horse that took us there, etc., etc."

I took those stories with me, deep inside, from my home town to university in Saskatoon, thinking I could leave them behind there. I took them with me during my seven years of teaching high school, during my studies for a Master's degree in Edmonton, and through several years as a poet on the road, taking up a writer-in-residence position in places like the Regina Library and the University of Toronto. The stories wouldn't go away; the place stayed with me. They kept finding words and images in my poems, no matter how far I traveled; they kept taking me back to the place I was born, the place that made my blood and bones and heart.

Saskatchewan has always been at the centre of my writing no matter what I've done and where I've lived, including in my present home on Vancouver Island where green invades the yard with vines and branches, and the rain always comes. My husband, the poet Patrick Lane, jokes with me about my need to cut down a tree every year in our yard. Soon, he says, all we'll have left is a level field ready for the sowing of wheat.

The weather of my birth-place, and all that "weather"

PHOTO BY BLAISE ENRIGHT-PETERSON
AND BARRY PETERSON

LORNA CROZIER

implies, has gone with me to poetry festivals in Chile, Malaysia, South Africa, Italy, France. It's found its way into major national anthologies like *Twentieth Century Poetry and Poetics* and *The Oxford Anthology of Canadian Poetry in English*. It's been with me in my classrooms at the University of Victoria, where I've been a professor since 1992 in the Department of Writing. The awards I've received—the Governor-General's, the Pat Lowther, the Canadian Authors Association Award for Poetry, the National Magazine Gold Medal, the Dorothy Livesay Award, the CBC National Literary Award—all have honoured where I come from and how it shapes my perceptions and the stories and images that grow out of them. It's a hard place, a demanding place, a place that never lets you go. Even though the whole province slips off the maps of the big publishing houses, the corporate executives, the Pope on his visit to Canada, the Rolling Stones Tour, it's a place that creates the dreamy, the sensitive, the larger-than-life, the sharp tongue and eye of the writer. It's the place my poetry still calls home.

About Writing... *One of the most difficult tasks for a poet is to open her eyes and actually see what's there: the small, close-fitting ears of the gopher, hoarfrost on the telephone wires, the hollow in the snow where a deer was sleeping. Just see, and the words will come.* —LORNA CROZIER

ROBERT CURRIE was born in Lloydminster in 1937. His parents, Duncan Currie from Delisle and Jean Mondy from Paynton, met in Ibstone, where Dunc ran the United Grain Growers elevator and Jean taught school. An interesting fact: among their close friends at the time were Alexander and Christena MacLeod, parents of writer Alistair MacLeod.

Currie spent his early years in Furness, Hendon, and Saskatoon before the family moved to Moose Jaw, where he received most of his schooling. As a kid he was already writing, winning occasional prizes in *The Canadian Boy*, a United Church paper; since prizes meant publication, he was hooked for life. Still, after high school, when a Kudor Preference Test suggested he become a cartoonist, he decided to be realistic and pursue a career in pharmacy. Along the way he worked as a ditchdigger, a hired hand on a feedlot, a construction laborer, a pharmacy apprentice, a CPR ice-gang worker and a drug gardener. At the College of Pharmacy he wrote much of the college paper, *The Tonic*, and in his final year took creative writing as his arts elective. Edward McCourt, the charismatic teacher of that class, had a profound influence on his desire to keep writing.

Upon graduation, Currie began an internship at Saskatoon's University Hospital, inspired partly by the chance to write for *The Hospital Pharmacist*, which was edited there. When offered a job as a sessional lecturer in Pharmacy, he took it, discovered he loved teaching, and decided to become a Pharmacy Professor. Then, in a crisis of conscience, during which he was influenced in no rational way by a Mark Harris novel, *The Southpaw*, he decided that if he was going to teach it had better be something he loved, namely literature. Back he went to the University of Saskatchewan, earning a B.A. in 1964, an Honours English diploma in 1965, and a B.Ed. in 1966.

One day in April of 1965, during the lull between final exams and inter-session, Currie bought his first poetry book, Irving Layton's *A Red Carpet for the Sun*. A few days later he discovered Raymond Souster's *When We Are Young* in the library. For the rest of his life he would be reading and writing poetry.

In 1966 Currie returned to Moose Jaw where he taught English for thirty years at Central Collegiate and led a creative writing workshop for grade twelves. Monday nights he tried to keep free for his own writing. By 1969 he was editing and publishing *Salt*, a little magazine of contemporary writing. In truth, "publishing" was pure hyperbole, for *Salt* was churned out on a hand-cranked gestetner borrowed from a friend. However, the magazine did publish numerous writers long before their first books appeared (Mark Abley, Kristjana Gunnars, Dave Margoshes, Carol Shields, Lois Simmie, and David Zieroth included). *Salt* also featured such luminaries as Ron Everson, Gary Geddes, Robert Kroetsch, Ken Mitchell, and Anne Szumigalski recalling how they began as writers. Meanwhile, Currie's own poems were appearing in "little mags" and in a slim volume from Montreal's Delta Press. Slim is right; *Quarterback #1* contained only six poems. Other thicker chapbooks would follow: *Sawdust and Dirt* and *The Halls of Elsinore* in 1973, and *Moving Out* in 1975.

Beginning in 1972 Currie spent five summers teaching and studying at Fort San. There he was greatly inspired by Ken Mitchell, Anne Szumigalski, Robert Kroetsch, Eli Mandel, and Rudy Wiebe and determined to make writing a bigger part of his life. In 1973, while attending his first Saskatchewan Writers Guild conference, Currie was stunned to be elected the organization's chairman. Two years later, after weeks of debate over the sanity of what they were about to do, he, Gary Hyland, Barbara

ROBERT CURRIE... AND A POETRY FAN, GRANDDAUGHTER JAYDEN.

Sapergia, and Geoffrey Ursell founded Coteau Books, which would eventually become one of Canada's most successful small presses. Later in 1975, he and Lorna Crozier decided they had to keep alive the spirit of Fort San and, with Gary Hyland, Judith Krause, Ed Dyck, Jim McLean, Byrna Barclay, and Ralph Ring, formed the Moose Jaw movement, a poetry group which, despite changes in personnel and name, continues today.

Three times during his teaching career Currie took unpaid leaves-of-absence to write full-time. Books and awards followed. Over the years he won three first and two second prizes in SWG Literary contests, plus third prize for poetry in the 1980 CBC National Literary Awards. In 1977 his play, *What About What I Want*, won the Ohio State Award for radio drama. He was honoured, along with Eli Mandel, Ken Mitchell, W.O. Mitchell, John Newlove, Sinclair Ross and Anne Szumigalski, with a Founder's Award from the Saskatchewan Writers Guild in 1984.

Currie's first book, *Diving into Fire* (1977), resulted from a chance remark about bridges in a CBC interview. His second, 1980's *Yarrow*, came about when the characters in one poem refused to die, but kept resuscitating themselves in poem after poem. In 1983 *Night Games* appeared, a book of linked stories, followed by *Learning on the Job* in 1986, a collection of occasional verse. With *Klondike Fever* in 1992 Currie tried fusing genres to achieve the strengths of fiction and non-fiction through poetry.

Since retiring from teaching in 1996, he

keeps busy writing and editing. Recent editing work includes books by Mary Bishop, Betty Dorion, Don Kerr, Rita Moir, and Arthur Slade. His own *Things You Don't Forget* was hailed in the Toronto *Star* as "to my mind the best book of stories published in Canada in the past decade." A comment not to be taken too seriously, he thought, but, oh, what fun to read. In the fall of 2002, after more drafts than he cares to admit, Currie published his first novel, *Teaching Mr. Cutler*. Though his own kids, Bronwen and Ryan, have long since departed, Currie lives with his wife, Gwen, in Moose Jaw, home of The Festival of Words, on whose board he serves. "Write on!" is his motto, and that he does.

About Writing... *One major difference between published and unpublished writers is the persistence with which they attempt revisions. When James Thurber's wife said of something he'd written, "Goddam it, Thurber, that's high school stuff," he told her to wait until the seventh draft, it would work out all right. Yes, but Thurber was a genius; most of us need more than seven drafts.*—ROBERT CURRIE

ELLY DANICA. At five years of age Elly Danica came to Moose Jaw from her birthplace, The Hague, Netherlands, with her parents, Ann and Peter vander Raadt and four siblings. Elly left behind a much loved grandmother (her mother's mother) in Holland and found the transition to life in Canada difficult. Since Dutch was her first language and her English was rudimentary, she felt stranded between two cultures. This resulted in both loneliness and isolation, and as soon as she could read, she turned to books. Growing up on the wrong side of the tracks in Moose Jaw meant her books were a small and well-worn collection of saints' lives at school, and the public library across town was for many years as distant as another country. She owned no books of her own, either in Dutch or English.

She read to learn about her new home, to try to make sense of her life and increasingly difficult family situation. More siblings were born, until there were ten children. Poverty, hunger, and winter cold were constant struggles. All of this meant that Elly lived as much as possible in the life of her imagination. Reading was never merely a childhood pastime: books were compulsion, escape, a lifeline, and a quest. The highlight of summer was the long walk across the Fourth Avenue bridge to the library to haul home as many of the Andrew Lang series of fairy tales as she could carry. By the time she was nine, she knew she would be a writer and with a clarity that her adult self finds astonishing, knew what she would write about.

School was a struggle, for the chaos at home left no physical or emotional space in which to do assignments. High school brought access to a larger library, and schoolwork took second place to grazing through the collection, reading Dickens and a biography of the Egyptian queen/pharoh Hatshepsut, over and over. Books were now her friends and her family; the characters in the books she read were vastly more important than anything in "real life."

In 1965, eighteen-year-old Elly married to escape her father's house and moved to Ottawa with her husband, a Lieutenant in the Canadian Army, Transport Corps. In 1970 her son Greg was born, a son who has grown into a very creative and caring young man and has inherited his mother's passion for writing.

She was accepted at the University of Regina in 1972 where she studied anthropology, sociology, and political science but did not complete her degree. In 1974 and after her divorce, she officially changed her last name to Danica. In 1975 she bought an old United Church in the village of Marquis, for $300 with her partner Barry Lipton, and installed her weaving studio there. She loved this huge space because it had so much room for her now ever-expanding collection of books. She finally had "a room of her own" in which to write. Over the next ten years Danica developed both her weaving skills and experimented with writing in an attempt to tell the story of her childhood experience. She often wrote all of her waking hours.

It took until the winter of 1987 to complete a manuscript which, Danica believed then, was not even a coherent first draft. A friend suggested she attend West Word III in Vancouver, a writing school for women writers to be held in August of that year. A generous grant from the Saskatchewan Arts Board made that possible. Within days of arriving at West Word III and meeting Nicole Brossard and Libby Oughton, she had two offers to publish her as-yet untitled manuscript. Libby Oughton made the best case and an agreement was reached that she would publish the book.

The following spring, *Don't: A Woman's Word* was published and it has never been out of print. What followed publication was overwhelming. Her long-time friend Barry Lipton wrote to Peter Gzowski about the book. Gzowski interviewed her in the basement of her church home for his CBC radio program, *Morningside*, and this award-winning interview launched the book in a manner beyond Danica's wildest hopes or dreams. She traveled the country to speak, give readings, and do interviews which ranged from the profound to the painful and the occasionally offensive. Eighteen months of continuous travel culminated in a seven week tour of Europe in support of Dutch, German, and Irish editions of the book.

A book about the experience of touring and speaking about such a difficult issue followed in 1996 and was called *Beyond Don't: Dreaming Past the Dark*. It was short-listed in the non-fiction category of the Saskatchewan book awards in 1997.

PHOTO BY PAULA MACKAY
ELLY DANICA

Danica has two completed and as-yet unpublished fiction manuscripts, *mcHarriet: An Adventure* and *The Orphaned Heart*. An excerpt of an early draft of *The Orphaned Heart* became a radio drama for CBC Regina.

In 1998 she realized her dream of moving to the Maritimes where she now resides in a 125-year-old Nova Scotia house, has a blue wood stove she's very fond of, a lovely kitchen, and writing, painting and weaving studios in which to play. The sea and several gorgeous beaches are ten minutes down the road. Elly Danica goes there often for long meditative walks and the wide horizon she misses from the prairies.

About Writing... *Don't let the inevitable flaws in the first, second, or even third draft discourage you. Each draft is better, truer, more the book it was meant to be. Trust in the process, be brave, write with passion, always.*—ELLY DANICA

JEANNE MARIE DE MOISSAC is best-known as a poet—she published *Second Skin* in 1998 and *Slow Curve* in 2004. Her works have appeared in *Grain, Dandelion, Arc,*

Fiddlehead, and even *Playgirl*. She has had her work broadcast on CBC Radio.

De Moissac was born and raised near Biggar and currently lives on a farm in the Bear Hills near that town. For many years a member of the poetry circle led by Anne Szumigalski in Saskatoon, Jeanne Marie has also studied at the University of Saskatchewan.

NIK BURTON

REX DEVERELL was born in Toronto in 1941 and raised in Orillia, Ontario. His father, Joseph, was a fourth-generation Canadian of English/Irish background who had grown up on a farm near Orillia. Deverell's mother, Ruby Gwendolyn Johnson, was a Barbadian immigrant who had come to Canada in the mid-1930s. She was a registered nurse and Joseph a soldier in WW II and, afterwards, a carpenter by trade. Their inter-cultural and often stormy relationship served as source material for Deverell's 1980 play, *Drift*.

During the fifties, two influences came to bear on the young Deverell's life direction. One was theatrical, including Tyrone Guthrie's numinous production of *Oedipus Rex* at the fledgling Stratford Festival. The other was theological: he found himself drawn towards faith and faith commitment.

He graduated secondary school in 1960 and entered McMaster University where he received degrees in liberal arts and theology. He also participated extensively in the McMaster Dramatic Society as a director and actor, and was given Honour Society membership for his work as president. He wrote his first play as a Divinity College thesis.

In 1966 and 1967 he went to New York's Union Theological Seminary for specialized study in the area of Theology and Theatre. He met his future wife, Rita Shelton, who was studying at Union and Columbia. They were married the day after graduation. He served as a pastor in St. Thomas, Ontario, for three years. During this time he was able to explore how drama as celebration and idea might be used in the church context.

At the end of this period Rita and he decided to take a year to explore possibilities in theatre. They worked for Ernie Shwartz' Toronto experimental group, Studio Lab, in 1970. In 1971 Rita joined Regina's Globe Theatre as a performer. Rex began to write plays at first for the school company and ultimately became the Globe's first permanent Playwright-in-Residence.

The Artistic Directors of the theatre were the late Sue Kramer and her husband Ken Kramer. Deverell's first work for the main stage was *Boiler Room Suite*, and Sue starred memorably in its premiere. Since then, *Boiler Room Suite* has received international productions, including translations in French and Japanese. The Banff New Music programme toured an operatic version of the play in the United Kingdom with music by Quentin Doolittle.

Ken Kramer encouraged the exploration of Saskatchewan stories and themes through the seventies and eighties. Deverell mined Saskatchewan history for plays like *Number 1 Hard*, a collective creation; *Medicare*, a play based on the introduction of a socialized medicare plan in

REX DEVERELL

the province and the resulting doctors' strike; and *Black Powder*, the story of the Estevan coal miners' strike and the killing of demonstrating strikers. He also wrote and directed the play *Prairie Wind*, a light-hearted romp through the history of the province's legislature, which was performed at a gala for Queen Elizabeth and Prince Phillip. For many of these projects, Geoff Ursell and Rob Bryanton collaborated with Deverell as songwriters and, in Rob's case, arranger.

Through these years Deverell's work included many styles of theatre: cabaret, satire, docu-drama, and personal, poetic works like *Drift*, or *Quartet for Three Actors*. He never lost his interest in writing for young audiences.

In 1974, a new critic (and source of material) appeared on the scene. The Deverell family celebrated the birth of their son, Shelton Ramsay. By 1981 he was able to proudly claim that he had managed to watch all four hours of his father's translation of *The Orestiea*.

In 1990 the family moved back to Toronto—Rita for the founding of *Vision TV*, a multi-faith cable television network, and Rex to freelance. Since Regina, Deverell scripts have been commissioned by The Golden Horseshoe Players, the Banff Music Theatre programme, Canadian Artists Workshop Theatre, and Mixed Company.

2002 saw a commission for "Ellis Portal: The City at Night" a libretto for the Talisker Chamber Music Players and composer Andrew Ager. In February and again in July, Deverell scripted two forum theatre pieces with Simon Malbogat (Mixed Company, Toronto) and two companies of street experienced youth: "Dream Park" and "Heat Exchange." He is currently working on yet another commission for a play for young audiences about ethics and decision-making.

Deverell's writing has won the Canadian Authors Association medal, the Chalmers award, a Major Armstrong, and a Banff Film Festival award.

In August of 2002, Rita accepted a three-year position at Aboriginal Peoples Television Network and both Rex and Rita relocated to Winnipeg.

About Writing... *A writer is someone who finishes his play, his story, his poem. This is the very slim difference that separates a writer from a non-writer. However, the difference between a writer and a good writer is something else. A good writer is someone who writes beyond—beyond common clichés—beyond his or her own clichés—and finally beyond herself (himself); and then starts the whole process all over again.*

Writing for Theatre is an art that allows a writer to gather a tangibly present community. There can be no imposition of a "message," only an invitation to come along on a voyage of discovery. The response may be negative or positive. At any rate, it is immediate!—REX DEVERELL

NORMA LOUISE DILLON (1948–1984)

was a poet and member of the arts community in both Winnipeg and Regina. Born in Winnipeg on December 16, 1948, she was the only daughter of Marjorie and Eldridge Dillon who was co-partner in an electrical firm in that city. She had one brother, Ronald.

After high school, Dillon read for an English degree at St. John's College, University of Manitoba. At the same time she was developing an interest in mass media and in this connection began to attend conferences and workshops, most notably one held in the summer of 1971 at the University of Winnipeg, and also six years later in Brandon where she had had poems published. Dillon was also attending creative writing workshops to develop her growing poetical talent and her poems were gaining recognition both on the CBC's *Anthology, Arts Manitoba*, and in the *Manitoba Writer's News Magazine*. In 1976, the deaths of first her brother and then her mother were to have a lasting and disturbing influence on her. She alludes to her mother's death in the title poem of her chapbook *Mother's Gone Fishing*, which was edited by Dennis Cooley and published in 1979.

In the late 1970s Dillon moved to Regina and was accepted by the University of Regina to do a Master's degree. Her first years in Regina were happy and productive. She soon became part of the writing scene and joined the Saskatchewan Writers Guild. Dillon also took a creative writing course from Mick Burrs, and she was the president of the Wascana Writers Group in 1980.

In the summer of 1979 Dillon attended a writing course at Fort San, that happy second home for so many Saskatchewan writers of the time, and so she further widened her circle of acquaintances. She read at the "Warm Poets For A Cold Night" series in January 1980, in the Sub Poetry reading series in Edmonton in March of the same year, and at various coffee-houses and locales in Regina. All this time she continued to write, and her work was published in small magazines, such as *FreeLance* and *Variety 11*, which was a publication of the Wascana Writers Group. Dillon became a vibrant part of a writing group convened by Brett Balon.

This period of relative tranquility ended when a relationship she had become dependent on ended. She moved from the small house on Angus Street near the railway tracks she had referred to as "our/two story/nest-egg cradle" in a poem called "Security," taking with her, her small dog, Tinker. But the bungalow she rented did not prove such a safe haven as she was subjected to the taunts of neighbourhood children and grew increasingly depressed. Although Dillon advertised herself as a poet, researcher, and reviewer, she was unable to find work. Nor could she form another satisfactory relationship. Beset by financial difficulties and more depressed than ever, she drove to Bridgewater, Nova Scotia, where her father (now remarried) was living. She was admitted to a psychiatric hospital there but after a brief spell discharged herself and returned with Tinker to Regina where her depression and paranoia worsened, and her eccentric behaviour grew. Finally, in November 1984, seeing no ending to her problems, Dillon committed suicide having first ensured her small dog and her collection of cats would survive. At her memorial service her father remarked, "I always believed that as long as she had her small family she would be safe." Sadly, this was not the case.

Dillon left a large volume of unpublished work, much of which was left to the care of the Saskatchewan Writers Guild. Deeply observant of the natural world, and with a rare

NORMA DILLON... WITH TINKER, 1984.

command of English, her poems are remarkable for their unusual allusions and metaphors, though it is easy to trace her growing despair in her later writing. Despite her depression, Dillon remained both gentle and generous. Almost childlike in her trust, she left small gifts on the doorsteps of anyone who had shown her a kindness. A tribute to Dillon by editor Andris Taskans was printed in the Manitoba publication *Prairie Fire*, together with poems selected by Mick Burrs and Marion Beck. Norma Dillon was buried in Fort Gary.

MARION BECK

HARRY C. DILLOW (1922–2004) was born in the South Bronx on August 17, 1922, and spent the first eight years of his life there. Around 1930 his family moved to Newburgh, New York, for a brief two-year hiatus. It was in Newburgh that he began his schooling and discovered the delights of Newburgh's parks, lakes and semi-rural atmosphere, so different from the big city. It is probably fair to say that Newburgh became for him a vision of Paradise, and it remains so to this day.

Back in New York the family moved to Washington Heights in Manhattan where he did most of his growing up. He attended George Washington High School, the City College of New York, and Columbia University where he received his M.A. In 1970 he earned his Ph.D. at the University of London. Through the efforts of Professor Marjorie Nicolson at Columbia he was able to gain a post as Instructor at Adelphi College on Long Island, where he began his teaching career. The greatest influence on his development at this point was Mark Van Doren, whose lectures on Homer and Cervantes made him aware of the poetic qualities of these works. An earlier influence that turned him toward poetry was that of Mary J.J. Wrinn, an English teacher at George Washington High, who gave a course on the writing of verse and encouraged his first awkward experiments.

In 1961, having taught for two years at Adelphi, he came to Saskatchewan initially as an instructor at Regina College, later to become the second campus of the University of Saskatchewan and, finally, the University of Regina. Dillow subsequently became Professor of English, specializing in the seventeenth century. He also taught, among the usual courses, a course in creative writing and found that this was of considerable help with his own writing. Dillow's poetry has been published in *Ariel*, *Fiddlehead*, *Grain*, *Quarry*, *Waves*, *The Antigonish Review*, *Prism International*, *Queen's Quarterly*, *Number One Northern*, and *Wascana Review*. He was also the editor of *Wascana Review* from 1970 to 1984. That year, his first collection of verse, entitled *Orts and Scantlings*, was published.

Dillow lived in Regina following his retirement and died in May 2004.

HEATHER HODGSON

ANNE DOOLEY was born and raised in a Chicago suburb, graduated from Grinnell College, Iowa, with a B.A., married, and had two children before she and her husband brought the family to Saskatoon where they had two more children and lived happily ever after.

Which is true, but leaves out some of the best stuff. Like the part about her initiative and involvement in early preschool education at a time when there were only a few kindergartens and no nursery schools or play schools in Saskatoon. And the part about her husband's fishing trip.

A bunch of friends went fishing each year,

and one year the pilots among them volunteered to fly them to a particular lake up north where perch and pike begged to be caught. Possessing a big old station wagon, Anne was delegated to drive around Saskatoon at an ungodly hour on a Sunday morning, to pick them up and deposit them and their gear at the airport. Loading the aircraft took forever, but finally, one by one, engines coughed to life and the little planes followed one another to the runway. They were just single engine Pipers that only held four passengers, but in the soft light of early morning they left the ground with an accumulated roar and climbed with grace. Turning north they became specks that gradually disappeared. And the airport was quiet. Anne had always been fascinated by planes and wanted to fly, and when she was little she sometimes bumped into fence posts and fire hydrants when she looked up to watch a passing aircraft. Instead of going right home she went into the hangar and signed up for lessons.

She flew, and earned Airline Transport and Class I Instructor ratings, and then taught others to fly. She proved that 'Nothing learned ever goes to waste,' by combining her undergraduate experience of being a campus radio disc jockey and an interviewer and reporter, with her love of flying when she became the CKOM traffic reporter/pilot in Saskatoon for the morning and evening 'drive times.' Anne flew later for CJWW. That was a great deal of fun except for the part about having to get up every morning at 4:30 A.M.

Anne also helped to launch and shape CASARA (Civil Air Search and Rescue Association) in the province. For CASARA she set up and ran the provincial dispatch system and held a variety of offices including provincial President, and served on the national board of directors. For many years she was an elected Saskatchewan Aviation Council Board member and she was also a member of the General Aviation and Airport Security Committees at Saskatoon's John Diefenbaker airport, before it was privatized. Anne owned and operated her own flying service, too. Then, almost twenty years after that fateful fishing trip, rheumatoid arthritis forced her out of the cockpit.

PHOTO BY PETER DOOLEY
ANNE DOOLEY... "LOCAL FLIGHT."

Arthritis was a bitter blow. It felled her and turned the easiest and most common of activities into painful and almost impossible chores. Just getting dressed took all morning and by then Anne was ready for a nap. Almost immediately she began aggressive treatment and learned everything she could about the disease. In typical Anne fashion, she became an arthritis advocate. Her theory is that if you can see what needs doing, then do it.

And 'doing it' is how she came to writing. Always an avid mystery reader she decided to try to write one, using a dinosaur of a computer, and teaching herself as she went. She didn't tell anyone what she was doing. Write a book? Bad enough she had arthritis, no point in convincing everyone she'd taken leave of her senses, too. It wasn't until she had a reasonable draft that she confessed to a writer friend, Gail McConnell, who convinced her to talk to mystery writer Suzanne North, who in turn graciously offered to read the manuscript. The result was *Plane Death*, which came out in 1996, and which is an aviation-based mystery that takes place in Saskatoon and northern Saskatchewan, published by NeWest Press. The book was shortlisted by Crime Writers of Canada for an Arthur Ellis Award in the Best First Novel category (1997), and it also placed as a finalist for The Brenda Riches (Best First Book), at the Saskatchewan Book Award in 1997. Anne is working on a second novel, but it's slow going. Competing for her time is her advocacy work for The Arthritis Society and as a member of the Canadian Arthritis Patient Alliance (CAPA) Steering Committee.

She and her husband, Peter, live in Saskatoon. Their four children are successfully established in their lives and careers, and there are five grandchildren to spoil. Now, when Anne flies she sits in the back of the plane.

About Writing... *Location, location, location! What does it look like? How does it smell? See it as the characters you create. See it as you want the reader to see it. Are there bugs? What kind? Do they bite? Location is as important as your hero and your plot.*—
ANNE DOOLEY

BETTY FITZPATRICK DORION is the author of two juvenile fiction titles, and a Young Adult novel. Her first book, *Melanie Bluelake's Dream*, was a finalist for the Silver Birch Award in Ontario, the Young Readers' Choice Award in Manitoba, and for two Saskatchewan Book Awards as well. *Bay Girl* won the Children's Literature Award at the Saskatchewan Book Awards and was a finalist for the Publishing in Education Award in the same competition. Her Young Adult title, *Whose Side Are You On?*, has been adopted for use by, among others, the Saskatchewan Federation of Labour for its youth summer school program.

Born, raised, and educated as a teacher in Newfoundland, Dorion moved to Saskatchewan in 1975. She lived and taught at a number of reserve schools in the north until moving to Prince Albert in 1980, where she continues writing and teaching to this day.

NIK BURTON

T/ED (E.F.) DYCK was dropped into the short-grass prairie (this is not a figure of speech) within sight of the South Saskatchewan River breaks SE Sec. 31 Twshp. 18 Range 11 W3 SK on 03.09.39. There is some dispute about the day: his mother (d. 1967) claimed it was 02; his father (d. 1989) registered it as the day WW II started. His parents were emigrants from Russia (father) and the United States (mother).

Dyck matriculated at Herbert and graduated from the universities of Saskatchewan, Minnesota, and Manitoba, with a plethora of degrees and even some honours. He has enjoyed two academic non-careers (mathematics and literature). He has taught in some ten universities and colleges, in three countries and two continents. At times and in places he has been rhetor, writer, editor, scholar, businessman, professor, pseudo-hermit, instructor, teacher, ranch-hand, brush salesman, and so on. The predictable life of the ne'er-do-well, in short.

He began writing in the 70s, about the time Berryman leapt into the Mississippi and a Russo-Canadian poet from Manitoba fell into his (Dyck's) over-easy eggs in Dinkytown Minnesota, one early morning. It is but one step from the languages of mathematical logic to poetry. He has continued to write in a variety of genres since then: poetry, fiction, non-fiction, criticism, essays, letters, etc. This writing has been praised by few, vilified by

PHOTO BY STEVEN ELMS
T/ED (E.F.) DYCK...
INUVIK, 2003

many. He continues, however, to publish in several modes: books, magazines, journals, etc. Increasingly, he has turned to electronic publishing, though he believes the technology of paper and pen is far from being equaled. He operates an Internet-based writing and editing service called WorDoctor.

Like Groucho Marx, Dyck eschews all cliques, clubs, schools, groups, and cults that would have him, especially of the literary type.

He has his other interests: fly-fishing, x-country skiing, snooker, Bach and Gould, the classical guitar, cognac—in no particular order.

T/Ed (E.F.) Dyck currently lives in Grande Cache and Wetaskiwin, Alberta, with his companion and partner, Penny Snelgrove, her children, Megan and Marc, and two dogs, Kita and Piper.

ELSIE ELLIS was born Elsa Adeline Klein, on Section 24, Township 12, Range 25, West of the Third Meridian, on December 30, 1930. She was the middle child of nine born to Sam and Lena Klein of Piapot, Saskatchewan.

A child of the prairies, she lived all of her life in southwestern Saskatchewan, where she attended country schools, and graduated from Maple Creek High School. After teacher's training at Moose Jaw, and classes at the University of Saskatchewan, she taught school for ten years.

In 1952 she married Lenard Ellis and they moved to their farm at Hazlet, Saskatchewan, on the eastern edge of the Great Sand Hills. They have three children: Diane, Randi, and Brad, along with five grandchildren: Rebecca, Renita, Renay, Rorie, and Craig, and great-grandsons, Cody, Carter, Konrad and Joshua. Grandchildren were the inspiration for much of her early writing.

After she retired, Ellis had time to devote to writing children's fiction and poetry. Her initial writer's workshop with Lorna Crozier in 1980 resulted in her children's story, "Saddle Patch," being published in *Canadian Children's Annual '83*.

She joined the Saskatchewan Writers Guild and attended many workshops to improve her skills and in 1985 Ellis won honourable mention in the Guild's non-fiction category.

Success inspired Ellis to continue. Her poetry was subsequently included in *Branch Lines* (1981), and later in the 1987 and 1988 volumes of *Premium Swift Review* and *100% Cracked Wheat* (1983). Ellis's poem, "Golfing," placed second in a national contest and was subsequently published in *Poetry '86*.

Over the years her by-line has appeared many times with both poetry and non-fiction in *Western People*, *Farm*

ELSIE ELLIS...
50TH WEDDING ANNIVERSARY,
APRIL 2002

Woman, Folklore, and other periodicals including FreeLance.

In 1986 and 1988 Ellis won first place for her poetry in Saskatchewan History & Folklore's writing competition. She was the recipient of a Canada Council Grant in 1987, and the manuscript that resulted from that project became her first book of poetry, Sand Hills and Sage, in 1988. In 1992 her second collection of Saskatchewan verse, Sand Script, was published. Friends and Fences, a collection of short stories by Saskatchewan authors (1994), included Ellis's "Separate Checks."

During both the 1994 and 1996 Provincial Senior Games her poetry won a Bronze medal.

Cowboy poetry is another genre that she has developed and shared for the past decade with an appreciative audience at the Maple Creek Gathering. As a member of the Range Writers, Ellis appeared with the cowboy poets at Regina's Agribition in 1993, and in 1996 to 1999 inclusive.

Ellis's signature poem "The Boss" is included in Sharon Butala and Todd Korol's Harvest: A Celebration of Harvest on the Canadian Prairies (1992) and in the anthology Running Barefoot: Women Write the Land (2001).

For the past twenty years, Ellis has shared her writing with people of all ages—from kindergarten to seniors, with students in Saskatchewan schools, libraries, and other venues. Her poetry is solidly rooted in the prairie around her. She writes about things she has seen, her life on the farm, and the hold the land has on her family. Her third book of Saskatchewan verse, The Land of My Undoing, is used in Saskatchewan schools. Her future project is to have a collection of her stories for children published.

About Writing... *At my first writers' workshop in 1980, Lorna Crozier asked each student what we expected from her sessions. My question was, "Do I have talent, or am I wasting my time?" Her reply: "Don't spend all of your time with your hands in the dishpan." Were it not for those words of encouragement, I would not have become a writer. In my scrapbook from that era, I treasure a note from Lorna which contains this advice: "Keep writing."*

I have learned that you must first be a dedicated reader before you can ever become a writer. My love of books began as a child in our country school, where I had read every volume (except the Encylopedia) in our limited library by grade three.

Books will never become obsolete. In this electronic age they may have taken on a different format, but the written word as we know it, and the writers who dream and create stories and poetry will always be an integral part of our lives.—ELSIE ELLIS

CHRIS FISHER's first short story collection, Sun Angel, was published in 1992, and received the Publisher's Prize at the very first Saskatchewan Book Awards. Two stories from that collection, "Sun Angel" and "Games," were award winners as individual stories. A subsequent collection, Voices in the Wilderness, was published in 1999 and a third collection, Third and Long, in 2004. His work has also appeared in numerous magazines and anthologies, and broadcast on CBC Radio.

Born and raised in southwestern Saskatchewan, Chris Fisher now lives in Lumsden and works in Regina.

NIK BURTON

THELMA FOSTER was born in Stockholm, Saskatchewan, to parents of Swedish origin. She taught school for a number of years and lived at Milden, Saskatchewan. A grant from the Saskatchewan Department of Culture and Youth enabled her to publish her novel, Wild

Daisies (1978), about life in a Swedish settlement in early Saskatchewan.

Foster's stories, poems and articles were published in *Grain, Canadian Children's Annual, Modus Operandi, Canadian Author and Bookman, Alberta Poetry Yearbook, Skylark, Western Producer,* and *Winnipeg Free Press*. Her poems were read on CBC Radio.

Thelma Foster died on April 19, 2001, at the age of eighty-six.

NIK BURTON

BERNICE FRIESEN was born in Rosthern hospital in 1966, ten minutes after her parents arrived, her mother Margaret Labach forcing her husband to eat a good lunch before allowing him to take her to town. Ukrainian on her mother's side, Dutch Mennonite on her father's, three of her grandparents were born in the Ukraine. She grew up on her grandparents' Henry and Sarah Friesen's homestead, where her father James was raised. The life of her great-grandfather's family has been written about in *The Mulberry Tree* by Victor Carl Friesen and his mother Anna Friesen (Sarah's sister).

Friesen's first moment of self-awareness came when she was in grade two, about seven years old. She thought to herself, "Here I am: I'm in grade two, on the school bus, and the bus is right here on the highway, and someday I will think back and remember being just here, just now." She built a teepee hideout in the bush, drew pictures of horses, wrote letters in code, tried and failed to teach herself Latin when she was ten, wandered in the alfalfa fields talking to God, and got her first cold sore the day Prince Charles married Lady Diana when she was fourteen.

She trained first as a printmaker and painter at the University of Saskatchewan, ending up with a B.F.A. and a B.Ed. by 1990. She took a creative writing course with Elizabeth Brewster, and in 1998 attended the Banff Writing Studio. She taught herself to read both French and Italian and has mostly forgotten both: there is only so much one can do while having babies. She has traveled in the British Isles, and in France, Italy, Greece, Korea, Hong Kong, China, New Zealand, Mexico, The Cook Islands, Fiji, the United States, and every province in Canada.

After odd jobs such as being a waitress, art studio lab assistant, project coordinator at A.K.A. Gallery, Saskatoon, odd-bod temp at Lloyds of London, England, and singing telegram girl, she got her first professional job as an art gallery educator in Estevan, Saskatchewan. She has also helped to mismanage a group home for adults with mental disabilities, taught Sage Hill Writing Experience for teens, and done a little editing and commercial writing. She has produced six works of art for the covers of Coteau's Open Eye poetry series, and her fiction and poetry has been published in anthologies and magazines in Canada and Europe.

The title story of her first book, *The Seasons are Horses* (1995), won the Vicky Metcalf Award for Best Young Adult Short

PHOTO BY COLIN BOYD

BERNICE FRIESEN... WITH SON ALEXANDER IN THE COOK ISLANDS SQUANDERING HER LITERARY EARNINGS ON ANOTHER FRIVOLOUS SEARCH FOR INSPIRATION.

Story in Canada. Her book of poetry *Sex, Death and Naked Men* came out in 1998.

Friesen wants to write big lush books that a reader can get lost in and regret the passing of the pages. She has been working on several novels recently, as well as a few odd poems, and a computer art project, a magazine satire called WOM.

Friesen lives and works mostly in Saskatoon, and sometimes in a lovely piece of rainforest on an island off the coast of British Columbia. Most recently she has been writing in New Zealand, on sabbatical with her professor husband and best friend Colin Boyd and their baby son Alexander.

She is a beginner belly-dancer.

About Writing... *Looking back upon past proclamations in other "About Writing" sections, I always seem to sound like an idiot. No matter: I'll share what I've learned most recently in my working habits. Yes, I do what writers are supposed to do, treating it like a job, sitting down five mornings a week and pounding away at the keyboard. I am one of those obsessive workaholic sorts of writers, and have only recently learned how to listen to my mind and body when they're sending me burnout signals. When I feel burnt out now, I stop writing instead of torturing myself at the keyboard and producing pages of material that have to be thrown away, which is very hard on the ego and only exacerbates the burnout. By enforcing a period of rest, I gain my writing momentum back and can eventually produce good work.*—BERNICE FRIESEN

CONNIE (HATLEY) GAULT was born in Central Butte in 1949, the granddaughter of pioneers of the area. Having a father in the air force, she spent her childhood moving from province to province. She attended three different schools in grade one and moved again to begin grade two. Every summer, the family drove many hundreds of miles to return to the wheat fields and sunny skies of southern Saskatchewan. While their skin and throats and noses grew drier with the change in climate, their mother sang "Highways are Happy Ways (when they lead the way to home)." Gault has lived most of her adult years in Regina.

After an early and lucky escape from nurses' training, Connie married Gordon Gault of Moose Jaw. While their two sons, Dylan and Brennan, were growing up, she completed her B.A. in English at the University of Regina. Her favourite writers, because of the unique ways they illuminate the inner lives of their characters, are Charles Dickens and Virginia Woolf.

Although she'd been inventing her own stories since she could read—and sometimes directed neighbourhood children in acting them out—Gault didn't begin to write seriously until her early thirties. Encouraged by Joan Givner of the University of Regina English department, she started to revise and complete her stories and began exchanging work with another Regina writer, Marlis Wesseler. Gault's first story was published in *Grain* in 1981 and fiction editor Brenda Riches became another writing colleague. Soon after that, Gault joined a local writers group: The Bombay Bicycle Club. The other core members of this group, who became comrades in the fight to get better, were Ven Begamudré, Bonnie Burnard, Chris Fisher, Dianne Warren, and Marlis Wesseler.

Some of Eve's Daughters, Gault's first collection of short stories, won a Saskatchewan Writers Guild Long Manuscript Award in 1986 and was subsequently published. In 1987 the Thunder Creek Co-operative, publisher of Coteau Books, invited her to sit on their board of directors. She served on that board for seven years, reading manuscripts from Saskatchewan and beyond, sharing in the excitement of publishing fine books. She edited three manuscripts for Coteau: Sharon Butala's *Queen of the Headaches*, Craig Grant's *The Last India Overland*, and Susan Andrews Grace's *Ferry Woman's History of the World*.

In the late 1980s Gault attended the Spring Festival of New Plays, an annual event put on by the Saskatchewan Playwrights Centre, and became intrigued by the possibilities in playwrighting. Her first play, *Sky*, received workshops at the SPC Festival and at Playwrights' Workshop Montreal. It was first produced in 1989 as part of an exchange of plays between 25th Street Theatre, in Saskatoon, and Theatre Network, in Edmonton. Her second play, *The Soft Eclipse*, premiered at Globe Theatre, Regina, later that same year. *The Soft Eclipse* and *The Making of Soft Eclipse*, videos produced by Reel Eye Media during the Winnipeg production of that play, are available for teachers and students through Saskatchewan Education. Gault has workshopped five plays through the Saskatchewan Playwrights Centre, benefiting from the opportunity to work with theatre professionals from across Canada and in particular with dramaturgs Michael Springate, Marina Endicott, and D.D. Kugler. Her plays have received amateur and university productions as well as being professionally produced and published. *Otherwise Bob* and *Red Lips* are her most recent plays. Several of her radio plays have aired on CBC and *Sky* was produced by the BBC as a World Service Play of the Week.

PHOTO BY GORD GAULT
CONNIE GAULT...
CYPRESS HILLS, 1999

For several years Gault taught creative writing classes at the Neil Balkwill Arts Centre, the University of Regina Extension Department, the Regina Senior Citizens Centre, and the Southeast Community College. She taught introductory fiction and playwrighting the last two years of the Saskatchewan School of the Arts at Fort San. She sat on the SWG Colony Committee and served for several years on the board of the Saskatchewan Playwrights Centre. From 1995 to 1998, she was prose editor of *Grain*.

Gault continued dividing her time between writing fiction and plays and published her second collection of stories, *Inspection of a Small Village*, in 1996. It was the recipient of the City of Regina Book Award. Gault's stories have been published in several anthologies, most recently in *Turn of the Story: Canadian Stories for the Millennium, The Oxford Book of Stories by Canadian Women, Inside Stories 111*, and *Donde Es Aqui*, a Mexican anthology of Canadian short stories translated into Spanish.

In 1999, Gault co-wrote the script for *Solitude*, a feature film directed by Robin Schlaht and based on her short story, *The Fat Lady with the Thin Face*.

Currently, she is working on a novel set in Regina.

About Writing... *Whenever I remember that I spend my days imagining the lives of others, I feel fortunate.*—CONNIE GAULT

— 79 —

JOANNE GERBER resolved to become a writer when she was nine years old. She had written an essay in which she explored belief and unbelief, a sense of meaning and the sensation of lostness, using light and darkness as metaphors. Being asked to present it at the Augustine Seminary, she was both terrified and exhilarated by the power of language to communicate one's deepest questions and concerns. She is still exploring those themes, working with those metaphors four decades later.

Gerber was born in Buffalo, New York, to Canadian parents, and grew up in Toronto. After starting a family, she spent four years in Ottawa, then in 1984 made her home in Regina, where she raised two sons, Christopher and Timothy. The vibrant artistic community has kept her in Saskatchewan, although she still travels to Lake Huron to write.

Gerber majored in Creative Writing at York University from 1977 to 1980. There she studied under some of Canada's finest writers. Her instructors included W.O. Mitchell, Don Coles, Clark Blaise, Frank Daveys, and Eli Mandel. Don Coles remained a long-time correspondent. Michael Ondaatje, Dennis Lee, Mavor Moore, Irving Layton, and Margaret Atwood were among the guest lecturers. York taught Gerber more about the life and discipline of writing than about the mechanics. She began to find her own voice and discovered the poetry and poetics of Osip Mandelstam, which have challenged her ever since. But uncertain about how to work with her own material, and torn between the demands of writing and family life, she agreed to take a hiatus from writing.

JOANNE GERBER

Gerber received a Bachelor of Arts in Interdisciplinary Studies from Carleton University in Ottawa in 1984. Her area of specialization was the effect of the Russian Revolution on writers, literature, and poetics in the Soviet Union, especially during the Stalinist Era. Her own writing at this time was confined to a poetry notebook. She went on to pursue a Master of Arts in Religion at the Canadian Theological Seminary in Regina. Still concerned about the uneasy relationship between ideology and artistic expression, religious belief and artistic practice, she concentrated on theology, Christian thought, and aesthetics; or art and faith. While serving as teaching assistant in theology, she began to form a poetics which would embrace both her faith and artistic freedom.

Gerber soon took up writing again, turning from poetry to prose. She attended two Saskatchewan Summer Schools of the Arts, working with Seán Virgo, then with Leon Rooke and Gordon Lish. Chastened and challenged, she began to write fiction in earnest, drafting rough stories that would later be incorporated into her first book. She started a writers group, and signed up for a correspondence class that evolved into a gracious mentorship by the late Brenda MacDonald Riches.

Regina composer David L. McIntyre asked Gerber to collaborate with him, first on songs, then on an opera. Initially hesitant, she has found the long-time collaboration a great joy. *Above An Abyss*, a song cycle for soprano, cello, and piano, premiered at Government House in 1987, and has had several professional concert and radio performances. A composer-librettist laboratory at the Canadian Opera Company informed her work on the libretto for *Sea Change*, an original chamber opera by McIntyre. In 1998, the Globe Theatre, Toronto's Tapestry Music Theatre, and Opera Saskatchewan co-sponsored a workshop performance at the Globe.

To support her creative work, Gerber works with words professionally. She has taught writing courses in Saskatchewan, Ontario, and British Columbia. She has lectured and read at universities, libraries, bookstores, symposia, and writing festivals across Canada. Since 1999, Gerber has been employed by Coteau Books, as an acquisitions editor, editorial assistant, proofreader, and copyeditor. She also edits novels and juvenile fiction. She has been involved in the Writers Guild as a volunteer, as a mentor, and as fiction editor for *Spring*. In September 2003 she assumed the position of fiction editor for *Grain* magazine.

Gerber credits many writers and programs for her development. At the Writing Studio in Banff (1994 and 1996), she worked with Edna Alford, Greg Hollingshead, and Isabel Huggan; Robert Kroetsch and Audrey Thomas also offered advice. She studied with Ven Begamudré at Sage Hill and with Dave Margoshes in Regina. She has taken the Simon Fraser University Book Editing Immersion Workshop, and Saskatchewan Playwrights Centre workshops. Notes from the Underground, a Regina writers group, has provided discourse and encouragement since 1993. Edna Alford has been an insightful editor and ongoing source of writerly wisdom.

Gerber's stories have appeared in *Grain*, and in several anthologies. CBC radio has aired her work, including five linked stories on *Between the Covers* and *Richardson's Roundup*. Individual stories received SWG awards for short fiction (1990, 1993, 1996), the City of Regina Writing Award (1995), The National Magazine Awards (1994), and a Journey Prize nomination (1994). The Globe Theatre's *On The Line* series performed "Je Me Souviens" in 1998, and "Mission" in 2001.

In the Misleading Absence of Light, Gerber's first book, was released by Coteau Books in 1997. Now in its third printing, the collection received favourable reviews in newspapers and journals across Canada. It also received a number of honours, including the Jubilee Award (1998) for Best Short Story Collection from the Canadian Authors Association, short-listing for the Toronto Book Award (1998), third place in the Danuta Gleed Award (1998) for Best First Story Collection from the Writers Union of Canada, and three Saskatchewan Book Awards (1997): Best Fiction Award; the Brenda Macdonald Riches Award for Best First Book, and co-winner (with Sandra Birdsell and Ven Begamudré) of the City of Regina Award.

At present, Gerber is working on her first novel, *Like Manna*.

HEATHER HODGSON

About Writing... *Learning to write has been as much about learning to look attentively at the world, to listen intently to my work, to love and to dignify my characters, as learning to craft sentences. I am still learning. I will always be learning. There is a just-audible music, a just-visible image that eludes me, some truth about what it means to be human. So I cast a net of words. It falls short. I recast and recast.... And that's enough.*—JOANNE GERBER

JOAN GIVNER was born Joan Mary Parker Short in Manchester, England, in 1936. She took an Honours degree in English at the University of London in 1958, and married

David Givner in 1965. Givner returned to London for a Ph.D. in 1972, following some teaching and graduate studies in the United States. In 1972 she resumed teaching in the English Department of the University of Regina, where she also edited the *Wascana Review* from 1984 to 1992. In 1995 Givner took early retirement and moved with her husband to British Columbia to write full-time.

Balancing her responsibilities as researcher, professor, and mother (she has two daughters), Givner began publishing her short stories in 1981. At the same time she also maintained a vigorous output of scholarly articles and conference papers. Her first book, entitled *Katherine Anne Porter: A Life*, was published in 1982 and reprinted in 1991, establishing Givner as a feminist biographer. A subsequent book, *Katherine Anne Porter: Conversations*, which was published in 1987, contains a collection of interviews with Porter that were edited and introduced by Givner.

Givner embraced a Canadian subject in *Mazo de la Roche: The Hidden Life* (1989), a serious examination of de la Roche's work and life with her cousin, life-companion, and amanuensis, Caroline Clement. De la Roche's books, although immensely popular, were typically regarded as eccentric at best and risible at worst by the intelligentsia (Dorothy Livesay being a significant exception). Givner argues that de la Roche's writings provide an essential transition from the nineteenth-century foremothers, Susanna Moodie and Catharine Parr Traill (both of whom were still living when de la Roche was born), to Margaret Atwood and Margaret Laurence, who were publishing at the time of de la Roche's death in 1961. Givner communicates her fascination with de la Roche's multiple ambivalences—"sexual, national, racial, and religious"—and with the necessity to "inscribe her own female desire obliquely" within the conventions of the novel. In 1992 Givner's play *Mazo and Caroline* was presented at the Saskatchewan Playwrights' Centre in Regina.

PHOTO BY ANNE BOMFORD
JOAN GIVNER... IN HER GARDEN.

Givner's first collection of short fiction, *Tentacles of Unreason*, published in 1985, is pleasing apprentice work that shows her exploration of the notion of "fictional fictions" and "fictions of autobiography," finding the female present in the "intertext between the two." For example, in the title story of her second collection, *Unfortunate Incidents* (1988), a literary biographer at work on the life of Rachel de la Warr, meets Rachel's adopted daughter Aimée, in a sophisticated reminder of de la Roche and her adopted daughter Esmée. The stories in *Scenes from Provincial Life* (1991) demonstrate a similar wilful assault on the sort of androcentric criticism that finds women's writing merely autobiographical.

Givner turned her life-writing talents to her own experience with *The Self-portrait of a Literary Biographer* (1993), focusing on her grammar-school beginnings and her growth into her own writing, incidentally presenting a brilliant depiction of the pettiness, appalling cosiness, and sheer meanness of the underclass way of English life.

Since then, Givner has published *In the Garden of Henry James* (1996), *Thirty-Four Ways of Looking at Jane Eyre* (1998), and the novel, *Half Known Lives* (2000), which is a satire based on so-called advances in biotechnology and partly inspired by a Regina anti-abortion case and its all-male participants.

Givner is a regular contributor to *Books in Canada* and *BC Bookworld*, and she writes and reviews for several other journals. A novel that will be called *Ellen Fremedon* is scheduled to be published in 2004. Another novel in the works is entitled *Playing Sarah Bernhardt*.

Joan Givner resides with her husband on the coast of British Columba, where she writes and works in her Mill Bay garden.

The December 1994 issue of the journal *A Room of One's Own*, edited by Cristina George, is devoted to Joan Givner's work.

PATRICIA WHITNEY

About Writing... *I write every day following the ballet-dancer's rule that if she fails to practice for one day she notices, two days and the company notices, three days and the audience notices.*—JOAN GIVNER

DAVE GLAZE was born on September 17, 1947, in New Westminster, British Columbia. By the time he reached his teens, he had lived in four provinces. His family—father Russell, mother Phyllis, and sister Sandra—moved every few years to meet the demands of his father's employer. His parents eventually settled in Tisdale, Saskatchewan, in the early 1960s.

Glaze attended the University of Saskatchewan in Saskatoon from 1965 to 1969 and graduated with a B.A. (Honours). While there, he helped edit the last editions of the Greystone yearbook. After graduation, he worked for one year in the field of social work in Calgary. He quit that position and for the next while earned his living in a variety of jobs, including landscaper and lumber mill worker in northern British Columbia. Glaze then bought a motorcycle and travelled across Canada to the east coast, and partway back. He later flew to England and spent the better part of a year travelling in Europe and northern Africa.

Returning to Saskatoon, Glaze worked at a number of temporary jobs, then helped found and edit a community-based newspaper, *The Saskatonian*, which was in print in 1974 and l975. Later, Glaze was employed as an on-air reporter for a local CBC television public affairs program for two seasons. He also freelanced for CBC radio.

In the late 1970s, Glaze went back to the University of Saskatchewan, this time to complete classes in the College of Education required for a teaching certificate, and later a Bachelor of Education degree. He taught for two years for the Sturgeon Lake Band and one year for the Whitecap Band. Since 1980, he has been employed by the Saskatoon Public School Division, first as a teacher and then as a teacher-librarian.

Glaze has written for and helped to edit three magazines, *Briarpatch*, *Green Teacher*, and *NeWest Review*. He has also contributed to *The Bulletin*, the journal of the Saskatchewan Teachers Federation.

Around the time of his fortieth birthday, Glaze committed himself to writing fiction. He was inspired by the success of local historian and young adult writer Geoffrey Bilson and was encouraged by writer-in-residence Lois Simmie. His first novel, *Pelly*, was published in

DAVE GLAZE... IN HIS BACK YARD.

1993. It tells the story of a girl who, forced to move to Saskatoon, befriends a young pelican on the river. Three years later *Who took Henry and Mr. Z?* was published. In this mystery, two children resolve to find out who stole their classroom's guinea pigs. Both books received the Canadian Children's Book Centre Choice Award. *Who Took Henry and Mr. Z?* was shortlisted for an Arthur Ellis award.

Waiting for Pelly, a sequel to Glaze's first novel, was published in 2004. Glaze is at work on a third and last book about Pelly and her human encounters in and around Saskatoon.

Glaze is married to Susan Gilmer, a scientist who works in the area of cell botany. They have two daughters, Sarah and Alice.

About Writing... *When the voice inside tells you to write, write. When it tells you not to bother, write then, too.* —DAVE GLAZE

BETH GOOBIE, who lives in Saskatoon, was born in 1959. She attended the University of Winnipeg in Manitoba. Graduating with a B.A., she was also the recipient of the gold medal in 1983.

Goobie is the author of *The Colours of Carol Molev* (1998); *Could I Have My Body Back Now, Please?* (1991); *The Dream Where the Losers Go* (1999); *The Girls Who Dream Me* (1999); *The Good, the Bad and the Suicidal* (1997); *Group Homes from Outer Space* (1992); *Hit and Run*; *I'm Not Convinced* (1997); *Kicked Out* (1995); *Mission Impossible* (1994); *The Only-Good Heart* (1998); *Scars of Light* (1994); *Sticks and Stones* (1994); and *Who Owns Kelly Paddik?* (1993).

She won the Joseph S. Stauffer Award in 1998, and the Pat Lowther Award in 1995 for *Scars of Light*. Goobie went on to win the R. Ross Annett Award in 1995 for *Mission Impossible*, the Our Choice Award in 1998 and 1999, as well as CBC's Write for Radio contest.

In 1992, she was nominated for the Alberta Fiction Award. In 1995, Goobie was nominated for the Governor General's Award for Children's Literature and that same year she was also nominated for the Gerald Lampert Award. In l998 she was nominated for an award for Saskatchewan's Children's Literature, as well as for the Canadian Library Association's Young Adult Novel Award in both 1998 and 1999.

Goobie wrote a radio drama entitled *Continuum*, which was broadcast on CBC's *Morningside*. In 1992, she wrote the play *Dandelion Moon*, which was produced by Catalyst Theatre and which went on tour in 1992 and 1994.

HEATHER HODGSON

LEE GOWAN was born in the Swift Current Union Hospital on November 3, 1961. His mother, Laureen Gowan grew up in the farming community of Allenford in Bruce County, Ontario. All nine of her siblings lived their entire lives on farms in the area, but Laureen nursed in Toronto for a year and was on the way to a nursing job on Vancouver Island when she stopped to visit relatives in Swift Current. Her father's cousin, Goldwin Gowan, was on the Union Hospital Board and found her a position there. She met Joseph Gowan, her second cousin, who was born (at the Swift Current Union Hospital) on Dec. 24, 1929, which, coincidentally, was also Laureen's birthday. They married a year later. They were both descendants of Joshua Gowan and Anna Braithwaite, who emigrated from Ireland in the 1840s to farm in the Eastern Townships of Quebec.

Gowan spent his first 21 years on the family farm, in the same house his father had grown up in, and where his father and brother still farm. After high school he stayed on the farm for three years, not having considered any other possibilities for a career, but finally decided that he was not suited to be a farmer. He attended his first writing workshop in October 1980 in a convent in Ponteix. Lorna Crozier was serving as writer-in-residence in Swift Current for the year, as part of a community Arts Board campaign initiated by the Saskatchewan Writers Guild and called The Southwest Writers Project. The workshop is notable in that so many prominent Saskatchewan writers attended it as students: Sharon Butala, David Carpenter, Liz Philips, Ven Begamudré, Geoffrey Ursell, Rick Hillis, and Sharon MacFarlane, to name a few. Gowan took an introductory workshop from Lois Simmie, and also developed a relationship with Jack Hodgins who became an important mentor for Gowan.

A week after the workshop ended, Gowan decided to become a writer. That winter, using one of his mother's textbooks he found in the basement, he taught himself to type, and began writing poems and short stories. In February 1981, he embarked on a three-month trip to Europe, where he traveled part of the time with his aunt Carmel Gowan (his father's sister) and his cousin, Kim. Kim is Vietnamese and had been adopted by Carmel while she was working at a nightclub in Saigon in 1964. Carmel was a World Champion trick-roper who roped at the Moulin Rouge in the 1960s. She taught her act to Kim, and Kim later became World Champion. They performed all over the world. Gowan followed them to clubs in Geneva, Prague, and Llubljana, Yugoslavia.

He returned to the farm in April 1981, and wrote a short story called "The Trestle" which won an Honourable Mention in the Saskatchewan Writers Guild's Literary Awards. This small success gave him the confidence to continue writing and taking workshops. The next two summers he attended the Summer School of the Arts, and took workshops there and in various other locales from Anne Szumigalski, Patrick Lane, Joe Rosenblatt, Lorna Crozier, W.D. Valgardson, Ed Dyck, and Caroline Heath. Heath was a particularly important mentor, and they remained close friends until her death in 1989.

In September of 1982 Gowan left Saskatchewan to enroll in the Creative Writing Program at the University of Victoria. He worked on fiction and poetry and did workshops with Jack Hodgins, Marilyn Bowering, David Godfrey, Derk Wynand, and Robin Skelton. In the summer of 1985 he married and moved to Vancouver, where he finished his undergraduate degree at the University of British Columbia, taking workshops with Robert Harlow and George McWhirter. After completing his degree he spent a year working as a courier for a stockbroker, before applying to the Graduate Program in Creative Writing at the University of British Columbia. He won the fellowship, which gave him a little money to write for the next two years. His first son was born in October of 1987, just as he was beginning the graduate program.

PHOTO BY ALISON HAHN
LEE GOWAN

One criterion of the program was that all students needed to write in at least three different genres, and the novel (Gowan had begun writing a novel by this time) and short story were both considered the same genre, so he was forced to learn the format for writing a screenplay. Fiction, though, was still his real interest, and in his second year at UBC Gowan polished a collection of short stories under the guidance of Jerry Newman. This collection was accepted for publication in February 1989, just before he completed his graduate degree.

In September of 1989 Gowan moved his family to Melfort, Saskatchewan, where he served as writer-in-residence for a year. In the spring of 1990 he launched his first story collection, *Going to Cuba*.

In the fall of 1990 Gowan moved his family to Swift Current, his "hometown," where he taught courses through extension from the University of Regina at the Cypress Hills Regional College. He also worked as a clerk at the Swift Current Branch of the Chinook Regional Library. It was during this time that he began writing his novel *Make Believe Love*. Meanwhile, though, his writing career took a sharp turn when he won a screenwriting contest sponsored by the National Film Board and administered by the Saskatchewan Writers Guild. His screenplay "The Playboy" was optioned and produced as a television movie for Global called *Paris or Somewhere*. The story was based on J.M. Synge's "The Playboy of the Western World," and it won two screenwriting awards and was nominated for a Gemini. While in Toronto for the Gemini Awards, Gowan was interviewed by the selection committee at the Canadian Film Centre and was chosen as one of five writer residents for their program. He moved to Toronto in the summer of 1996 and attended the program for the next ten months.

During this time his marriage fell apart, and though he returned to Saskatchewan for two months in 1997, he soon went back to Toronto. He has since remarried and has a second son.

Though he has had half a dozen film projects in development, Gowan has had little success in the film business since coming to Toronto. His focus has shifted back to fiction. His novel *Make Believe Love* was published in 2001 and was nominated for Ontario's Trillium Award. His new novel, *The Last Cowboy*, was published in January 2004.

Gowan lives in Toronto and directs the Creative Writing Program at the University of Toronto's School of Continuing Studies.

About Writing… *One of my students won a contest and when she was asked about my teaching she said the best advice I ever gave her was to let her characters stop and have a look around.*—LEE GOWAN

GREG GRACE. Although, for the most part, Grace has not lived his life in chronological sequence, the following is an outline of his life employing such a framework. Greg Grace was born on June 22, 1947, and raised in the rough-and-tumble of North End Winnipeg by a working class family. After he grew up he was employed at various jobs, including working as a dishwasher and as a research consultant as well as a teacher in a federal penitentiary. He received a Bachelor of Arts from the University of Winnipeg, a Master of Arts from the University of Manitoba, and a Master of Divinity from the Vancouver School of Theology.

Since completing theological college, he has worked for the past twenty-two years in various locations in Manitoba and

Saskatchewan as a United Church minister. As a spiritual leader, Grace is not only interested in Christian spirituality, but has also taken a deep interest in Sufic and Cabbalistic–Hasidic spirituality as well as Zen Buddhism. These spiritual traditions have in a variety of ways influenced his writing. In his writing Grace attempts to penetrate the depths of his own soul through explorations of the soul of the world and the world's soul through explorations of his own soul.

Grace's artistic interests include writing and painting. He had two chapbooks of poetry published in the seventies, as well as a larger volume of poetry published in the early eighties. At this time he also has publications in over two dozen literary magazines and his writing had been supported by Canada Council and Saskatchewan Arts Council grants. Apart from a spiritual journal that was published in the late eighties, Grace did not write very much for almost two decades. However, he has recently had material published in a number of literary magazines.

Grace has privately sold many of his drawings and paintings and he has also had a one-month exhibition of his work at the Art Gallery of Southwest Manitoba in Brandon, Manitoba. Many of these pieces include within their contours jagged fragments of poetry.

Grace has two children—Damien and Heather—who are pretty well grown up; he is married to Ruth Card, a social worker who is employed in Swift Current.

GREG GRACE... ANOTHER DAY AT WORK.

About Writing... *According to the mystical tradition of Cabbalism, buried within the conventions and petrified perceptions of the world are divine sparks that wait to be ignited and set the world to a new awakening. I feel that one of the functions of poetry, as well as the other arts, is to help free stylized matter and conventionalized language from its chains. Poetry can break open worlds into their latent possibilities through the unexpected collisions of words, through the energy of raw and subtle rhythms, and through the surprise of imagery that shatters the presented images that have cast their pervasive spell upon our culture and the souls that inhabit that culture.*—GREG GRACE

REBECCA GRAMBO. Rebecca Lynn Yost grew up in the small town of Beresford, South Dakota. By the age of three, she was reading books and riding horses. Both of these interests were to have a lingering influence on her life. In those long ago pre-Internet times, books let a prairie girl escape to far away lands filled with fascinating animals. Riding and training horses took Rebecca outdoors and taught her a great deal about animal behavior.

Grambo's mother, Delores, gave her the most precious gift any parent can give a child: time. Delores was never too busy to examine Grambo's latest discovery, be it pheasant feathers or rabbit droppings. If Grambo was reading a science or nature book, her mother excused her from setting the table or doing dishes. On several occasions, Delores took her daughter out of elementary school in the afternoon for a "dentist appointment." The principal might have become suspicious had he glanced out the window and seen the fishing rods in the back seat of the car. With a change of clothes and a bag of sandwiches, the truant pair headed for the nearby Vermillion River. Together they would sit for hours, watching the birds and insects, and sometimes catching fish. Grambo learned a great deal of biology cleaning fish and game, and in those hours by the river acquired the patience to sit and observe that would serve her so well later on.

From 1981 to 1985, Grambo lived in Rapid City, South Dakota, where she attended the South Dakota School of Mines, graduating with a B.Sc. in Geological Engineering. She missed the graduation ceremonies because she was driving to Houston, Texas, to begin work as a geophysicist. It was a difficult time in her life. Two months earlier, Delores had died, creating a gaping hole in Grambo's world.

A year of Houston's pollution and people proved to be more than enough. Rebecca decided to return to the surreal but safe world of academics to pursue a Ph.D. After investigating several options, she decided to enroll at the University of Saskatchewan in Saskatoon—a place of which she had never heard. Grambo did not finish her doctorate but did gain something important from the university. In 1989 she got married; Glen Grambo was a fellow graduate student.

Glen's interest in photography rubbed off on Rebecca. She decided to leave engineering behind and try a new "poor but happy" lifestyle as an outdoor photographer. Writing did not come into the picture until 1994 when natural history writer Candace Savage helped Rebecca get her first project, *The Nature of Foxes* (1995). After that, Grambo's writing took over, eventually forcing her to temporarily set aside photography and her other career as a needlework designer. Grambo became the originator and author of a series of *Amazing Animals* books for children. She also wrote several other children's books, including *Weird Science* (1998), *Dinosaurs* (2000), *Kids' Nature Question and Answer Book* (2000), *Is That Robot Really My Doctor?* (2001), and *Birds of Prey* (2002). In addition, she researched and wrote for adults: *Eagles: Masters of the Sky* (1997), *Mountain Lion* (1998), *Eagles* (1999), *Seasons in the Rockies* (2000), and *Wapusk* (2003).

REBECCA GRAMBO...GETTING ACQUAINTED WITH 5-WEEK-OLD WOLF PUPS

One of the world's best wildlife photographers, Daniel J. Cox, became a good friend during this time. After collaborating on *Mountain Lion*, the two decided to tackle an idea that Grambo had been carrying around for some time. *Bear: A Celebration of Power and Beauty* (2000) combined extensively researched myths, legends, art, and science with breathtaking photographs to produce a truly unique look at the bear/human relationship. Grambo was thrilled when *Canadian Geographic* chose it as the year's best wildlife book. Now Grambo is hard at work on a follow-up volume on wolves to be released in the fall of 2004. Grambo and Cox are also putting together a new series of children's books. The first of these, *Borealis: A Polar Bear Cub's First Adventure*, will be out in the fall of 2003.

When she is not writing, Grambo can be found photographing, designing needlework, or gardening. Often in demand as a speaker and teacher, she greatly enjoys traveling to photograph and research. With her love of the outdoors, Grambo would rather be outside than in, so time spent in the field is precious. After spending the past two summers in the

Arctic, she has become bewitched by the remarkable landscape and the life that flourishes there. She hopes to return next year.

Grambo lives in Warman, Saskatchewan—a town much like the one where she grew up—with her husband, Glen. They share their small home with three guinea pigs, four rabbits, two rats, and two chinchillas.

About Writing... *I write to share my sense of wonder in our world with others. I have the curiosity of a child and hope I never lose the "Wow!" feeling I get when I find out how something works or learn of an unexpected link between two dissimilar things. Conveying that passion in words is both my greatest challenge and my greatest reward.*—REBECCA GRAMBO

CRAIG GRANT was born on a pool table in Val Marie in June of 1955. This is badlands prairie. Why the nuns in the cloister of Marie decided to settle in this particular vale of tears is anyone's guess: not much there, then, except buttes, hoodoos, rattlesnakes, prairie dogs and—despite the previous reference to moisture—the constant promise of drought.

At the time, there was a doctor who did the circuit through southwest Saskatchewan, and he liked to hit Val Marie on the weekends since it held his favourite bar. By all accounts, he was drunk on gin and fresh from a poker game when he brought Grant into the world.

At age sixteen, while rolling up barbed-wire from a torn-down fence, Grant ignored the thunderheads rolling in. It was almost supper. Just one more strand to roll. The lightning bolt hit the wire about half a mile away. And knocked him to the ground. He's not sure how long he was unconscious. The spirit of his dead grandfather who materialized from the ether during the experience said it was only for a few minutes. But when Grant opened his eyes, hailstones were pelting down. Hours later, as he watched spirits dance in the depths of the cracked mirror he found himself staring at, Grant decided he'd just experienced something akin to a major paradigm shift.

Grant lost his virginity in a graveyard while listening to the Grateful Dead. This, he decided, was his second major paradigm shift. Soon thereafter, the girl in question graciously agreed to be his grad escort—and showed up wearing a mini-skirt, instead of a gown, and sunglasses, to mask an eye infection. Grant stared at his reflection in those sunglasses—and decided on the spot to get the hell out of those drought-stricken, snaked-infested badlands. His third major paradigm shift.

At the University of Saskatchewan, in Saskatoon, he met Brenda Niskala and joined the Saskatoon Poets Coterie, a motley crew of degenerates if ever there was one. And, despite that, he somehow managed to emerge from that beautiful institution with a B.A. in English.

With that valuable diploma in hand, in 1978 he flew to London and hopped on a tour bus to Kathmandu. Just to see the world. What he saw were Exxon gas stations burning in Iran and Russian soldiers marching into Afghanistan.

While recovering from the trip on the island of Koh Samui, off Thailand's east coast, he got this idea for a novel. Working title: "Deadhead in India." One

PHOTO BY BRENDA NISKALA
CRAIG GRANT...WAITING FOR ANOTHER PARADIGM SHIFT

novel. 443 small print pages entitled *The Last India Overland* (1989). Eight years to write it. Not bad. Most recent royalty cheque: eighty-seven cents. Not good. And people always ask him where his second novel is....

Well, he's still working on it. It's called *Shambolica*. Ostensibly, it's about an outlaw biosphere, deep in the Rocky Mountains. But it's actually about meeting the One Great Love in your life. Probably the peak experience of his life. Definitely another paradigm shift, that. Its appendix—its massive appendix—contains the complete archives of Brenda Riches. (See her bio elsewhere in this tome.)

Most peaks in life, however, have a deep, dark valley lying just beyond them. The novel—a "pseudo-memoir," as he calls it—is also about the One Great Sorrow. And about how life seems to be merely a series of epiphanies disguised as paradigm shifts, or vice versa.

Grant won three Saskatchewan Writers Guild literary awards, two for poetry for *After the Honeymoon's Over* (1988), and *A Date With the Butcher's Daughter* (1985), and one for prose, *Sally's Last Breakfast* (1982). He also received the City of Regina Writing Award in both 1989 and 1993. In 1990, Grant received a Canada Council Explorations grant to write a screenplay, *Comes a Cropper*, which was optioned in 1993 by Bradshaw & McLeod, of Calgary. He has also been the recipient of several Saskatchewan Arts Board grants (1980, 1981, 1984, 1986, 1987, 1990, 1992, 1995), two Canada Council Project grants (1988, 1991), and an Arts Council of Ontario grant (1984) for most promising out-of-province writer and on the recommendation of *New Quarterly*. In January 2001, he received a grant for $10,000 from BC Film for the development of *The Long Hot Summer of Ought 6*.

Shortly after New Year's Day 2004, Grant disappeared into the Valhalla range of the Kootenay Mountains, west of Nelson, British Columbia, where, some say, there's an outlaw biosphere being built.

Never to be seen again, said the note he left behind—along with a dog-eared copy of that "pseudo-memoir"—for his literary executor, yours truly, Garrett Coulson.

Let me see if I can glean anything about the nature of writing, from his little 'pseudo-memoir'... Well, yes, seems I can... .

About Writing... *In the chapter called "Fort Yewetee Blues," Grant writes about attending several prose and poetry workshops, in a former tuberculosis sanitorium that he claims is haunted. The lead character, one Breydon Dunne, dramatizes the most singular thing he's heard in the two weeks he's been at the writing school, from an instructor named Patricia Mahoney.*
"Her shirt was open to the navel and a full inch of ash was about to fall off her cigarette onto the green felt of the pool table. She squinted at me as she lined up the shot. 'What you have to remember, kid, is that the Word is a very powerful tool. You have to use it carefully. Damn carefully. Because it's one tiny little letter away from being 'the World', and if you ain't careful, soon you'll find that you're not writing about the world. No. It's the world that's writing you....'"
And then she scratched on the eight ball.—CRAIG GRANT

FRANCES GREENSLADE was born in 1961 in St. Catharines, Ontario, close to where four generations of ancestors lived. She grew up on the land next to her grandparents' farm, a place she thought would always be home. But at age ten, her family moved to Winnipeg and began a migration that covered four provinces and brought her eventually to Regina.

Frances' mother, Kathleen (Smith), was an independent-spirited woman with a love of the outdoors. Her father, Arthur, was not formally educated, but loved reading and collected a large library. The youngest girl in a family of five girls and one boy, Greenslade began writing stories early. She was convinced early, too, that she would only be happy if she could write. Still, she had no idea how to make it a career. Instead of enrolling in university after high school as her parents encouraged her to do, Greenslade moved from their farm into the city, got a tiny, one-bedroom apartment in St. Boniface, and worked as a credit union teller for a few years, writing on lunch hours, during late nights, and sometimes at her teller's wicket. She took a night course before enrolling full-time in English at the University of Winnipeg. There, she was fortunate to take writing classes with Winnipeg writer Uma Parameswaran. Parameswaran's supportive workshops focused both on writers' weaknesses and strengths. Greenslade realized she was no poet, but also learned that she was good at dialogue. She has loved writing it ever since. She received her B.A. in 1985.

After graduation, Greenslade traveled to Portugal. She lived in a rented cottage in Conceicao in the Algarve and worked fitfully on an ill-conceived novel, which was never finished. She traveled in Morocco, Italy, and France before following her family to Vancouver where she got work as a "station editor" for *TV Guide*. There, Greenslade learned to write so concisely that she would later have to unlearn some of it. In the evenings, fuelled by strong coffee, she wrote stories. The first one was published in the *NeWest Review* in 1989. *NeWest Review* published a second story in 1992.

In 1990, Greenslade spent a few months traveling in Mexico and Guatemala. Not long afterward, she began the M.F.A. program in Creative Writing at University of British Columbia. Her trip to Mexico provided the framework for her thesis, an unpublished novel called *Fear is Not An Animal*, which she worked on under the guidance of author Keith Maillard. Maillard inspired through his unequivocal remarks about moving the plot along, and through his lavish encouragement, but most of all, through the fact that when students knocked on his closed door, they would find him bent over his desk, hard at work on his next book. His enthusiastic pursuit of authenticity for the tiniest details of his fiction gave Greenslade a new appreciation for the joys of research. Maillard's advice about writing has stayed with her: *Don't feel you have to start writing at the beginning; start wherever you're interested*. In fact, she has since used her own engagement with the writing as a barometer of whether or not it's working. If she finds herself bogged down, she abandons it and starts somewhere else.

Greenslade worked as fiction editor for the department's literary journal, *Prism International*. The flood of submissions they received from all over the world helped her to understand more about what makes a story tick (or not tick). Editorial board meetings were passionate, sometimes acrimonious debates that had the effect of forcing writers to define their own writing style.

PHOTO BY DAVID JOYCE

FRANCES GREENSLADE...
MAP-READING IN GLACIER NATIONAL PARK, U.S.A.

The UBC writing program was an invaluable opportunity to be among other writers and to be validated for those hours spent bent over the desk, writing into the morning.

Students were required to write in several genres in the M.F.A. program, and Greenslade's creative non-fiction class with author John Munro, combined with her love of travel writing, spurred her to begin reading and experimenting with creative non-fiction. She became fascinated especially by women writers like Sharon Butala, Karen Connelly, M. Wylie Blanchet and Theodora Stanwell-Fletcher, who seemed to avoid the "voice of authority" when writing about place, and instead acknowledged their doubt. They took readers along on their personal searches for understanding and did not force answers where there were none. Inspired by their rich storytelling style, she decided to write about one of her own journeys, a quest for home that led to Ireland.

A Pilgrim in Ireland: A Quest for Home was published by Penguin in 2002 and won the Saskatchewan Book Award for Non-Fiction that year. In it, Greenslade uses the techniques learned from writing fiction to shape her journey into stories, with plot, conflict and characters. *A Pilgrim in Ireland* began a growing interest in research into the myths that shape us. One of the biggest challenges when writing the book was to integrate that research without spoiling the story. She continues to be interested in non-fiction that is narrative-driven, but enriched by an exploration of a wide range of research sources.

Her current project again delves into the myths we inherit. *A Rough Guide to Motherhood: An Adventurer's Tale* explores the bizarre landscape of new motherhood. The book's title reflects a re-thinking of motherhood myths, using the quest motif. Her own experience, a severe bleeding crisis a few weeks after the birth of her son, forms the narrative framework for the book. The subject of the book, however, is not only her story, but also the psychic baggage that accompanies us on the journey to motherhood.

Greenslade lives in Regina with her husband and young son, and teaches English at Luther College.

About Writing... *If you're going to write autobiographical non-fiction, you have to realize that your own small life is both everything and nothing. Like a good novel, vivid details are essential. If you can be truthful about your experience (and that's no easy task), it will resonate with readers. But one small life is nothing without context. There must be a larger picture, and the writer's job is to reveal it without ruining the story.*—FRANCES GREENSLADE

GREY OWL. Born in Hastings, England, on September 18, 1888, Archibald Stansfeld Belaney was raised by two maiden aunts who insisted on proper behaviour for a young gentleman but indulged Archie's love of animals. Estranged from his father, Belaney buried himself in adventure stories and organized games of "cowboys and Indians" at school. When Buffalo Bill came to Hastings in 1903, fourteen-year-old Belaney imagined that his father—who had once lived in the States—was a performer with the show.

Belaney left Hastings Grammar School at the age of fifteen and got a job as a clerk in a local lumber yard. He lasted less than two years before being dismissed for setting off an explosion in the office chimney. He decided to expand his horizons and, on March 29, 1906, he set sail for Halifax from Liverpool.

When Belaney arrived in Canada, he worked as a clerk for Eaton's department store in Toronto before taking the train to northern Ontario, where he worked at the Lake Temagami Inn. In the summer of 1910, he married Angele Egwuna, a member of the Bear Island Ojibway band. By the summer of 1912 he had left Angele and his daughter, Agnes, and was working as a fire ranger out of Biscotasing. In the winter, he trapped. Year round, he drank.

Belaney sent back stories of his adventures to his old school magazine, *The Hastonian*, and began to tell people that he had been brought up in the American Southwest by a Scottish father and Apache mother. On May 6, 1915, he signed up for the Canadian army in Digby, Nova Scotia, noting on his application form that he had previous military experience with the Mexican scouts, 28th Dragoons. He left behind a Metis girlfriend, pregnant with his child. He was shot in the foot at Ypres Salient in 1916 and sent to Hastings to convalesce, where, on February 10, 1917, he married a childhood acquaintance, Ivy Holmes.

Belaney returned to Biscotasing alone in the fall of 1917 to discover that his girlfriend had died after bearing him a son, Johnny Jero. He kept his distance from Johnny and, after a brief reconciliation, left Angele and Agnes for good. Ivy, when she learned of Angele's existence, promptly divorced him for bigamy.

From the fall of 1917 to the spring of 1925, Belaney worked around Bisco as a ranger and trapper, learning more about the Indian way of life from another Ojibway family, the Espaniels. Then one day in the late summer of 1925, on the shores of Lake Temiskaming, he met nineteen-year-old Gertrude Bernard, a beautiful Iroquois woman whom the world would come to know by Belaney's name for her: Anahareo.

SAB / R-A22531
GREY OWL AND ANAHAREO

With beaver on the decline in Ontario, Belaney and Anahareo moved to Quebec, where he trapped until one day in 1928 when Anahareo insisted that they bring home two orphaned beaver kits. The two babies wormed their way into Belaney's affections and that summer he declared he would trap beavers no more. Instead of earning his living off their fur, he would turn his hand to writing about them.

In the spring of 1929 the British magazine *Country Life* published one of Belaney's articles about life in the bush. That summer he was also published in *Canadian Forest and Outdoors* and was invited to give a talk to local residents on the subject of conservation. To illustrate his point, he brought along a young beaver kit named Jelly Roll.

Belaney realized that his message would have more punch if it was accompanied by a suitably dramatic persona and he began signing off his letters to *Country Life* using the name "Grey Owl." On January 23, 1930, he gave his first public performance using his new identity, when he gave a presentation to the Canadian Forestry Association. By now "the beaver man" had come to the attention of the Canadian Parks Branch, which was looking for a way to raise the profile of the new national parks system. Belaney was offered a post as caretaker of animals at Riding Mountain National Park in Manitoba. Water levels were particularly low that year and by October Archie, Anahareo, and their beavers had moved to a new cabin specially built for them on the shores of Ajawaan Lake in Prince Albert National Park. That fall Grey Owl's first book, *Men of the Last Frontier*, was published.

For the next four years, Grey Owl looked after his beavers and entertained such celebrities as soon-to-be prime minister John Diefenbaker and the governor general of Canada, Lord Tweedsmuir. He wrote two more books with a new publisher, Lovat Dickson, while Anahareo looked after their daughter, Shirley Dawn, and, eventually, fell out of love with him. The winter of 1935 to 1936, Grey Owl undertook a four-month tour of Britain to promote *Pilgrims of the Wild* and *The Adventures of Sajo and Her Beaver People*, speaking to more than half a million people. Returning to Beaver Lodge in the spring, he did not adapt well to life alone and in December 1936 he married Yvonne Perrier, a French-Canadian he had met while touring.

In 1937, Grey Owl completed another book, *Tales of an Empty Cabin*, and made two films to celebrate the Ontario wilderness. He also learned that the North Bay *Nugget*, alerted by Angele, had discovered his true identity in 1935 but had been sitting on the story so as not to upset his conservation work. He realized it was only a matter of time before someone broke his cover.

He undertook another grueling book-promotion tour in Britain, this time getting an audience with King George VI. Yvonne came along, but as his secretary, because he did not want to disappoint a public used to seeing Anahareo as his companion. He continued to tour for another three months when he returned to North America. On April 7 he arrived, exhausted, at Beaver Lodge. Three days later he was taken to Prince Albert, where he died of pneumonia on April 13, 1939. His books are still in print today.

JANE BILLINGHURST

About Writing... Grey Owl was fiercely protective of his text. Here is what he had to say about the editorial process: *A story, once it was on paper, became a palace of dreams the structure of which was studded with rich gems, not one of which was to be on any account removed. Any suggestion that some of these be extracted for the general good, aroused a state of mind bordering on the mildly homicidal.*—GREY OWL

DENNIS GRUENDING was born in St. Benedict. He holds an honours degree in English from the University of Saskatchewan, and a Masters in Journalism from Carleton University.

Gruending is primarily a writer of non-fiction, but has also published a book of poetry entitled *Gringo: Poems and Journals From Latin America* (1983), as well as various pieces of short fiction.

Gruending has worked as community organizer for the Roman Catholic Archdiocese. He has also been a contributing editor for *Content* magazine, a contributor to the *Prairie Messenger* and other religious publications, and contributing editor for *NeWest Review*. He has won national awards for farm writing and religious journalism.

In 1980, Gruending was the recipient of the first City of Regina Writing Grant. He also received a Saskatchewan Arts Board grant for travel and study in Latin America.

As a journalist, Gruending has worked for three newspapers as well as for CBC radio as a host and producer. He also worked as a television reporter.

Gruending's articles, stories, and poems have appeared in *Canadian Forum, This Magazine, Canadian Dimension, Grain, Salt, Fort Sanity, NeWest Review, New Internationalist, Maclean's* and *Reader's Digest*. His poetry has also been broadcast on

CBC Radio. In 1981, Gruending won the Saskatchewan Writers Guild Award for Creative Journalism.

Gruending has published *The Middle of Nowhere: Rediscovering Saskatchewan* (1996), *Promises to Keep: A Political Biography of Allan Blakeney* (1990), and *Emmett Hall: Establishment Radical* (1985). He has also published poetry and articles in *The First Ten Years* (1974), *Number One Northern* (1977), and *Canadian Newspapers: The Inside Story* (1980).

HEATHER HODGSON

KRISTJANA GUNNARS was born in Reykjavik, Iceland, in a house on Sorlaskjol by the ocean. She grew up on that street and the shoreline was her playground. Her father was also from Reykjavik, descended from a clan in northern Iceland, but her mother was Danish, and her parents in turn were descended from landowners in Jylland and Fyn, but had relocated in Copenhagen. As a result of this bilingual upbringing, a great deal of traveling between Reykjavik and Copenhagen took place during Kristjana's childhood. Since a relative of her father's was captain of a cargo/passenger ship between the two cities, she traveled frequently with her mother and sister at sea. For Kristjana, in fact, growing up at sea is the nearest description she can find for what her early years were like. The ship she traveled on was the closest thing to a home country.

In 1964 her family moved to the United States in what has become known as "the brain drain," meaning the good scientists of Europe and elsewhere ended up in better paying jobs in the U.S., with better facilities and connections than could be had at home at the time. Kristjana's father became a professor in three departments at once, which testified to his adaptability and flexibility: the departments of Mathematics, Physics and Oceanography all claimed him, and when Kristjana had to find her father on campus, she had to run between three buildings and three offices before he could be located. Her father was a pioneer in geothermal energy, which Iceland is famous for, and one of the scientists who brought the geothermal heating system in Iceland into effect. He was later a consultant for the United Nations to countries looking for alternatives to gas, coal, and oil.

Kristjana attended Oregon State University and married a fellow student. Together they immigrated to Canada in 1969, because, in light of their political beliefs, it was the only "noble" thing to do. They lived first in Vancouver, then moved on to Toronto and eventually had most Canadian provinces covered. They lived in Saskatchewan for a good many years, and their son Eyvind was raised as a prairie boy. It was also in Saskatchewan that Kristjana found a viable, dynamic, and vibrant writing community, which threw her into the writing life. The landscape and climate of Saskatchewan had a profound effect on Kristjana, and she continues to consider that her other home, after the North Atlantic island where she grew up.

Eventually Kristjana became professor of English at the University of Alberta, where she taught Creative Writing for a good many years.

KRISTJANA GUNNARS...AS WRITER-IN-RESIDENCE AT THE REGINA PUBLIC LIBRARY IN 1989.

She translated and studied the work of Stephan G. Stephansson, another Icelandic writer who ended up in Alberta a century earlier. Kristjana has, since she first came to Canada, been involved with the Icelandic-Canadian community, and while living in Manitoba, Saskatchewan, and Alberta, had opportunity to be engaged on many levels—as editor, writer, and cultural worker. She marvels at the vicissitudes of fate that took her from the sea to the heart of the continent, and is appreciative of the fact that she has spent much of her adult life as far from the sea as it is possible to go.

Kristjana now lives in British Columbia and has a view of the ocean, at about the same distance from her window as was the case in her childhood. She is now writing full-time, and consolidating a number of years spent learning and absorbing. She began publishing poetry in 1981, and has been active publishing poetry, fiction and non-fiction since. Her first books concentrated on the mythos of Icelandic immigration to Canada historically, but eventually she published lyrics that were more personable and less historical. She began to write short stories in the eighties, and has continued to enjoy the craft of short fiction writing, although she finds it most challenging. In 1989 she published a cross-genre work on her childhood memories, *The Prowler*, which became a kind of template for five books that were a cross between a meditation and a form of poetic or lyrical prose. Other titles in that series are *Zero Hour* (a meditation on her father's death); *The Substance of Forgetting* (a novel set in the Okanagan); *The Rose Garden* (a meditation on her sojourn in Germany); and *Night Train to Nykobing*, a novelized essay on her return to Denmark.

Kristjana is writing short stories and editing books on Canadian writers she admires. She will finally get a chance to write novels in her new life, and is grateful for her beginnings in Saskatchewan, which did so much to mold her thinking about writing.

About Writing... *If you want to write, you must find a subject that will stay with you through thick and thin; you must need to go there every day for at least five hours; and never give up on your story if it means something to you. Read as much as you can: it is by reading we become members of our community.—* KRISTJANA GUNNARS

TONJA GUNVALDSEN KLAASSEN was born in a snowstorm in Saskatoon in April of 1968. She lived with her mother, Lonnie Wailing, at her grandparents' farm near Manitou. Later that year her mother married Martin Gunvaldsen, and the family moved to Calgary where Lonnie taught elementary school.

Both sets of grandparents and two great-grandmothers played a significant role in Gunvaldsen's early life, and they appear later in her poems. The Gunvaldsens were urbane, genteel; Kaare Gunvaldsen was a professor of languages at the University of Saskatchewan and a Kafka scholar who spent much of his time researching and writing "The Undiscovered Franz Kafka," a manuscript which remained unpublished. His wife, Ruth Gunvaldsen, forced a cellar garden of violets and worked a large wooden loom.

The Wailings lived a harsh and physical life by contrast. They were married on Hallowe'en night in 1944, and their union was volatile from the outset. Gordon Wailing was a farmer, trucker, and a trapper; Evelyn Wailing was a maker of headcheese, flapper pie, and relish. At the age of five, Gunvaldsen spent the summer of 1973 at the home of her maternal grandparents where she learned the secrets of yeast and of making relish; this made for a somewhat reluctant return to Calgary when she had to begin school. By June of 1976, the family left Calgary and returned to farm again in Saskatchewan.

From 1986 to 1992 Gunvaldsen studied at the University of Saskatchewan where she was drawn to Commonwealth literature. This included the poetic novels and short stories of Jean Rhys, J.M. Coetzee, Amos Tutuola, Chinua Achebe, and Janet Frame. She also got involved in theatre and during the drought in the spring of 1988, Gunvaldsen toured Saskatchewan with the Greystone Players' production of *Dracula*. On the tour she met James Klaassen. The two married in 1989 and spent the winter of 1990 in Redhill, Surrey, where Gunvaldsen Klaassen taught third-form English literature. On the weekends and during holidays, she and her husband travelled through southern England, France, and Italy.

After all their money was spent, they returned to tent near the North Saskatchewan River where Gunvaldsen Klaassen wrote poems and stories. In the fall of 1990, she returned to the University of Saskatchewan to study with Lorna Crozier and David Carpenter. She also honed her skills under the guidance of Patrick Lane and Dennis Cooley at the Sage Hill Writing Experience, where she met the poet Sylvia Legris.

Working part-time at the Meewasin Centre in Saskatoon, and with the help of Saskatchewan Arts Board grants and the Canada Council Explorations program, Gunvaldsen Klaassen continued to write. In 1994, she began consulting Betsy Warland, writer-in-residence at the Saskatoon Public Library. Later that year, she was invited to attend an informal gathering of poets at the home of Anne Szumigalski. At that time Hilary Clark, S. Padmanab, John Clark, and the Welsh poet, Robert Minhinik, were also included. During this apprenticeship, Gunvaldsen Klaassen's poetry and short stories began to appear in several Canadian journals including *Grain*, *NeWest Review*, *Prairie Fire*, *Border Crossings*, and *Malahat Review*. Her stories were also included in anthologies such as *Vital Signs*, *eye wuz here* and *Under NeWest Eyes*. Gunvaldsen Klaassen's poetry received Honourable Mention in the Bronwen Wallace Poetry Competition and was included in the anthology *Breathing Fire: Canada's New Poets*. On January 1, 1996, her poetry was featured on the CBC program, *The Arts Tonight* hosted by Eleanor Wachtel.

These early poems, collected in *Clay Birds* and published by Coteau Books in the spring of 1996, attracted considerable critical attention. The book was short-listed for the Gerald Lampert award and the Saskatchewan Book Award for first book, and it won the Saskatchewan Book Award for poetry. In this first collection, the search is for home; the poems return to Manitou for a sense of identity and belonging on the prairies, a place where the wind leaves "a hundred, a hundred hundred // tiny erasures."

In 1997, after the birth of her first son, writing time was in short supply, but the constant state of fragmented concentration

TONJA GUNVALDSEN KLAASSEN...AND IRA

invited an exploratory approach to language, imagery, and formal arrangement. Whether writing about birthing or insomnia or courting sleep and dreams, the poetry lost much of its narrative composure, and became increasingly dependent on intuitive leaps. Influenced by late-night and naptime readings of Kafka, Celan, Plath, Mouré, Gwendolyn MacEwen, Gustaf Sobin, and Gaston Bachelard, the fractured logic of sleep deprivation became a familiar. The poems return again to Manitou and to Horse Lake where "the night is barbed," filled with pitchforks, pencils, fence posts, and the ditches "shot with selves, bent stalks, ponies, snow." These poems' first audience was the Saskatoon poets' coterie which, after the death of Anne Szumigalski, continued to meet at the home of Elizabeth Brewster. Gunvaldsen Klaassen read a selection of these poems for the CBC Saskatchewan program, *The Arts Wrap / Gallery*. Completed in 2000, the collection titled *Ör* won an inaugural John V. Hicks prize for unpublished manuscripts, and was accepted for publication in spring 2003.

In March 2001, Gunvaldsen Klaassen moved with her husband and son to Halifax. Since the birth of a second son, she has been at work on new poems.

About Writing... *For me, poems come from the same place as dreams. A faithful response requires acute listening, a surrender of self to reverie's rests and stresses, even long silences. Sometimes I falter—it's difficult to be patient—but if forced, words, the tools of poetry, become unwieldy weapons.*—TONJA GUNVALDSEN KLAASSEN

LOUISE BERNICE HALFE's Cree name is Sky Dancer. She was born on the Saddle Lake Reserve in Two Hills, Alberta, in 1953. At the age of seven, she was sent away to the Blue Quills Residential School in St. Paul, Alberta. She left residential school of her own accord when she was sixteen, breaking ties with her family and completing her studies at St. Paul's regional high school. It was at this time that she began writing a journal about her life experiences.

Halfe made her debut as a poet in *Writing the Circle: Native Women of Western Canada*, the acclaimed anthology of life-writings by Native women. In 1993 she was awarded third prize in the League of Canadian Poets' national poetry contest.

LOUISE BERNICE HALFE

Louise Halfe has published two books of poetry. *Bear Bones & Feathers* was published in 1994 and received the Canadian People's Poet Award. It was also a finalist for the Spirit of Saskatchewan Award that same year. Her second book of poetry, *Blue Marrow*, was published in 1998, and was a finalist for both the Governor General's Award for Poetry and the Pat Lowther Award. *Blue Marrow* was also a finalist for the 1998 Saskatchewan Book of the Year Award, and the Saskatchewan Poetry Award.

Her work has also appeared in various anthologies and magazines, notably *NeWest Review*. She has been on CBC Radio's *Morningside*, *The Arts Tonight*, and *Ambience*.

Louise Bernice Halfe lives in Saskatoon with her husband and two children.

NIK BURTON

GILLIAN HARDING-RUSSELL was born in Toronto. No, the story begins earlier. Her parents—both brought up in England—were born on the prairies and both *their* fathers were Anglican clergymen. Her mother was born in Humbolt and her father near Vermillion, Alberta. Both her mother and father returned to England at ages six and five years old, respectively, after their clergymen fathers had completed their residencies in Canada. Both her parents considered themselves English, and her mother admitted a technical Canadian citizenship only if pressed. Her mother retained her English accent, even after forty years living in Canada after World War II; but her father, who joined the Canadian army (because he was too young for the English army), lost that "effeminate" accent and acquired other "bad habits" (in her mother's view) while under the influence of the "force."

When Harding-Russell was two years old, her family moved to St. Jean, Quebec, where her father taught English Literature and coached soccer at the Collège Militaire Royal. She attended Dorchester School, St. John's High School, and then commuted to St. George's School in Westmount for grades nine and up. From there she moved on to College d'Enseignement Général Et Professional and then to McGill University where she earned her first degree—a B.A. with first class honours—and then an M.A. She completed her M.A. dissertation on Dickens' last darker novels.

To work on her Ph.D., she moved on to the University of Saskatchewan. Although she had been promised a teaching fellowship at the University of York, and admission to several other universities, she accepted a scholarship at the University of Saskatchewan. Her married sister had already moved with her geologist husband to Saskatoon, and so her decision to attend the University of Saskatchewan seemed to have been made without her. She spent the next seven years attending graduate classes, eventually teaching English 100, and trying to convince herself and others that she wanted a Ph.D. What else could she do? After picking up and discarding many areas of study, she settled on post-modern Canadian poetry, and did eventually find her niche. She had been writing poetry many years earlier, and had her first two poems published in *CVII*. Unfortunately, that area of her life—writing poetry—had been languishing in the academic environment, and life in a university can be unreal at the best of times.

Prince Charming—Peter Russell from the Agriculture Department—came to the rescue. But not before she had completed a Ph.D. dissertation—"Open Forms of Mythopoeia in Three Post-Modern Canadian Poets" (under the direction of Elizabeth Brewster, now poet laureate)—did she leave Saskatchewan and move to Surrey, British Columbia, where her husband had been offered a job with the federal government. There she made a connection with David (Dale) Zieroth and *Event* magazine and began as a Reader. Two years later, Zieroth asked her to accept the poetry editorship. Her daughter, Celia, and her son, Gareth, were both born during those years in Surrey.

GILLIAN HARDING-RUSSELL...
"DON'T TAKE A PICTURE NOW!"
(TO HER SON)

When her husband was transferred to Regina, she welcomed the chance to be with her aging parents, and two years later her father passed away. Her son, Laurie—named after her father—was born two days after what would have been her father's birthday, and ten days after he died. (The coincidence of this birth happening on the heels of her father's death was traumatic and became the shaping inspiration for her first poetry collection, *Candles in my head*.) Two years later, her mother died, seemingly in sympathy—which becomes a focal theme in *ghosts and aureoles in the winter night*.

Although she had been scribbling intermittently for years, Harding-Russell's first book was published by Ekstasis Editions only in 2001. The manuscript had been lost after two years, and then re-sent and finally accepted; it took another two years before the collection finally came out. The cover design comes from a painting of the publisher Richard Olafson's wife, Carol Sokalov—painted by her sister after Carol had given birth to her own son. Harding-Russell's own idea for a double exposure with candles superimposed on a woman's face, or alternatively for a photograph of a dark puddle during an electrical storm with lightning reflected inside of it, proved difficult to manage on a slim publishing budget. (Thunderstorm imagery predominates in *Candles in my head*.) Her second poetry collection, *Vertigo~*, was published in 2004.

Some of her poems have been published in the following anthologies: *Waiting to Hear You Speak* (1999), *No Choice but to Trust* (2000), *Swimming in the Ocean at Night* (2003), *The Common Sky: Poems against the U.S.-Led Invasion of Iraq* (2003), and *Land/Space: an anthology of speculative prairie literature* (2003). More poems are scheduled to appear in *Let Yourself Go: Poems of loss and grief* (2004). Throughout the years she has won several awards, including three Saskatchewan Poetry Prizes (1984, 1993, and 1995). In 1995, she also earned an honourable mention for "Letter to a Ghost" in the *Prairie Fire* poetry contest. In 1999, she won the Livesay-Sandburg prize (second place). The same year, a poem placed second in the *CV2* contest, "Shades of Light, Shades of Colour." In 2003, her poetry was short-listed for the CBC award.

She is now working on several other poetry and prose collections: *Usual Lives* (a collection of poems, prose poems, and dramatic monologues with various speakers—interspersed with poems by the poet-speaker that appear as confessional *trompe d'oeil*) and a growing mass of miscellaneous odds and ends filling a couple of collections, tentatively entitled, *Poems for a lesser Gethsemane* and "*I forgot to tell you.*" She is also working on a young adult novel entitled *Spirit Virus* and a play about King Sullyman and the Queen of Saba, tentatively entitled "Land of Snakes and Scorpions." A fragment of the play was produced at the Globe Theater under the title "Donkey Legs" during the Sandbox Series (January, 2004). Harding-Russell reviews books and writes articles of interest, and other contract work, usually of an editorial nature. After fifteen years, she is still poetry editor for *Event*.

Although she lives to write (cannot stop writing)—or writes to live—(not sure which), and has had numerous poems published in literary magazines across the country, she still finds it difficult to find book publishers for her poetry. Either the funding is not there for more than a prescribed number of poetry collections and all those are filled. Or unsolicited work is not accepted. Or something. Not enough people read poetry, it seems, for a larger output of poetry books. Also, she is somewhat of a lone wolf—unknown except to her closest friends—and had unintentionally managed to remain on the periphery of the writing community, perhaps to her own detriment. Nevertheless, she persists in hoping against hope to leave some little behind her after she is dead. (Not to be too dramatic!) In the meantime, she will continue to express all that's human in herself and in others she sees around her.

About Writing... *Never, never give up. Write only for your own soul and for those souls out there who matter to you. At some point, someone somewhere out there will hear.*—GILLIAN HARDING-RUSSELL

MARY HARELKIN BISHOP was born in Michigan and moved to Saskatoon as a teenager. She is a teacher-librarian in the Saskatoon Public School system. The books in her juvenile fiction "Tunnels of Moose Jaw" series—*Tunnels of Time*, *Tunnels of Terror*, and *Tunnels of Treachery*—are the fastest-selling books in Coteau history. In addition to her fiction writing for children, Mary has published poetry and short fiction in the Courtney Milne book, *Prairie Dreams*, and in *Green's Magazine*.

NIK BURTON

NORMA JEAN HAWKINS was born on May 2, 1923, in Yorkton. She is the daughter of Henry and Chrissie Beck who were married in England at the end of World War I. Hawkins' father owned a small dry goods store in Yorkton in which she worked during her elementary and high school years. Hawkins had an older sister, Ruth, and a younger brother, Harvey.

After graduation from the Yorkton Collegiate Institute in 1942, Hawkins was receptionist in the medical office of Drs. Clarence and Sigga Houston for four years. She then attended the University of Saskatchewan, graduating in 1949 with a Bachelor of Arts.

In 1956, after working as a clerical assistant at the Saskatoon Public Library for seven years, she received her Bachelor of Library Science degree from the University of Toronto. That year she was awarded first prize for both fiction and non-fiction in a university-sponsored contest judged by Robertson Davies.

Returning to Saskatoon, Hawkins worked in the Saskatoon Public Library for three more years, where she met her husband-to-be.

On August 12, 1959, she married a newly-graduated and ordained seminary student, the Reverend David Geoffrey Hawkins, who came from London, England, to study at Emmanuel Theological College in Saskatoon. After a five-month stay with David's parents in London, during which time he did deputation work on behalf of the Colonial and Continental Church Society which had sponsored his training at Emmanuel College, they returned to the Anglican Diocese of Saskatchewan.

Their first parish was centred in the town of Birch Hills in the northern part of the province. Her novel *Chokecherry* was published in 1996.

The mythical town of Chokecherry, with a population of 500, is

NORMA JEAN HAWKINS... AND THE REV. DR. DAVID HAWKINS. LIFEBOAT DRILL ON A CRUISE SHIP.

the quintessential northern Saskatchewan town. Becky arrives as a young bride with her newly-ordained husband to take over a parish covering 200 square miles. *Chokecherry* is their story. They learn to cope with no running water and outside plumbing, and an ancient car that they drive with one hand on the horn, frequently into ditches and trees. Finding that she is expected to provide the music in church, she at first learns to play the organ with one finger. She churns out the parish newsletter on a rickety mimeograph machine, pours tea at bazaars and disastrous rummage sales, and deals as well as she can with the pastoral visits of an austere bishop.

Coming to Vancouver in 1953, Hawkins' husband took doctoral studies while she worked first as a children's librarian and later as a branch head at the Vancouver Public Library. She retired in 1986.

In 2002, excerpts from *Chokecherry* were read on CBC, both on *Sunday Showcase* and *Monday Playhouse*, and repeated a few weeks later on *Richardson's Roundup*.

Thirty-five articles and stories written by Norma have been published in magazines and newspapers such as *Chatelaine*, *Queen's Quarterly*, *Western Producer* and *The Vancouver Sun*.

About Writing... *I have been a scribbler from my early days, learning the thrill of finding the right word or phrase. My writing skill was honed by carrying on a voluminous correspondence with family and friends. I feel strongly that everyone should write a book about his or her life's experiences. Otherwise all these marvellous stories will be lost. It isn't any more difficult to write a book than to write a long letter home. It just takes longer. Even if your book is never published, your children and grandchildren will bless you for it. I had a dear old professor, Carlyle King, at the University of Saskatchewan, who used to say about writing essays,* "Begun is half done," *and the same applies to writing a book. So take a pen and paper and write just one sentence of your memoirs; the rest will follow.*—NORMA JEAN HAWKINS

CAROLINE HEATH (1941–1988). Born in 1941, in Eugene, Oregon, Caroline first came to Saskatchewan in 1962. It was just a stopover on her way to Europe where she spent the next four years living and studying in England and Germany, with her husband Terrence Heath. She settled in Saskatchewan in 1966, began a master's degree in German Literature, but was soon completely engrossed in the writing being done in Saskatchewan. This interest eventually led her to abandon her academic work and, in 1973, to become editor of the newly-founded *Grain* magazine. For the next ten years this magazine occupied almost all the time she could spare from raising three children, Paul, Joseph, and Simon, and running a house in the country. She set difficult but important guidelines for herself and for her associate editors, insisting that all

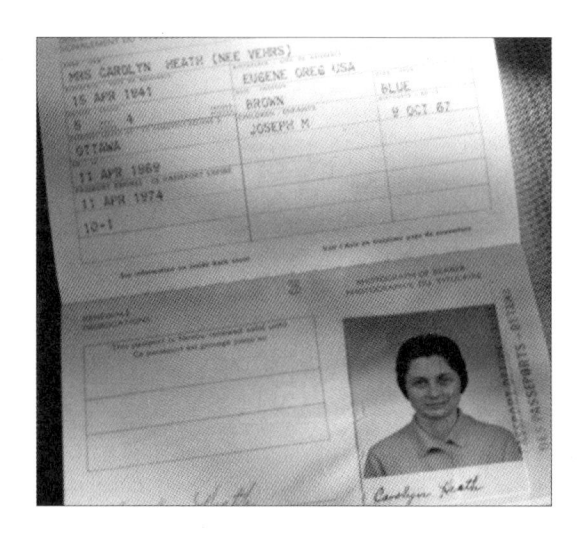

CAROLINE HEATH

submissions be critiqued, with personal letters written to the writers, and that all submissions be returned within six weeks. She felt that an editor's job was not only to judge good and bad but also to encourage and help. These guidelines helped make *Grain* into a literary magazine that many Canadian writers credit for their first publications. It was an accomplishment of which she was very proud.

In 1982, she decided to take a further step and found a literary press. Fifth House, named for the astrological house of creativity, was established to seek out especially young and promising Canadian writers. Her "discoveries" included Sharon Butala, whose first novel, *Country of the Heart*, was published by Fifth House. Caroline also had a particular interest in the work of First Nations writers. Fifth House quickly established itself as an important literary press in Canada. She ran the entire operation out of her basement, spending long hours reading manuscripts, designing the books, working with printers, finding ways to secure distributing and marketing, and otherwise make ends meet financially.

By 1986, however, she was diagnosed with breast cancer. She fought the disease for two years before succumbing to it on April 13, 1988. Her ashes were spread on the land she had grown to love.

Apart from her vigorous support for writing in Saskatchewan, Caroline began to write poetry late in her life. In 1994 her poems were gathered together, edited by Anne Szumigalski and published by Coteau Books under the title, *Why Couldn't You See Blue?* In 1989, the Saskatchewan Writers' Guild instituted the Caroline Heath Memorial Lecture. In 1999, she was posthumously honoured with the Saskatchewan Arts Board Lifetime Award for Excellence in the Arts.

JOSEPH HEATH

TERRENCE HEATH is an independent writer, curator, and consultant. He has curated, reviewed, and written catalogue essays for exhibitions at art galleries across Canada.

Heath was executive director of the Western Development Museum and director of the Winnipeg Art Gallery. He writes both articles and columns for art magazines in Canada and has just completed a retrospective exhibition of the drawings of Tony Urquhart. Heath is presently curating a retrospective exhibition for the Mackenzie Art Gallery and the National Gallery of Canada and writing a biography on the life and work of the Canadian sculptor Joe Fafard.

TERRENCE HEATH

Heath is a co-founder and is also presently on the board of the Centre for Canadian Contemporary Art. He was also chair of the governing board of the Ontario College of Art from 1993 to 1999. He served on the taskforce of the City of Toronto which re-established the Museum of Canadian Contemporary Art (formerly North York Art Gallery) in Toronto.

Heath's books include: a novel, *The Last Hiding Place* (1982); a biography of the Canadian painter Ernest Lindner, entitled *Uprooted: The Art and Life of Ernest Lindner* (1983); a collection of short stories, *The Truth and Other Stories* (1972); and three books of poetry, *Journey/Journée* (1988), *Interstices of Night* (1979), and *Wild Man's Butte* (1979). *Journey/Journée* and *Wild Man's Butte* were co-authored with Anne Szumigalski.

Born and raised in Saskatchewan, Heath presently lives in Toronto.

LALA HEINE-KOEHN was born in Poland, and spent her early childhood in Zakopane, in the Tatra Mountains, where she attended the first few grades of public school.

Forced to leave her native country, she was relocated to Germany where she studied International Law at the University of Munich, and Voice at the Händel Conservatory in Munich. Heine-Koehn and her family then immigrated to Canada and settled in Saskatoon for more than twenty years. While raising a family of five, Heine-Koehn found time to pursue her artistic interests and studied art at the University of Saskatchewan with Rita Cowley, Andrew Hudson, Otto Rogers, and Don McNamee.

Heine-Koehn's first book of poetry, *Portraits*, was published in 1977. *Sandpoems*, her second book of poetry, was published in 1979. Her third collection, *The Eyes of the Wind*, was published in 1981. *Forest Full of Rain* was published in 1982, and *The Spell of the Chaste Tree* was published in 1994. *Through the Mashrabiya Screen*, a chapbook, was released in 1995, and *The Certain Days of Abstinence* was published in 1998.

Currently, Heine-Koehn has completed two manuscripts. *I Should Like to be a Piece of Cheese* is a whimsical collection of fables, fairy tales, and animal stories. *The Seduction of the Written Word* is a collection of love poems, part of which was entered into the League of Canadian Poets chapbook for competition which earned second place.

Her poetry has been published in various literary magazines, such as *Writer's News, From an Island, Rattle Moon, Malahat Review, Poetry Canada Review, Grain, Salt, Other Voices, Manitoba Review, Arc, Nebula, Wot, Dandelion, Corfu News, Dalhousie Review, Prairie Fire, Voices Israel, Mythic Circle, The Mythopoeic Society*, and others.

Her work has also been included in several anthologies, including *Number One Northern, Best of Saskatchewan, Draft, Tributaries, The Best of Grain, Anthology of Magazine Verse (Yearbook of American Poetry,* USA*), Arrivals (Greenfield Review,* New York, USA*), Dancing Visions, New Quarterly, Sudden Radiance,* and *Skelton at Sixty,* among others.

Her poetry has been broadcast on CBC Radio and it was also included at *Teledon's Great Canadian Poetry Machine Canada Pavillion* at Expo 1986, and in the *Casette Gazette*, an audio magazine of Polish poetry in Paris, France.

Heine-Koehn has been a guest reader at the world famous Edicion de la Fiesta de la Cultura Iberoamericana in Holguín, Cuba. Another anthology, the Holguín-based *Ambito Literary Magazine*, also included Heine-Koehn's poetry.

About Writing... *Writing is like the colour of your eyes. It stays with you whether you are pleased with it or not (contact lenses are a temporary cure only).*—LALA HEINE-KOEHN

LEE HENDERSON grew up in Saskatchewan and Calgary and in his teenage years experimented with acting, drawing, radio hosting, and computer animation—a highlight was his animation work on a rock video for Sonic Youth. The quirky, engaging stories in his much-heralded debut collection, *The Broken*

LALA HEINE-KOEHN

Record Technique, are both afflicted and inspired by the psychic rootlessness of the world of talk-show television, mega-malls and suburban sprawl.

HEATHER HODGSON

TREVOR HERRIOT was born in Edmonton in 1958 during a brief Alberta tour of duty made by his parents. Norman Herriot met Jeannie McRae at a dance in Edmonton, where they discovered they were both Saskatchewan refugees. Norm, the youngest of five sons, was born in 1931 on the edge of the Great Sand Hill on a wheat farm near Hazlet that was profitable until the drought hit. By the time Norm was eight years old, his parents had made the move north to the refuge of the boreal forest at Christopher Lake where his father was able to secure some land as a veteran of the Great War. Jeanne, also the youngest in a large Scottish family, was born in 1927 on a farm in the eastern Qu'Appelle Valley where the drought was less severe. Her parents, Jock and Amelia McRae, figure strongly in the final section of Herriot's first book, *River in a Dry Land: a Prairie Passage*.

Returning to Saskatchewan soon after Trevor was born, Jeanne and Norm moved several times in those early years from town to village to city, with Norm advancing from one position to another in potash mining and other industries. After a brief stay in Tantallon, the village near Jeanne's family farm, the Herriots moved to the town of Esterhazy in 1963, where Trevor entered school that same year. Five years later they had moved to Saskatoon, now with four children: from eldest to youngest, Jacqueline, Trevor, Scott, and Lisa. Trevor took the remainder of his schooling in that city, attending public school at Georges Vanier, and high school at Holy Cross. In the fall of 1976, he entered the Fine Arts program (visual arts) at the University of Saskatchewan through St. Thomas More College. After a year of trying to not look too directly at the models in figure studies, Herriot decided it would be a good idea to switch to English.

He graduated with a B.A. (honours) in English in the spring of 1981, happy to be away from university. That fall he took a job as a technical writer at SaskTel, where he has continued to work as a professional writer, producing everything from technical procedures to speeches, annual reports, magazine articles, and briefing notes. Herriot believes that his success in creative writing has in part come from writing habits he developed over the years at SaskTel, following a daily discipline of practical composition, working out the common problems of communication within narrow boundaries of form and content.

In the mid-1980s, Herriot began publishing small articles and essays as a freelance journalist, writing for Saskatchewan publications such as *Briarpatch Magazine* and *The Prairie Messenger*. During this period, he was developing a keen interest in natural history, traveling on vacations to experience the birds, plant life, and landscapes of the Northern Great Plains as well as other parts of Canada, the United States, and

PHOTO BY KAREN HERRIOT
TREVOR HERRIOT...
SUMMER 2002 IN REGINA.

Mexico. But his interest in landscape and wild places probably began with his early experiences in the Eastern Qu'Appelle Valley and in the boreal forest and lake country just south of Prince Albert National Park—places he visited whenever the family returned to the homesteads of his grandparents. His father took him bird hunting each fall as soon as he was considered old enough to handle a shotgun. Early fishing and canoeing trips, including one on the South Saskatchewan River and another into remote lakes of the national park, also left a strong impression.

As a child, from age eight onward, Herriot spent a good deal of his free time teaching himself to draw. In adulthood, while learning the birds of the province, he began to draw and paint them, in pencil, ink, and watercolours. Given the choice, he still would rather spend his time drawing, and enjoys it more in fact than writing, which always feels more like work.

Herriot's interests in writing and natural history converged when he began writing about environmental issues for national magazines in the late 1980s. He has had several articles published in *Canadian Geographic* and *Nature Canada* magazines and continues to write the occasional article of this kind.

In 1996, Herriot officially started work on a book of non-fiction he had been mulling over in his mind for years. After winning the City of Regina Writing Award to make time for the initial research and writing, he began working closely with Edmonton writer Myrna Kostash to revise drafts of the manuscript that became *River in a Dry Land*. Published in the fall of 2000 by Stoddart, *River* was well received, took several national and provincial awards, and spent a number of weeks on Canadian best-sellers lists. Herriot wrote and narrated a radio documentary based on one of the stories contained in *River*, and it was aired on CBC's *Ideas* in 2000.

He is currently finishing the manuscript of his second book, *Jacob's Wound*, a non-fiction narrative exploring the boundaries between religion and wildness. *Jacob's Wound* is due to be published by McClelland & Stewart in the fall of 2004.

Herriot married Karen Sutherland in Regina in 1984, and together they have raised four children: Kathryn (Kate), Jonathon, Sage, and Maia. Karen, who has an honours degree in English from the University of Regina, works out of their Cathedral area home as a doula (birth assistant), has been a La Leche League leader for many years, and plays a prominent role in home-schooling and mothering circles in the city. The family is active in the Roman Catholic parish of Holy Rosary. They grow a garden in the city and keep bees at their weekend acreage in the Qu'Appelle Valley.

About Writing... *Some suggestions for writers: write with pen and paper for at least the first two drafts, take long walks, avoid the noise of mass media, pray, keep an eye out for creatures you have never seen before, carry a pen and index cards in your pocket, read nothing but the strongest poetry and the bravest narratives.*—TREVOR HERRIOT

JOHN V. HICKS (1907–1999) was born in London, England, on February 24, 1907. He spent his early years in Montreal and in Alberta, and then moved to Saskatchewan where he was a long-time resident of Prince Albert. Hicks' wife, Marjorie Kisbey Hicks (1905-1986), was an organist, pianist, piano and vocal teacher, and a composer, too.

Hicks wrote and published poetry for more than half a century, mentoring many writers and poets along the way. For many of those years he also worked as an accountant and church organist and he was choirmaster for the city of Prince Albert. The biggest influences on Hicks' writing were the great classics of music and literature.

Hicks' first book was called *Now is a Far Country* and it was to be followed by many more volumes thereafter. His poetry was published widely in many major literary journals and newspapers all across North America. Hicks also published many short stories and these appeared in various school textbooks and anthologies, including the *Canadian Children's Annual*. Hicks' poetry was broadcast on CBC radio and was set to music by the composer Elizabeth Raum of Regina.

His other books include *Winter Your Sleep* (1980), *Silence Like the Sun* (1983), *Rootless Tree* (1985), *Fives and Sixes* (1986), *Side Glances: Notes on the Writer's Craft* (1987), *Sticks and Strings: Selected and New Poems* (1988), *Month's Mind* (1992), *Overhead by Conifers* (1996), and *Renovated Rhymes* (1997).

Anthologies containing his work include *Number One Northern*, *Sundogs*, *A Sudden Radiance*, *Anthology of Magazine Verse and Yearbook of American Poetry*, *Dancing Visions*, *Canadian Children's Annual*, *Draft*, *The Maple Laugh Forever*, *100% Cracked Wheat*, *Contexts*, and *Saskatchewan Gold*. Literary magazines and periodicals containing his work include *Salt*, *Poetry*, *Quarry*, *New York Herald Tribune*, *Wascana Review*, *Kansas Quarterly*, *Dalhousie Review*, *New York Times*, *Malahat Review*, *Michigan Quarterly Review*, *Grain*, *The Washington Post*, *Antigonish Review*, *Ohio Journal*, *Fiddlehead*, *Mademoiselle*, *FreeLance*, *Chicago Review*, *Canadian Forum*, *Event*, *Waves*, *Canadian Literature*, *Ariel*, *Prism International*, *Nimbus*, *Prairie Journal of Canadian Literature*, and many others.

Hicks was Honourary Fellow of the University of Emmanuel College in Saskatoon, and he was awarded an honourary LL.D. from the University of Saskatchewan. He received the Saskatchewan Arts Board Lifetime Achievement Award in 1990, and the Saskatchewan Order of Merit in 1992.

His first book of poetry was published in his 71st year. *Overhead by Conifers* was nominated for two prizes at the Saskatchewan Book Awards. Hicks' tenth book was entitled *Renovated Rhymes* and contains sonnets based on nursery rhymes. The book was illustrated by Victor Gad.

HEATHER HODGSON

About Writing... *Truth, like a name on tongue-tip, stands poised, fervent to be spoken.* (from "Within a Whisper I Was" in *Now Is a Far Country*)— JOHN V. HICKS

GERRY HILL. "It was hot, it was dirty, it was awful," Alice Hill would admit, years later, of the summer of 1951 when her son Gerry was born in Herbert, just a short Saturday's drive east of Swift Current. She'd been seven months pregnant when she and Don arrived from Wynyard, where they'd lived since the war. Born and raised in farming communities, Don and Alice had married in '38, when Don was already seven years into his career as an educator that, after ten years as Superintendent of Schools in Herbert, would take him to the University of Regina until his retirement.

As on old-style schoolteacher, Don Hill knew dozens of poems from memory, could at least claim to have read the classics of English literature, owned a bookcase full of leather-bound Dickens, loved to hold forth in the manner of some bard declaiming his cadences, and loved Louis L'Amour to boot. Out of all that, somehow, Gerry Hill acquired his love of language, although it took many years before it would show up as published writing. First came ten years of boyhood, much of it alone, under the open sky around Herbert, and another ten as a terrified teen in Regina. He wrote rhyming verse, read widely (fiction, not poetry), dug jazz, and engaged in the stuff of the counter-culture—sex, drugs, and rock 'n roll, in short—as much as a shy guy could, but by the early 1970s he hadn't a clue what he was about, literarily or otherwise.

PHOTO BY LUCY HILL

GERRY HILL... AFTER FRISBEE WITH HIS YOUNGEST DAUGHTER.

Surviving two or three dark years, Hill surfaced full of motivation to become a teacher, and he completed a B.Ed. at the University of Calgary in 1975. After two years teaching junior high Language Arts in Rocky Mountain House, Alberta, Hill shipped out to Papua New Guinea as a CUSO high school teacher in 1978. He loved it over there but by 1981 had become homesick for God knows what—Hill certainly didn't know—which is when an old high school friend from Regina came to his rescue.

Throughout the 1970s, when they both lived in Calgary for most of the time, he'd shown her his notebook jottings (which is all they were). She was literally his *only* reader for seven or eight years. And she, even before he did, sensed that he was some kind of latent writer. "Better latent than never," she told him. By 1981, she lived in Nelson, B.C., home of a small fine arts college, David Thompson University Centre (DTUC). She wrote and told Hill about it; eight or nine months after leaving Papua New Guinea, he showed up there to begin a year of Creative Writing studies in the fall of 1981.

The writing program at DTUC featured three writers whose influences figure prominently in Hill's poetics to this day: Fred Wah, for whom language itself is content and the conventional lyric poem an empty Modernist relic; Tom Wayman, who insisted that there was enough mystery in the world already without adding to it by writing incomprehensible poetry; and Dave McFadden, always willing to de-centre any supposed sacredness of the writing act with chance, play, sheer goofiness. Hill instantly took to their varying approaches. He was hooked.

A year later, now certain he'd be a writer, and with his first publication—a poem in *Dandelion*—under his belt, Hill moved back to Regina, reasoning that he'd write himself into the world, and *vice versa*, from his home base. Supporting himself with various forms of teaching work, he joined the Saskatchewan Writers Guild and attended his first Writers and Artists Colony at Fort San in November of 1982. There he met the theatre artist Ruth Smillie. Within a year or two he'd joined her and her daughter Emmaline, whom he adopted, in Saskatoon, and a year or two after that, in 1985, they were married and living in Edmonton, where Ruth ran a theatre company and Hill taught adult education. A son Thomas was born in 1986 and a daughter Lucy in 1989.

In the meantime, Hill's publishing career was moving right along. His first poetry collection, *Heartwood*, was published in 1985. By the early 1990s, his work had been published in more than two dozen literary magazines and several anthologies. His second collection, *The Man From Saskatchewan*, however, did not see the light of day until 2001. Echoing the thank-you speech delivered by Dalton Trumbo at the 1971 Oscars—at which he'd won a second Oscar for Best Screenplay (for *M.A.S.H.*) twenty-seven years after winning his first one—Hill declared, "At last there's some structure to my life: every sixteen years I publish a book of poems."

In the meantime, he'd gone to grad school, earning an M.A. (English) from the University of Alberta and embarking on his Ph.D. work. He published academic articles on Gail Scott, Robert Kroetsch, Daniel Defoe, and Hélène Cixous and earned a Social Sciences and Humanities Research Council of Canada doctoral fellowship. Various freelance writing and editing projects provided both income and time demands during that period, as they have since. His marriage broke up in 1992, and although it took three or four years, during which time Hill taught at Red Deer College, by the mid-1990s he and his ex-wife and their children all lived near one another in south Regina, not far from where Hill had lived in the 1960s. And he was teaching English at Luther College, University of Regina.

Having published both *The Man From Saskatchewan* and (with Doug Chisholm) a collection of mini-biographies of Saskatchewan men killed in World War II, called *Their Names Live On*, in 2001, Hill has stepped up the pace of his book publications. A third poetry collection, *Getting To Know You*, was published in the fall of 2003, and a fourth collection, *Prayers For and After Rain*, which are prayers for love, loosely speaking, as much as rain, will be the book after that.

Meanwhile, the spring and summer of 2003 saw him building a long poem about a building—a kind of poem cam, loosely based on a major construction project on the University of Regina campus. At about the same time, he became poetry editor of *Grain*, one of the country's finest literary magazines.

But whatever the project is, it's a matter of language, as Hill sees himself both directing, and taking direction from, his next few words. Which reminds Hill of a bit of advice about writing.

About Writing... *To make the world happen in writing, he says, or to make writing happen in the world, PAY ATTENTION. Over and over again. As profoundly as possible. Until, in the end (which is never an end) you can let one shape the other.*—GERRY HILL

JEAN ROBERTA HILLABOLD was born in 1951 in Redwood City, California, to Jane (nee Ward) and Arthur Hillabold, who was then doing graduate work at Stanford University. In 1955, the family moved to southern Idaho, where two younger children, Susan and Nancy, were born. In 1967, Arthur Hillabold joined the faculty of the University of Saskatchewan, Regina campus, and the family moved to Saskatchewan.

Jean Hillabold was encouraged to write as a student in the Fine Arts Program at Central Collegiate, Regina. In 1969, in her last year of high school, she was the provincial winner in a national student writing contest sponsored by the Canada Permanent Trust Company. During a year in England (1973–74), she met a Nigerian student, Pepple Ikiriko, whom she sponsored into Canada and married in 1975. The marriage lasted until 1981, and produced a daughter, Elizabeth, born in 1977.

In the early 1980s, as a graduate student in English, Hillabold wrote a collection of poems, including a set inspired by her baby daughter, which were eventually published as half of *Double Visions*, co-authored with Thelma Poirier. Throughout the 1980s, she wrote reviews and articles for feminist and leftist journals such as *Briarpatch* and *Network*, journal of the Saskatchewan Action Committee on the Status of Women. She continued to write poetry and fiction. In 1984, her short story "Snowflakes" won first prize, Short Fiction Category, in the annual writing competition of the Saskatchewan Writers Guild, and it was published in *More Saskatchewan Gold*. In 1987, another of her short stories appeared in *The Old Dance: Love Stories of One Kind and Another*, and one appeared in *Wascana Review*, a literary journal produced by the Department of English, University of Regina.

Hillabold performed in several amateur plays, beginning in the 1980s, including *The Funny Pages: An Evening of Improvisational Theatre* (1986), for which she wrote a skit which satirized the current Canadian federal cabinet. She also performed in several plays produced as part of AIDS Awareness Week by the educational health organization AIDS Regina. In the late 1990s, she was a member of L.I.F.E. (Little Improvs for Education), a popular-theatre troupe under the direction of Mirtha Rivera, which performed educational skits on AIDS and related issues in high schools and for various organizations.

In 1988, Hillabold began writing under the pen name "Jean Roberta" when her collection of lesbian stories, *Secrets of the Invisible World*, was published by a one-woman press in Montreal.

JEAN HILLABOLD... THE OLD WITCH WITH HER ANIMAL FAMILIAR (TO CELEBRATE TURNING 50).

The book was favourably reviewed in various lesbian and feminist journals, but it went out of print when the publisher went out of business in 1990. Two stories from that collection were republished in anthologies: "The Ballad of the Deep Blue Sea" in *Dykeversions* (1986), and "Secrets of an Unkosher Home" (originally named "Sisters") in *The One You Call Sister* (1989).

In 1989, Hillabold received a Master's degree in English from the University of Regina; her thesis analyzes the *Children of Violence* novels by British writer Doris Lessing as a *bildungsroman*, or multi-volume novel of development. She was hired to teach Creative Writing in the Seniors Education Centre, University of Regina, and for the Saskatchewan Writers Guild. In 1991, she was hired to teach first-year English courses at the University of Regina.

As she acquired teaching experience, her alternative writing persona, Jean Roberta, developed in other directions. In 1988, she attended the third International Feminist Book Fair in Montreal, where she saw a call-for-submissions for erotica by women. She wrote three stories in response, and received a letter of acceptance before the American publisher went out of business. Discouraged, she did not write again in this mode until 1998, when she acquired a computer and joined the on-line Erotic Readers and Writers Association.

Since 1999, she has had numerous erotic stories published in anthologies such as the *Best Lesbian Erotica* and *Best Women's Erotica* series, two *Wicked Words* anthologies, *Shameless*, *Best Bisexual Erotica 2* (which was nominated for a Lambda Award, given each year for the best books with gay, lesbian, bisexual or transgendered subject matter), the *Amatory Ink Fantasy Anthology*, *Desires*, and others. Her work has also appeared in various websites and print journals. Her erotic novel, *Prairie Gothic*, is available in electronic form from the website Amatory Ink (www.amatory-ink.co.uk).

In February 2001, aware that her colleagues in the Department of English, University of Regina, were curious about her unorthodox "research," she gave a talk on the history of erotica and censorship as part of a monthly academic discussion series organized within the department. The script of this lecture is available on request. She has also given brief talks on the history of erotica followed by readings. Since 2002, she has been writing reviews of erotic books and films for various websites and at the request of fellow erotic writers. She is an irregular columnist for *Perceptions: The Gay/Lesbian Newsmagazine of the Prairies* (Saskatoon).

About Writing... *Too many fledgling writers pride themselves on being True Artists rather than literary whores (writers for money). All writers are influenced by their cultural milieu, and what is almost unthinkable in one generation becomes a stale cliché in the next. Don't try to write for the ages; write what feels true for you now, and enjoy the rewards available to you.*—JEAN HILLABOLD

DORIS HILLIS (née Bennett) was born in Epsom, Surrey, England, and was educated at the City of London Freemen's School. Her mother and father were both Londoners. Her father served in the First World War and was badly wounded at the Battle of Somme. After a good recovery, he worked for Lloyd's Bank for most of his life. Hillis's mother was a bookkeeper before marriage and later became a full-time homemaker. Their family of three, Phyllis, Peter and Doris spent their growing-up years, which included the Second World War years, in the Epsom-Ewell district. They experienced the brunt of the Blitz from 1940 to 1941.

After spending a year at Portsmouth College in 1948, Hillis proceeded to the University of Nottingham to read for an English Honours degree. Following graduation, she returned to the south of England where her parents then lived and she attended the University of Southampton to obtain a Professional Teaching Certificate.

Her first job was in St. Peter Port, Guernsey, Channel Islands, where she taught at the Guernsey Grammar School for Girls. This beautiful island close to the coast of France was not only idyllic in itself but a wonderful "jumping off" spot for trips to the other Channel Islands and to Europe. Hillis and a teacher friend spent Christmas and Easter holidays travelling in France and Austria.

Then in 1955, Hillis and her friend decided they would set forth on an adventure abroad. They made applications for teaching positions in Saskatchewan and were both accepted, Hillis to teach at the high school in Langenburg, and her friend to teach at the collegiate in Kamsack. Their first winter on the prairies, its huge snowfalls and low temperatures, was a thrilling experience for them and they enjoyed the challenge of teaching eager Canadian students. However, they missed city living and so the next year took positions with the Winnipeg School District No. 1.

Their original intention was to spend several years in Canada and then return to the British Isles, but immense changes were in the offing. Hillis's friend was married in 1957 and Hillis, having started part-time M.A. studies at the University of Manitoba, completed them in 1958 and then moved to Vancouver to enroll in a Ph.D. program at the University of British Columbia. She also taught university students for two years as well as summer semester courses.

Shortly after, Hillis was faced with another major turning point in her life. She had met her future husband, Bill, in 1957. He farmed in Saskatchewan, south of Macklin, near the Saskatchewan/Alberta border. When they decided to marry in 1960, this was a great adjustment for Hillis from an urban university milieu to life in a small rural town. It meant, too, that she would be settling in Canada, thousands of miles from family and friends in England and would, in fact, be cutting close ties with her homeland.

Despite these difficulties and buoyed by shared dreams and plans, Hillis began to find great satisfaction in farming. Bill was a progressive and inventive farmer and together they set about making a comfortable home and modern landscaped farmstead. And in time, Hillis discovered that farming and the quiet, regulated pace of seasonal activities were the necessary matrix for her creative inspiration. But this did not happen immediately. The everyday work, participation in a new business, and the birth of her daughter filled her hours... and years.

Hillis did not participate in other activities until 1967. Then she was asked to join the Macklin Park and Recreation Board, the Overture Concert Series Committee, and later the Adult Education Committee. She also taught a grade twelve evening class and took two off-campus university courses. In 1975, she was appointed Board Member of the newly-formed Prairie West Community College, serving west-central Saskatchewan.

Doris Hillis

Her interest in literature and the arts was channeled into establishing a marionette club for school students. The youngsters devised shows, made marionettes, and learned the skills of manipulation. They performed on an ingenious table-top stage, designed and built by Hillis's husband. The club was active for several years and gave presentations in Macklin, Provost, and Saskatoon.

Hillis was in her late forties before she began to write. She started with appreciative studies of the work of Brian Johnsrude and Klaus Walch—both talented Macklin residents—which were published in *Arts Canada* and *The Craft Factor*, respectively. She also wrote profiles of Myrna Kostash and Patrick Friesen, accepted by *Canadian Author and Bookman*, and, thereafter, she started the major project of interviewing Saskatchewan writers for literary magazines. Hillis also had work published in *Dandelion*, *Descant*, *West Coast Review*, and *Prairie Fire*, later collated into the books *Voices & Visions* and *Plainspeaking*. As well, Hillis did considerable book-reviewing.

A further pivotal event was the formation of the Macklin Literary Club. Hillis and friends Darlene Kidd and Susan Conly brought together a group of local people who were interested in literary appraisal and creative writing. They also joined the Saskatchewan Writers Guild and with Guild support were able to invite excellent, established writers to the community to give workshops. In the early eighties—out of the blue—Hillis was moved to write poetry. This came as a great surprise and would never have reached fulfillment without the wise advice of an unknown Saskatchewan Arts Board mentor and the encouragement and expertise of visiting poets Byrna Barclay, Glen Sorestad, Lorna Crozier, and Anne Szumigalski. Hillis learned the necessity of studying contemporary styles and forms and practising the assiduous task of revising and crafting language. She also learned to look within for inspiration and thus assembled the manuscript *The Prismatic Eye*, published in 1985. In these poems Hillis spoke of her English childhood, the war years, the immigrant experience, her re-rooting in Canada, and revealed personal insights that proved, at last, she was finding her own voice, her own unique mode of expression. Ten years later, she published a more reflective collection, *Wheelings*. With the publication of each book, Hillis gave public readings in rural Saskatchewan as well as in Moose Jaw, Saskatoon, and Calgary, Alberta. She also conducted workshops in Macklin and Rosetown.

Other exciting events occurred during the eighties, nineties and into the new millenium: many broadcasts of her poems and short stories were heard on CBC Regina. Some of her poems were accepted, and she was one of eight Canadian poets chosen by Michael Horwood for the libretto of his five-part Choral Symphony No. 2, which premiered in Sarnia in 1996. Three of her poems were also included in a series of windows (acid etching on glass) by Toronto artist Doreen Balabanoff for the Freeport/Grand River Health Centre in Kitchener in 1996. Hillis also published two playscripts: *Fuse* and *Waiting*, and she gave dramatic readings from these last works in Macklin, Regina, and Saskatoon.

Hillis has now retired from farming after thirty-eight years. She resides in Saskatoon where she enjoys ready access to literary readings, concerts, theatre, and the diverse programs sponsored by the University of Saskatchewan. Her daughter and grandson also live in the city. Hillis has recently completed a third manuscript of poetry and is giving tentative thought to a memoir.

About Writing... *Write from your own experience. Find your own voice. Don't get discouraged.—* DORIS HILLIS

RICK HILLIS's grandparents homesteaded in Saskatchewan in the 1930s—his mother's parents lived around Saltcoats in southeastern Saskatchewan, and his father's parents lived up north near Tisdale. His own parents, Lyle Hillis and Joyce Morgan, met when they were sixteen when Lyle was working for the Saskatchewan Power Corporation, stringing new line. They were married two years later and a year after that, when they were nineteen, Rick was born in Nipawin in the winter of 1956.

His father's employment with Saskatchewan Power took the family from Tisdale to Aneroid in the southern part of the province, where they lived from 1957 to 1967, then to Gull Lake from 1967 to 1970, and finally to Moose Jaw from 1970 to 1974. In Moose Jaw Hillis attended Riverview High School. There he had the good fortune of being a student in the prominent poet and publisher Gary Hyland's senior English class. Hillis graduated in 1974, the first person on either side of his family to complete high school.

For the next year Hillis toiled on a natural gas construction crew, going from small town to small town around Saskatoon and Prince Albert, running gas services to houses. It was a job he hated but continued for two summers while he attended university in Saskatoon where he was studying education (Physical Education and English). In the winter of 1976, while delivering a paper to class on a sub-zero morning, Hillis had a vision he has never fully comprehended. The next year—1977—he transferred to the balmy University of Victoria where he begged his way into his first creative writing workshop. It met for three hours each Wednesday afternoon, led by Derk Wynand. While Hillis did not learn until years later that there was a lecture component to the class that took place on Tuesday afternoons, or maybe because he didn't know there was such a component, the class had a powerful, lasting effect on him. With the exception of his tenth grade typing class, no academic experience would prove as useful for his future writing.

Hillis returned to Saskatoon and graduated from the university in 1979 with a B.Ed. He landed a job teaching middle school in Rosetown, and during the winter he commuted to Saskatoon to take a creative writing class at the Saskatoon Community College. The class was taught by the wonderful poet, publisher, teacher, and force of nature, Glen Sorestad. It resulted in Hillis's short story, "First Kill, Last Day," being accepted by Wayne Schmalz and broadcast on CBC Radio's *Ambience*.

It was during this time that Hillis fell under the spell of two books of fiction: W.P. Kinsella's *Shoeless Joe Jackson Comes to Iowa*, and John Irving's popular literary novel *The World According to Garp*. From the liner notes he learned about the Iowa Writers' Workshop, and applied. He was too late for the deadline but Iowa responded that they liked his work and he should apply the next year.

RICK HILLIS

The next while was spent substitute teaching in Saskatoon and trying to figure out what to do with his life. Hillis applied to train as a Federal Corrections Officer. He'd worked during the summers of 1977 and 1978 as a sports coordinator at corrections institutions and had enjoyed it. At the same time, he tried Iowa again.

The acceptance from the Federal Corrections Program arrived in March. He had two weeks to notify them of his decision. A week later the acceptance came from Iowa. Three months later he was driving through the corn.

Hillis attended the workshop in 1984, living, by chance, in a room in the basement of a house owned by W.P. Kinsella, who was living elsewhere at the time. He only lasted a year in Iowa, though, before fleeing to Montreal where he enrolled in Concordia University's M.A. program in English. In 1986 Hillis returned to Iowa and completed his M.F.A.

The following year he was back in Saskatoon, teaching at the Saskatoon Community College, the Psychiatric Center, and elsewhere. During this time he began to publish stories and poems in literary journals and anthologies. In January of 1988, his son Cullen was born. A short time later he learned he had been awarded a Stegner Fellowship to attend Stanford University and write fiction. That same year his book of poems *The Blue Machines of Night* was published and was a finalist for the Gerald Lampert Award.

In 1990 Hillis's book of fiction, *Limbo River*, was published. It was awarded the Drue

Heinz Prize and a medal from the Commonwealth Club of California. After teaching fiction writing at Stanford from 1990 to 1992, he was offered a fellowship to Universal Studios to write screenplays for a year. That June his daughter Cassidy was born in Santa Monica.

Hillis had some success in Los Angeles—his original screenplay *Mandible Gorge* (based on a canoe trip he took on the Churchill River in 1978) and an adaptation of his short story "Rumors of Foot" were both optioned. For visa reasons, however, Hillis had to return to Stanford to complete his teaching contract. In 1994 Chesterfield Films purchased the screenplay adaptation of "Rumors of Foot" and that same year he was hired to be writer-in-residence at Reed College in Portland, Oregon. He stayed there, except for brief departures to teach writing at Lewis & Clark College, and the University of Oregon in its M.F.A. program, until 2003.

In 2003 Hillis was granted a Green Card in the category of Alien with Extraordinary Ability in the Arts. Currently, he is an assistant professor of screenwriting and literature at DePauw University, teaching during the summers at the Iowa Writing Festival, and writing primarily screenplays.

About Writing... *I have one 3x5 card on the wall by my typewriter that sums up what writing means to me at this moment in my life. It's a quote from a Guy Clark song, "Boats to Build": "I'm gonna build me a boat with these two hands, it'll be a fair curve from a noble plan. Let the chips fall where they will; I got boats to build." Makes sense to me.*
I think it's important to remember that writing is not the same as literature. Writing doesn't have that sort of heavy responsibility. Writing is just a game of its own design; a form of diversion for the writer, and the reader. Literature is for someone else to decide.—RICK HILLIS

BRITT HOLMSTRÖM (-Ruddick) was born in Malmö, Sweden, in 1946. Malmö remained her permanent address apart from 1965 and 1967 when she lived for longer periods in London, England. It was here, in 1965, that she started writing her first novel (in Swedish) at age nineteen. The book, which was set in London, was called *Peppermint Gin* and was published by A. Bonniers Förlag (Stockholm) in 1967. She and the editor (who was in London for a conference) fittingly sealed the deal over a beer in a Soho pub.

While this book is her only novel in Swedish, she did in fact write one more, the second one occurring somewhere in between 1967 and 1969, the title of which is long since forgotten. Holmström's editor at Bonniers sent it back with a lengthy letter. Holmström assumed that the manuscript had been rejected and, not very happy with it, threw it out. A year or so later, via a writer colleague who had been to Stockholm, her editor sent a message wondering where the revised novel was. Holmström was not particularly upset. In 1969 she sold the film right to *Peppermint Gin* to Minerva Film (Stockholm) and, although the movie was never made, received what seemed like a fortune at the time for merely signing her name on a piece of paper. Wasting no time, she immediately cashed the cheque and took off for southern Spain. Here she truly planned to continue writing but somehow never got around to it. It was in Spain that she met her first husband, a Canadian from Hamilton, Ontario. Like most Europeans she knew nothing about Canada.

The following year Holmström arrived in this unknown country with two suitcases, got married, and talked her husband into returning to Spain where they spent the winter of 1971. During this time she did do some writing, still in Swedish, but never finished it. She returned to Canada, got depressed, then divorced, all the while working as a medical secretary. She still did not write at all, but did think about it a lot. And, as always, she read voraciously.

A few years later, Holmström met her second husband. Somehow, considering that she's not exactly fashionable, she managed to obtain a degree in Fashion Design and Technique from Sheridan College in Oakville, Ontario, and proceeded to design knitwear as a part-time business. Eventually, via New Brunswick and Manitoba, she and her family arrived in Regina, Saskatchewan, in a covered wagon, or perhaps a moving van. In Regina, where she still lives, she continued to design knitwear part-time. She assumed she had long ago stopped being a writer.

In the late eighties, Holmström got the sudden notion that she should study science. She gave up designing and enrolled in classes at the University of Regina, where she ended up with a Bachelor of Science (Honours) and a Master of Science in Microbiology. From this she concluded that life is strange, and not only from a biological point of view. She was once again writing, but only scientific stuff. Writing fiction more than ever appeared a thing of the faraway past.

In 1994, she proceeded with a two-year contract at the Agriculture Canada Research Station in Regina, where one day towards the end of her contract, feeling bored and under a strange kind of pressure, she sat down by her desk in the lab and began writing a book. She did not stop. A year later the book, dealing with a disturbed man, the son of a Nazi sympathizer, and eventually titled *The Man Next Door* was completed. It was published in 1998, won The City of Regina Book Award, and was nominated for the Book of the Year Award.

PHOTO BY MICHAEL TRUSSLER

BRITT HOLMSTRÖM... REACTING TO THE SUGGESTION THAT SHE *TRIES* TO LOOK LIKE A SERIOUS WRITER.

Holmström writes only in English these days, with one exception. Back in 1996, she went on a horseback-riding trip down to Grasslands National Park and fell in love with the vast empty landscape full of craggy buttes and winding coulees, pronghorn antelope and rattlesnakes. It's still her favorite part of Saskatchewan. During her first trip there, she and her friends got caught in a tornado. It also resulted (apart from hypothermia and destruction of the base camp) in Holmström writing a piece of non-fiction in her native tongue for a Swedish Women's Magazine that was thrilled to publish a true Saskatchewan adventure.

In 1999, Holmström was lucky to get a Canada Council Grant to write her next novel and, believing you should always visit the places you write about, traveled to Zagreb, Croatia, and Vienna, Austria, to do research. She spent the next year and a bit writing full-time. The book, entitled *The Wrong Madonna*, was published in April 2002 and received rave reviews. It was also nominated for two Saskatchewan Book Awards: The City of Regina Award and Fiction of the Year Award.

Her latest novel, *After We Crossed the River*, is due out in the fall of 2004. It is set mainly in Canada and Latvia. Before writing it, Holmström took off to Latvia to familiarize herself with the city of Riga with the aid of wonderful and accommodating helpers like the writer Nora Ikstena and the poet Knuds

Skujenieks. Holmström fell in love with Riga and hopes to go back one day.

Meanwhile, Holmström is working on a collection of short stories. She is also into the early stages of researching her next novel, which will deal with both modern Canada and 17th-century Scotland. And somewhere there hovers yet another vague idea for a novel.

While Holmström lives in Regina, in her mind she is usually far away in a world of her own, in the company of people who don't exist. She is a formidably boring and antisocial person who does not spend time in the here and now unless she has to.

About Writing... *The writing process for me is an addiction if anything, one I finally succumbed to late in life, but it is, in truth, something I never think about or try to analyze.* —BRITT HOLMSTRÖM

LEWIS HORNE was born on April 14, 1932, in Mesa, Arizona. He is the son of Ben and Dorothy (Blackbun) Horne. He has one brother and two sisters. Horne is married to Sandra Lindsay and they have four daughters.

Horne was raised in Mesa, Arizona, and received a B.A. from Arizona State University, as well as an M.A. and Ph.D. from Michigan.

He immigrated to Canada in 1971, and taught in the English Department at the University of Saskatchewan until he retired in 1996.

Horne is author of two collections of stories, *The House of James and other stories* (2001) and *What Do Ducks Do in Winter?* (1993), and a collection of poetry entitled *The Seventh Day* (1982). His poems and stories have appeared in various periodicals in the United States and Canada, and in some anthologies, among them, *Prize Stories: The O. Henry Awards* (1987), *The Hopwood Anthology: Five Decades of American Poetry* (1981), and *Best American Short Stories* (1974).

HEATHER HODGSON

KEN HOWE was born in Edmonton in 1960. His first poetry recollections are of his mother reading from *A Child's Garden of Verses*. He recalls being made uncomfortable by the word "bosom." This is because the first "o" can be pronounced like "book" or like "boot." How do you decide?

It is said that his father could recite the prologue from *The Canterbury Tales* by heart, though Ken's never heard it himself.

Shortly after he learned to read he became a disciple of Lewis Carroll, which he remains to this day.

When Ken was nine they moved to Beaverlodge, which is a small town. His brother fit in there but he didn't, really. Peter Faris lived up the street and played the flute in the Beaverlodge Band, so Ken asked if he could get an instrument, too. His parents said yes and he told them he wanted to play the saxophone. The band people said they didn't want a saxophone player; they wanted a French horn player. His first teacher told him that it shouldn't be called a French horn though—it should be called "the horn."

In Beaverlodge he also started writing poetry and publishing it by photocopying his new stuff and leaving it at the entrance to the school. He also became obsessed with the classical guitar and practiced it constantly, at least three hours a day. He read T.S. Eliot, Ezra Pound, Earle Birney, and Margaret Atwood and decided he would become a poet.

He went to Grande Prairie Regional College and the University of Alberta as a music student, choosing eventually the horn over the guitar. He dreamed of a small professional orchestra where most of the work was chamber music but you still got to play the great music that was written for orchestra. He did many auditions—none for the kind of job he wanted—but unfortunately didn't win any.

In the meantime he had been having apprehensions of God. He had actually read the Gideon's *New Testament* they gave out in grade five. Though his parents were lapsed Unitarians, he had seen God in a bicycle wheel on a dirt road once, and another time above a crabapple tree in front of the Jubilee Auditorium. In 1982 he sold his possessions (except his horn and music) to be like Francis of Assisi, then joined the Catholic Church. In 1985 he decided to quit music and become a Jesuit. While in the Jesuits he discovered the work of Tim Lilburn and stayed up two whole nights reading and re-reading *The Names of God*. It revolutionized his writing, which had been floundering under the influence of Renaissance and German romantic poets. The novice master, Doug McCarthy, advised him to submit this new work to literary magazines. He did.

Then he read Bertrand Russell's *Why I am not a Christian*, had a crisis of faith, and left the Jesuits. He tried to become a French and German teacher but couldn't handle the classroom. Then he started a Master's Degree in French Literary Translation. He got a horn and played part-time in a military band. He published his first poems (after 35 rejections). When one of his professors told him there were no jobs in literary translation he decided to join a full-time military band.

KEN HOWE... JURA CREEK, ALBERTA, MAY 2003.

While he was waiting for an opening he did auditions for real orchestras. The Saskatoon Symphony had an opening for a principal horn where most of the work was chamber music but you still got to play the great music written for orchestra. He auditioned and was runner-up! When he told a horn student at the University about it, the student said "The Regina Symphony's better." At the time it seemed twitish, but when he won the principal horn job in the Regina Symphony that summer, a job in which most of the work was chamber music but you still got to play the great music written for orchestra, it seemed prophetic.

His whole life was now a success. He hooked up with the writing group "Notes from the Underground." He wrote texts for the Regina Symphony children's shows. The Regina literary community was supportive and welcoming. In 1998 he attended the Sage Hill Poetry Colloquium in order to meet the glorious Don McKay. The following year Tim Lilburn himself was writer-in-residence at the Regina Public Library, and with the help of these two he eventually finished a manuscript that was published in 2001 as *Household Hints for the End of Time*.

In his eight years with the Regina Symphony he had the privilege of performing the most glamorous and challenging pieces written for the horn in orchestra. He performed twice as a soloist in the orchestra's Masterwork's series, and played much of the exciting chamber music that features the horn, including chamber versions of concertos on CBC radio. Several composers wrote music featuring him. In his last two seasons the

Regina Symphony Chamber Players chose him to perform as a soloist in eighty concerts for schools. He also appeared as a soloist in 2001 at the Prairie Festival of new music, premiering a concerto dedicated to him.

In May of 2001 he was dismissed for musical reasons.

Howe moved to Toronto where he remains to this very day. In the fall of 2001 he returned briefly to receive the Saskatchewan Book Award for poetry for *Household Hints*. He won the principal horn audition in the Oshawa Symphony. His second book, *Cruise Control: a Theogony*, came out in 2002. He now lives with Elaine Huth and two abandoned cats.

About Writing... *Mushrooms are not just there to be eaten—they are first and foremost objects of contemplation. Don't let your dog stick its head out the window when you're driving. Marx was the greatest poet.*—KEN HOWE

GARY HYLAND was born in Moose Jaw in 1940 and continues to live there. His parents were James Kenneth Hyland (known as "Tec") and Iris Frances Bourassa. She was a hairdresser and he was a clerk and labourer. His father came from a railroading family, his grandfather being an engineer and well-known sportsman. His mother descended from a farm family in the Woodrow region of southern Saskatchewan. He has one brother, Ron, who changed his name to Jherryd.

When he graduated from Moose Jaw's St. Louis College in 1958, the first on either side of his family to finish high school, he worked in the CPR roundhouse and general office for a year to finance his education. He studied at Campion College in Regina for his first year of university, worked that summer and each thereafter, and then attended the University of Saskatchewan in Saskatoon where he received a B.A. (1962) and a B.Ed. (1964). He married Linda Bell in 1962 and, after graduating as a teacher, declined an offer from an Edmonton school board, decided instead to return to Moose Jaw and take a position at the new Riverview Collegiate, a high school just two blocks from Home Street where Hyland grew up.

Mark, the first of his sons, was born in 1964, followed by Michael in 1965 and Miles in 1970. In 1984 he and Linda divorced. In 1988, he married Sharon Nichvalodoff, daughter of Paul Nichvalodoff and Mable Metin.

Hyland recalls always being sensitive to words, even to the song lyrics he heard as a child on the family radio. The first writing he can recall was at the age of ten or eleven as proprietor, journalist, columnist, and delivery boy of the *Home Street Clarion*, each issue of which he wrote by hand. The third issue was the last, containing as it did a news item that one of the neighbourhood couples belonged to a "nature camp" or nudist colony. And so the budding writer learned a lesson in censorship via his mother.

Around the same age, he won, to his chagrin, a book of poetry at a church bazaar. His friend snickered that the book was the same one his sister carried as a high school text, *Poems Worth Knowing*. What was worse, the book was defective; some of its pages were blank. Months later, bored on a long winter evening, he began to read this book and soon found himself completing the poems that should have been continued on the blank pages. The next step was to write his own poems, so soon his own "perfect" first drafts were side by side with Shelley and Tennyson. He continued to write poetry sporadically from then on, never telling his classmates or the guys on his hockey, baseball, or football teams, one of whom was to become one of Saskatchewan's leading writers, Ken Mitchell.

Hyland began sneaking off to the public library to read books of poetry in the stacks, his assumption being that any volume in such an august setting must be good poetry. And most of it was. He recalls reading Poe, Edith Sitwell, Conrad Aiken, Bliss Carman, Robert Graves, and E. J. Pratt, among others. But one of his earliest conquests was *The Divine Comedy*. After reading in his high school history text that Dante was one of the greatest poets of all time, he dashed straight to the library to sign out the book, much to the consternation of the librarian. It took him two months to complete the book, which was weighted with erudite footnotes that he nonetheless understood better than most of the poetry. The experience is recounted in more detail in "Deke and Dante," one of the poems in *Just Off Main*. Years later, in his twenties, he returned to Dante's poem and read it with much more appreciation. It remains one of his all-time favourites.

After high school, while working in the CPR general office, Hyland became a genuine closet poet. Having achieved some efficiencies in performing his chores, two or three times a week he would slip away for half an hour or so and read and write poetry in a large seldom-used storage closet for which he had been entrusted with the key. Lots of free white paper and a few secreted books of poetry kindled his imagination and many early and completely forgettable poems were composed beneath the dusty overhead bulb.

His first poems were published in the university newspapers under pseudonyms and in *The Chelsea Annual*, a publication of St. Thomas More College in Saskatoon, having placed second and received an honourable mention in one of their contests. His work also appeared in the *Alberta Poetry Annual* for a few years after winning a third place and honourable mention in the contests run by the Alberta branch of the Canadian Authors Association.

By this time he was developing a taste for certain poets to whom he would return many times over the years. These included Coleridge, Donne, Blake, Browning, Frost, Eliot, Auden, Dickinson, Rilke, Layton, and Birney. Later, while working in Toronto, he attended his first poetry reading, a knockout performance by Gwendolyn MacEwan who recited for over forty minutes without opening the book she clasped at her side. He was both intimidated and inspired.

Though he had some early success with short stories in a few journals and won a provincial short story contest sponsored by Credit Union Central as well as writing articles and columns, poetry has been his passion. His early post-college work appeared in *Salt*, Bob Currie's journal out of Moose Jaw, and in *Skylark*, the magazine of the Saskatchewan English Teachers Association.

PHOTO BY HEATHER HODGSON

GARY HYLAND... "YES, ME—I'M FROM MOOSE JAW."

By 1972, he had joined the newly-formed Saskatchewan Writers' Guild and met such writers as Anne Szumigalski, Glen Sorestad, John Hicks, and Lois Simmie. In 1973 Andy Suknaski published Hyland's first chapbook, *Poems from a Loft*. In 1974, he partnered with Bob Currie, Barbara Sapergia, and Geoffrey Ursell to found Coteau Books, and his chapbook *Home Street* was one of the company's two inaugural publications. While teaching high school English and garnering several teaching awards, Hyland remained with Coteau until the company moved to Regina in 1986. During that time he published poems in several leading literary magazines and he also co-edited the poetry anthologies *Number One Northern* (1977) and *A Sudden Radiance* (1987). He then edited the humour collections *100% Cracked Wheat* (1983) and *200% Cracked Wheat* (1992). Hyland retired from teaching high school in 1994 but continued to teach English part-time for a few more years, this time for the University of Regina's Department of English.

He was a founding member of the writing group called the Moose Jaw Movement which included such people as (T)Ed Dyck, Bob Currie, Jim Mclean, Judy Krause, Byrna Barclay, and Lorna Crozier. The group later morphed into The Poets' Combine when some of the originals moved away. Paul Wilson and Bruce Rice eventually joined Barclay, Currie, Krause, and Hyland. That group remains active to this day. Along with Currie, Hyland was named Poet Laureate of Moose Jaw in 1991. These were lifetime appointments involving no special recognition beyond an awards night and no requirements or expectations of the laureates.

Just Off Main (1982) was his first full-length book of poetry, followed by *Street of Dreams* (1984), *After Atlantis* (1992), *White Crane Spreads Wings* (1996) and *The Work of Snow* (2003). *After Atlantis* and *White Crane Spreads Wings* won Saskatchewan Writers' Guild long manuscript awards, and *The Work of Snow* received the John V. Hicks Memorial Award sponsored by Thistledown Press. Hyland has won several other poetry prizes. His work has also appeared in more than twenty literary magazines and more than thirty anthologies.

Known as an activist and builder, Hyland was a founding member of Saskatoon's CJUS-FM radio (now the local community station), the Moose Jaw Community Hockey School, Moose Jaw Rink Action Committee, Sage Hill Writing Experience, ArtSchool Saskatchewan, CineView Saskatchewan, LiveMusicCity, Great Plains School of the Arts, Moose Jaw Centennial Committee, the Festival of Words (Artistic Coordinator), Moose Jaw Arts in Motion (Executive Director) and Wide Skies Film Festival (Executive Director). He continues to serve on the boards of the last six and also the Moose Jaw Cultural Centre Builders (Chairperson) and the Moose Jaw Cultural Centre Board of Directors. All positions are voluntary. He is a former director of Saskatchewan Film and Video Development Corporation and the City of Moose Jaw Ad Hoc Committee for a Cultural Centre.

In 1977 at the Saskatchewan Summer School of the Arts, Hyland took a two-week writing workshop with Eli Mandel and later taught creative writing there himself from 1982–1984. At the time of writing he has begun work on a sixth poetry manuscript and a how-to book for beginning writers based on columns he wrote for several years.

About Writing... *Learn the craft of writing with extreme humility; write with supreme assurance.*—
GARY HYLAND

VICTOR JERRETT ENNS was born three weeks late in Winnipeg in April 1955, having been to see *Gone with the Wind, in utero*, a space he shared with his alter ego Jimmy Bang. Jimmy was the subject of a first chapbook of poetry by the then young, unestablished, local poet (so identified by the CBC) known as Victor Enns, published with the inspired title *Jimmy Bang Poems* in 1979. This collection of poems, described as "punk poetry" by the *NeWest Review* and "misogynist" by Douglas Barbour in the *West Coast Review*, was the inadvertent result of finishing an advanced creative writing course while under the influence of Robert Kroetsch and George Ballantine. Other mentors included Dennis "Mr. Prolific" Cooley, E.F. "I'm not a Mennonite" Dyck, Andrew "Wood Mountain" Suknaski, "No longer two people" Patrick Lane and Lorna Crozier, and David "Goliath" Arnason who was heard to say "he's crazy as a shithouse rat" in reference to the erstwhile Enns who graduated with a B.A. in the fall of 1979 to the relief of the University of Manitoba.

Regaining consciousness in 1981, Enns hosted a bacchanal at his brother's hobby farm in Aubigny on the Red River during which time the Manitoba Writer's Guild was founded to a bluegrass gospel rendering of the Hallelujah chorus. Six months later he was the executive director of the Saskatchewan Writers Guild in Regina. Grant Devine was elected one month later. He spent a fabulous six years wallowing in lottery money, expanding Guild programs and staff. His second poetry collection, a real book, *Correct in this Culture*, edited by Caroline Heath, was published in 1985. This was to be his last book publication for over 20 years as he devoted his time to therapy, making a living, and raising a family of three children with his wife Sheila Jerrett. They had married soon after his divorce in 1982. He presented her with an epithalamium on the night before their wedding. She married him anyway, when they joined their names among other things. General manager of the Globe Theatre for three years, he returned to Winnipeg with his family in a misguided attempt to run a musical theatre in 1991. Grant Devine was defeated a month later.

There were several anthology and journal publications in the nineties and the release of a self-published chapbook, *a poem of pears*, which was one of the two poems that won the SWG poetry award in 1989. The other was from *the involuntary tongue*, a massive work of violence, profanity and seething sexual repression and its impact on the development of language, which has become an unpublishable life's work. It will join the very pleasant and much rejected *Lucky Man*, a collection celebrating family life and suburban green grass, in his collected papers.

Jerrett Enns has held posts as the executive director of the Manitoba Arts Council, The Manitoba Periodicals Association, and The Winnipeg Film Group. He was able to spend thirty days at the Patricia Blondal Memorial Writers retreat, a farmhouse north of Gimli, courtesy of the Manitoba Writers Guild in July 2003, discovering that, given scotch and solitude, he would still write poetry, which he

VICTOR JERRETT ENNS

found oddly reassuring. Less so the departure of his wife six months later, taking half his surname with her to her place above Prairie Sky.

About Writing... *Writing is a bitch barking to keep the black dogs at bay.*—VICTOR JERRETT ENNS

SHERRY JOHNSON was born in Craik in 1972. She grew up in Eastend, an area that has deeply influenced her. Eastend has become, she says, a template for her sensibility. Johnson has had poems published in a number of Canadian literary magazines. Her books include *Pale Grace* (1995), and *Hymns to Phenomena* (2001). Johnson won the 2001 ReLit Award for Poetry.

HEATHER HODGSON

TERRY JORDAN was born in Central Butte, but moved almost immediately to Humboldt with his parents, Denise and Donald. One of his earlier memories is finding a copy of *To Kill a Mockingbird* on a closet shelf in his parents' bedroom. "It's as if it was hidden. Though I don't know why it would've been, I've never asked, I don't think I ever will. Just to leave the quiet mystery of it intact is important. The things that cause you to wonder, to question, however small, are only friends to a writer."

Jordan moved from Humboldt to Melfort when he was fourteen years old, and finished high school there. "These places, each in their way, shaped who I am now. Both were made mythical when you took the time to get to know them. As were friends I grew up with—creative, musical, political, magical—I was very lucky. We invented our own language, our own stories; we tried, at least, as we should have, to do the same with rules.

"My family lived, at least for part of the time, on the edges of those towns. With a view across the prairie all the way to the horizon, poplar bluffs and animals and the far-away buildings of the next town falling back into the curvature of the earth. It was as though you could mail your thoughts out to those places, and they would respond in kind. So I grew up looking outward, conversing inward—searching, watching, pondering—isn't that a good part of what writing is? Maybe that's one of the secrets that prairie writers hold."

After high school he spent most of a year travelling in California and Mexico. He went on to live in different parts of Canada and the United States. Attending university, playing music for a living, building houses, working as a technician on films. Travelling to Mexico, Central and South America, Europe. He spent a year living in Sweden, part of it working on a film about Grey Owl's companion, Anahareo.

Jordan began writing when he was thirty-one. "I had just moved from Toronto to Vancouver at the time. The film business was slumping; I was seeing plays then that I was very alive to, reading writers who made me want badly to do what they were doing, but to do it myself—Marquez, Sinclair Ross, Dave Godfrey, Joyce's *Dubliners*, Pinter and Caryl Churchill. I started to write stories, and short pieces for the theatre, at night." The first workshop he attended was with Robert Kroetsch at David Thompson University in Nelson, British Columbia. The

PHOTO BY ALISON SCOTT

TERRY JORDAN... WITH DAUGHTER, CAMILLE.

two following summers were spent at Fort San with Seán Virgo and Leon Rooke. Jordan participated twice in the Banff May Studio as well as in a Dramatic Writing workshop with Bena Schuster. His first stage play, *Reunion*, was produced by the New Play Centre in Vancouver in 1990. The year after, *Movie Dust* was staged at the Quebec Drama Festival in Montreal, and *Close Your Eyes* was performed in Saskatoon at the University of Saskatchewan's Greystone Theatre. Different productions of these plays have been staged across the country in the years since.

Jordan's first book was a collection of stories, *It's a Hard Cow*, published in 1995. It won the Brenda MacDonald Riches Award at the Saskatchewan Book Awards and was nominated for a Commonwealth Writers Prize. His first novel, *Beneath That Starry Place*, was published both in Canada and in the United States, and as *Une Constellation D'escrocs* in France and Quebec. Jordan is finishing a novel, *Been in the Storm So Long*, and will also publish a collection of natural history essays in 2005.

Jordan was awarded the initial fellowship at the Wallace Stegner House in Eastend, Saskatchewan, in 1991, and received the first Margaret Laurence Fellowship at Trent University in 1996. He has held writer-in-residence positions and headed writing workshops in Canada and the United States, and he has taught in the English and Creative Writing department of Concordia University in Montreal.

Jordan now lives in the town of Allan, Saskatchewan, with his wife, Alison Scott, and their daughter, Camille. "I probably define myself more as a father than a writer these days, and consequently I work harder than ever shaping my story and prose because I hope that some day my child will read what I have written. I want clarity, and whatever power I can bring to it now to be there, then. So she has become my Everyone, and I write for her."

About Writing... *I love Gertrude Stein saying she learned about rhythm in writing, the difference between a sentence and paragraph, by listening to her dog drink water at its bowl. I admire William Gass's critical thinking, and the ringing truth of Joy Williams' comment on the beauty of our imperfect language, our wonderful failure of expression: "None of this is what I long to say. I long to say other things. So I write stories in my attempt to say them."*—TERRY JORDAN

DON KERR was born in 1936 in Saskatoon, of Irish and Scottish parents. He married Mildred McNamee in 1960 and they have three sons, David, Robert, and William. Kerr received a B.A. Honours degree in English from the University of Saskatchewan in 1958, and an M.A. from the University of Toronto in 1961. He went to London, England, to do a Ph.D., but went to movies and plays in London instead: five movies and one play a week. He's taught English at the University of Saskatchewan—from 1964 until now—and teaches what he learned in London: modern drama and film.

As a writer Kerr was first a poet, and for many years he was both a romantic and a poor poet, until he learned, partly from Al Purdy, that you could write plainly about your own place. Then an involvement in politics and the invention of irony got him out of himself.

Kerr has published six volumes of poetry: *A New Improved Sky* (1981), *Going Places* (1983), *Talkin Basie* (1990), *In the City of our Fathers* (1992), *Autodidactic* (1997), and *Smoke/Screen* (2003).

He began writing plays in the 1980s, all of them collective and historical in form and influenced by the great play he'd seen in London in 1963—Joan Littlewood's *Oh What A Lovely War*. His first play, *The Great War* (1985), was an eight-actor play about World War One, and covers the years from 1914 to 1919. Like his first three plays, it was performed at 25th Street Theatre under the direction of Tom Bentley-Fisher. Kerr's second play, *Talking Back, the Birth of the CCF* (1988), covered the years from 1932 to 1939, and was published in 1992. *Talking West*, performed in 1992, was more farcical and mythical, and is about ordinary Canadians defending themselves against British and American imperialism. The last full-length play Kerr had produced was *Lanc* (1996), about the crew in a Lancaster bomber, in raids over Germany in the winter of 1943 and 44. It was based on interviews with sixty Bomber Command veterans. The play was performed to celebrate the Greystone Theatre's 50th Anniversary and was directed by Henry Woolf.

Kerr has written plays for the Fringe Festival in Saskatoon, notably *Single Mom in the land of the Bureaucrats* (1992), which is a nativity play about justice being more important than mercy. He also wrote *I'm All Ears* (1996), which is a one-woman biography of pain overcome. His *The Smoking Cabaret* (1998) is about the pleasures and pains of cigarettes.

Kerr has had several short pieces aired on CBC radio: "I'm All Ears" (1993); "My Town," a celebration of Saskatoon, jazz, and the terrors of time (1988); "Swingtime Count" (1988) from *Talkin Basie;* and "The Railroad Blues" (1991), which is about the Liberal government's dismantling of VIA Rail.

Most recently, Kerr has been writing fiction, first a collection of short stories, *Love and the Bottle*, which was published in 2000. He began writing the stories after he had read a collection of W.P. Kinsella's baseball stories, some of which he thought were splendid, some terrible, and he thought, if he can write stories anyone can. And if Kinsella wrote about Indians and baseball, Kerr would write about sex and liquor; thus *Love and the Bottle*. Kerr also published a teen novel, *Candy on the Edge* (2001); he continues to write novels about Candy.

His editing reflects his writing interests. He has edited two collections of poetry with Anne Szumigalski: *Heading Out*, an anthology of new Saskatchewan poetry (1986), and an issue of *Grain* (1990) which contained Saskatoon poetry and prose. He edited two collections of plays with Diane Bessai of Edmonton: *Showing West* (1983) and *NeWest Plays for Women* (1987). Other books Kerr edited reflect his serious political involvement, first in the NDP, and then as an Independent Socialist in John Richard's 1975 campaign. He edited *Western Canadian Politics: The Radical Tradition* (1981) and, with John Richards, *Canada What's Left? a new social contract pro and con* (1986).

Kerr has had a lifelong interest in Saskatoon, which is present in his poetry but most notably in a book co-written with Stan Hanson, *Saskatoon: The First Half Century* (1982), and in his involvement in the heritage movement since 1973, originally under the inspiration of Bill Sarjeant. He was the first chair of the Saskatoon Heritage Society established in 1977, and he was first chair of the Saskatoon Municipal Heritage Advisory Committee from 1981 to 1986, and from 1997 to 2000. Most recently he has become the

PHOTO BY DAVID MANDEVILLE

DON KERR

Saskatchewan Governor of the Heritage Canada Foundation—the major heritage organization in the country. On heritage, his heart says: save everything. Then his mind interferes.

Kerr has been involved in a number of cultural and arts organizations: World University Service of Canada, from 1968 to 1971, where he learned the pleasures of committee work— "the pleasure of politics and the politics of pleasure," as he says in a poem. He also served on the Saskatoon Public Library Board, from 1971 to 1982, and was Chair from 1977 to 1982. He was active with the Meewasin Valley Authority from 1979 to 1983 (to which he was appointed by one government, the NDP, and dis-appointed by another, the Conservatives). Kerr served on the Saskatchewan Arts Board from 1991 to 1996 and with Sask Film from 1997 to 2000.

Kerr was an editor of *Grain* from 1973 to 1983. He brought *NeWest Review* to Saskatoon from Alberta in 1981, and edited it for five years. He has been on the boards of two of the most important regional presses in the prairies: NeWest Press in Edmonton from 1983 to the present, and Coteau Books in Regina, from 1983 to 1995 and from 1997 to the present. He feels that their service is crucial for writing from this part of the earth.

Kerr has been a press editor for more than fifteen books, of which the most important was Stan Rowe's *Home Place, Essays on Ecology*, published in 1990 and recently reprinted. Working with Stan convinced him that saving the earth was more important than any of his other pursuits. He's working with him on a new book, *Earth Alive*.

Kerr has seen two important literary organizations become victims of funding cuts because of Saskatchewan Arts Board decisions: 25th Street Theatre and *NeWest Review*.

He is currently involved in two projects: a biography of the Regina sculptor Vic Cicansky, and a history of Saskatchewan Public Libraries (at the request and with the sponsorship of the Saskatchewan Library Trustees).

Much of his writing is done in transit, in cars especially, but also in The Roastery Coffee House and Amigos, which is his local bar in Saskatoon.

About Writing... *Writing is a way to scheme freedom, slow time, and feel important, and happy. If I'm not writing, I'm not happy. It's as if I'm driven to write. As a member of writing groups, notably Anne Szumigalski's prose group, reading my work to a peer group felt like publication and relaxed me. Yet if I didn't publish would I keep up the work? Would I have that much character?*—DON KERR

ROSS KING was raised in North Portal. He obtained his B.A. (1984) and his M.A. (1986) in English at the University of Regina and later completed his Ph.D. at York University in Toronto. He has lived in England since 1992, and is now a full-time writer based near Oxford.

PHOTO BY JERRY BAUER, USED WITH THE PERMISSION OF WALKER & CO.

ROSS KING

King is the author of two novels, *Domino* (1995) and *Ex-Libris* (1998), as well as two works of non-fiction about Renaissance art and architecture: *Brunelleschi's Dome: How a Renaissance Genius Reinvented Architecture* (2000) and *Michelangelo and the Pope's Ceiling* (2002), which was shortlisted for the 2003 Governor-General's Award for non-fiction.

NICHOLAS RUDDICK

BARBARA KLAR was born in Saskatoon in 1966, the third and youngest child of kind, hard-working post-war German immigrants. Her father, a cabinet-maker, and her mother, a home-and-garden-maker, taught her that perfectionism and a love for the beauty of nature *can* co-exist. Klar began writing around the age of eight, filling small notebooks with rhyming poems and creative essays about the things that moved her.

BARBARA KLAR

Days after writing her last Grade 12 exam at Nutana Collegiate, Klar headed to the Saskatchewan School of the Arts at Fort San to take the Introduction to Creative Writing, a two-week course that changed her life. She began to want to be a poet more than anything, although at the time she had little idea just what that would entail in terms of life, thought, and work. Klar became a Fort San junkie, attending poetry workshops for the next four summers under such instructors as Patrick Friesen and Paulette Jiles. She also obtained a B.A. in English from the University of Saskatchewan, taking writing courses there under Patrick Lane, Lorna Crozier, and David Carpenter.

Klar's poems began to appear in literary journals such as *Prairie Fire*, *Border Crossings*, and *Grain*, and in the anthology *Breathing Fire: Canada's New Poets*. In 1993 her first collection, *The Night You Called Me A Shadow*, was published. It went on to co-win the League of Canadian Poets' Gerald Lampert Award for the best first book of poetry published in Canada that year. Her second collection, *The Blue Field*, was published in 1999.

Klar has worked as a baker, bookseller, small-town barmaid, and bush cook, but it was her nine years as a tree planter that most influenced her work. She had always felt most comfortable in the landscape of the forest, and this intense work in the northern bush not only deepened her connection to the land, but also taught her a great deal about the limitations of the human mind and body. Tree planting also introduced her to the Cypress Hills, the subject of a new poetry manuscript in which Klar further explores our relationship with nature. Her greatest courage is coming from visionary writers such as Tim Lilburn, Trevor Herriot, Mary Oliver, and Galway Kinnell.

Klar lives on an acreage near Ruddell with her partner Hal Gates and a Scottish Deerhound, Uisge Beatha. She is also a workshop leader and editor, orchardist, and chronic insomniac, all of which lead to poetry and truth.

About Writing... *I make a practice of walking in the North Saskatchewan River valley to be with the real world: the hills, trees, and stones which tell their stories if a person is open, vulnerable, and unselfish.* —BARBARA KLAR

BILL KLEBECK was born in 1955 in Foam Lake. His father owned a farm implement and automobile business and was also a farmer. His mother worked as a nurse/receptionist at the local doctor's office. Klebeck was raised in Foam Lake as a town kid but, because his father operated a farm north of town, he also spent considerable time on the farm. He actively farmed with his father until his father passed away in 1986 and he still owns farmland in the Foam Lake area.

Klebeck graduated from high school in

1973 and took his first year of university at the University of Calgary. The next year he worked at a pulp mill in Prince George, British Columbia, and traveled to Australia, South America, and Europe. He returned to the University of Saskatchewan and obtained his B.A. (Honours) in English in 1978. He received his LL.B. from the University of Saskatchewan in 1981 and was admitted to the Law Society of Saskatchewan in 1982. Klebeck has been a lawyer in private practice in Saskatchewan since that date.

Klebeck always wrote. In grades five through seven, he had notebooks filled with short stories at school that classmates would often ask to read instead of library books. By the end of grade nine, he had completed a 210-page novel entitled *Hawk*. He has published poetry and short fiction in many CanLit magazines, including *Grain*, *NeWest Review*, *Canadian Fiction Magazine*, *Prism International*, *Prairie Fire*, *CVII* and *The Capilano Review*. His fiction has also been anthologized in such works as *What's Already Known*, *Stag Line: Stories by Men*, *The Grand-Slam Book of Canadian Baseball Writing*, *Open Windows*, *The Farm Show: A Documentary*, *Heading Out*, and *More Saskatchewan Gold*.

From 1978 to 1981, Klebeck was a member of the Saskatoon Poets Coterie, which included other now-published writers such as as Brenda Niskala, Susan Andrews Grace, Craig Grant, Kim Morrissey, Alan Barr, and Lorne Kulak. In 1980, the Saskatoon Poets Coterie published an anthology of the group's work entitled *Blue Streak in a Dry Year*, edited by Anne Szumigalski. Klebeck's first book of fiction, *Where the Rain Ends*, was published

BILL KLEBECK... "PRAIRIE BOY UP AGAINST THE WALL"

in 1990 and his second book of short fiction, *Down Milligan Creek Way*, was published in 1995. It was nominated for the Saskatchewan Book of the Year and the Saskatchewan Fiction Award in 1995. Klebeck received awards for his fiction in the Saskatchewan Writer's Guild Literary competition, Short *Grain* contest and the *Capilano Review* short story contest. He was awarded the Saskatchewan Writer's Guild Member Achievement Award in 1993.

Klebeck has also been actively involved in many literary arts and cultural organizations. He served as President of the Saskatchewan Writers' Guild in 1980–81, was President of the Saskatchewan Council of Cultural Organizations in 1989–91, and was a member of the Saskatchewan Arts Strategy Task Force Implementation Management Committee 1991–93. Klebeck was also a member of the Saskatchewan Writers/Artists Colony Committee, 1985–1995; was President of SaskFilm in 1996–97; and was Director of Access Copyright from 1999 to the present.

Since publication of his second book in 1995, Klebeck has been working on five projects including an historical noir novel set in Saskatchewan *circa* 1932 and a manuscript of "long" short stories situated in "Milligan Creek" milieu. Klebeck continues to live in Wynyard with his wife, Glenis, and his two children. He continues to practice law as his family is not prepared to give up their middle-class lifestyle for his art quite yet.

About Writing...

If you're 'writing west', using plainspeak, tapping the anecdotal with the right measure, you can achieve art that endures. —BILL KLEBECK

TREENA KORTJE CARSON was born in 1971 and grew up in Yorkton and Saskatoon. She now resides in Melfort with her husband Mark Carson and her three children. Although much of her published work is under the name Kortje, her surname is now Carson.

She is the author of the poetry collection *Variations of Eve* (1999), which was shortlisted for both Best First Book and Book of the Year at the 1999 Saskatchewan Book Awards. In 2000 she was the first Saskatchewan writer ever to receive the Canadian Authors Association Air Canada Award for being the most promising writer in the country under thirty.

Carson's work has been published in numerous literary magazines, heard on CBC Radio, and included in the anthologies *200% Cracked Wheat* and *Friday After Five: The Feast*. In 1999 she performed and produced a staged version of her long poem *Variations of Eve* at the 25th Street Theatre's Women's Festival, the North Battleford "On the River's Edge" Festival, and at the 1999 Saskatoon International Fringe Festival.

Carson has taught creative writing and performance art workshops for students and adults of all ages and she has also given numerous readings and stage performances herself.

She has served as a board member (1998–1999) and as president (1999–2000) of the Saskatchewan Writers Guild.

JUDITH KRAUSE was born in 1952 in Regina, where she currently teaches on a full-time basis in an adult education program at SIAST. She is the daughter of Regina writer and former broadcaster, Pat Krause.

Judith studied languages and literature at the University of Regina and the Université de Caen, France, as well as studying and teaching in Switzerland. She holds a bilingual B.A. from the University of Saskatchewan (Regina Campus), a Bachelor's degree in Vocational/Technical Education from the University of Regina, and a Master of Fine Arts in Creative Writing from Warren Wilson College in Asheville, North Carolina.

Her informal education in writing began in childhood. Her mother taught her to read before Judith started kindergarten, and fostered her love of books. Nothing was off limits.

In 1971, mother and daughter signed up together for an introductory course in creative writing offered through the University of Regina Extension Department. The instructor was Ken Mitchell. This was an exciting time in the development of the Saskatchewan writing community. Through Ken's involvement in the foundation of the Saskatchewan Writers Guild, both Pat and Judith became Guild members very early on.

Over the years, Judith participated in a number of informal and non-credit writing workshops and classes led by well-known Canadian and American poets such as Patrick Lane and Paulette Jiles. Her first poetry instructor at the Saskatchewan School of the Arts was Anne Szumigalski. Friendships forged in the early days of Fort San writing classes led to the creation of one of Saskatchewan's longest running writers' groups—The Moose Jaw Movement, now known as The Poets' Combine. Judith is a founding member of this group, going into its 28th year.

In the mid-1990s, Judith completed two poetry workshops at the University of Iowa through its Summer Writing Festival program. One of her Iowa instructors, Jane Mead, suggested Judith look into the M.F.A. Program for Writers at Warren Wilson College. More recently, as a member of the 2002 Paris Writers' Workshop, Judith had the opportunity to work with Sharon Olds.

A past president of the Saskatchewan Writers Guild, Judith has worked as a Literary Arts Consultant to the Saskatchewan Arts Board, and coordinated the Creative Writing Program at the Saskatchewan School of the Arts. She also taught creative writing classes for the University of Regina, Extension Division, the Saskatchewan School of the Arts at Fort San, and the Sage Hill Writing Experience.

Judith served as member-at-large on the Sage Hill Writing Experience Board of Directors from 1993 to 1996. She is currently a member of the *Grain* advisory committee and acts as an advisory editor for Tupelo Press, a new literary press based in New England. In 1999, she served as a co-judge for the League of Canadian Poets National Poetry Contest, and in 1996 she was one of the Gerald Lampert Award judges. Judith represented the Saskatchewan writing community on the provincial Poet Laureate Search Committee in 2000, and in 2001 she worked as a mentor in the Saskatchewan Writers Guild Apprenticeship Program. In 2002, Judith served as one of the Pat Lowther Award judges.

Judith has been active in publishing, as an editorial assistant for *Salt* magazine, as a poetry editor for three terms for *WindScript*, and as a member of Thunder Creek Publishing Cooperative. In 1993–94, she assumed the *Grain* poetry editorship on an interim basis, and edited six issues. Together with Ven Begamudré, she edited a prose and poetry anthology called *Out of Place*, published in the spring of 1991. In 2000, she served as poetry editor for a new

PHOTO BY BRENDAN QUINLAN
JUDITH KRAUSE...
ON THE GULF OF MEXICO

anthology of Saskatchewan writing, *Sundog Highway*, which was specifically designed for high-school teachers and which features the writing of many new Saskatchewan voices.

Her first poetry collection, *What We Bring Home*, was published in 1986; her second collection, *Half the Sky*, came out in 1994. Judith's third poetry collection, *Silk Routes of the Body*, appeared in 2001.

A two-time winner of the City of Regina Writing Award (1988, 1998), Judith was the first recipient of the Robert Kroetsch Scholarship to the Saskatchewan School of the Arts. She has also received several Individual Assistance awards from the Saskatchewan Arts Board. Her poems have appeared in many Canadian periodicals and journals including *Grain*, *Prairie Fire*, *Event*, *Quarry*, *Fiddlehead*, *Canadian Literature*, *The Windsor Review* and *Border Crossings*. Her work has also been aired on CBC, and is included in several textbooks and in a number of anthologies. *Half the Sky* and *Silk Routes of the Body* were both shortlisted for Saskatchewan Book of the Year awards, and individual poems have won prizes at provincial and national levels.

Judith is currently at work on her fourth collection of poems, tentatively entitled "Secrets of the Flesh." Her chief regret as a poet is that it takes her so long to put together a collection.

About Writing... *Writing is a lot like gardening. It requires hard work, patience, a passion for creating, a willingness to experiment, ruthless weeding, acceptance that there are no guarantees, and a crazy desire to keep trying.*—JUDITH KRAUSE

PAT KRAUSE is in her third decade as a writer and her seventh decade on earth. Lucky numbers, she hopes. Mary Patricia Blair was born Sunday, January 26, 1930, in Druid City Hospital, Tuscaloosa, Alabama. Her father, Dr. Allan Blair, whose hometown was Regina, was on the medical faculty of the University of Alabama in Tuscaloosa. Her mother, the former Florence Wilson of Indian Head, earned a B.A. in 1923 from the University of Saskatchewan, where her parents met. There is a snapshot of newborn Miss Mary Pat on her father's lap howling her head off. Under it, in the neat letters he used to label slides, her father printed: Daddy Doc and a sack of holler. Krause credits early practise for her distinctive voice. The Blair family moved home to Canada in 1934 and lived in Winnipeg, Indian Head, and Toronto, before moving to Regina in 1939.

Krause's girlhood dream was to become a foreign correspondent, complete with dirty trench coat, glamorous movie star Veronica Lake's hairdo, and Katharine Hepburn's sophistication. She thought she'd cover the war-torn capitals of Europe surrounded by Hemingway-like lovers, sip goblets of wine in sidewalk cafes and flourish a French cigarillo in a long ivory holder to emphasize her blasé attitude to the Pulitzer prizes she'd won. Instead, she married her high school sweetheart in 1950 and only part of the dream came true. For a number of years, daily life did resemble living in a war-torn environment raising four children and trying to toilet train other flying, slithering, wiggling, crawling, joyously jumping, defecating creatures.

PHOTO BY PAUL JOHN STEIN
PAT KRAUSE... IN HER ROLE AS FAIRY GODMOTHER, CALGARY, 2001.

In 1970, the adage that life begins at forty became a personal hope. Her eldest daughter, poet Judith Krause, signed them both up for a creative writing class with Ken Mitchell to revive her mom's dream of becoming a writer. Beginner's luck helped Krause sell some short stories and articles, broadcast commentaries on CBC Radio, and win the first W.O. Mitchell Bursary in 1975 to attend the Saskatchewan School of the Arts writing workshops at Fort San as an apprentice writer and future teacher. In the latter half of the seventies, Krause coordinated and taught Fort San workshops and worked for CBC Radio as a writer, researcher, reporter, and host of an open-line show. Krause learned that writing is a lifetime apprenticeship.

In 1980, she won a major award in the book-length category of the Department of Culture and Youth Literary Competition for the manuscript of *Freshie* (1981).

During the 1980s, she won the City of Regina Writing Award, Saskatchewan Writers Guild literary awards, an Honourable Mention from *Prism International* for a true story about her father's black widow spider experiment titled "Webs," and she had stories published in various anthologies. In 1988, her collection of short stories, *Best Kept Secrets*, was published.

The nineties brought sorrow. Krause's husband, Frank, was diagnosed with non-Hodgkin's lymphoma in 1991 and had surgery that his oncologist thought "got it all." Frank was a "responder" to a series of chemotherapy treatments he took at the Allan Blair Cancer Clinic, named for Pat's father after he died of a heart attack in 1948. When chemo damaged Frank's heart in the fall of 1994, he underwent radiation therapy that did not change his terminal prognosis. Frank was only bedridden for five days before he died at home on January 24, 1995.

Inspired by Michigan undertaker and poet Thomas Lynch's description of mourning as a romance in reverse, Krause wrote a memoir about Frank's death. "Acts of Love" won a 1999 non-fiction award from Douglas College and was published in their literary magazine *Event*. Judge Tom Wayman said it was, "Magic. An intricate weave of a tale imaginatively and movingly portrayed." It was a finalist in the National Magazine Awards that year. In 2000, "Acts of Love" was published in the anthology *Going Some Place*, edited by Lynne Van Luven, and received excellent reviews. In September of the luckily numbered year 2003, the book-length manuscript of *Acts of Love* was one of the winners of the John V. Hicks non-fiction award.

Today, Krause says, "I did not burst into the Canadian literary galaxy as a child prodigy. Nor as a happy housewife who ended her grocery lists with: Surprise for me! The hot flashes I mistook for imminent stardom in middle age when I first got published were menopause. I was destined to become that little old lady in gold running shoes who wants to be a famous writer someday. Sometimes my muse is a gargoyle who squats on my back and hisses: *Freshie*'s as stale as bobby socks and *Best Kept Secrets* would have been best kept to yourself."

About Writing... *I am old now and I stand on my head trying to find words to inspire agile young writers to keep doing cartwheels. It's true I cannot make anonymous obscene telephone calls to editors who reject my work, but it's important to keep my own voice as a writer. So in a voice more like Bogart's than Bacall's, I can only repeat: If you want anything, all you have to do is whistle. Wish for magic while you whistle for good luck, do a wolf whistle when your fairy godmother waves her wand and grants it, and write your heart out.*—PAT KRAUSE

ROBERT KROETSCH was born and grew up in Alberta and presently lives in Manitoba. He feels that the resolution of this geographical confusion makes him a citizen of Saskatchewan. He was born near the village of Heisler, in the mixed-farming area of central Alberta. His father and his father's parents were born in Bruce County in Ontario, in the town (Formosa) of German-Catholic settlers made famous by Jane Urquhart's novel, *The Stone Carvers*. Just after the end of the nineteenth century they sold the family watermill and moved from Bruce County to homestead in the west. Paul Kroetsch, Robert's father, first homesteaded north of Shaunavon, but soon after moved to join his parents and siblings in the Alberta section of the Battle River country. Kroetsch's mother (Hilda Weller) was born in Spring Lake, in that same area, in the District of Alberta before Alberta became a province. Her parents had moved from St. Cloud, Minnesota, to homestead in 1901.

Kroetsch was born in a tarpaper homestead shack, a fact of which he has made a lot of hay, but in fact, while he was being born, the family's large and rather elegant farmhouse was under construction just a few yards away. He attended the Heisler Public School, then earned his B.A. at the University of Alberta. He was the first student from his agricultural area to study something as useless as English and philosophy. By way of justification he announced that he was going to become a writer. In the quest for writing experience, he went into the Canadian North and spent six years working first on Mackenzie River riverboats, then on the shore of Hudson Bay, then in Goose Bay, Labrador. At the end of that period he had accumulated a great deal of experience. And he felt he had learned almost nothing about writing.

After six years in the North he spent six years in graduate school. He went first to Middlebury College, Vermont, for a master's degree, then to the University of Iowa for a Ph.D. After that he took a position as professor at the State University of New York at Binghamton.

During his seventeen years in Binghamton he wrote most of his novels, including *But We Are Exiles* (a riverboating story), and his prairie novels *The Words of My Roaring*, *The Studhorse Man*, *Badlands* and *What the Crow Said*. During that same time (he was in his forties; rather along in life to become a poet, he was told) he began to write poetry, and published his first long poems, *The Ledger* and *Seed Catalogue*. About that same time (in the 1970s) he began to teach summer courses at Fort San, in Saskatchewan. While at Fort San he had the good fortune to work with or in the presence of writers as various as Byrna Barclay, David Carpenter, Lois Simmie, Robert Currie, Lorna Crozier, Geoff Ursell, Barbara Sapergia, Anne Szumigalski, and Ken Mitchell. The sudden, beautiful landscapes of the Qu'Appelle valley became for him the equivalent of Saskatchewan's blossoming literature.

In 1978 Robert Kroetsch returned to Canada, becoming professor of English at the University of Manitoba, where he taught until 1995. During that time he continued to write fiction, poetry, and essays, including his two collections of essays, *The Lovely Treachery of*

PHOTO COURTESY THE OFFICE OF PUBLIC AFFAIRS, UNIVERSITY OF ALBERTA

ROBERT KROETSCH... THE AUTHOR LEARNS TO IGNORE HIS COMPUTER.

Words and *A Likely Story*. Kroetsch has published something like twenty-five books, including nine novels, a travel book, and a collection of journal entries. He received the Governor General's Award for Fiction for *The Studhorse Man* in 1969. He is a Fellow of the Royal Society of Canada. He has received three honourary doctorates and was the first Canadian writer to receive the Distinguished Achievement Award from the Western Literature Association of the United States. His most recent long poem, *The Hornbooks of Rita K*, was nominated for a Governor General's Award in 2001. Kroetsch's daughter Laura lives in Wellington, New Zealand, and his daughter Megan lives in St. Petersburg, Florida. Kroetsch lives with Dawne McCance, professor and writer, in Winnipeg. He has given and continues to give readings around the world. During the first years of the new century he has had the good fortune to teach the novel colloquium in the Sage Hill Writing Experience held in Lumsden, Saskatchewan; he continues to meet the makers of the Saskatchewan writing tradition.

About Writing... *The merest need is hanging in. One writes and then one re-imagines and rewrites. One listens to what one has written and then one re-imagines again and rewrites again. The actuality of blank sheets of paper becomes the mystery of a readable book.*—ROBERT KROETSCH

PATRICK LANE was born in 1939 in Nelson, British Columbia. He has worked at a variety of jobs, from common labourer, cat skinner, miner, truck driver, and Industrial-First-Aid-Man in a number of sawmills, to salesman, office manager, and corporate industrial accountant. Much of his life has been spent as an itinerant poet, wandering over three continents and many countries. He began writing with serious intent in 1958. In 1966 he established with bill bissett and Seymour Mayne the publishing house Very Stone House, which produced a number of important collections of poetry in the 1960s.

In 1971 he decided to devote his life exclusively to writing and travelled to South America, where he lived for two years. On his return he settled on the west coast of Canada in the small fishing village of Pender Harbour. In 1978 he left the coast and took up a writer-in-residency at the University of Manitoba. Since then he has been writer-in-residence at Concordia University, the University of Ottawa, the University of Alberta, the Saskatoon Public Library, and the University of Toronto. Previous to moving to British Columbia, he lived in Saskatoon, where he taught at the University of Saskatchewan in the English Department, sharing a position there with his permanent companion, the poet Lorna Crozier. He has taught writing at Concordia University, the University of Saskatchewan, the University of Ottawa, the Banff Summer School of the Arts, the Saskatchewan Summer School of the Arts, the Victoria Writing School, and at numerous other writing schools across the country. He is presently retired from the University of Victoria Writing Department, where he taught for ten years. He teaches a number of private master classes in fiction and poetry. He is the father of five children and the grandfather of five. He is a member of PEN, the League of Canadian Poets, and the Writer's Union of Canada.

Lane has published numerous volumes of poetry over the past forty years, including: *Poems, New & Selected* (1978); *The Measure* (1981); *Old Mother* (1982); *A Linen Crow, A Caftan Magpie* (1984); *Selected Poems* (1987); *Milford & Me* (1989), a collection of children's poems; *Winter* (1990); *Mortal Remains* (1991); *Too Spare, Too Fierce* (1995); *Selected Poems 1977–1997* (1997); *The Bare Plum of Winter Rain* (2000); and *Go Leaving Strange* (2004). Other publications include a collection of short fiction, titled *How Do You Spell Beautiful? And Other Stories* (1992), and a series of meditations on life, art, poetry, and gardens, titled *There is a Season: A Memoir in a Garden* (2004). *Short Stories—New and Selected* will be published in 2005.

Lane is the co-editor (with Lorna Crozier) of *Breathing Fire* (1995) and *Breathing Fire II* (2004), two anthologies of Canada's new poets, and *Addicted: Notes From the Belly of the Beast* (2001), an anthology of personal essays on addiction.

Lane has received a number of Canada Council Arts Awards, along with awards from the Ontario Arts Council, the Saskatchewan Arts Board, the Manitoba Arts Board, and the B.C. Arts Council. Lane received the Governor General's Award for poetry in 1979 for *Poems, New & Selected*; the Canadian Authors Association Award for poetry in 1988 for *Selected Poems*; and the Dorothy Livesay Prize in 1995 for *Too Spare, Too Fierce*. Both *Winter* and

PHOTO BY KATE HILL
PATRICK LANE

Mortal Remains were nominated for the Governor General's Award.

The radio script *Chile*, co-written with Lorna Crozier, won the National Radio Award's Best Public Radio Program for 1987. In 2004 Lane was given an award for the best radio political commentary in Canada. He has been nominated several times for the National Magazine Award and has won twice: once, in 1989, for a group of poems appearing in *Border Crossings*, and again in 1987 for his short story "Rabbits," which appeared in *Canadian Forum*. In 1991 Lane's short story "Marylou Had Her Teeth Out" was selected for the anthology *Best American Short Stories*.

Lane has lived and travelled extensively around the world and has read and published his work in a number of countries including England, France, Czechoslovakia, Italy, China, Japan, Chile, Colombia, Yugoslavia, The Netherlands, South Africa, and Russia. His poetry appears in all major Canadian anthologies of English literature.

A critical monograph by George Woodcock on Patrick Lane's life and writing has been published as part of *Canadian Writers and Their Works* (1985). Lane is considered by most critics and scholars to be one of the finest poets of his generation.

KATHERINE LAWRENCE. Some women turn forty and go back to school, or file for divorce, or get an ankle tattoo—a rose, a seahorse, a humming bird. It's change they seek, something permanent and lasting.

Katherine Lawrence decided to write a book of poetry. She approached the task the way she might stitch a row of buttons down the back of a dress, quietly and alone, one poem at a time.

It took five years to write the poems but when Coteau Books of Regina published *Ring Finger, Left Hand* in 2001, Katherine felt as though she had taught herself how to live out the rest of her life as a writer. The book won the Brenda Macdonald Riches Award for best first book from the Saskatchewan Book Awards. Most of the poems had been previously published in Canadian journals or broadcast on CBC radio.

Not that the writing life had escaped Katherine up to the age of forty. It's that she had spent the previous twenty years engaged in another kind of writing, namely journalism and public relations. Creative writing, as she understood it, was not an acceptable avenue for a Hamilton girl raised by hard-working, ambitious parents.

Ron Lawrence and Marion O'Hanley were married in Hamilton in 1952. They had two daughters, Katherine and Barbara. Marion stayed at home to raise the girls and worked part-time as a model during fashion seasons. She returned to school in 1968 after separating from Ron. Marion then worked full-time, first as a dental assistant and later as a dental educator. During these years Ron built a medical supply business and remarried. He retired in 1987 after selling the business to an international firm.

It's never difficult for a girl to learn from the example of her mother, and Katherine was a watchful daughter. More education and a career would have saved her mother from some lean and difficult years after the divorce. Katherine was encouraged to take a critical view of marriage or, at the very least, prepare to embrace the institution as an equal partner. She told herself that creative writing was a hobby, much like flower arranging.

Katherine headed to Ottawa after high school to study journalism and English at Carleton University, graduating in 1978 with a

B.A. She studied with poets Christopher Levenson and Robert Hogg, both of whom were encouraging. Occasionally, an acceptance letter from a literary magazine would arrive, but the money was never as good as what Katherine was beginning to realize she could earn as a journalist.

After graduation, Katherine worked as a reporter for the Hamilton *Spectator*, a job that earned writing awards for her from the Ontario Newspaper Association. But she was restless. She left after 2½ years to work for the Whitehorse *Star* in the Yukon, took up freelance writing for CBC Northern Services, and also filed stories on northern affairs for daily newspapers in southern Canada, including *Maclean's* magazine. She was listed on their masthead as Whitehorse correspondent.

A journalism career appeared to be taking shape but her personal life was somewhat chaotic because a man she had met at Carleton remained in touch despite their geographic distance. By now, Randy Burton had moved from Ottawa to Saskatoon where he was working as a reporter. He invited Katherine to join him. She agreed to leave Whitehorse "for just one summer." They were married in 1984.

Twenty years later, Katherine remains in Saskatoon. During the first ten years she worked for CSP Foods (a former division of the Saskatchewan Wheat Pool) as manager of public affairs, and later for the Saskatchewan Research Council as their communications manager. She and her husband had their first daughter but by now the poetry had fallen away from her, proof that it had been an adolescent fad. It was replaced by a busy family life, a respectable career, and a numbing, low-grade depression. Something was missing from her life.

Katherine left the Saskatchewan Research Council after her second daughter was born and started a freelance writing business. At home, with two young children and a small business, she began to address her nagging unhappiness. She realized she needed to write for herself again. She discovered the Sage Hill Writing Experience where she took a poetry workshop. Writing colonies followed, friendships in the writing community bloomed, poems filled her desk, and her first book was published.

Today Katherine lives with her husband, their two teenage daughters, and writes regularly. She is working on another manuscript of poems and exploring short fiction. She also maintains a part-time job doing public relations for a former client, the Royal University Hospital Foundation.

Daughters will always watch their mothers and Katherine believes there can be no better role model for a teenage girl than a mother who clears her own path.

About writing... *A woman who heeds the call of a writing life must learn to become gloriously selfish. She must sit at her desk for a few hours every day and say, this is where I belong. The rest of her life will look after itself.* —KATHERINE LAWRENCE

PHOTO BY RANDY BURTON
KATHERINE LAWRENCE... AND RHUBY

SHELLEY ANN LEEDAHL was born on April 2, 1963, in Kyle, to Jim and Helen Herr. Her father's work as a Co-op General Manager took the family to the Saskatchewan towns of Turtleford, Wilkie, and Meadow

Lake. She has four siblings—Heather, Kirby, Ron and Crystal—and her childhood was enriched by the twenty-five children her parents fostered over the years.

Leedahl knew from an early age that she wanted to spend her life writing. She studied Journalism Arts at SAIT in Calgary, but quickly realized that poetry and fiction were her passion. A recession, a few months of unemployment in Medicine Hat, and a return to Saskatchewan ensued.

Leedahl worked at various Saskatoon Co-op locations—she particularly enjoyed the Farm Centre and remains a small town girl at heart—and found her future husband, Troy, in the plumbing aisle of the Westview Co-op, where they were both employed. The young couple became the parents of Logan Thomas in 1984, were married in 1985, and rounded out the family with daughter Taylor Rae in 1986.

In her early twenties, while parenting toddlers and operating a home daycare, Leedahl began crafting stories and poems around the edges of her busy days. This work found its way into publications like *Fireweed*, *NeWest Review*, and *Western People*, and onto CBC Radio Saskatchewan.

Leedahl joined the Saskatchewan Writers Guild, sought out the editorial advice of other new writers in the Saskatoon Poets Coterie, began taking creative writing classes (with Lorna Crozier, Fred Stenson, Gloria Sawaii and, later, David Carpenter), attended Saskatchewan Writers Guild colonies and entered creative writing competitions. She had early luck with the latter. *A Few Words For January*, her first book of poetry, was released on a Cinderella night in 1990. It promptly sold out and was reprinted one month later.

Leedahl continued to write and publish in various genres while she worked at various part-time jobs: church secretary, shoe salesperson, cleaner, radio advertising copywriter. In 1995 she took the leap of faith necessary to become a full-time writer and has been writing ever since for a number of commercial and literary markets.

She has been active in the Saskatchewan writing community in various capacities: regularly presenting in schools and libraries; leading creative writing classes and residencies; serving as a poetry, fiction, and non-fiction editor for Saskatchewan magazines; judging competitions and mentoring. Her work—frequently broadcast on CBC Radio and widely published—has earned numerous awards and nominations. Korean rights have been sold for *The Bone Talker*.

Leedahl was one of five Canadian writers selected to participate in the Canada-Mexico Writing/Photography exchange in Mérida, Mexico (2002) and Banff (2003). Another career highlight was working with Innu and Inuit children in Labrador. In 2004, she was awarded a fellowship to attend the Hawthornden Castle international retreat for writers in Scotland.

Her poetry books are *Talking Down The Northern Lights* (2002, 2001), and *A Few Words For January* (1998, 1990, 1990). Other books include the novel *Tell Me Everything* (2000); an illus-

PHOTO BY TAYLOR LEEDAHL

SHELLEY LEEDAHL... "FIRST I RUN 10K; THEN I HAVE THE ENERGY TO TACKLE THE HARDER WORK OF SITTING AT MY DESK.

trated children's book, *The Bone Talker* (1999); a juvenile novel, *Riding Planet Earth* (1998, 1997); and a short story collection, *Sky Kickers* (1994). *Orchestra of the Lost Steps*, a short fiction collection which earned a John V. Hicks Manuscript Award in 2001, was released in 2004. *Doce Maneras de Mirar la Luna*, a collection of stories, poems, journal entries, and photographs, is forthcoming with Ediciones Monte Carmelo in Mexico.

Leedahl continues to enjoy the challenge of writing in multiple genres and for readers of all ages. Other interests include long distance running, cycling, beach volleyball, tennis, gardening, studying Spanish, camping, and travelling. She divides her time between Saskatoon and her writing retreat home in Middle Lake.

About Writing... *I've always been curious—in grade five the other girls called me nosy—about people's lives. What do they think about? What are their fears and desires? As a writer I get to live many lives. My poetry is mostly confessional, but my fictional characters form an eclectic cast—from 12-year-old boys to 70+-year-old women. I don't know where these people come from, or, often, where they're going. I may begin with a first paragraph, but soon the characters take over the story and I'm just the woman at the keyboard, tripping over the keys in order to keep up. Writing is an adventure, and it's still as much fun today as it was the first time I put pencil to paper.*—SHELLEY LEEDAHL

TIM LILBURN was born in Regina in 1950 to Walter and Winnifred (Blaylock) Lilburn. His father was a letter carrier, later working in the post office's city sortation department, while his mother was employed as a sales clerk in a series of women's clothing stores. He grew up in the northwest part of the city, attending Benson School and Luther College. After leaving school for a period in his late teens, he completed his high school at the University of Regina in the senior matriculation program run by Dr. Les Crossman.

Lilburn subsequently majored in philosophy and English, receiving a B.A. from the University of Regina in 1973; one year later, he qualified for a Saskatchewan Teacher's Certificate. He joined CUSO in the summer of 1974 and was sent to northern Nigeria, where he worked as a teacher of English composition and literature for two years at General Murtala Mohammed Secondary School in Yola, Gongola State. There he developed an interest in such African writers as Chinua Achebe, Wole Soyinka, Amos Tutola, and the poets Christopher Okigbo and U'Tamsi.

Lilburn continued to write while in Africa, and managed to publish his first work (two poems) in *Prism International* shortly after his return to Canada. He published nothing else for ten years, though he did not cease to write or submit his work to magazines. In 1978, he joined the Jesuits, a Roman Catholic religious order, and moved to Guelph where he made his novitiate. While with the Jesuits, he worked as a hospital and prison chaplain, a farm labourer, an instructor within the novitiate, a retreat director, and a writer on social justice issues. He received an M.A. in philosophy from Gonzaga University, Spokane, Washington, in 1982. Lilburn left the order in 1987, and worked for a number of years as a farm labourer and part-time university lecturer at Wilfrid Laurier University in the Department of Religion and Culture, in the Guelph-Kitchener area.

His first book of poems, *Names of God*, was published in 1986; this was followed in 1988 with *From the Great Above She Opened Her Ear to the Great Below*, where his poems appeared alongside reproductions of installation pieces by Susan Shantz. Lilburn was appointed writer-in-residence at the University of Western Ontario in 1988–89, sharing this position with the late Bronwen Wallace. In 1989 he published *Tourist to Ecstasy*, for which he received a Governor General's Award nomination.

Lilburn returned to Saskatchewan in 1990 to teach philosophy and literature at St. Peter's College in Muenster, Saskatchewan. Over the next thirteen years, he produced six books, including three collections of poetry: *Moosewood Sandhills*, *To the River*, and *Kill-site*. He also published one essay collection, *Living in the World as if It Were Home*, and two anthologies on poetics: *Poetry and Knowing* and *Thinking and Singing: Poetry and the Practice of Philosophy*, where he appeared as both contributor and editor. Lilburn also published a chapbook with Helen Marzolf which is a long poem called *Kill-site*.

Lilburn has served as writer-in-residence at St. Mary's University (1995), the Regina Public Library (1998–99) and the University of Alberta (1999–2000). He has taught at the Sage Hill Writing Experience and at the Banff School of Fine Arts, and has read his work at venues across Canada, in China, and in the United States. His work is widely anthologized, and is included in *Twentieth Century Poetry and Poetics*, *15 Canadian Poets x 3*, and *A Matter of Spirit: Recovery of the Sacred in Contemporary Canadian Poetry*. It also has been translated into Chinese and Polish. Lilburn delivered the inaugural Anne Szumigalski Memorial Lecture to the League of Canadian Poets in 2002 and the twenty-fourth Nash Memorial Lecture on art and the sacred in the same year. He currently lives in Saskatoon, near the South Saskatchewan River, and is at work on new poems: a long study of desire in the Western intellectual tradition, tentatively entitled *Going Home: Eros in Plato and Early Christian Platonists*, a Philosophical Poetics, and a collaborative thought experiment with the poet-philosopher Jan Zwicky called *Contemplation and Resistance: An Exchange*.

PHOTO BY ALLAN SAFARIK

TIM LILBURN... AT THE INAUGURAL ANNE SZUMIGALSKI MEMORIAL LECTURE TO THE LEAGUE OF CANADIAN POETS, SASKATOON, 2002.

2002–2003 was a fruitful year for Lilburn. *Thinking and Singing: Poetry and the Practice of Philosophy* was published in the fall of 2002 and contains essays by Dennis Lee, Don McKay, Jan Zwicky, and by Lilburn, all of which deal with poetics. In April of 2003, his sixth book of poetry, *Kill-site*, for which he received the Governor General's award, was published.

About Writing... *I've always resisted the notion that poetry is chiefly decorative: it's a way of knowing. Some forms of poetry are possibly the most trustworthy way of knowing. Writing is listening and obedience—and hoping you will be visited by something worth saying.*—TIM LILBURN

ALISON LOHANS. Born and raised in Reedley, California, in the agricultural heart of that state, Alison Lohans felt drawn to move to Canada during the Vietnam war era. With a B.A. in music, completed at California State University, Los Angeles, Lohans and husband

Michael Pirot moved to Victoria, British Columbia, in 1971. Pirot did graduate studies at the University of Victoria and Lohans, after several years of working as a pharmacy assistant, completed her Postgraduate Diploma in Elementary Education. A job offer for Pirot at the University of Regina brought the couple to Saskatchewan in 1976. Following many years of part-time study, Lohans defended her M.Ed. thesis at the University of Regina in 2002.

Saskatchewan quickly became the literary home where Lohans' lifetime commitment to writing began bearing fruit. Apart from two early pieces of the 1960s, all of her published work has been crafted in Regina. Her husband's lengthy battle with cancer and eventual death made it impractical for her to participate in the many workshops that were available in Saskatchewan, so she worked primarily as a self-taught writer, in regular correspondence with another developing writer friend, Kathy Kennedy Tapp, who she knew from her university days in California. This semi-isolation changed in 1982 and 1983 when she was able to work in-depth with Janet Lunn, who was writer-in-residence at the Regina Public Library. During that same year Lohans' first young adult novel, *Who Cares About Karen?*, was published. Seán Virgo influenced Lohans' fiction a decade later, with the editing of *Laws of Emotion* and *Don't Think Twice*.

Lohans has published thirteen books for children and young adults, short stories for audiences ranging from children to adults, several poems, and a variety of non-fiction pieces. She created the story scripts for Regina Symphony Orchestra's children's concert series from 1999 to 2001. Nine of Lohans' books have appeared on the Canadian Children's Book Centre "Our Choice" List over the past twenty years. Her novel *Don't Think Twice* was shortlisted for both the 1997 Saskatchewan Book of the Year Award and the Canadian Library Association Young Adult Award. Other titles shortlisted for awards at national and provincial levels include *Waiting for the Sun*, *No Place for Kids*, *Getting Rid of Mr. Ribitus*, *Nathaniel's Violin*, *Laws of Emotion*, and *Foghorn Passage*. *Can You Promise Me Spring?* and *Mystery of the Lunchbox Criminal* won the South Saskatchewan Reading Council/SWG Young Readers' Choice Award in 1994 and 1996. Lohans has also won awards for her short fiction and, more recently, academic non-fiction. Her books have been translated into French, Swedish, and Norwegian.

Teaching of one sort or another has occupied some of Lohans' time over the years. In the 1970s she taught beginning band in Regina public schools. Later, busy with a growing family, she began working with developing writers: first as peer mentor, then correspondence instructor and manuscript evaluator, and eventually as instructor for the Regina Sage Hill Teen Writing Experience. These years of mentoring brought Lohans full circle when she was offered the position of writer-in-residence at Regina Public Library for 2002 and 2003.

Winner of the 1996 Saskatchewan Writers Guild Volunteer Leadership Award, Lohans is active in writing- and book-related organizations at local, provincial, and national levels. She founded the Saskatchewan Children's Writers' Round Robin

ALISON LOHANS

in 1984, and co-ordinated the Regina Young People's Literature Roundtable for many years. She has served on the boards of the Saskatchewan Writers Guild, the Writers' Union of Canada, the Canadian Children's Book Centre, and other Saskatchewan-based arts groups.

Lohans' fictional work evolves from her fascinations with character development and setting. Passions for music and reading claim some of her time. She also does intermittent contract work for the University of Regina in the areas of educational research and program development. Other family members in Regina include son Chris Lohans and partner Stewart Raby. She has several novels in various stages of completion, some of which include *The Tangled Braid*, *Time of the T'laaure*, *River Rat*, and *Thee, Alyssa*.

About Writing... *We all strive to create something exquisite, crafted with hope, dedication, and much labour. Using the medium of fiction we try to illuminate human truths, larger-than-life. Often the aesthetic impulse, and its manifestations through our work, don't fare very well in the commercial reality which tends to devalue the arts. Consequently we find ourselves needing ever-thicker skins to protect and preserve that spark which makes it all possible in the first place. Time and time again we must pick ourselves up, dust off the bruises, and simply keep going. Because this is something we feel called to do, something we must do, in order to be alive and whole.*—ALISON LOHANS

HOLLY LUHNING was born in Regina on New Year's Eve, 1977. She and her younger brother Nathan grew up on the family farm near Lumsden. Her parents are both from rural backgrounds; her mother, Norma (Jacobson), grew up near Kyle and her father, Rod Luhning, is from the Lumsden area. They met in Regina while pursuing post-secondary studies. In addition to farming, Rod is involved in municipal governance, as well as educational governance at the local and provincial levels; Norma is a registered nurse. Nathan currently lives in Regina with his wife, Alison.

At 17, Holly briefly travelled through western Europe as a musician with the Canadian Youth on Tour concert and jazz band. She attended the University of Regina for a year, and then transferred to the University of Victoria. During her time at UVic, she worked at CFUV radio, and was on the editorial team for *Chaos*, an undergraduate writing journal. She wrote for the women's centre newspaper *The Emily* (now *Third Space*), and started to belly dance. She spent a summer in Whistler facilitating a youth chamber music camp, and another summer studying French in Montreal. In 1999, she graduated with a B.A. in English.

That July, Luhning attended the introductory workshop at the Sage Hill Writing Experience with teachers Dave Margoshes and Liz Phillips. She returned to Sage Hill for the next couple of years as an on-site assistant, and eventually came back as an "experient."

Later in 1999, Luhning left Canada for New Zealand. While there, she worked as an usher, housekeeper, and waitress in Auckland, and as a kiwi fruit picker in Kerikeri. She also backpacked in Australia and Fiji before returning to Canada to begin graduate school at the University of New Brunswick in the fall of 2000.

At UNB, Luhning was an editorial assistant for *Studies in Canadian Literature*, and served on the editorial boards of *Qwerty* and *Fiddlehead*. She was also a teaching assistant, and a student writer for the public relations department. In 2001, she received her first journal acceptance, from *Grain*. Luhning completed her creative thesis, a version of her first book, under the supervision of poet, editor, and professor Ross Leckie. She obtained her M.A. in English and Creative Writing in 2002.

While in Fredericton, Luhning was involved in community radio as a co-host of the CHSR FM music and talk show "Cold Fuchsia." She also worked with a group that gave dating violence prevention workshops in rural New Brunswick high schools. Luhning was a winner of the 2002 NB Acts short playwriting contest, and her play *Hibiscus* was performed at the 2002 NB Acts festival. She continued to belly dance, and was part of a folk-influenced troupe that performed in New Brunswick and Maine.

Luhning returned to the prairies later in 2002. She continued to work on her poetry manuscript, and published more work in literary journals. In 2003, she won third place in *This Magazine*'s Great Canadian Literary Hunt, and attended the Booming Ground Writers' workshop with Roo Borson, and the Sage Hill workshop with Betsy Warland. Her first book, *Sway*, was published in the fall of 2003. *Sway* is about home, travel, dislocation, and the navigation of the personal, domestic sphere.

From late 2002 until early 2004, Luhning worked at the University of Regina as a research coordinator and a sessional instructor. During that time, she belly danced in the Zarifah dance troupe. She continues to dance-and performs with the dance name Firuze (which is Turkish for turquoise, her birthstone). Luhning spent the summer of 2004 travelling throughout Eastern Europe. She is currently working on her second manuscript, a project inspired by the life of sixteenth-century Hungarian countess, Elizabeth Bathory, and she is also studying towards her Ph.D. in English at the University of Saskatchewan.

PHOTO BY BEN CHECKOWY AND BOB McDONALD

HOLLY LUHNING

About Writing... *Pay attention to the sinuous and the sensual, and be aware of your landscapes—geographical, emotional, physical. Don't be afraid of writing bad poems—sometimes you have to wade through the muck to get the good stuff.* —HOLLY LUHNING

RANDY LUNDY, a Scorpio, was born in November of 1967 in the mining community of Thompson, in north-central Manitoba. His father, Elmer Lundy, was the son of a Minnesota-born man of Norwegian descent, who had moved to northern Saskatchewan to homestead, and a Saskatchewan-born woman of Irish descent. Lundy's mother, Marguerite Bighetty, is a Cree woman born in northern Manitoba near the community of Brochet, home base to the Barren Lands First Nation. According to the official record, Lundy's mother is the daughter of a Cree woman and a Scottish man, who was a trapper and miner. However, there is an apocryphal, oral story that his mother was born of a Cree man and woman but was adopted by a Scottish couple.

When his parents separated, less than amicably, in the early 1970s, Lundy moved with his father to the logging community of Quesnel, in the interior of British Columbia. In 1974, Lundy and his father relocated to the logging community of Hudson Bay, in northeastern Saskatchewan, where he graduated from high school in 1986. After graduation and after a year of outdoor, minimum-wage work in Hudson Bay, Lundy applied to join the

Canadian Air Force. He was accepted but, after deciding that a first contract of nine years was far too large a commitment, he turned the offer down in favour of attending university. In order to explain such an apparently impractical decision to a father who had spent his entire life working in the agricultural, mining, and forestry industries, Lundy invented the dream of law school, a dream he had little, if any, intention of following. He moved to Saskatoon to attend the University of Saskatchewan in the fall of 1987 and drifted somewhat aimlessly but rather pleasurably between the English, Philosophy, and Religious Studies departments. He finally completed a B.A. (Hons.) in 1993. After some hellish time spent working for minimum wage once again, Lundy decided to return to the University of Saskatchewan as a graduate student. He completed an M.A. in Native Canadian Literature in 2001. While a graduate student, Lundy won a Graduate Teaching Fellowship and other academic awards, and in spite of the grumblings of some fellow students about "racial politics," the simple fact was that Lundy's grades were superior to those of the grumblers. Also while a graduate student, he began working first as a writing-clinic instructor and then a Sessional Lecturer at the Saskatoon Campus of the Saskatchewan Indian Federated College.

In spite of what he had told his father, Lundy's true motivations for attending university were simply to avoid low-paying, mind-numbing work and to have an opportunity to read (not necessarily for classes) and to write, primarily poetry, something he had been doing secretly since his mid-teens. In the fall of 1999, all of his lies and deceits paid off with the publication of his first collection of poetry, *Under the Night Sun*. The publication of this first book also provided the opportunity for Lundy to move to Regina, Saskatchewan, to take up a year-long position as writer-in-residence at the Saskatchewan Indian Federated College, on the University of Regina campus. After completing the residency, he took on a one year term appointment in the S.I.F.C. English Department, where he is currently employed as an Assistant Professor. As of the fall of 2002, Lundy has completed a second manuscript of poetry, currently titled *Gift of the Hawk*, and has begun a foray into short fiction, which he is not yet convinced will lead to anything remotely worth reading.

To the extent that Lundy has learned anything about the craft of poetry, he has learned the craft primarily from being a reader. In his mid-teens when he began writing poetry to relieve adolescent boredom and to try a new strategy to get a date, it was the discovery of Archibald Lampman's nature sonnets that gave the first impulse to his writing. However, it wasn't until his first year at university that Lundy actually learned how to read. During his early years at university, Lundy actually regressed in terms of the influences on his writing. From writing poor imitations of Lampman, he regressed, at least chronologically, to writing poor imitations of 17th-century English poets. Later, and, of course, inevitably, came his brush with the English Romantics.

PHOTO BY BURYL BERNARD

RANDY LUNDY... POE-TREED ON THE BANKS OF THE SOUTH SASKATCHEWAN.

But it was a class in Canadian Literature taught by Canadian poet Patrick Lane that introduced Lundy to the richness of contemporary and local poetry. Later, in a Canadian Poetry seminar, Professor Susan Gingell actually taught Lundy to read poetry well, and he is still indebted to these teachers for any craft that is apparent in his writing. It was also in Gingell's seminar that he first became acquainted with the poetry of Native Canadian writers, such as Maria Campbell, Beth Cuthand, and Louise Halfe. The best of contemporary Canadian and Native poetry, both north and south of the 49th parallel, has been and continues to be the most significant literary influence on his craft.

Aside from the literary influences on his writing, if asked, Lundy would probably suggest two even larger influences: his cultural backgrounds and the geography of the landscapes in which he grew up. As for his cultural backgrounds, if we are not aware of the dispossession of Native peoples on this continent at the hands of its settler populations (both historical and contemporary), then that is a shameful ignorance. On the other hand, Lundy, perhaps romantically, likes to think of his paternal family as farm-folk who lived in awareness of a close dependence upon the land and its rhythms, until they were colonised by the pressures and temptations of post-World War II industrialisation in Canada. As for the geography of the landscapes in which he grew up, the primary one would be the edge of the northern boreal forest in north-eastern Saskatchewan, a landscape similar to that his maternal ancestors knew. Lundy grew up near the confluence of the Etamomi, the Fir and the Red Deer rivers just south of Hudson Bay, Saskatchewan. Having inhabited this particular landscape for many years, he has found that this landscape has also come to inhabit him. Hence his poetry is filled with recurrent images: water, stones, birds, animals, the earth, the moon, and the stars. These creatures, these non-human relations who witness our passing and with whom we share the experience of our lives, if we are lucky enough, are also the subject and the dwelling place of Lundy's poems.

About Writing... *As far as I can tell, poetry has something, perhaps everything, to do with paying attention to what is around and within you, whatever that may be, and being honest with yourself about what it is you see and/or hear. I say this with the following caution: neither of these things is as simple or straightforward as they may seem. Beyond this, there is the difficult and lonely labour of sitting down with your attention and honesty and practising the craft: what is the right word? is this image what it should be? where in the hell does the line break? Attention, honesty and craft will, with a great deal of luck, make the poem live.—*
RANDY LUNDY

RODERICK PETER MACINTYRE was the oldest of five children. His mother was Frances Germaine from Burr, Saskatchewan, a first-generation immigrant from St. Petersburg, Russia; his father, Duncan MacIntyre from East Bay, Cape Breton, Nova Scotia, was orphaned just before the Second World War. Stationed at Camp Dundurn during the war, he met Frances and they were wed shortly after. Roderick Peter was born in Saskatoon on February 18, 1947, in St. Paul's Hospital when the population was 46,028 and horses still towed milk wagons, water wagons, and "honey" wagons, and trolley cars ran up and down 20th Street.

MacIntyre went to St. Mary's School on the west side, then to Holy Redeemer College in Edmonton, a juvenate, where, for his first two years of high school, he thought about becoming a priest. He finished high school at St. Paul's High in Saskatoon. After a year of driving truck for a drug company, he attended the University of Saskatchewan for five years, where he obtained an honours degree in English and Sociology in 1970. It was during this time he met and began living with Sharyn Swann.

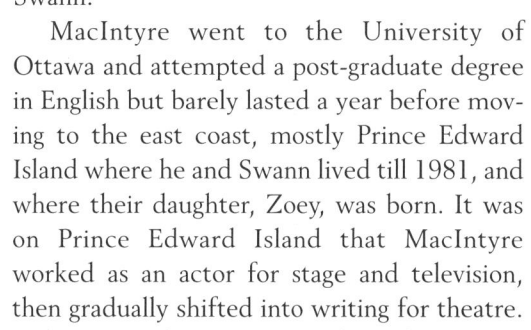

ROD MACINTYRE

MacIntyre went to the University of Ottawa and attempted a post-graduate degree in English but barely lasted a year before moving to the east coast, mostly Prince Edward Island where he and Swann lived till 1981, and where their daughter, Zoey, was born. It was on Prince Edward Island that MacIntyre worked as an actor for stage and television, then gradually shifted into writing for theatre.

During the 1980s and early 1990s, MacIntyre still worked as an actor and playwright in Saskatoon before writing the first of his young adult fictions, *Yuletide Blues* (1991). Since that time, he has published three more books: *The Blue Camaro* (1994), *The Crying Jesus* (1997) and *Revved* (2002), and he has edited two anthologies of young adult fiction: *Up All Night* (2001) and *Takes* (1996). As well, he edited more than fifteen other works of fiction in all genres. MacIntyre received the Vicky Metcalf Award for his short story "The Rink" in 1993, and the inaugural Saskatoon Book Award for *The Crying Jesus* in 1997, among others.

MacIntyre and Swann currently make their home in the resort village of Candle Lake where he remains active as a writer and activist within the provincial and national arts community.

About Writing... *Whoever said that writing is ninety percent perspiration and ten percent inspiration is ninety percent right (write?). It is a process, not an event. It remains as difficult and elusive as in grade three when first asked to write what you did on your summer holidays. The terror of invention, of learning how to dream while you're awake and then going back and reinventing it all again without any knowledge of its worth makes writing a most peculiar activity. It is a dangerous and uncertain place. Beware all ye who enter here.—* ROD MACINTYRE

ELI MANDEL (1992–1992). Elias Wolf Mandel was born on December 3, 1922, in Estevan and died on September 3, 1992, in Toronto. Mandel was the second child and only son of Charles and Eva (Berner) Mandel. He had one sister named Rita. In 1949 Mandel married Miriam Minovitch (they divorced in 1967) and they had two children, Evie and Charles. He married Ann Hardy in 1967 and they had a daughter, Sara.

Mandel is the author of ten volumes of poetry: "Minotaur Poems" in *Trio* (1954), *Fuseli Poems* (1960), *Black and Secret Man* (1964), *An Idiot Joy*, (which won the Governor-General's Award in 1967), *Stony Plain* (1973), *Out of Place* (1977), *Mary Midnight* (1979), *Life Sentence* (1981), and two selected editions: *Crusoe* (1973) and *Dreaming Backwards* (1981). He published two essay collections, *Another Time* (1977) and *The Family Romance* (1986), two full-length critical works, *Criticism: The Silent-Speaking Words* (1967) and *Irving Layton* (1969). Mandel also published articles and reviews on literature, including Canadian literature, literary theory, art, and cultural politics.

He edited *Contexts of Canadian Criticism* (1971) and, with David Taras, *A Passion for Identity* (1987), in addition to numerous anthologies featuring work by Canadian, British, and American poets.

Mandel spent his early years in Estevan, moving to Regina with his family in 1935, where he attended Central Collegiate. After graduation, he worked for a time as a drugstore clerk (his writing is replete with images of sickness, madness, and violence), before joining the Canadian Army. Mandel served overseas with the Canadian Army Medical Corps from December 1943 to the end of the war. Following his return to Saskatchewan in August 1946 (he had spent part of the previous year studying at Khaki College in England), he enrolled at the University of Saskatchewan, where he earned a B.A. in 1949 and an M.A. in 1950. He then began his Ph.D. at the University of Toronto, completing his dissertation on Christopher Smart in 1957. Smart had also been the subject of Mandel's M.A. thesis.

Mandel taught at Collège Militaire Royal de St. Jean from 1953 to 1957. Once his doctorate was completed, he joined the faculty in the department of English at the University of Alberta, in Edmonton, where he remained until 1967. That year he moved to York University in Toronto (he had taught at York in 1963 and 1964).

Mandel became a fellow of the Royal Society of Canada in 1982. His work won various awards in addition to the Governor General's Award: the University of Western Ontario's President's Medal for Poetry (1963), a Centennial Medal (1967), a Silver Jubilee medal (1977), as well as several Canada Council and Ontario Arts Council Awards.

ELI MANDEL

Eli Mandel was widely recognized throughout Canada as a teacher and, later in his career, as a public lecturer, accumulating several writer-in-residence and visiting professor appointments. Mandel served as the Regina Public Library's first writer-in-residence in 1978–79.

JUDY CHAPMAN AND ANDREW STUBBS

DAVE MARGOSHES grew up in the United States, where some of his childhood was spent in New York City, and some in rural New Jersey. His father, an uncle, and his grandfather were journalists but Margoshes had no intention of following in their footsteps until, after university, he found himself working for a newspaper. What he did want to do, from an early age, was write fiction. Even as a young child, he was always making up stories in his head.

Margoshes soon began writing his stories down. Later on in high school he began to write poems but he really always thought of himself as a novelist. He published his first novel, in fact, very recently.

As a journalist, he lived a somewhat itinerant life for several years, working on nine daily newspapers (and some lesser publications) in the United States and in Canada before shucking it for full-time writing of his own in 1986. This shift in focus was coincidental to his move to Saskatchewan, where the fates seemed to be pulling him. Since then, he's been a "literary hustler," publishing a dozen books, and doing whatever it takes to pay the bills: some teaching, some editing, some freelance writing.

Some of Margoshes' stories and poems

spring from his days as a journalist, when he covered everything from politics to murder to cat shows, and during which time he also ghost-wrote a column for actress Jayne Mansfield (a story Bob Currie stole).

Although he went to public schools in New York City, he finished high school in Somerville, New Jersey. He attended Middlebury College in Vermont for two years (where he also attended the Breadloaf Writers Conference along with Samuel Delaney) and distinguished himself by flunking French several times. In self-defence, he followed Huck Finn's advice by hightailing it for the territories, and barely managed to get a B.A. at the University of Iowa, also spending some time at San Francisco State College. Later, he would return to Iowa and its famous Writers Workshop, for an M.F.A., working with Vance Bourjaily, Dick Yates, and Robert Coover, among others.

First, though, he started a career in newspapers at the *San Francisco Chronicle*, where he was a copyboy. Over 20 years, he worked for papers in Chicago, New York City, New Jersey, Iowa, Colorado, and Monterey, California, before moving to Canada in the early 1970s. In Canada, he worked for both newspapers in the city of Calgary where he also taught journalism at Mount Royal College and the Southern Alberta Institute of Technology (SAIT). Twice he was a city editor and he also lived and worked as a journalist in Vancouver.

His latest novel, *Drowning Man*, was published in the spring of 2003. He has also published the novel *I'm Frankie Sterne*, and a novella entitled *We Who Seek: A Love Story*. His other books include the story collections *Fables of Creation, Long Distance Calls, Nine Lives,* and *Small Regrets*. He has three books of poetry, *Walking at Brighton, Northwest Passage,* and *Purity of Absence,* and he is the author of a biography of Tommy Douglas. Margoshes published a resource book about Saskatchewan that is now used in schools across the country and also in the United States.

His stories and poems are published in dozens of magazines and anthologies in Canada and the United States. They have been included five times in *Best Canadian Stories*. His work has been broadcast on CBC and he has given readings across the country. Along the way, he has also won a few awards, including the Stephen Leacock Prize for Poetry in 1996 and the John V. Hicks Award for fiction in 2001.

Margoshes has taught creative writing at the University of Regina and he has led creative writing workshops at various places for various groups (including at Sage Hill). He has participated in the Writers in Electronic Residence program, which links professional writers with high school students, and he was writer-in-residence in Winnipeg in 1995–96. In 2001–02, he filled a similar post at the Frances Morrison Public Library in Saskatoon. He has mentored many younger writers.

Active in the writing community in Saskatchewan and across Canada, Margoshes helped found the writers guild in Alberta, and took part on the board of the

TOMMY DOUGLAS, JUST RIGHT OF... DAVE MARGOSHES

Saskatchewan Writers Guild several times, serving twice as vice president. He has been a member of the Saskatchewan Writers Guild colony committee as well as other guild committees, and he has served on the boards of the Sage Hill Writing Experience and the Moose Jaw Festival of the Word. Margoshes helped to organize the Saskatchewan Book Awards, for which, in fact, he was the original chairman. That effort was formally acknowledged in 2000 when he was presented with the Saskatchewan Writers Guild Volunteer Award. As vice-president of the League of Canadian Poets, Margoshes chairs the national organization's membership committee. He also belongs to the Writers' Union of Canada and the Manitoba Writers' Guild.

About Writing... *I go along with Frost's notion of the poet as a trickster, making use of a bag of tricks. When I'm writing poetry I'm a juggler, a card shark, a tightrope walker. With fiction it's much the same, except that the primary focus is on telling a story. Story is what it's all about.*

As to what poetry is, I subscribe to Emily Dickinson's definition: "If I feel physically as if the top of my head were taken off, I know that is poetry." That's also the true test of great fiction – when I'm writing, I want to knock the reader's head off.

To new writers, young or old, I have this simple advice: Write! Read!—DAVE MARGOSHES

RON MARKEN is a Professor of English at the University of Saskatchewan. He is married and has three daughters, two sons, and nine grandchildren.

In 1960, he earned his B.A. (Honours) in English from Concordia College, Minnesota, going on to complete M.A. and Ph.D. degrees in English from the University of Alberta with studies of Gerard Manley Hopkins' poetry.

Marken has taught at the University of Saskatchewan since 1966 and during his tenure there has been head of the English Department, acting head of the Department of Native Studies, chair of the English graduate programme, and director of the Gwenna Moss Teaching and Learning Centre.

He taught English 110 and Creative Writing in the Prince Albert Penitentiary in the 1970s, an experience that resulted in his editing the convict anthology, *Don't Steal This Book* (1977). In 1987, he helped develop and teach a live television credit course in first-year English; the class is still operating successfully. He has also taught spring and summer courses at the University of Victoria, Brock University, and the Northern Teacher Education Programme in La Ronge, Saskatchewan.

In 1985, Marken was presented with the University of Saskatchewan Master Teacher Award, and in 1987 the Society for Teaching and Learning in Higher Education awarded him the 3M National University Teaching Fellowship. He was given the Paul Harris Award by Rotary International in 1995.

Marken has served on several professional and community boards, including the Executive Committee of the International Association for the Study of Irish Literature, the Canadian Association for Irish Studies, and Persephone Theatre in Saskatoon. As a consultant, he has advised most of the crown corporations on effective communication practices and has served as reviewer and commentator for CBC radio since the early 1970s.

Since joining the University of Saskatchewan faculty, he has conducted research at Oxford, Cambridge, Trinity (Dublin), University College Dublin, University of Ulster, University of Galway, Wuppertal University (Germany), and the

WOULD YOU BUY AN ACATALECTIC TROCHAIC HEXAMETER FROM THIS MAN?
(RON MARKEN)

University of Sydney, Australia.

Marken has published scholarly articles, book chapters, and reviews in academic journals in Canada, Ireland, Northern Ireland, West Germany, and the United States on Contemporary Irish Poetry, Canadian Native Literature, W.B. Yeats, Gerard Manley Hopkins, Thomas Hardy, Henry David Thoreau, Walt Whitman, Frank Lloyd Wright, William Blake, and aesthetics. He has presented conference papers and plenary addresses on Hardy, Yeats, the psychology of literature, and contemporary Irish and Native poetry in Canada, West Germany, Ireland, Northern Ireland, and Australia.

In 1987, Marken co-authored, with Gail Bowen, *1919: The Love Letters of George and Adelaide* (an historical novel). The book was later re-cast and published as a play, *Dancing in Poppies*, and performed at Regina's Globe Theatre, and the Grand Theatre in London, Ontario. Another play, *Flights of Angels*, was produced by 25th Street Theatre, Saskatoon, in 1986. In 1985, he edited a collection of satire, *The Easterners' Guide to Western Canada*. He has two small volumes of poetry: *Dark Honey* (1974) and *Cycles of Youth and Age* (1976).

Three of his radio plays have been produced on CBC radio and he has also published articles about Canadian theatre, Canadian poetry, and theatre photography in *Maclean's*, *Canadian Forum*, *Photo Canada*, *Canadian Theatre Review*, *NeWest Review*, and other journals.

As a teacher—his first love—Marken specializes in Irish literature (particularly poetry), poetics, and freshman English.

About Writing... *As a writer, I'm hardly a craftsman, but I am a workman. I labour part-time to shape a few doors and windows in my walls, giving access to other people and worlds—and even shedding a bit of occasional light.*—RON MARKEN

JENI MAYER was born in Coleville, Saskatchewan, and now lives in Dodsland.

When at twelve years of age she decided to become a writer, she and her friends were interested in witches, ghosts, seances, and graveyards. Later in life, when she began to write mystery novels for children and young adults, it seemed natural to focus on the themes that had fascinated her when she was young. Her mysteries have Canadian settings, another "theme" dear to her heart. She is dedicated to promoting Canada—and Saskatchewan—to Canadian school children. She does so, not only through her writing, but also through school visits and readings across the province and the country.

JENI MAYER... AT A SASKATCHEWAN WRITERS GUILD CONFERENCE.

Mayer has three young adult mysteries published: *The Mystery of the Turtle Lake Monster* (1990), *The Mystery of the Missing Will* (1992), and *Suspicion Island* (1993).

Mayer took several years' hiatus from writing—from 1996 to 2002—to recover from some life difficulties. She also started her own business in 1999. Mayer is the managing editor of *Body Mind Spirit Magazine* at www.saskworld.com/bodymindspirit and she is also the operator of the Holistic Health World website at www.saskworld.com/holistic.

Mayer is still actively involved with the writing community as the director of the Write On Speakers' Bureau. This Speakers' Bureau promotes the workshops and speaking services of over 100 Canadian and American writers and storytellers.

In 2003, Mayer wrote another young adult mystery which is now in the hands of a publisher. She continues to do readings and workshops across Canada.

Mayer received the Manitoba Young Reader's Choice Award for *The Mystery of the Missing Will* (1995).

About Writing... *Writing is cathartic. A healing process begins when ink flows from the tip of the pen. Haunting memories lose their power to hold you captive as they are arranged and rearranged, sculpted and resculpted on the page. Writing gives life to new worlds and softens the places of the past.*—JENI MAYER

JOANN MCCAIG was born on August 6, 1953, in Moose Jaw. She is the author of *The Textbook of the Rose, a tale*, and *Reading In: Alice Munro's Archive*. McCaig was the winner of Calgary Writer's Association Short Fiction Competition in 1995, and the Jack Hodgins Scholarship to Sage Hill that same year. She was also shortlisted for a Canadian Literary Award in the Fiction cateogory in 1998.

McCaig was the fiction co-editor for *VOX* from 1993 to 1996. She received a Bachelor of Arts in 1983 from the University of Victoria. She received an M.A. in 1988 and Ph.D. in 1997 from the University of Calgary.

McCaig teaches literature and composition at the University of Calgary. She is also the mother of three sons: Kevin, Andrew, and Michael.

HEATHER HODGSON

EDWARD ALEXANDER MCCOURT (1907–1972) was born in 1907 in Mullingar, Westmeath, Ireland, and grew up on a homestead near Kitscoty, Alberta. He received a B.A. (Honours) from the University of Alberta and an M.A. from Merton College, Oxford, where he was a Rhodes Scholar. Between 1935 and 1944 he taught at Ridley College, St. Catherines, Ontario; Upper Canada College, Toronto; Queen's University; and the University of New Brunswick.

In 1944 McCourt joined the English Department at the University of Saskatchewan in Saskatoon, where he remained until his death in 1972.

McCourt married Anna Margaret Mackay in 1938, and they had one son named Michael William.

McCourt was the author of several novels, including *Music at the Close* (1947), *Home is the Stranger* (1950), *The Wooden Sword* (1956), *Walk Through the Valley* (1958), and *Fasting Friar* (1963). He also wrote short stories for the CBC and various periodical publications. McCourt also wrote scholarly books, including *The Canadian West in Fiction* which was a pioneering study of the subject (1949;

revised 1970). In 1967 he wrote *Remember Butler*, a biography of William Francis Butler, an Irishman whose journeys across the prairies produced two important books about the region: *The Great Lone Land* (1872) and *The Wild North Land* (1873). McCourt also wrote an introduction to a new edition of the latter book in 1968.

At the time of his death McCourt was working on a biography of Sir William Gregory, the husband of Lady Augusta Gregory, patron of William Butler Yeats.

McCourt produced three books for young adults about the period of the Riel Rebellion of 1885: *The Flaming Hour* (1947), a novel, and *Buckskin Brigadier* (1955) and *Revolt in the West* (1958), both historical accounts.

His travel books were *The Road Across Canada* (1965), *Saskatchewan* (1968), and *The Yukon and Northwest Territories* (1969).

McCourt's papers, including an unpublished autobiography, are to be found in the archives of the University of Saskatchewan.

PAUL DENHAM

JUDY BERLYNE MCCROSKY was born in Aberdeen, Scotland, in 1956. She is married, is the mother of two young adults, and lives with her family in Saskatoon, Saskatchewan. McCrosky has lived in Canada since 1961, and is a Canadian citizen. She writes and teaches creative writing full-time, and while she has written in many genres, her current focus is on literary and speculative fiction.

McCrosky attended university at McGill and Queen's, where she studied psychology, and worked on the psychiatric ward of Kingston General Hospital. She eventually became burned out and, after stints as a classical musician and weaver, she discovered—with a sigh of relief—writing.

McCrosky has published two collections of short stories, *Spin Cycle & Other stories* (1990) and *Blow the Moon Out* (1995), and one romance novel, *Lake of Dreams* (1992). *Blow the Moon Out* was shortlisted in the Best Fiction category at the 1995 Saskatchewan Book Awards and her novel was a finalist in the Best Traditional Romance category of the 1992 RITA Awards.

In addition to her books, McCrosky has had many stories and non-fiction articles published in magazines, anthologies, and textbooks, and her work has also been broadcast on CBC Radio. Her fiction has been translated into French, German, and Italian.

Recently, McCrosky ventured into book editing, through her work as editor of an anthology of speculative fiction and poetry by prairie writers in Canada, the United States, and Australia. This collection, called *Land/Space*, was co-edited with Candas Jane Dorsey, and was published in January 2003.

McCrosky is an experienced teacher and workshop leader. She has taught classes in Creative Writing at the University of Saskatchewan, has taught basic and advanced level courses for several years, and taught regularly at the YWCA. She has also led many writing classes and workshops at schools and libraries, where her students have spanned in age from kindergarten to senior citizens.

McCrosky is active in the writing community—provincially and nationally. She served on the Board of the Saskatchewan Writers Guild for a total of seven years, and two of those

JUDY MCCROSKY

years she served as President. She founded the Saskatoon Romance Writers group, and was co-founder of Critical Mass, a province-wide group of writers of speculative fiction. She also served on the National Council of the Writers Union of Canada, and represented the prairie region. McCrosky is a member of the Saskatchewan Writers Guild, PEN Canada, TWUC, the Science Fiction and Fantasy Writers of America, and Science Fiction Canada.

About Writing... *Writing, for me, is an exploration, a chance to become other people and have experiences different from my own. Everything I write, including futuristic science fiction and fantasy set in other worlds, is an attempt to better understand the wide range encompassed by being human in contemporary society. My writing process is filled with free association, seeking images, emotions, and memories out of my subconscious. I play with them, ask myself questions about them, and wait for the magic 'click' when disparate pieces come together to form a story. The more I write, the more I experience, and the more life experiences I have, the more I have to draw on when I write. I love to write because it helps me to more fully live life. And, I love to teach because I always have something to learn.* —JUDY MCCROSKY

J.S. (JIM) MCLEAN's first poetry collection, *The Secret Life of Railroaders*, was published in 1982. His hilarious railroad poems place him in the great tradition of Saskatchewan literary humorists. He was also one of the editors of the humour collection *100% Cracked Wheat*. His writing has also appeared in a number of anthologies and periodicals.

McLean is also well-known as a wildlife illustrator, chiefly for contributing the artwork to the classic publication, *Wildflowers Across the Prairies*.

Born and raised in Moose Jaw, McLean worked for the Canadian Pacific Railway in that city for twenty-five years. After a period of working with the company in Ontario, McLean retired to Calgary, where he now resides.

NIK BURTON

JAMES MISFELDT was born on June 18, 1946, in Melfort. He is the eldest of six sisters and two brothers, of a teacher mother, Doreen, and ex-WW II RCAF father, Jim, turned civil servant, now retired.

Misfeldt grew up on the wrong side of the tracks of Melfort, an early life of dirt-hot, swimming-hole summers and skate, toe-frozen winters. He grew up on Saturday morning peewee hockey games and movie matinées and Saturday night dances in places like Fairy Glen and Crooked River.

Before starting classes at the University of Saskatchewan in 1964, he spent the summer in northern Saskatchewan where he worked on a fire crew with Cook and Boots and the ex-convict (whose name he now forgets). "I had brought books in my backpack and was given the name Professor." Misfeldt, majoring in English and the visual arts, holds a B.A. from the University of Saskatchewan.

Married young and with three children, Rondy, Renee and Rian, to raise, Misfeldt taught in rural schools, the experience fictionalized in *Pretty Mama Blues*, a novel he is trying to get back to and finish. He left teaching and worked for a number of years as a communications consultant with the provincial Department of Agriculture. He has since left the department to write full-time. He and his wife, artist Betty Tomasunos Sellers, live at Regina Beach.

His novel *the half-finished christ* was

published in 1987. His short stories have appeared in *Grain* and been broadcast on CBC. His short story "Ex-Soldier" was anthologized in *More Saskatchewan Gold* (1984). Misfeldt has also written a collection of short stories, *A Harlequin's Romance*, and he is working on the novel, *why do you believe me when I tell you I love you when you know I've been a liar all my life*.

Misfeldt's short stories, published in *Grain* and in *More Saskatchewan Gold*, are rooted in the minimalism of the prairie landscape. "My characters are still trying to find their place in the landscape."

"I can't keep up with the life stories of everyday people. The old woman who, at fourteen, during the depression, had to leave home to find work. The story of a little brother being taken to the mental hospital because there was no money to go to the doctor to see about a broken nose from playing ball, and how it took years for him to finally get himself out of the institution. A ninety-year-old Ukrainian, in broken English, telling me his story about being conscripted into the Austro-Hungarian Empire army, captured by the Italians, and released from the mountain prisoner-of-war camp, sick with malaria, two years after WWI. The story of an immigrant from Holland who, as a boy, jumped off a moving train to escape having to fight for the Nazis. A Canadian soldier from Melfort, in the muddied trenches on the Holland front, telling his buddy to get down and have a look at the image of a girl back home, and the machine gun bullets ripping into the bank where they had stood. I have the story of my brother, killed in a DNR plane crash, juxtaposed on the front page of the *Star Phoenix* with the story of alleged corruption by a senator."

JAMES MISFELDT... WITH THREE OF HIS THIRTEEN GRANDCHILDREN, KADE, AVA, AND LIAM

Misfeldt's play, *The Arrangement*, was staged by Standing Room Only in 1987 in Regina and later performed at the Edmonton Fringe Festival. His five-part radio play, *Walk the Line*, was broadcast on CBC in the early eighties, and his one-act play, *Chasing the Wind*, was given a stage reading at the 1998 Saskatchewan Playwrights Centre Spring Festival and at the University of Regina's Theatre Department's 2000 Playwrights Reading Series. Misfeldt's play *Saint Jimmy* was selected for the 2001 Spring Festival, and his short play *And Then You Die* was given a stage reading in Globe Theatre's 2001 On the Line. *Birds of Paradise* was staged in the Saskatoon Fringe 2002.

These days, Misfeldt is working on a couple of plays, *The Crabapple Tree* and *One-Eyed Jacks*. He chairs Saskatchewan Stage, a collective from the theatre community, mandated to stage Saskatchewan plays.

About Writing... *On the prairies, you had better have a grip on reality, or freeze to death.*
To write about the prairie, you first have to get down on your knees and dig in the soil underneath the surface.
Prairie people are skeptical of words, they want action. —JAMES MISFELDT

KEN MITCHELL was born on December 13, 1940, in Moose Jaw. He is the eldest in a family of ten children who were raised on the family farm near Moose Jaw. Mitchell graduated from grade twelve at Central Collegiate in Moose Jaw, and then went on to receive both a B.A. with Great Distinction and an M.A. (Saskatchewan, Regina Campus, 1965, 1967). Mitchell has taught in the University of Regina English Department since 1967, though he has also been a visiting professor at the University of Edinburgh, University of Victoria, Nanjing University, China, and the Foreign Affairs College in Beijing, China.

He has published more than twenty books, including the novels *The Heroic Adventures of Donny Coyote* (2003), *Stones of the Dalai Lama* (1993), *The Con Man* (1979), *The Meadowlark Connection* (1974), and *Wandering Raffery* (1972). He has also written short story collections, journalistic articles and documentaries, history, radio dramas and television dramas, as well as much poetry, including *Witches and Idiots* (1990) and *Through the Nan Da Gate* (1986). He edited an anthology for Oxford University Press titled *Horizon: Writings of the Canadian Prairie* (1977), which became a standard reference work of the period.

Perhaps Mitchell is best known for his stage dramas, beginning with the prize-winning one-act play *Heroes*, first produced in 1971. Since then, he has had over a dozen stage plays successfully produced and published, including the acclaimed country opera *Cruel Tears*, written with Humphrey and the Dumptrucks, first seen in 1975. Most of the plays are Saskatchewan-based dramas, such as *The Great Electrical Revolution* (1996); *That'll Be the Day* (1996); *Melody Farm* (1987); *The Plainsman* (1985); *Laffin' Jack Rivers Show* (1983); *Year of the Moose* (1982), co-written with Geoffrey Ursell and Barbara

PHOTO BY HEATHER HODGSON

KEN MITCHELL... IN THE VILLAGE.

Sapergia; *The Shipbuilder* (1978); *Davin the Politician* (1977); and *Wheat City* (1973).

In 1980, Mitchell wrote the screenplay for the film *Hounds of Notre Dame*, which garnered him a Genie nomination (1981). His drama about Norman Bethune, *Gone the Burning Sun*, premiered at the Guelph Spring Festival in 1984, and won the Canadian Authors Association Award that year for Best Canadian play. Mitchell performed as Bethune himself in later productions, and presented the drama across Canada, as well as in Ireland, Scotland, Germany, China, and India.

He has lectured abroad extensively on various aspects of Canadian literature, and was instrumental in the creation of many key arts institutions, including the Saskatchewan Writers Guild (1969), *Grain Magazine* (1973), Saskatchewan Playwrights Centre (1982), Playwrights Union of Canada (1984), and the Cathedral Village Arts Festival (1992). He was honoured for his work as a "literary ambassador" by induction into the Order of Canada in 1999, and into the Saskatchewan Order of Merit in 2001.

About Writing... *I have never felt comfortable offering advice or philosophy on the mysterious process of writing, except to keep on truckin'. I try to avoid analyzing what is essentially an organic and unconscious response to life, for fear of losing it. I see it as nonintellectual activity, and most productive when it is least cerebral.*—KEN MITCHELL

WILLIAM ORMOND MITCHELL (1914–1998). W.O. Mitchell—writer, performer, and teacher—is best remembered for *Who Has*

Seen the Wind and the Jake and the Kid stories which grew out of and defined Saskatchewan prairie.

Mitchell was born on March 13, 1914, in Weyburn. Two events in his early life indelibly marked him and, he claimed, made him a writer. When he was seven his father died, and his memory of this event was the genesis for his first novel, *Who Has Seen the Wind*, a lyrical, episodic work knit together by recurring motifs of birth and death. A deep sense of man's mortality lies behind all of Mitchell's writing although his vision of life is fundamentally optimistic.

The second pivotal event occurred in 1926 when he contracted bovine tuberculosis of the wrist and was withdrawn from school. Forced in upon himself, he often wandered alone on the prairies becoming acutely attuned to the "poetry of earth and sky." Out of this grew his remarkable ability to describe the prairie in all its moods and sensuous particularity. As one of the first Canadian writers to valorize his own region, he paved the way for others to write about their own place and people. The prairie landscape and what he called "the energy of death" are central to his exploration of loneliness, the quest for "how to be," and, most importantly, the bridging of one human to another.

To cure his tubercular wrist, he and his family spent the winters of 1927 to 1931 in California and then St. Petersburg, Florida. However, each summer they returned to Saskatchewan to spend time at their cottage at White Bear Lake. Here he met Sheepskin, the Assiniboine chief of the reserve, and developed a sympathy for native peoples which later led to his concern for the Stonys of the Alberta foothills and inspired his novel *The Vanishing Point* (1973).

From 1931 to 1934 he majored in philosophy at the University of Manitoba. After two years taking courses in journalism and play writing at the University of Washington (Seattle), he landed in Alberta in the middle of the depression. For the next four years he survived by selling magazine subscriptions, encyclopedias, insurance and radio advertisements, even doing a high-dive clown act for a carnival.

In 1940 in Edmonton he met Merna Hirtle whom he married two years later. He completed his B.A. at the University of Alberta and obtained a teaching certificate. With Professor F.M. Salter as his creative writing mentor and Merna as his first editor, he began writing seriously. His first two published short stories in *Maclean's* and *Queen's Quarterly* (1942) showed his talent for both the humourous and the more philosophically serious.

In 1945, after two years as principal in Castor and New Dayton, Mitchell moved to High River, a small town in the foothills of Alberta where he turned to freelancing and completed *Who Has Seen the Wind* (published simultaneously in Canada and the United States in 1947). Reviewed as one of the best Canadian novels ever written, it remains the classic Canadian prairie novel.

From 1948 to 1951 Mitchell lived in Toronto where he was fiction editor of *Maclean's*. Here he began writing the Jake and the Kid radio series for CBC which ran from 1950 to 1956. Drawing on the oral narrative

PHOTO COURTESY ORMOND MITCHELL
W.O. MITCHELL

tradition of the prairies, he produced over two hundred episodes about a hired man, a fatherless boy and his mother who live on a farm near the fictional town of Crocus, Saskatchewan. Mitchell's humorous portrayal of Crocus and its eighty citizens entered the imaginations of Canadians across the country and, at the height of its success, the series was described as a power in the land and Canadian culture in the making. Mitchell adapted the Jake and the Kid stories for a CBC television series (1961), but his most successful television plays were *The Devil's Instrument* (CBC, 1962) and *Back to Beulah* (CBC, 1974) which won the ACTRA award for best script.

Similarly Mitchell exploited his Jake and the Kid material for the stage. His first play was a one-act adaptation of "The Day Jake Made Her Rain" for the drama workshop at Qu'Appelle (1953). *Royalty is Royalty*, premiered by the Greystone Players of Saskatoon in 1959, was his first full-length play. Based on Jake and the Kid stories about the visit of the Queen to Crocus, it was later adapted as the musical, *Wild Rose* (1967). The most popular of his nine plays, *The Black Bonspiel of Wullie MacCrimmon*, was first performed by Regina's Stoneboat Theatre in 1976. His other stage plays include *The Devil's Instrument*, *Back to Beulah* (which won the Chalmers Prize in 1977), and *The Kite*.

Mitchell thought of himself as a teacher as well as a writer and devoted much of his time to working with beginning and developing writers. In his first writing workshop in 1952 at Qu'Appelle for the Sasktatchewan Arts Board, he began teaching his "freefall" process, a spontaneous gathering of sensory and autobiographical fragments which go into the making of stories. He later established the creative writing program at the Banff Centre, which he headed from 1974 to 1986, and from 1968 to 1986 he held five writer-in-residencies at universities across Canada.

In 1968 the Mitchells left High River, where they had raised their three children, to move to Calgary. By this time he had become one of the most publicly recognized authors in Canada, and he was sought after to perform readings from his novels and from his semi-autobiographical tales such as "Melvin Arbuckle's First Course in Shock Therapy" and "Take a Giant Step." These reminiscential pieces became the genesis for the highly successful *How I Spent My Summer Holidays* (1981), a dark sequel to *Who Has Seen the Wind*, in which Mitchell returned to his prairie and Weyburn community roots. These two novels, along with *The Vanishing Point*, established Mitchell as one of Canada's most accomplished novelists. His other published work includes *The Kite* (1962), *Dramatic W.O. Mitchell* (1982), *Since Daisy Creek* (1984), *Ladybug, Ladybug...* (1988), *Roses Are Difficult Here* (1990), *For Art's Sake* (1992), *The Black Bonspiel of Wullie McCrimmon* (1993), and *An Evening With W.O. Mitchell* (1997).

Mitchell was admired and honoured by his home province, receiving his first honourary degree from the University of Saskatchewan (Regina, 1972) and the Lifetime Award for Excellence in the Arts from the Saskatchewan Arts Board (1989). He received eight other honourary degrees, two Stephen Leacock Awards for humour, and was made an officer of the Order of Canada in 1973 and named to the Queen's Privy Council in 1993.

Mitchell died in Calgary on February 25, 1998. He will be remembered as the writer who put the Saskatchewan prairie on the literary map of Canada. But, recalling his Weyburn roots and the words inscribed on his father's gravestone, he expressed a wish that he, too, would be remembered as a caring, honourable man, "Loved by all who knew him."

ORMOND AND BARBARA MITCHELL

REFERENCES: Latham, Sheila and David, ed. 1997. *Magic Lies: The Art of W.O. Mitchell*. Toronto: University of Toronto Press. • Mitchell, Barbara and Ormond. 1999. *W.O.: The Life of W.O. Mitchell, Beginnings to Who Has Seen the Wind*. Toronto: McClelland & Stewart. • Mitchell, W.O. Papers. Ms. 19. University of Calgary Special Collections, Calgary, Alberta.

LYNDA MONAHAN was born in Prince Albert in 1952 where she still resides on an acreage just outside of the city in the pines of the Nesbitt Forest. She lives there with her husband of over thirty years, Don, and their spoiled dog, Max. Her family includes their son, Shawn, daughter-in-law Jill, and three gorgeous grandsons, Joshua, and twins Connor and Kyle of Saskatoon. Monahan and her family spend much of their summers at Waskesui Lake at the family cabin. She has traveled extensively and visited many exotic locales. New Zealand is a special place for her, in particular a little shack set high on a cliff that overlooks the Pacific where she and her husband have spent many idyllic weeks.

Monahan cannot remember a time when she didn't have an interest in writing. It has always been her grand passion. As a child she was always scribbling poems or stories. In high school she worked for the now defunct (not her fault she hopes!) *Prince Albert Weekly News* for which she wrote a series of children's stories and editorials about teenagers.

Monahan first took a creative writing workshop with Mick Burrs (a.k.a. Steven Michael Berzensky) in 1977 in Regina during a brief stay in that city. Around that time she saw publication of her first poem. She later studied English through University of Saskatchewan distance education at S.I.A.S.T. in Prince Albert and creative writing with Lorna Crozier at the University of Saskatchewan in 1990–91. She also attended a Sage Hill Writing Experience Fiction workshop and a few years later, the poetry colloquium led by Patrick Lane. Monahan was the recipient of both a Saskatoon Media Club Scholarship and the John V. Hicks Scholarship to attend Sage Hill. She also attended Emma Lake Kenderdine Campus writer-in-residence program with Glen Sorestad where she finished work on her second manuscript.

In the early 1990s, Monahan began publishing her work in CanLit journals and having her poetry broadcast on CBC radio. Her first collection of poems, *a slow dance in the flames*, was nominated for a 1998 Saskatchewan Book Award in the publishing category. Monahan has worked collaboratively with visual artist Gwen Duda McBride and has given a multimedia exhibition of poetry and paintings at the Grace Campbell Gallery titled *staring straight into the sun*. She has also written from the work of artist Lorraine Beardsworth; they gave a joint show at Lakeland Art Gallery in the summer of 2002. Monahan has had several suites of poems filmed for SCN television's *Story Album*, produced by Donna Caruso. She has written and performed work for *Voices on the Treeline*, a multimedia performance of poetry, song, dance, and photography, and was involved in *Transmissions*, a multimedia event for which she worked with visual artist Karen Cay on an installation piece combining poetry and artwork. Monahan's framed poetry is displayed at Gallery on the Lake at Waskesui and Lakeland Art Gallery at Christopher Lake.

For the past nine years, Monahan has taught creative writing classes at SIAST Woodland Campus in Prince Albert. As well, she has facilitated workshops and classes in creative writing, journaling, and life-story writing for McNally Robinson Booksellers in Saskatoon, the Prince Albert Arts Center, Saskatoon Writers Co-op, Moose Jaw Festival of Words, and various school groups from kindergarten to university level. She has given writing workshops through the Eagle Program and the Prince Albert Youth Outreach Program and recently co-facilitated a photo-journaling workshop for the Youth Activities Center. These writing programs for at-risk kids are of special interest to her.

PHOTO BY DON MONAHAN
LYNDA MONAHAN... LOOKING OUT ON THE SHELL RIVER IN HER YARD SALE WILLOW CHAIR.

She has served on the board of directors for Sage Hill Writing Experience for four years and on the board of directors for the Saskatchewan Writers Guild for a two-year term. Lynda was also on the committee which was instrumental in achieving funding for the John V. Hicks long manuscript awards. As well, she was on the planning committee for the Saskatchewan Writers Guild spring conference "Voices on the Treeline." She is a longtime member of the Saskatchewan Writers Guild, a member of Moose Jaw Festival of Words, Saskatoon Writers Co-op, and a full member of the League of Canadian Poets.

Monahan is a founding member of the poetry group "sans nom" which has been meeting regularly for the past nine years in Prince Albert. She credits the members of "sans nom" for giving her their unfailing encouragement and friendship. Monahan's influences were her teachers and mentors, Lorna Crozier, Patrick Lane, Mick Burrs (a.k.a. Steven Michael Berzensky) and her good friend John V. (Jack) Hicks who shared poems and bad coffee. Her perspective on writing is very much influenced by the work of Canadian poet Alden Nowlan, whose advice was to write about what we feel deepest and hardest. Lynda tries to remember that always in her own writing and she instills much of his advice in her own students of writing.

Monahan's second book, *what my body knows*, was published in the fall of 2003. She is also presently at work on a collection of original lullabies which she has written and performed, entitled *through a sea of stars*, which she hopes to produce as a compact disk in the near future.

About Writing... *Have a staring contest with truth and be the last to blink. Be courageous in your writing and, above all, be honest. Never be afraid to take risks.*—LYNDA MONAHAN

KIM MORRISSEY is a Saskatchewan poet and playwright. Her first book, *Batoche* (1989), was a co-winner of the Saskatchewan Writer's Guild poetry manuscript award, judged by Gwedolyn McEwan and D.G. Jones (co-winners were Patrick Lane and Lorna Crozier) in the summer of 1987. In the autumn of 1987 the cycle placed third in the CBC National Literary Awards (Lorna Crozier's cycle placed first). A poem from the *Batoche* cycle also won an earlier SWG single poem category, judged by bp nichol. Since its publication in 1989, *Batoche* has been used as a Canadian Studies text in Canada, Britain, Germany, Norway, and Denmark, and as a secondary school text. It is now in its fourth printing and had its debut as an opera (by composer William Pura) at the Saskatoon New Music Festival, on April 21, 2001.

Kim's second book, *Poems For Men Who Dream of Lolita* (1992), has also had poems set to music at the New Music Festival and has been taught at university. Five of the poems from the book were selected for *Mythic Women/Real Women* (edited by Lizbeth Goodman). Kim's black comedy about Freud, *Dora: A Case of Hysteria* (1994), was one of the first plays workshopped at the Saskatchewan Playwrights Centre, with director Steven Gregg. It was produced by Steven Gregg at Regina's Wheatland Theatre in 1987. Since then, *Dora* has been produced in Canada, America, Australia, Britain, and Germany and is a suggested text for the Open University in England.

Clever As Paint: The Rossettis In Love (1998) premiered in London, England, and was a theatre choice for *The Guardian*. Kim has written critically-acclaimed documentaries and dramas for both CBC and BBC Radio, and was a commissioned writer on BBC's political satire sketch show *Week Ending* (executive producer, Gareth Edwards), also broadcast on the BBC World Service.

As well as having a radio broadcasting degree from Mount Royal College in Calgary and a B.A. Honours degree in English Literature from the University of Saskatchewan, Morrisey was taught poetry by Eli Mandel and Patrick Lane at the Fort San Summer School of the Arts (1979). She is one of the original members of the Saskatoon Poets Coterie, *circa* 1979 (which included, amongst others, Allan Barr, Susan Andrews Grace, Craig Grant, Bill Klebeck, Lorne Kulak, and Brenda Niskala). She is a founding member (with fellow Coteau writers Roy Morrissey, Rex Deverell, Sharon Butala, Geoffrey Ursell, Barbara Sapergia, Ken Mitchell, Diane Warren, and Connie Gault) of the Saskatchewan Playwrights Centre.

In 1998, Kim took part in the Hypertext Poetry Workshop project, with London (U.K.) poets Cahal Dallat, Jane Draycott, Chris Hedley-Dent, Elizabeth James, Duncan McGibbin, Leona Medlin, Richard Price, and Sudeep Sen. She was one of the writers invited to the official Writers' Opening of the new British Library in 1997, in London, England.

In the late seventies and early eighties, Kim and her husband were a successful writing team, and were amongst the first Saskatchewan playwrights to write for the *Morningside* drama series ("Hammersmith" in 1983 and "Turbine Time" in 1987). She also wrote dramas for radio on her own, including "Peter Gzowski, Peter Gzowski" (a two hander, for Anne Wright and Peter Gzowski) and *The Soul of A Poet* (a retelling of the Sarah Binks story, with the novel's original "Sarah Binks" poems put to music by Sheldon Corbett). Although her cycle of poems, *Batoche*, took her eight years to research, mostly from her farm near Batoche, since the death of her husband Roy (L.J. Morrissey) in 1987, Kim has spent most of her time in England. In addition to writing her own work, she has taught creative writing, served as writer-in-residence in Saskatchewan schools (Grades K-12), taught play analysis at Rose Bruford College for Drama in London, England, and has been a regular guest lecturer at the Open University's Summer School in York, England. Her latest feminist play, *Mrs. Ruskin*, rehearsed in August 2003, premiered in London in September 2003.

KIM MORRISSEY

About Writing... *Patrick Lane taught me two things: ambiguous line breaks. Thanks Pat.*—KIM MORRISSEY

HELEN SENECAL MOURRE was born in the farming community of Rosetown on March 14, 1949. She arrived ten minutes sooner than her fraternal twin sister. Her parents were Marion Olson and Albert Senecal, whose father immigrated to Saskatchewan from Quebec in the early 1900s and took out a homestead.

Mourre received a classical education from the nuns at St. Joseph's Convent in Rosetown, choosing to study Latin instead of typing. She then attended the University of Saskatchewan, beginning an English degree. In 1969 she married Paul Mourre of Sovereign, Saskatchewan, where they continue to farm today.

In the latter part of the 1980s Mourre resumed her studies at the University of Saskatchewan, finishing up her English degree in 1991. During this time period, Mourre took a class in Western Canadian Literature from David Carpenter and was blown away by the writing that had been going on around her. She studied authors like Sinclair Ross, Margaret Laurence, Wallace Stegner, Robert Kroetsch, and the emerging Guy Vanderhaeghe. All of them were writing about this place.

About this time Lorna Crozier began teaching a creative writing class at the University of Saskatchewan. Mourre had joined the Rosetown writers group by then and had had a few poems published. She applied to Crozier's class and was lucky enough to get in. Under Crozier's skillful and compassionate mentoring, Mourre was able to find her voice. Another creative writing class taken from David Carpenter at the University of Saskatchewan moved her further along on the path to becoming a writer.

Mourre's first big breakthrough was a story broadcast on CBC radio in 1993. The Sage Hill Writing Experience was also a great influence on Mourre's writing. She took classes from Judith Krause, Dave Margoshes, Ven Begamudre and Bonnie Burnard. Mourre began publishing short stories in such magazines as *Grain*, *Western People*, and the *NeWest Review*. In 1996, she won a Saskatchewan Writers' Guild award for the short story, "No Turning Back."

In 1997, Mourre had her first collection of short stories, *Landlocked*, published. As the title suggests, the stories have a strong sense of place. *Landlocked* was a finalist for the First Book Award at the Saskatchewan Book awards in 1998. The book has also been listed on the grade twelve English bibliography for Saskatchewan Education.

A new collection of Mourre's stories entitled *What's Come Over Her* is forthcoming in the fall of 2003. As well as writing and farming, Mourre worked for several years in the area of special education and has taught creative writing courses at Prairie West Community College. She has served on the boards of both the Saskatchewan Writers' Guild and the Sage Hill Writing Experience. She is currently a member of the University of Saskatchewan Senate.

About Writing... *Writing is a compassionate act whereby the writer must completely enter the worlds of the characters.*—HELEN MOURRE

FARLEY MOWAT was born in Belleville, Ontario, on May 12, 1921. He is the son of Angus McGill and Helen (Thomson) Mowat. Mowat has written over thirty books in the genres of autobiography, non-fiction, and novels for juveniles. His work has been published in over 40 countries.

Mowat spent his childhood in Ontario before his family moved to Saskatoon in 1933. There, he wrote a birdwatching column for the *Star-Phoenix*. While completing his degree at the University of Toronto, he moved to the Arctic and spent two years there working as a field biologist.

After he graduated, he became a freelance writer. His first book, *People of the Deer* (1952), is about the Inuit. The north and its people have remained sources for Mowat's writing.

Farley Mowat's books include, *People of the Deer* (1952); *Lost in the Barrens* (1956), winner of the Governor General's Award; *The Dog Who Wouldn't Be* (1957); *Ordeal by Ice* (1960); *The Regiment* (1961); *Never Cry Wolf* (1963); *The Polar Passion* (1967); *Canada North* (1967); *This Rock Within the Sea* (1968); *The Boat Who Wouldn't Float* (1969), winner of the Leacock Medal for humour; *A Whale for the Killing* (1972); *Tundra* (1973); *Canada North Now: The Great Betrayal* (1976); *And No Birds Sang* (1979); *My Discovery of America* (1985); *Virunga: The Passion of Dian Fossey* (1987); and *The Farfarers* (1998).

HEATHER HODGSON

JOHN NEWLOVE (1938–2003) was born in Regina on June 13, 1938, and was raised in Kamsack and various other small towns throughout Saskatchewan. Newlove took classes at the University of Saskatchewan in Saskatoon. After that, he embarked on a cross-country tour of Canada.

Before that, Newlove had worked briefly as a high school teacher in Birtle, Manitoba, and he also worked as a social worker in Yorkton. In addition to teaching and being a social worker, he took other jobs that included working for radio stations in Weyburn and Regina, and working as a labourer in British Columbia and Saskatchewan.

Between 1970 and 1974 Newlove was the editor at McClelland and Stewart in Toronto. He also served as writer-in-residence at various universities, including Loyola College in Montreal, Quebec, and at the University of Toronto in Ontario. In 1979–80, he served as the Regina Public Library's second writer-in-residence (Eli Mandel was the first). Newlove taught for a year at David Thompson University Centre in British Columbia in 1982. After 1986 he was employed as a federal public servant in Ottawa, Ontario.

Newlove's *Lies* won the Governor General's award for poetry in 1972. He also won the Saskatchewan Writers' Guild Founders Award in 1984, and the Literary Press Group Award in 1986. His poetry has been published in journals, magazines and literary anthologies in both Canada and the United States as well as in several countries abroad.

In the 1960s and 1970s he and Eli Mandel, were thought to be among the dominant voices of Canadian prairie poetry.

Newlove's books include: *Apology for Absence: Selected Poems 1962–1992* (1993), *Poems* (1993), *The night the dog smiled* (1986), *Three poems* (1985), *The green plain* (1981), *The fat man: selected poems, 1962–1972* (1977), *Lies* (1972), *7 disasters, 3 theses, and welcome home: click* (1971), *The cave* (1970), *3 poems* (1968), *Black night window* (1968), *What they say* (1967; reprinted 1968) *Burn* (1967), *Notebook pages* (1966), *Moving in alone* (1965 and 1977), *Elephants, mothers & others* (1963), *Grave sirs; poems.* (1962).

Newlove also edited various publications including *Canadian poetry: the modern era* (1977), and Joe Rosenblatt's *Dream craters* (1974).

John Newlove died December 23, 2003, in Ottawa.

HEATHER HODGSON

BRENDA NISKALA is a poet and fiction writer and she is currently the Executive Director for the Saskatchewan Publishers Group. She's been employed as a crisis counsellor, bush plane lawyer, writer-in-residence, and a branch representative for the Alliance of Canadian Film, Television and Radio Artists (ACTRA). Since 1998 Brenda has been the mentor for the Survivors Writers Group, a street-oriented group which began as a writing class for sex-trade workers, and evolved into a large and diverse collective of self-proclaimed survivors, of very potent writers who are doing much more than surviving. Hagpapers (an imprint of Underwhich) published *Emma's Horizon*, Niskala's chapbook, in 2000. In 1998 Brenda toured across Canada, from Fredericton to Nanaimo, with four other poets—Joe Blades from Frederiction, rob mclennan from Ottawa, Anne Burke from Calgary, and Dennis Reid from Victoria—and their co-authored collection, *Open 24 Hours* (1997). The tour resulted in a radio documentary about the trip, and another about Niskala and her writing life, both by Robert McTavish, for CBC radio.

Her book of poetry, *Ambergris Moon*, came out in 1983. A chronic underachiever, a painstaking perfectionist or a perfect procrastinator, Niskala has other full-length manuscripts (poetry and fiction) which have been heard and read by more people than usually buy a book of poetry. She will be sending them out to publishers someday, but she is drawn more to the building of the literary community and the raising of her children, Nathan and Aidan. Niskala's home is often the refuge of itinerant writers, including Kim Morrissey, Tim Lander, Wilma Riley, Joe Blades, Lala Heine Koehn, rob mclennan, Tekyla Friday, and Craig Grant. Niskala also frequently harbours people from the north who are making the transition to the city. She was foster-mom to Harlan Obey, son of the recently deceased Marlyn Obey, poet and member of the Survivors writers group.

In 2003 Niskala was selected by the League of Canadian Poets to attend the Lahti International Writers Reunion in Lahti, Finland, and invited to read at the Wayzegoose Festival in Nelson, British Columbia. Niskala's poetry was the *Arc* Poem of the Year Editor's Choice for 2000, and won a Sterling Award for Poetry 1999, and a Saskatchewan Writers Guild Literary Award 1991. Her manuscripts were shortlisted for the CBC/Saturday Night Awards for poetry in 1998 and 2002.

Niskala's work has been featured on CBC every three years or so, and she's been published in several anthologies including *Siolence, Lodestone, Sky High, Dancing Visions, Heading Out, Bridges4, What is Already Known*, and in numerous magazines.

She has served on the editorial boards of *Grain, Briarpatch*, and *NeWest Review* magazines, as well as Coteau Books, the executive of the League of Canadian Poets and the Saskatchewan Writers Guild. Niskala represented writers on the Canadian Reprography Collective (CanCopy/Access), the Minister's Advisory Committee for the Status of the Artist in Saskatchewan, the Film/Video Professional Development Co-ordinating Committee and the Regina Arts Commission. Niskala has been a juror for the Quebec

Writers Federation and Alberta Book Awards, the National Chapbook Competition, and the Lowther Award, among others. She has judged poetry slams, including the famous Cathedral Village Arts Festival Free House Slam. She taught Creative Writing for the University of Regina Extension Department, the Saskatchewan Writers Guild, the Moose Jaw Festival of Words, and Sage Hill Writing Experience, and she has presented hundreds of readings and workshops in schools and libraries throughout the last twenty-five years.

PHOTO BY SHELLEY SOPHER

BRENDA NISKALA... ST. MICHAEL'S / ARTHUR'S MOUNT, MAY 1996.

The Writing Program at Fort San in the late seventies and early eighties opened the door to a vibrant and welcoming writing community province-wide. The weeks spent at the Fort remain Niskala's most profound writerly experiences. Writers groups have kept Niskala enthralled with the literary scene. In the late 1970s she was part of the group of writers meeting regularly at poet Anne Szumigalski's home in Saskatoon—Caroline and Terrence Heath, Shanoo Padmanahb, Lala Heine Koehn, Allan Barr, Mark Abley, Nancy Senior, and Elise Yeats St. George, among others. Szumigalski soon insisted Niskala start her own group, and the Poets Coterie was formed. This group had chemistry! Bill Klebeck, Allan Barr, Lorne Kulak, Craig Grant, Kim Morrissey, Charlie Taylor, Susan Andrews Grace and others produced a chapbook, *Blue Streak in Dry Year*, with cover by visual artist Gary Young, Niskala's husband at the time. Niskala's second former husband, Kenneth Carriere, became involved in the book world too, ultimately writing *The Bulrush Helps the Pond* (2002) in English and Swampy Cree. Friendships from writers' groups have outlasted two marriages, and spawned such writerly adventures as the great Cornish eclipse escapade of 1999. The solar eclipse hid behind clouds, but Saskatchewan writers read in the stone and earthen theatre on the most westerly tip of Cornwall, and Ken Kesey regaled them as he sat on the front bumper of The Bus. Niskala's partner from the Cotswolds, Mick Beard, writes but does not declare himself a writer—yet.

Having participated in writers' groups in La Ronge, North Battleford, and Prince Albert, Niskala currently meets regularly with the Survivors (Marianna Feschke, Tina Hannah Munns, Dennis Acoose, Jackie Lay, Margaret and Jim Foley, Simon Ash, Preston L'acaine, Corrine Herne and others), the Erratics (Karlene Gibson, Bernadette Wagner, Marie Mendenhall, Alison Lohans, and others), and Three Babes with Dave and Currie (Pat Krause, Byrna Barclay, Dave Margoshes, and Bob Currie). The support, friendship, and inspiration offered through these groups form a core component of who Niskala is: her community. This connection has lasted through weddings and funerals, through childbirth and empty nests, from Pat Krause's wacky cards with words of wisdom, to Mick Burrs stopping by to ask, as he does regularly, if the poetry has been sent out yet, to Anne Szumigalski literally twisting Niskala's scarf around her neck and saying, "Niskala, if you don't send that manuscript out, I'm going to kill you."

Always a Saskatchewan resident, Niskala has lived in Regina, Saskatoon, La Ronge, Prince Albert, North Battleford, Davidson, and Moose Jaw. She was raised on a farm in the Big Valley-Rock Point area of Saskatchewan, which is a Finnish-Canadian community a mile or two down the road from the homestead of the shipbuilder Tom Sukanen.

About Writing... *The often astonishing process of expressing oneself, of tapping into the words you didn't even know were there, is the first step. Sharing it is the second. In the process of sharing, the writer is enriching the collective intelligence, contributing to the vitality of human thought, and entering into a relationship which inspires. Audience count doesn't matter. Interaction does. If you have moved one person with your words, your job here is done. It feels good so keep on doing it.*
Hanging out with writers keeps you young. Join a group. Recognize it as a community. By celebrating other writers, you are celebrating yourself. —BRENDA NISKALA

ROSEMARY NIXON was born Rosemary Deckert in 1952, the baby in a family of seven children—two older brothers and four big sisters, the last four all of whom were supposed to be boys. So one can only imagine the delight Rosemary's arrival must have brought. Her mother was of Swiss Pennsylvania Dutch heritage and her father of Polish German stock from Yorkton. He came to the little village of Guernsey, Saskatchewan, with "five borrowed dollars in his pocket," and worked as a hired man for seven years until he saved the money to buy his own farm and marry Rosemary's mom, for whom he had to wait to grow up.

Nixon spent her own growing-up years climbing plum trees in the back yard, playing Scrub and "Anti-I-Over" with her sisters, having sleepovers in the barn loft with her friends, and generally doing no work whatsoever. All she ever dreamed of was being a teacher, and various family photos of a spindly-legged Rosemary teaching her dolls strewn about the lawn attest to the fact. She left home at seventeen to attend first-year university at the University of Waterloo, Ontario, spent a second year at the University of Alberta, and her third and fourth years at the University of Calgary. She managed to graduate with an education degree in 1974, despite having chased about the country after various boyfriends and having endured jobs ranging from chambermaid in Jasper, Alberta, to working at K-Mart, to an Opportunities For Youth job that involved puppets and considerable humiliation.

Nixon taught Junior High in Calgary for four years before setting off on an adventure to Europe and Africa. She spent one year in Belgium and France perfecting (well, okay, getting passable in) French, and then two years teaching in a little village on the equator in Zaire which is now the Democratic Republic of Congo. The experience was wonderful and terrible and fodder for her second book, though not yet being a writer, she didn't know this at the time. She returned in 1981 and taught for four more years before catching the writing bug.

In 1988 Nixon had a conversion of sorts (not religious, she'd already been saved seven times, evangelical meetings being the social event of the year in the '60s in Guernsey, Saskatchewan) which, without warning, tossed her into courses at the University of Calgary. Nixon studied under Aritha van Herk for two years, then later, for short stints, under Robert Kroetsch in Red Deer, Paulette Jiles at Strawberry Creek, and Jane Urquhart at Sage Hill, where she later returned to teach herself for three years, pairing up with Bill

Robertson, reconnecting with her roots, and making fast friends with fellow Saskatchewanites, as well as writers from across Canada, the United States, and even Europe. She later returned to Saskatchewan for a memorable two weeks at Emma Lake, again developing lifelong friendships that have greatly enriched her life.

Nixon's first book of fiction, *Mostly Country*, came out in 1991. *Mostly Country* was shortlisted for the Howard O'Hagen Short Fiction Book of the Year Award. Her second book of fiction, *The Cock's Egg*, published in 1994, won the Howard O'Hagan Short Fiction Book of the Year Award. *The Cock's Egg* takes place in Africa and explores the complexities of characters trying to find a foothold on the shaky geography of foreign soil. Nixon was honoured, as well, when in 1994 she won *Grain's* Postcard Fiction contest, and has harboured fond feelings for its judge, David Carpenter, ever since (only now made public). Nixon's work has also appeared in numerous anthologies across the country.

Nixon has served on various Writers Guild of Alberta committees, as well as acting as a member of the board for two years. She has judged Writers Guild of Alberta book competitions, the Grant McKewan Alberta Book of the Year Competition, and a variety of other short fiction competitions, both in Alberta and Saskatchewan. She has spent the last fifteen years teaching Creative Writing at the University of Calgary, Extension Program, and at Chinook College, and also teaches numerous private classes for students who have progressed beyond. She continues to be delighted at the talent roiling under Chinook winds. Rosemary spends her days as a consultant for the Calgary Board of Education, teaching teachers how to teach writing creatively. All in all, she has generally done a lot of not writing during these years (not counting the many letters that have crisscrossed Canada to and from her writing friends). She has, nonetheless, finally finished her third work of fiction, a novel, *Half Way Round The Sun*, which is presently out on spec.

ROSEMARY NIXON... POSING IN HER UNTIDY HOUSE IN LIEU OF CLEANING IT UP.

About Writing... *A story is like a child. To manipulate a story is to fail it and yourself. Allow it its own telling. But as you rewrite, focus on its underlying structure: sculpt the shape and rhythm of its sentences until the spirit of the work emerges. And don't stop the editing process one moment too soon.*—ROSEMARY NIXON

SUZANNE NORTH was born and raised in Calgary, Alberta, and now lives in Saskatoon with her husband Donald Buckles, an arachnologist.

Before turning to writing mystery novels, she wrote for CBC television and various magazines, and worked as a bibliographic searcher, a television announcer, a waitress, and a professional horse player.

North is the creator of the Phoebe Fairfax mystery series. In 1995, *Healthy, Wealthy & Dead* (1994) was nominated for an Arthur Ellis Award for best first novel. Other novels in the series are: *Seeing is Deceiving* (1996) and *Bones to Pick* (2002).

HEATHER HODGSON

S. PADMANAB was born in Bangalore, India, in 1938. He studied medicine in India, the United Kingdom, and Canada. Padmanab worked as the Director of Laboratories at St. Paul's Hospital in Saskatoon, and was also on the staff of the Saskatoon Cancer Clinic. Padmanab lived in Saskatoon with his family until his death in 2004.

He served on the Executive of the Saskatchewan Writers Guild and was an associate editor of *Grain Magazine*. He is a member of the League of Canadian Poets and the Saskatoon Poetry Group. His poems have appeared in *CVII*, *Grain*, *Writers News Manitoba*, and in a number of anthologies.

Padmanab's book publications include *Ages of Birds* (1976), *A Separate Life* (1974), and *Songs of the Slave* (1977).

NIK BURTON

KAY PARLEY was raised on a farm in a Scots Pioneer community near Wolseley. She spent her life pursuing various careers from commercial artist to country schoolteacher to secretary. In 1948, she graduated from the prestigious Lorne Greene's Academy of Radio Arts in Toronto. She was set on becoming an actress but learned at the Academy that she not only loved the dramatic arts, but also was intrigued by the writing, which sparked her creative muse.

When Parley returned to Regina, she enrolled in business school and was subsequently hired as a secretary. For three years she worked as a writer for the Saskatchewan Arts Board and then spent eight years working in Regina Little Theatre.

KAY PARLEY

At the age of thirty-five, Parley decided she wanted to be a psychiatric nurse, so in 1956 she enrolled and trained at the infamous Weyburn Souris Valley Centre. At that time the hospital was in the midst of changing the approach towards the treatment for mental illness and health patients. During her training and work period, group therapy was introduced, and the term "psychedelic" was coined at Weyburn. By 1958 Parley was a full-time employee at Weyburn, actively participating in the transformation of the mental health system. She was still writing.

After a few years of working as a psychiatric nurse, Parley acquired an interest in teaching and developing training courses for psychiatric nurses. While working at University Hospital in Saskatoon she completed a B.A. Honours in Sociology and a Bachelor of Education. For the next eighteen years Parley taught social sciences at the Kelsey Institute of Applied Arts and Sciences in Saskatoon.

In 1987 Parley retired and also published her book *The Monkey Vault* (1987). Throughout this time she had been writing for several church and farm papers, nursing magazines, and had been published in periodicals such as *Epic*, *Folklore*, *Western People*, and *Western Producer*. Since 1964 Parley has also published *They Cast a Long Shadow: The Story of Moffat* (1964, 1994), *The Grass People* (1980), and *The Scots Line* (1992).

Her writing interests relate to family, local history, old fieldstone buildings, the Scots culture, and community. Her portfolio demonstrates her interest in biographies, creative non-fiction, long fiction, and non-fiction.

Parley now lives in Saskatoon, where she continues to write and never ceases to paint.

She celebrated her eightieth birthday in 2003 and continues to maintain her own home and lead an active life.

MICHELE SEREDA

About Writing... *Don't ever park your sense of humour on the shelf. Don't ever write just for money. Avoid fads. Love the sound of words and rhythm. Trust your subconscious.*—KAY PARLEY

LIA PAS was born in Saskatoon on the Winter Solstice of 1971. She grew up in Saskatoon, combining music, movement, and text at a young age. She started studying ballet at the age of three, piano at the age of seven, flute at the age of nine, and oboe at the age of ten. She has a copy of the first poem she wrote at age seven.

While she was a child, her Aunt Ellie met and subsequently married poet bp nichol. Pas' relationship with bp became a mentorship when she was about 14. She would share poems with him and he would critique them late into the night. In 1988, bp died, but Pas kept on with her writing. Her first published poem, "skin" was about bp's death, and was published in *WindScript* magazine.

In grade nine, Pas had entered into a correspondence course through the Saskatchewan Writer's Guild with Brenda Macdonald Riches. She met Riches face to face a few years later at Fort San while Pas was studying oboe and Riches was teaching Creative Writing. Once she was old enough, Pas went to Fort San to study poetry with Steve Scriver and then with Judy Krause.

After high school, Pas took a year off and applied for various universities. She was offered a chance at a full scholarship for the classical music program at Queen's but declined as her heart was set on studying at York, where bp had taught Creative Writing and collaborated with music professors David Mott and Casey Sokol.

At York, Pas switched from pure classical music to more edgy forms. She studied improvisation on oboe, voice, and piano with Casey Sokol, who introduced her to Meredith Monk's extended vocal and movement work (which was later to become a major influence in Lia's theatre pieces). She studied composition with James Tenney (who had worked closely with John Cage and Philip Glass) and with David Mott, who encouraged a more meditative and multi-disciplinary approach to composition. She studied Karnatak (South Indian) music with mrdangam master Trichy Sankaran and was his first voice student at York. She also began studying voice with Richard Armstrong of the Roy Hart Theatre.

PHOTO BY MARIE BROWN
LIA PAS

Pas was a musician in the York University Dance Ensemble, performing text/rhythm/movement pieces with eight dancers and four other musicians. She also sat on the board of *Existere*, York University's literary magazine. At this time she began volunteering at *Musicworks Magazine*, and after leaving Toronto, continued writing reviews for the magazine, and eventually becoming an editorial advisor.

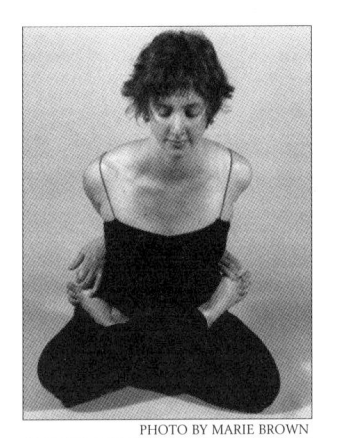

Once her degree was finished, she moved back to Saskatoon with her husband, artist and graphic designer Ed Pas (they married in 1992). Soon after renovating their first home, she became pregnant. Jarrod Griffin was born in November 1995.

Earlier in 1995, Pas had studied Creative Writing at the University of Saskatchewan with Maria Campbell, who encouraged her to apply for a grant to attend Sage Hill. Pas attended the Sage Hill Poetry Workshop with Di Brandt and received a Saskatchewan Arts Board grant later that year to work on a manuscript of poetry. In January 1996, she began work on what would become *what is this place we have come to*.

Once Pas moved back to Saskatoon, she began performing with DUCT, Saskatoon's premier improvisational ensemble founded by Steven Ross Smith. Pas also began to perform her own musical work and eventually became a part of the Saskatoon Composer's Performance Society, through which she was able to have a number of compositions performed by both the Saskatoon and Regina Symphony musicians.

In 1997, becoming disillusioned with the prospect of making a living as a music teacher, Pas began to train as a yoga instructor. She quickly became adept at it, having studied so much dance while younger, and has been an in-demand teacher, integrating Sanskrit chants and philosophy into her classes.

In 1999 Pas formed the group Mundi to perform her more text-based compositions, and enjoyed moderate success. But mere months after forming the group, it dissolved, so Pas put her energy to other creative endeavours.

In 2000, she hooked up with dancer Paulette Bibeau and director Beata Van Berkom and together they created a multi-disciplinary piece titled and based on the Sumerian myth *The Descent of Inanna*. This piece enjoyed great success in Saskatoon.

In the winter of 2000, Steven Ross Smith approached Pas about publishing a chapbook with Underwhich Editions; *vicissitudes*, parts of which had been broadcast on CBC Saskatchewan's Gallery program, became that chapbook. The book deals with conception, pregnancy, and birth as a spiritual process rather than a purely physical one.

After the success of *The Descent of Inanna* Pas, Bibeau and Van Berkom planned another show based on the Russian folktale "Vasalia the Wise." However, creative differences arose and Pas ended up writing and performing the multi-disciplinary piece *Baba Yaga's Hut* herself. This work enjoyed great success as well.

Pas attended the 2001 Sage Hill Fall Poetry Colloquium with Erin Mouré where she began work on *Gray's Tala*, a book incorporating found text and images from *Gray's Anatomy* combined with yoga philosophy.

Gray's Tala was put on hold when *what is this place we have come to* was accepted for publication, and around the same time there was interest from other potential publishers in *From the Book of The Pythia*, poems about the life of an oracular priestess in ancient Greece. *What is this place we have come to* will be published in 2003, as part of the New Leaf Series.

Currently, Pas and her family are moving to Japan. The couple will be teaching English on the JET Programme and experiencing the culture of Japan. Pas hopes to study shakuhachi, tea ceremony, and Japanese calligraphy and she also plans to continue her creative work in writing, music, and movement while she is there.

About Writing...
Your physical body is as important as the mental body you put down on paper. You will learn things about your work from your body: If you're writing about food and you get hungry, or writing about running and you get sweaty, you're on the right track. Read your work out loud while editing. The

way the work sounds will affect the way it looks on the page and often it is the differences in tonality that will let you push the edges of the look of the work.—LIA PAS

ELIZABETH PHILIPS was born in Winnipeg, Manitoba, in 1962. She grew up in Gimli, Manitoba, on the shore of Lake Winnipeg. In 1980, she moved to Saskatoon, where she now lives with her partner, visual artist Doris Wall Larson.

Philips began writing poetry at the age of 16, as the result of an in-class assignment by her English teacher. She knew very quickly that she wanted to be a writer, and has been writing poetry ever since.

Philips began her education as a writer with workshops at the Saskatchewan Summer School of the Arts in Fort San, Saskatchewan, in 1979, at the age of 17, when she took a two-week intensive workshop, Introduction to Poetry and Fiction, taught by Lorna Crozier and Lois Simmie. She returned to the Summer School in the beautiful Qu'Appelle Valley to take further workshops in succeeding years with Patrick Lane, Anne Szumigalski, and Paulette Jiles.

Philips has a B.A. (Honours) in English from the University of Saskatchewan (1985). She won a Hannon Travel Scholarship upon completion of her degree, allowing her to travel in Europe for four months, from October 1985 to February 1986.

She is the author of four books of poetry. Her first book, a chapbook, *Breaking Through Ice* (1982), was published when she was 20. All the poems in the chapbook were written between the ages of 17 and 18. Her first full-length collection, *Time in a Green Country* (1990), was written after she completed her English degree. The manuscript was edited with the help of Anne Szumigalski.

Her second poetry collection, *Beyond My Keeping* (1995), followed five years later. This collection won the first-ever Poetry Book Award at the Saskatchewan Book Awards. This collection includes poems about the poet's nurturing relationship with the natural world, though in its domesticated form, through fish-keeping and gardening. It also contains elegiac pieces, such as the last poem in the collection, "The Path of the Deer." This collection was edited by Patrick Lane.

A Blue with Blood in it (2000), her third and most recent collection, received the Poetry Award for 2000 from the Saskatchewan Book Awards. This collection, edited with the assistance of Don McKay, includes more narrative pieces, a few poems on gardening, complemented by pieces about the wild. This collection is concerned with that juncture, the line between domestic and wild nature. Many of the poems are interconnected in terms of narrative and theme.

Philips' poems have appeared in Canadian literary magazines such as *Malahat Review, Event, Arc, Prism International, Prairie Fire,* and *Grain*; as well, she's published poems in *The River King Poetry Supplement* and *Manoa* in the United States, and *Poetry Wales* in the U.K. As well, she has worked as a freelance editor and journalist, and her non-fiction has been published in many magazines, including *Western Living, WestWorld,* and *Equinox,* and in the anthology, *Fresh Tracks: Writing the Western Landscape* (1998). Her journalistic production, never a central focus, has all but ceased in the last two years.

Philips was the editor of the literary magazine *Grain* from December 1998 to July 2003. She has taught creative writing in many different programs, through Saskatchewan's Sage Hill Writing Experience, the Banff Wired Studio program at the Banff Centre for the

Arts in fall 2001 and fall 2003, and at the Metchosin International Summer School for the Arts in July 2002.

Philips has also developed skills as an editor of poetry manuscripts. She has edited a number of poetry collections to date, and is a member of the collective that runs Brick Books, one of the few Canadian publishers devoted exclusively to poetry.

Her poems deal with a wide variety of themes: nature, wilderness, gardens, sexuality, love, childhood, birth, and death. She has been influenced by her teachers—Lorna Crozier and Patrick Lane, in particular—and by her wide reading in Canadian and American poetry. Some of her more recent influences are Robert Hass, Jorie Graham, James Galvin, Jan Zwicky, and Don McKay. Her work has also been influenced by the Saskatchewan landscape, in its wild and domestic forms.

Her present project is another poetry collection, as yet untitled, including poems on youth, maturity, and death. She is exploring, for the first time, her childhood—some of the poems deal with gender roles, with issues of power and powerlessness, with illness and self-invention. She is also exploring the "long poem." This tendency toward narrative may, or may not, eventually lead her to write fiction. This is a possibility she would like to explore after the completion of her present project.

Philips loves living in a province that is underpopulated, where human constructs do not always dominate the landscape; where it is possible to drive for two or three hours and be in wilderness. Saskatchewan is an ideal place to live considering her interest in the natural

PHOTO BY DORIS LARSON
ELIZABETH PHILIPS... WITH HER MENTOR, JAZ.

world. The province is also very supportive of its writers and artists, and is a more affordable place to live than the traditional cultural centers, making it more practicable to live and work as an artist.

For Philips, the decision to live a life steeped in language—to partake in a lifelong devotion to poetics—was not so much a choice as a necessity. She believes that the difficulties involved in condensing ideas and experience into the idiosyncratic, intense, and intensely particular speech that is poetry enables her to define, if only intermittently, a coherent path toward personal and professional clarity.

About Writing... *Read as much contemporary poetry as you can; poetry is, above all, a specialized language in which it is possible to gain fluency. Be open to criticism, but balance that openness with a commitment to your own vision. Develop disciplined work habits—work even when you don't feel like it in an effort to keep the portal to the poetic imagination open.*—ELIZABETH PHILIPS

THELMA POIRIER was born at the home of a Red Cross nurse in southern Saskatchewan. Her parents, Leonard and Aquina Anderson, were pioneer ranchers on Rock Creek. She grew up in a home filled with siblings, music, faith, and concern. Her family has informed much of her poetry and creative non-fiction. One of her first long poems, "reunion," tells of sibling struggles and the pleasures of riding seven miles each way to attend a country school. The poem was published in her first book, *Double Visions*.

Poirier's first venture into independence

came with enrollment at Mount Royal College in Calgary where she completed high school. From there she attended teacher's college in Moose Jaw. As her first teaching experience she deliberately chose a multi-grade country school in southern Saskatchewan. Then came marriage to Emile, three sons, and more teaching.

After leaving her teaching position in 1976, Poirier became move involved in ranching and at the same time took up weaving and became a closet writer. The combination of colour, texture, and rhythm in front of the loom prompted many of her first poems. Finally in 1979 she joined other would-be writers at a workshop in Ponteix where she was encouraged by Lorna Crozier and Patrick Lane. There she began her first exploration of voice.

After attending a second workshop with Anne Szumigalski at Fort San, Poirier submitted a collection of poems which became the core of *Double Visions* (1984). During the 1980s Poirier began to write plays for local production, the first being *Wood Mountain, 1875*. During the same time she also began working as a research historian and, though playwriting and history were engaging, poetry demanded her attention.

Under the guidance of Robin Skelton and Kristjana Gunnars, she put together a second book of poems, *Grasslands*, which was published in 1990. Ranch life and Wood Mountain history were the basis for the poems. That book of free verse was a paradox in the world of rhyming cowboy poetry, but oddly enough it led her to that world, and Poirier took part in the National Gathering at Elko, Nevada, as well as at other places.

Poirier's first children's book, *The Bead Pot*, grew out of a lifelong relationship with a Lakota Elder in the Wood Mountain community. It is a story for children, a story of a woman's spirituality and relationship with the people and the land.

In 1991 Poirier began an exploration of Rock Creek, a solitary adventure which led to a journal and to a manuscript, which received a Saskatchewan Book Award for creative non-fiction in 1996. *Rock Creek* was published in 1998. The book celebrates her life along the creek and explores her relationship to it.

Through the years Poirier has published many poems in many journals and anthologies. She has also taken part in library tours and conducted workshops. In 1998, CBC Radio broadcast a long poem entitled "New Orleans, Saskatchewan" which is about a trip to New Orleans to visit a niece dying of AIDS. Poirier is developing a manuscript based on that experience.

GARRY RADISON was born in Kamsack in 1949. His early life was filled with dogs and relatives who eventually made their way into some of his early poems. At the end of grade ten he moved with his parents, Peter and Mary Raddysh, to Regina, where he finished high school in 1967.

In 1969 Radison married Joanne Cook of Regina. They had a family of three, Tricia, Amy, and Damon.

He attended the University of Regina and has a vivid memory of a classroom visit by poet Irving Layton. Despite feeling stifled by the courses, Radison graduated with a B.Ed. in 1971, and during his career as a high school teacher he became interested in drama. He worked with several adult groups as a director and actor.

At the age of 23, Radison began writing poetry and had three poems accepted by *Grain* for its second issue in December 1973. He also joined the Saskatchewan Writers

Guild, serving on various committees and as vice president. In 1977 his poem "Grandmother: The Waiting" won first place in the Guild's poetry contest.

In 1978 his first book, *Eye of a Stranger*, was published. The poems in it reflected a young man's concern with his childhood and ancestry, and the land that shaped him. Though his style and technique was developing, his voice was tentative.

After the publication of his early work, Radison abandoned the ideas of publication and audience, writing only to hear his own voice on the page. After two intense years, a slim manuscript, *White Noise*, was accepted and published in 1982. One review praised the book for its "voice in conversation."

In 1984 Radison read his poems on a *Grain* television program hosted by editor Brenda Riches. During 1985 and 1986 he served as the poetry editor for *Grain*. His own poems were published in magazines such as *Fiddlehead*, *West Coast Review*, *Ariel*, and several anthologies, as well as in a self-published chapbook, *Songs of the Elephant Man* (1986). After a trip to Europe in 1981, Radison's themes became more complex and wide-ranging. The resulting collection, *Jeffers' Skull*, was published in 1988.

As the internal pressure to write poems subsided, Radison found time to indulge an early interest in the Old West and wrote *Last Words: Dying in the Old West*. During the long delay until its publication in 2002, he continued his indulgence, producing a companion volume, *Last Words of the Civil War*. He then formed Smoke Ridge Books to publish and market the volume. *Last Words of the Civil War* appeared in 2001 and went on the market

GARRY RADISON

at fifty locations in twenty states. The books may be the first of their kind, a new book form based on thematic last words.

While researching *Last Words*, Radison realized that the events at Frog Lake in 1885 had never been published in the United States. He took time out to write a feature article, "The Frog Lake Massacre," for the December 2002 issue of *Wild West*.

Since 1988 Radison has resided in Yorkton, Saskatchewan, in a two-and-a-half storey home (now 91 years old) with a veranda. The veranda itself has appeared in a recent poem as have the neighborhood crows and the dying, gnarled tree that he refuses to cut down as long as it produces a living limb or two.

Radison's reading continues to take him in odd directions. Unconcerned with making a writer's reputation, he continues to write what pleases him; his only concern being to find the form that fits the idea.

About Writing... *Poet, don't fall in love with words. They lie. Only sound (and echo) can make them tremble, like orbiting electrons, above the page, giving form to some aspect of the mystery that enshrouds us. One false sound and, instantly, the poem fails, falls, and becomes mere words that lie on the page.*—GARRY RADISON

R.E. (RICHARD ERNEST) RASHLEY (1909–1975) was born September 16, 1909, in Leicester, England. Educated in Saskatoon, he received his B.A., B.Ed., and M.A. at the University of Saskatchewan. He served in the army in World War II. For many years, he taught in Saskatoon high schools and in his later years was assistant professor of English at the University of Saskatchewan. Rashley and his wife Laura had three children. His poetry collections include *Voyageur and other poems* (1946), *Portrait and other poems* (1953), *Moon Lake and other poems* (1959), *Paso por aqui* (1973), and *Rock Painter: poems* (1978). Rashley's *Poetry in Canada: the first three steps* (1958) traces the development of Canadian poetry. R.E. Rashley died on November 11, 1975.

R.E. Rashley: A Remembrance

Most writers have a mentor somewhere in their writing lives. Often a teacher, sometimes a fellow writer. For me, Mr. Rashley was both (and he was never Richard or Dick, but always *Mr.*). When he died, suddenly, on November 11, 1975 at the age of 66, I can only describe my feeling as one of abandonment. He had been for me something of an ideal—a marvelous poet, a quiet, humorous teacher, a man of immense curiosity and many passionate interests and accomplishments, and, most importantly, a guide and supporter as I wandered in the wide fields of literature.

He was a quintessential prairie poet—spare, direct, seeing the detail in the universal and the universal in the detail. He was a modernist, perhaps the first in prairie writing—the whispering of prose rhythms set against the echoing and re-echoing of vowel sounds and the breaking of lines for multiple meanings. The list of his books of poems is not long: Five poetry books in thirty years. And, one major study of Canadian poetry from its beginnings. His guide was I.A. Richards: read the poems, not the biographies and studies. The poem was all.

He was one of those teachers students remember all their lives. He was a large man, once on the university wrestling team, it was rumoured. He spoke quietly, but with a sort of passion that you felt, and at the same time knew would not burst forth into rhetorical outpourings. He played the violin in the school orchestra, towering over the other players even when seated. And, year after year, he collected the wannabe writers from the student body for a weekly "literary club" meeting. Some students were fortunate enough to be invited to his home where they got a glimpse of a life refined by music, literature and painting.

He was an amateur archaeologist, instrumental in the discovery and excavation of the Oxbow site in southern Saskatchewan. He was a bibliophile, whose library of first editions of largely Canadian writing was constantly being upgraded through the purchase of better copies or new discoveries. He was a bookbinder of some accomplishment. He raised prize gladiolas. These are just the activities I was aware of over the years of sporadic meetings.

But, what he instilled in me was a passion and understanding of the prairies, its land, its history, and, most importantly, the creative power of its people. In some ways, he died at the beginning of his life—just retired from his position as Assistant Professor at the University of Saskatchewan and finally finding the time to pursue his interests with no more essays and exams to correct, no more meetings, and no more daily treks to campus. He had just completed his first volume of poetry since retirement when he died. It is a major work.

TERRENCE HEATH

LLOYD WILLIAM RATZLAFF was born in 1946 in Saskatoon and grew up in the village of Laird, the eldest of three children of Albert and Elsie Ratzlaff. His parents farmed for most of their working lives, and although this occupation never appealed to him, Lloyd felt very much at home in the landscape of the prairies. In 1961 when he was fifteen he bought an Oliver typewriter for eleven dollars, a cast-iron beast patented in 1896 and requiring two strong men and a boy to haul it. On this machine, with help from a one-volume home encyclopedia, he learned to feel his way around a "qwerty" keyboard. Shortly afterwards, a Mennonite author in the Springfield school district hired him to type a three-hundred-page novel for twenty dollars, and he knew that he would rather become a writer himself than a harvester of oats and feeder of chickens. The old Oliver sits, retired, on his office shelf, reminding him now of the joys of finding words and putting them in a line.

For eight years in the 1970s he lived in Manitoba, but otherwise Lloyd has been a Saskatchewan citizen. His early non-agricultural jobs involved delivering bread for Express Bakery by day and pumping gas at night for Eastview Motel, installing carpet for an Eaton's flooring contractor, and working as an accounting clerk with Massey-Ferguson Industries. His post-secondary education was divided between Saskatchewan and Manitoba, earning him degrees in arts, theology, religious studies, and counselling psychology. He spent a decade as a minister in four churches, fifteen years as a counsellor, and twenty overlapping years as a part-time university lecturer. Throughout this period his writings were published in professional and academic journals, and while working for Saskatoon Catholic Schools he authored *Bruised Reeds and Flickering Wicks*, a monograph on student discipline which formed the basis of professional seminars in many Saskatchewan school divisions. He was briefly an extension course writer at the University of Saskatchewan, and for some years served as an assistant editor of *Guidelines: Journal of the Saskatchewan Guidance and Counselling Association*. He also became a popular exponent of certain kinds of depth psychology, and developed workshops on the clinical and educational facets of dreaming, whose reception prompted the publication of several articles.

In the mid-1990s he began disengaging from former professions to become a full-time freelance writer. Since then his literary work has appeared widely in Canadian and American magazines, in a monthly column for the Catholic journal *Prairie Messenger*, and in his first book *The Crow Who Tampered With Time*, published in 2002. Most recently, he worked as a literacy coordinator for senior adult writing groups, and edited an anthology entitled *Seeing It Through*.

In 1992 Lloyd married Larraine, an ESL teacher with Saskatoon Catholic Schools. His daughters, Shannon and Sheri, live in Winnipeg and Saskatoon with their husbands Ramsy Unruh and Rob Porrelli, and five grandchildren, Katy, Tom, and Jane Unruh, and Nik and Tate Porrelli.

Lloyd's work has been characterized as an imaginative exploration of the natural world and spiritual experience, driven by the mystic's thirst for inclusion and for creation. His themes range geographically between city and country, philosophically between state and church, and psychologically between surface and depth. He is currently working on a second book of literary non-fiction that probes liminal regions between the outer worlds of nature and culture and the inner world of soul.

He lives in Saskatoon, near the Saskatchewan River Valley where he grew up.

About Writing... *Writing is an opportunity to re-dream words consciously.*—LLOYD RATZLAFF

BRUCE RICE was born on November 3, 1951, in Fort St. John, British Columbia, just eighteen miles from the end of the Alaskan Highway. The highway was snowed in when his mother, Margaret (Pearl) was in labour and she had to be taken to the hospital in a jeep. She had started a mail order library in Fort St. John, and on her way to hospital calmly gave her husband instructions on how to run the library and the mysteries of the Dewey Decimal System. Bruce was the fifth child in a family of ten children.

Rice's family moved to Prince Albert when he was five years old. They stayed in his uncle's cabin at Christopher Lake during the summer until the family bought a house in town. It was the start of a lifelong love of the northern forest that is reflected in both the imagery and the density of Rice's work, and perhaps the sense of risk.

His father was a teacher by profession, but in the early 1960s was appointed director of the Prince Albert Training School, an institution for people with intellectual disabilities. At the time, Saskatchewan was in the forefront of a revolution in mental health and the beginnings of de-institutionalization. These struggles were a part of the conversation in the home. There were many books in the house. His father wrote plays and several unpublished books. Pearl Rice, his mother, was a war bride from Glasgow. During the Depression, she won, but had to decline, a university scholarship for mathematics in order to help support her family. Nevertheless, she grew up with in a city where even children saw professional performances of Shakespeare and there were regular trips to the National Gallery.

Rice's family moved to New Brunswick when he was seventeen years old. In the fall he entered Saint Thomas University, a small Catholic Liberal Arts university in Fredericton. He received a B.A. in Psychology from Saint Thomas. He later moved to Halifax where he lived for ten years. There he did community development work and received a Master's in Social Work from Dalhousie University.

Rice was a late bloomer as a writer. He did not begin writing seriously until he returned to Regina in 1978. He began to write short stories but soon moved to poetry. He took university extension courses in writing and attended the Summer School of the Arts at Fort San. His instructors included poets Joe Rosenblatt, Paulette Jiles, Garry Geddes, and American Margaret Gibson.

Rice's first collection of poems, *Daniel* (1988), is a long poem that traces his family history through five generations. The book is written in a series of first person narratives. About a third of it was written by dictating the characters' monologues into a tape machine and transcribing them directly. One of the major themes is the ways that the struggles of one generation are transformed and carry on in the next generation. *Daniel* received the Canadian Authors Association Award for a collection of poetry in 1989. The judges said that the book "portrays life's hardships with an elegance and simplicity of language that is stunning." It was the first time the prestigious CAA award was given for a poet's first collection.

PHOTO BY DON HEENAN

BRUCE RICE… GAZING THROUGH A STEREOSCOPE IN WASCANA PARK

Rice's second collection, *Descent Into Lima*, was

published in 1996 and edited by Tim Lilburn. The book is a descent into self in which the poet more freely explores his own voice and experience than was possible in *Daniel*. The book includes a series of travel poems based on a trip to Ecuador and Peru, and the "Mad Anne" poems, which are an exchange of imaginary letters between a psychiatric patient and Mexican artist and cultural icon, Frida Kahlo. The collection is dominated by prose poems and is more lyrical than *Daniel*, but perhaps not as dramatic.

The Illustrated Statue of Liberty, Rice's third collection, began as a playful extension of the "Mad Anne" character in *Descent Into Lima*. The writing process began with a series of poems about Faith, who is obsessed with painting the Statue of Liberty. The book is an exploration of the exile of the artist and the immigrant. A major portion of the book is a recovery and validation of the stories and lives of those in institutions for the mentally ill. Many of the poems were inspired by or include allusions to art. The book includes a number of photographs including stereoscopic images from museums and the author's collection. The manuscript was essentially completed before September 11, 2001. It is not apologistic. Rather, it reveals the intolerance, the curtailment of civil rights, and the mistrust of the "alien" that followed those events as an inevitable extension of history. *The Illustrated Statue of Liberty* received the City of Regina Award at the 2003 Saskatchewan Book Awards. The award is presented for the best book in any genre by a Regina author.

A cousin, Lynda Monahan, is also a poet. The same family characters inhabit the works of both writers.

Rice's work has appeared in several anthologies including *Heading Out: The New Saskatchewan Writers*, *Beyond Borders*, and *Facing the Lion*. It has also appeared in *Grain*, *Canadian Author and Bookman*, *Prairie Fire*, *Fiddlehead*, *NeWest Review*, *Event*, and *RedNeck*. Excerpts from *The Illustrated Statue of Liberty* (2003) received *Grain Magazine*'s Anne Szumigalski Award for the best poem or series of poems published in 2002. His work has been adapted for live performance and broadcast on CBC radio. He has been a member of three writing groups, The Correction Line (dissolved), The Poets Combine, and Notes from the Underground. Rice served as a president and vice-president of the Saskatchewan Writers Guild, and also served as president of the Sage Hill Writing Experience.

About Writing... *My poems are stronger than I am. People are subject to human weakness, to compromise and uncertainty. A poem never forgets. If it is true it will always remain so. Even human weakness is turned into virtue for what it reveals, what it evokes in the reader, and what the poet is prepared to face on behalf of us all. I believe that poetry is useful and has force in the world. One of its tasks is to prepare us for the future, to have the words ready—their grace and their grieving—for the times when the weight of events is too great and our own words fail us.*—BRUCE RICE

MALCOLM RICE spent most of his life in Saskatchewan small towns. On his eighteenth birthday, he started working in the mines in Esterhazy. Longing for more adventure, at twenty-one he enlisted in the Canadian Army. When his tour of duty was

MALCOLM RICE

over, it was back to the mines. After another ten years, he changed his trade to boiler operator and moved to Regina.

In Regina he got interested in writing and started to create long essays about people he had known and stories they had told him. Before he knew it, he had written several novels and screenplays in the fiction genre. By making the stories fictional, he could always add his own special flavors to the tales. Rice's published books include *Wreck of the Penny* (2002) and *My turn to be king* (2003).

Rice has also had articles and stories published in local papers and magazines.

DAVID RICHARDS was born, raised, and schooled in Melfort. His maternal grandparents were well-off German colonists in Russia who were driven out by the Revolution and arrived on the Saskatchewan plains to start again from scratch, facing significant hardships. But they thought themselves lucky to have escaped the full horrors of the Revolution. His paternal grandparents were English homesteaders, one of whom lived in a hole in the side of a hill on his homestead. But they thought themselves lucky to be able to own land and keep the money they earned. His parents, children of the homesteads, depression, and WWII service, could only borrow sufficient money to dig and finish the basement of their home in Melfort. After a winter underground they finished the house and moved upstairs. But they thought themselves lucky to have a steady government job and (eventually) a nice house.

Richards actually *was* lucky. He grew up small town–middle class–good health–functional family Canadian, which, on a global perspective, is a major lottery win.

At eighteen, Richards left home, joined the Regular Army, and was sent to Military College, graduating from R.M.C., Kingston, with a B.A. in Commerce. In 1975 he arrived at 1 Service Battalion, Calgary, as an educated, fit, trained, eager, and horribly grass green Lieutenant. The next twenty-four months were spent crashing through the bush with trucks, guns, and some very forgiving soldiers who cured him of the worst of his "grass greenness". There were also six weeks with NATO in north Norway (cold war was on) and three months in Montreal in 1976, moving and guarding athletes. On a blind date in Calgary, he met his future wife, Stella. (Richards' 115th blind date, Stella's first). They did two good years in Ottawa with 450 Helicopter Squadron then: quit the army in 1979; moved to Calgary in 1980; started work as an accountant (going to school at night); had son in 1980; had daughter in 1982; became a C.G.A. in 1984; moved to Moose Jaw in 1984; and began instructing accountancy at S.I.A.S.T. in 1984. (David, Stella, and their beagle are still in the Jaw; the kids are gone to university and work).

Richards started writing in 1985 at the age of thirty-two. An avid, but very much amateur historian, he won the 1988 SWG long non-fiction award for a manuscript on the Riel Rebellion. Twenty-nine publishers saw it, four liked it, none published it. Using the research and an urge to write fiction he produced a young adult novel about the Rebellion

DAVE RICHARDS... HIKING IN BANFF WITH HIS WIFE, STELLA.

called *Soldier Boys* that was published in 1993 and which caused huge excitement in the Richards' home. The book is currently in its second printing. The sequel, *Lady at Batoche*, was published in 1999 and won the Children's Lit category that year at the Saskatchewan Book Awards. In between, many stories, a novel about the Front de Libération du Québec (FLQ), and a variety of articles were attempted, and two Sterling writing awards were won: Short Non-fiction, 1997 and Short Fiction, 1999, both of which were short story competitions. A longtime ambition to write a novel about the homesteaders has been satisfied. *Warm in Winter* is scheduled to be released in the spring of 2004.

About Writing... *This is not for those who write "for a living." This is for those of you who write "for the rush." Ten o'clock at night, alone upstairs at your desk, Loreena McKennitt on the CD player, four cups of coffee downstream, you write 300 consecutive words that no editor, no legitimate critic can touch. Read them and re-read them; hug yourself and think what a lucky beggar you are to get to do this once in a while. The next rush may not come for another 10,000 words, but it's out there if you keep chasing it.*—DAVID RICHARDS

HARRIET RICHARDS is a first generation Canadian. Her Welsh father, J. Howard Richards, was stationed in southern Ontario as a meteorologist for the RAF, and later joined the Canadian army. Her American mother, MaryHelen Keele, a nurse, was commissioned as a second lieutenant in 1944, and was later sent with the Red Cross to Okinawa and one of the bloodiest battles to disgrace the earth.

Her parents first met in 1941 through mutual friends in Michigan and, after the war, decided to marry and have lots of babies. She was born in Toronto, 1953, the fifth of seven: David, Anne, Alun, Pegi, Harriet, William, Thomas. Her mother claims her father used to vanish sometimes as they walked, but that she soon learned to look for him up in trees.

Richards is named for her Welsh grandmother, Harriet Protheroe Richards, who was 80 at the time of her birth and died at 97, the year they lived on the Gower Coast in Wales. The family in *The Lavender Child* is named for her grandmother's.

As a child, she thought she might become a zoo keeper, veterinarian, or psychiatrist. Grade seven aptitude tests—gender-specific, of course—revealed that her talents were "clerical." She thought this meant she should become a nun. Creative writing was a fast, often enjoyable, way to get good marks. She kept a diary once, when she was ten, and filled very little of it. At thirteen or so, she discovered to her amazement that she drew very well in an odd way (but never drew fashion models or horses). That became her quiet passion for many years. At first she tore out the blank end pages from books in her parents' library, but eventually had sketchbooks and india ink. She believes the years of reading under covers and staying up until 3 a.m. on school nights to draw or write was Boot Camp for creative life as an adult. In later years, those hours of isolated concentration in the studio made the transition to writing fiction quite painless; plus she was already trained for survival in the gamey maze of creative false starts and external rejection of efforts.

She developed her craft through the act of writing those first few years, employing almost every mistake possible, and making good use of the writers-in-residence at Saskatoon's Frances Morrison library. She took her very first stories to Armin Weibe, near the end of his residency, and a few more the following year to Betsy Warland, who encouraged her to write a book. In 1994, she began what became *The Lavender Child*, and brought those slightly confused beginnings to Welsh poet/essayist Robert Minhinnick. He introduced her to Anne Szumigalski's homemade biscuits and marmalade plus prose group—an entertaining mix of Don Kerr, Alison Muri (who was working on *Histry of the Broken Fether*), Bill Robertson, Dave Carpenter (working on *Courting Saskatchewan*), Marie Elyse St. George, and occasional others.

To these meetings Richards, then unpublished village girl, brought double-spaced title-paged faded dot-matrix-printed copies of works-in-progress. At home that year, she had four kids (Dagan, Jeremy, Robin, and Glyn), a husband (Neil McMillan), Oscar (a Mexican student), various pets, occasionally a nephew, and often kids' friends to feed or trip over in the morning. Soon, two of her stories were published, and she began writing articles as well. Sandra Birdsell helped her enormously with *The Lavender Child* (Thistledown Press, 1997, Saskatchewan Book Award, 1998) and, when Thistledown Press accepted it, she discovered the talents of Seán Virgo, who became her editor and friend.

When she first began to write fiction, Richards made a deal with herself: if things became too serious, if she wasn't having fun, if the stifling powers of grant-givers and editors made her miserable, then she would quit writing. There has been only one, terrifying time when she came close; after finishing a very unsatisfying second novel, she completely lost faith in herself. Finally she scratched out a little story and sent it to John Barnie (poet, blues musician, and editor of *Planet in Aberystwyth*), who published her twice before, and he took it right away. If he hadn't? But she did write that story, and was already working on another. A couple of years later the collection *Waiting for the Piano Tuner to Die* (Thistledown Press, 2002) was published.

HARRIET RICHARDS

Richards was always a vivid night-dreamer and careless daydreamer and a hot-headed giggler and voracious reader, and for the most part despised school. She wouldn't have made a good nun.

As for becoming a writer, the operative word in the previous paragraph is reader. She generally reads for love, and sometimes laughs as she reads, usually in appreciation of a beautifully, maybe ironically, observed moment on the page. Sometimes she reads the books of her childhood: *Wind in the Willows*, *The Jungle Books*, the *Narnia* series, *Tistou of the Green Fingers*, *The Little Prince*. To present a random list of writers admired: she has recently, or once again, enjoyed Robertson Davies, Kurt Vonnegut, Douglas Adams, Guy Vanderhaeghe, essay collections by both John Barnie and Adam Gopnik, hand-me-down *New Yorker* magazines, *The Shipping News*, and Peter Mayle's *Provence* books.

About Writing... *Do not expect to write well unless you read a lot, and read for love, and read the best.*—HARRIET RICHARDS

BRENDA MACDONALD RICHES (1942–1994) was born in India in 1942. Her British father, Jack, and mother Audrey, born in India but of Scottish ancestry, met in Bombay. Both were teachers and keen readers with romantic spirits whom Riches considered to be her earliest influences. Following Indian independence, the family moved to England in 1945, first to Ipswich and then to the County of Somerset.

It was here that Riches received the first part of her formal education before moving on to Cambridge University to study languages—German and French. While at Cambridge, Brenda met her first husband, Graham. During this time she also developed a passion for writing. Studying foreign languages and being exposed to great writers such as Verlaine and Rilke, as well as Emily Dickinson, Marcel Proust, and Gabriel Garcia Marquez, gave Riches a greater insight into the complexities of language and sharpened her awareness of her own work.

From 1965 to 1974, Riches taught English and imaginative writing and began a family—two daughters, Naomi and Rebecca, and one son, Stefan. During this period, she and her family lived in London, Hong Kong, and Liverpool. Liverpool was where she met with a monthly gathering of writers, musicians, and artists called Jabberwocky, and found encouragement for her writing.

In 1974, Riches moved to Canada, landing in Saskatoon. Here she came in contact with a group of poets, including Alan Bradley, Theresa Heuchert, Mary Wood, and Anne Szumigalski. A great mentor and friend, Szumigalski would look at her apprentice's work and say, "No, you can't send that out, not

PHOTO BY CRAIG GRANT
BRENDA MACDONALD RICHES... BANFF, 1988.

really," until one day she said to Riches, "Now you're ready." Shortly after, her work began to be accepted by a number of Canadian literary magazines and anthologies such as *Grain*, *The Capilano Review*, *The Canadian Short Fiction Anthology*, and *Saskatchewan Gold*. Riches also found support and constructive criticism while attending the Summer School of the Arts and writing retreats at Fort San. Here she was further exposed to the Saskatchewan approach to poetry, which moved her away from high-flown English and the tendency to abstraction and didacticism, and towards concentrating on the image and present moment.

Although Riches rarely spoke of actual place or landscape in her work, the Saskatchewan landscape loosened something inside her. She saw the prairies as a place that leaves room around objects, driving the writer back inside the mind, undistracted. She also believed that, for her, the exterior world was real only to the extent that it affected what was inside. In a statement of her poetics, Riches declared that her goal was to tell the truth of the imagination. These beliefs and experiences, combined with the influence of one of her favourite writers, Virginia Woolf, caused a focus on the interior, on the human psyche, and led her to develop a stream-of-consciousness style of writing which is evident in much of her prose.

The Irish novelist Edna O'Brien, whom Riches read in the mid-1970s, was also a major influence. O'Brien's style was to develop a paragraph and conclude it on a subsidiary note. In the next paragraph she would pick up on that note and develop it as the main idea. This literary device, called "wit-walking," suited Riches, a mother of three young children, as it enabled her to leave a piece of writing and come back to it later without breaking the continuity. Her short story "Strings," an examination of the emotional tension between men and women, reflects this style.

In 1980, Riches released *Dry Media*, the first of three books. The poetry collection was the culmination of her work since arriving in Canada. At the time, Riches was still teaching, both creative writing and in the public school system. Her exposure to children in the classroom, her experiences as a mother, and the memory of her own childhood influenced such pieces as "Demeter's Daughter," "Gall," "Spider," and "Seth," in which children are portrayed as devious and cunning, while in others Riches explored the depth and range of children's emotions in a way that gave respect to their independence, their need to feel empowered, and to their secret desires.

During this time, Riches also became involved with the Saskatchewan Writers' Guild, serving as its president. Shortly after the release of *Dry Media*, she became the fiction editor of *Grain* and became editor-in-chief in 1983, a position she held until 1987. This experience sharpened her critical judgment and because she was not a prolific writer, served to exercise her critical eye. It also increased her appreciation of the necessity for writers to take a professional approach to their work, studying grammar and the craft of writing before submitting to periodicals.

By the time her second book, *Rites*, was released in 1988, Riches was divorced and living with her common-law husband, writer Craig Grant. The collection of short stories included "When Helen Wakes," an attempt both to exorcise her grief following the suicide of her sister-in-law and to get inside the world of a clinically depressed woman. Another, *The Maid*, was inspired by the Tom Robbins' novel, *Still Life with Woodpecker*. Instead of telling the tale of a princess and a bomber, Riches chose an angel and a ragpicker, and after seeing an Alex Colville painting, added the maid. Through these metaphorical characters, Riches explored and challenged traditional Christian values espoused by the church. Despite the prosaic narrative structure of a significant portion of the book, Riches, more interested in the sounds and rhythms of language than her subject matter, and with a devotion to exploring syntax, considered herself a poet rather than a storyteller.

In 1989, Riches was diagnosed with cancer. Her final collection of poetry, *Something to Madden the Moon*, released in 1991, deals in part with her attempt to heal herself. For the last few years of her life, Riches continued to write furiously, the writing doing more to numb the pain than any prescribed narcotic. She filled a dozen journals with the intimate details of her plight, written from the point of view of a narrator that had first appeared in *Something to Madden the Moon*, for a manuscript she called *Scorpio Rising*. She also continued to teach English and Creative Writing at the University of Regina and across Saskatchewan, serving as mentor to the next generation of Saskatchewan writers.

On July 12, 1994, Riches passed away in Vancouver, leaving *Scorpio Rising* unfinished. Though she was born on the other side of the world and died on the other side of the country, she considered Saskatchewan her home, and with its wonderfully supportive community of writers, the best place to develop her craft. Following her death, the Saskatchewan

Book Awards named the award for Best First Book, the Brenda Macdonald Riches Award, fittingly won in 1997 by Joanne Gerber, a former student.

In the last few months of her life, she somehow managed to maintain, wondrously, her sharp sense of humour, and her zest for living had developed an intensity that amazed all who came into her presence.

STEFAN RICHES

About Writing... *Writing has its own sense of direction, and sometimes the writer can be a real impediment by not seeing the signs. I once asked a writer friend where he thought I should go, now that my first book was published. "To the nearest bar," he suggested. Wine is a faithful inspirer, not only when I drink it, but when I look at it in the glass, especially by candlelight.*—BRENDA RICHES

WILMA RILEY was born on an extremely cold winter day in the General Hospital of Regina. Her father worked for the CN Railroad and she grew up in a working class village called North Regina. Riley says that it was unique and wonderful, multi-cultural, generous and kind. Her parents believed strongly in the worth of ordinary working people. She feels that the 1950s saw a flood of American propaganda and values which eroded the virtues and solidarity of small communities everywhere and her village was absorbed into the city and changed.

Riley lived in France for three years. She was a single parent when her children were just six, four, and two years of age. Thanks to the new policy of student loans, she was able to attend the University of Saskatchewan in Regina and obtained her Bachelor of Arts degree (with distinction). She later earned a Bachelor of Education degree. She taught school in Regina and Edmonton and she also taught a summer course in China. She speaks English and French and has a tourist's knowledge of Spanish. Riley has also mastered a few phrases in Mandarin.

Her childhood and youth were shadowed by the Second World War and as a result, she feels that the events and places of one's youth are always glorified somewhat by the simple optimism and acceptance of youth itself. She remembers feeling lonely and depressed even as a young child and has concluded that such feelings were probably prompted by the cruelties and anxieties of wartime which touched her family closely.

The life and events of Riley's childhood shaped her perceptions and sparked her interest in history and literature. They also inspired many of her stories which have been published in several anthologies. One of them—"Pies"—appeared first as a short story and then as a National Film Board animated film. It was also published with illustrations by Sheldon Cohen (who also created the art for the film) as a children's book. "Pies" appeared in *100% Cracked Wheat*, *Shoes and Shit* and (originally) in *Sundogs*. The story was broadcast on CBC radio.

Riley's novel *Cut-Out* is a story of espionage and enlightenment. It is under option for a film and while it has the basic structure of a spy novel, it is also a story of liberation.

"Fowl Supper" and "The Girl in Rose Brocade" won awards in Saskatchewan Writers Guild competitions. Other stories have appeared in *100% Cracked Wheat*, *Journal of Canadian Fiction*, *Canadian Fiction Magazine*, and *Sky High*. "From the Dark Wood," a horror story based on the grim war history of northern France and Belgium where she lived for three years, was published in *More Saskatchewan Gold*. Riley's novel *Cut-*

Out is based in the same region. Her articles have been published in the Regina *Leader-Post* and *Island Tides*. Her poems have been read on CBC radio, and "Winter Watch On The Great Wall" appeared in *Garden Varieties, An Anthology of the Top Fifty Poems from the National Poetry Contest of 1988*.

Some of Riley's stories have been inspired by her village, by the War of 1939 and by the great depression, of which she heard so much. Some of her stories just appear in her head, she says, almost written, while others have to be worked and sweated over. She rewrites and revises which usually means a great deal of research, some of which never appears in her books but all of which will be used somehow. Riley considers all artists, including writers, to be witnesses to history, which is why she is insistent that their work must contain the truth. Some day the testimony of writers may be called upon, and she subjects the authors of fairy tales and fantasy to the same high standard. To illustrate this, Riley points out how, by examining Grimm's fairy tales, we find not only the beliefs of people who lived long ago, but something about their everyday life and values. We learn a great deal about those people, including something about the dark truths held by human beings.

Riley can't remember any close brushes with greatness but she has had three memorable brushes with death. Death, she has come to understand, is another kind of greatness and she agrees with whoever said that death focuses the mind wonderfully.

Riley likes to scuba dive. The peaceful underwater world is a three-dimensional experience that also focuses the mind. "The fish" she says, "come to look at you curiously and you realize that you are the goldfish in their bowl."

In contemplating other writers, Riley likens herself to Colette. Colette wrote that her mother was an inspiration to her and that her most important word was 'regard.' "I never want to be afraid of what there is to see."

She is currently working on two novels and a collection of her short stories. She lives on the west coast because, she says, she cannot afford to break any more bones on the ice and snow of Saskatchewan. Yet she misses the plains and they remain in her bones, broken and unbroken. Riley thinks a winter trip to the spa at Watrous and the healing waters of Manitou Lake would help both her bones and her homesickness.

WILMA RILEY... "I'VE BECOME SO MUCH A PART OF THE LANDSCAPE, NOW HUMMINGBIRDS LAND ON ME AND FROGS HITCH A RIDE ON MY SHOULDER."

About Writing... *It's something I have to do, it seems. There is no advice that is universal because everybody is different. The human brain is the most powerful thing in the world, but it's often in shackles. Free the mind as best you can, prepare to be lonely and misunderstood and also poor if fiction writing is your main support. You may not be any of these things, but the truth is both hard to write and hard, sometimes, to take, but it is the only thing worth doing.*—WILMA RILEY

WILLIAM ROBERTSON was born in Tokyo, Japan, in 1954 to United Church missionary parents both of prairie immigrant stock. His father, Stewart, was born in Watrous, of Scottish immigrants, and his mother, Ruth, was born in Parkland, Alberta, of English

WILLIAM ROBERTSON...
WILLIE "WHEELS" WADENA (NEW YEAR'S EVE POLYESTER PARTY, 1996).

immigrants. His mother's family, the Peats, stuck it out in Alberta till his mother was six months old, then moved to the Gorge area of Victoria. Robertson was actually conceived in Lake Cowichan, British Columbia, where his father had his first ministerial charge, but his parents decided to become missionaries, learned Japanese, and flew to Japan. He lived the first five years of his life in the mountain town of Matsumoto, where he attended his first half-year of kindergarten.

Robertson switched to a Canadian kindergarten in Richmond, British Columbia, while his parents were home on furlough. Then he went to an American air base school for grade one and half of grade two while he lived in Hino, which is a suburb of Tokyo. While in Japan he was joined by two sisters.

His parents decided they'd had enough of missionary work and relocated to the tiny town of South Mountain, Ontario, where Robertson completed grade two in a one-room schoolhouse. He then bussed to grades three and four at nearby Hallville. In 1964 his father wanted a change, so the family camped across Canada to Cumberland, on Vancouver Island, British Columbia, where Robertson got his grades five and six. In 1966 his father wanted an even bigger change, so he left the ministry and joined the John Howard Society, working out of Nanaimo, British Columbia. Here Robertson went to Departure Bay Elementary for grade seven.

Disillusioned with the John Howard Society, Stewart Robertson moved the family to Shaunavon in 1967, where Robertson managed to get through his final five years of public schooling without a move. He graduated in 1972, worked a year in the oilfield and in the local General Motors garage, and then moved north to Saskatoon to do a B.A. in English. After a year of grain bin construction, selling CB radios, and then selling auto parts, Robertson returned to the University of Saskatchewan to earn his M.A. in English in 1981.

In the summer of 1977 as a teaching assistant at the University of Saskatchewan, Robertson discovered teaching and was hooked. He taught his way through his master's program, and for a couple more years after that. After a nine-year break to raise children and write, he returned to teaching in 1994 and has been teaching freshman English, creative writing, and grammar and composition in Saskatoon, Prince Albert, and Muenster for the University of Saskatchewan. He also teaches for Gabriel Dumont College, for St. Thomas More College, for the Indian Teacher Education Program, and for St. Peter's College.

In 1986 Robertson published his first collection of poetry, entitled, *Standing On Our Own Two Feet*. In 1991 he published *Adult Language Warning*, and in 1997, *Somewhere Else*. In 1992 he published a biography entitled *k.d. lang: Carrying the Torch*. While he was a student at the University of Saskatchewan, Robertson worked for the student newspaper, *The Sheaf*, and in 1979 parlayed that experience into a job with the Saskatoon *Star Phoenix* as a music reviewer. Since that time he has branched out into book reviews and since 1994 has reviewed theatre and music for CBC Saskatchewan. Since 1998, Robertson has reviewed books for CBC national's morning program.

For about ten years Robertson was the music editor of *NeWest Review* and he was also a member of that magazine's editorial collective, contributing editorials, book and music reviews, and feature articles.

Though Robertson taught writing for the Sage Hill Writing Experience and at St. Thomas More, he has neglected to take a creative writing class. He credits, hugely, his experience of working with writers-in-residence at the Saskatoon Public Library, particularly Patrick Lane, Betsy Warland, and Edna Alford, and at the University of Western Ontario, with Leon Rooke. Without the help of these writers, and others in writing groups, such as the late Anne Szumigalski, he'd still be fooling around at home.

Except for a year each in Kingston and London, Ontario, home since 1973 has been Saskatoon where, on his desk, sit uncompleted poetry and short fiction manuscripts. Any day now he'll deliver these to a publisher.

About Writing... *I recently had a student in a university freshman English class tell me that reading was helping her to become a better writer. When she arrived in my class she could barely put three sentences together. I asked her if she'd like to do some extra writing for me. She did, but along the way she made the discovery that reading—reading the literature I'd assigned and also other works I suggested—was helping her learn how to write. I am constantly amazed and occasionally appalled at the number of novice writers who would just like to get writing and get published, bypassing the part where they find out what's already been written. We certainly can't read it all, but I believe that to have at least a rudimentary idea of where we have been, we can more clearly know where we are going. So read, read, read.*—WILLIAM ROBERTSON

J. JILL ROBINSON (the "J" is for Jacqueline), was born in Langley, British Columbia, on June 16, 1955. She dropped out of school in grade eleven, and spent the next decade in a variety of pursuits—working for B.C. Tel, bartending, and cocktailing. Hitchhiking home from Calgary in 1974 she stopped at Radium Hot Springs, and then stayed, living in the Windermere Valley for four and a half years, but travelling to Nelson to attend Notre Dame University in 1977 and 1978.

She moved to Calgary in 1979, where she began university, earning first a B.A. in Canadian literature and drama (she wanted to be an actor), and then an M.A. in English literature, focusing on American poetry and Canadian fiction. She worked as a bartender to help put herself through school.

Robinson married in 1985, and taught at the University of Calgary until 1988, when she started work towards an M.F.A. in creative writing at the University of Alaska in Fairbanks. She graduated in 1991 and taught again at the University of Calgary. In 1993 she attended the Sage Hill Writing Experience, lured to Saskatchewan by the opportunity to work with Jane Urquhart. In December of that year she moved, dog, books, and chesterfield, to Saskatoon, where she has lived ever since with the poet Steven Ross Smith. They have one child, Emmett H Robinson Smith, born in 1995. They married in 1999.

PHOTO BY JENNIFER STILL
J. JILL ROBINSON

Robinson was the editor of *Grain*

Magazine for three and a half years. She now teaches creative writing, composition, and literature at St. Peter's College in Muenster.

She has published four books of short fiction, including *Saltwater Trees* (1991), *Lovely In Her Bones* (1993), *Eggplant Wife* (1995), and *Residual Desire* (2003).

Her work has won the *Prism International* short fiction contest (1989), *Event*'s non-fiction contest (1992), and has been short-listed for Best American Short Stories (1998). *Saltwater Trees* was awarded the Alberta Writers Guild Howard O'Hagan prize (1991); *Lovely In Her Bones* was included in the Toronto *Globe & Mail*'s "books we couldn't put down in 1993," and *Eggplant Wife* was short-listed for a Saskatchewan Book Award (1995). *Residual Desire* won two Saskatchewan Book Awards in 2003: Best Book from a Saskatoon author, and Best Book of Fiction.

About writing... *I first came to writing as a way to confront despair. Now, however, I am propelled by desire that is wider in scope—to understand what it means to be human. For me, Faulkner put it best when he said that "the problems of the human heart in conflict with itself...alone can make good writing because only that is worth writing about...."*—J. JILL ROBINSON

MANSEL ROBINSON was born in the rail and lumbering town of Chapleau, Northern Ontario, in 1955. His mother, Isabel (b. 1929) is the youngest daughter of Evadna Elliott, the post-mistress in Chapleau, and George Collinson, a supply driver in World War I with the 5th Canadian Field Ambulance who saw action at Vimy Ridge. Robinson's father, Mansel (1923–1998), an activist in the trade union movement and in politics, was the son of Rachel Legault and Hamel Robinson and retired as a conductor after 42 years with the CPR. His parents were active members in their community, serving on church and library committees, the Royal Canadian Legion, the school board and various charities. Robinson has two sisters, Wendy MacLeod, an interior designer, and Verlie, a sales representative and executive assistant for a tubing manufacturer.

Very nearly graduating from Grade 13 in 1972, Robinson hitchhiked to Mexico, then worked as a gravedigger, railway signalman, on fire crews and on the green chain before attending the University of Western Ontario. He studied English literature but for the most part read the books suggested to him by various heads and rounders. Shortly after reading Eugene O'Neill's *Long Day's Journey Into Night*, he started his first play. (Nothing he wrote would see production for 17 years.) After a year at the University of Ottawa, he lied his way into a gig as a stage carpenter with a small Ottawa theatre company. For about 15 years he made his living as a stagehand with theatres from Pictou, Nova Scotia, to Vancouver, including an eye-opening stint shoveling horse manure for the RCMP Musical Ride. Following an extended trip to Tibet, China, and southeast Asia, he enrolled in 1990 in the M.A. program at Concordia University in Montreal. His thesis was the writing of *Colonial Tongues*, a play which, thanks to the actor Sharon Bakker, premiered in 1993 at 25th Street Theatre in Saskatoon.

Robinson moved to Saskatchewan in 1992 with the sculptor and artist Ellen Moffat, who had been accepted into the M.F.A. visual arts program at the University of Regina. The move to the prairies resulted in a crucially productive and long-standing relationship with the writers and dramaturges associated with Saskatchewan Playwrights Centre, a nationally recognized play development centre. All his

MANSEL ROBINSON... CONTEMPLATES MOVING HIS BOOKS TO YET ANOTHER APARTMENT.

stage plays, with the exception of *Downsizing Democracy* (which premiered in 1998), have been developed at the SPC: *Collateral Damage* (1994), *The Heart As It Lived* (1997), *Spitting Slag* (1998), *Street Wheat* (2001), *Ghost Trains* (2001) and *Scorched Ice* (unproduced).

Benefiting from the work of dramaturges such as D.D. Kugler, Ben Henderson, Peter Smith, and Bob White, these plays have moved from the SPC onto stages across the country: Alberta Theatre Projects (Calgary), Theatre Network (Edmonton), Northern Light Theatre (Edmonton), Theatre & Company (Kitchener), The Globe Theatre (Regina), 25th Street Theatre (Saskatoon), Dancing Sky Theatre (Meacham), The P.A. Community Players (Prince Albert), The SummerWorks Festival (Toronto), The Great Canadian Theatre Company (Ottawa), and at York and McMaster Universities. The plays have also been published. Robinson's book of short fiction and poetry, *Slag*, was published in 1997.

From the start, Robinson's playwriting has focused on the lives of working people (miners, railroaders, farmers) and on politics and power (usually in the family or around the kitchen table). Recent collaborations with Big River songwriter Rocky Lakner and with Edmonton songwriter Stewart MacDougall have allowed him to expand his interest in a heightened stage language into experiments with song and music. And the curious act of a live, sweating actor telling her story to a living, coughing audience (especially in this age of the film and the internet) continues to intrigue him.

At the time of writing, and accompanied by Saskatoon actor and playwright Pam Bustin, Robinson is headed to the University of Windsor for a 9-month gig as writer-in-residence. He is at work on three new plays: *Picking Up Chekhov*, *Murder Museum*, and *Dodge City*.

About Writing... *I like the guy who said that "the only way to write is well and how you do it is your own damn business." And when George F. Walker counters the "write what you know" dictum with the idea that it's more exciting to write what you don't know, that you write to discover, I like that too. But as the American cultural blitzkrieg crunches across the country and the world, and as our self-styled elite sell off our water and sell out the rest, I think it is increasingly necessary to write where you know—Vancouver, Bienfait, Mississauga. It's a holding action to be sure, but a battle worth fighting, if only to force the bastards to note our passing.*—MANSEL ROBINSON

MILDRED A. ROSE (1912–2003) was born at Pike Lake, and spent her entire life in Saskatchewan. She was a graduate of Bedford Road Collegiate, Saskatoon, and earned B.Ed and M.A. (English) degrees from the University of Saskatchewan. Mildred and her husband Ted were both teachers in Regina.

Rose was writing poetry when she was still in high school. In June 1975, Rose was selected to be the Poet of the Month by the United Amateur Press in the United States. Her poems appeared in *Calliope, Repository, Dragonfly, Saskatchewan Poetry Book, Battersean, FreeLance, Alberta Poetry Book, Salt, Skylark, Driftwood East, Glowing Lanterns, Meanderings, Modern Haiku, Modus Operandi, Tangelo Trails, Janus/Seth Tower by the Sea Anthology, MS/B*, and other small magazines, and were read on CBC radio and at the Globe Theatre Noon Show.

Rose received the Saskatchewan Writers Guild "Founders Award" for her many years of dedicated service to the organization. She was also active in the Wascana Writers Group and the Saskatchewan Poetry Society. For many years she was a creative writing instructor with the Regina Public Library and University of Regina Extension.

Mildred Rose published a number of chapbooks including *Esor Derdlim, Second Story, The Fuchsia Tree, Old Belly Dancing Moon,* and *Inukshuk*.

PAUL WILSON

SINCLAIR ROSS (1908–1996). James Sinclair Ross was born on a farm in the Wild Rose school district twelve miles north of Shellbrook on January 22, 1908. His parents were Peter Ross and Catharine Foster (nee Fraser) Ross, who had purchased the quarter-section.

Ross attended the first grade at Wild Rose School before his mother separated from Peter, and took the boy with her to live at Indian Head, in southern Saskatchewan. She obtained work as a housekeeper for a district farmer, Bob Livingstone, and later worked for other farm families. They were joined a year later by Ross's older sister Effie, who married a local farmer, Matthew Price. During this period, Mrs. Ross obtained a brief housekeeping position in Regina, and during the winter of 1918, young Ross attended Connaught School in that city.

Young James Sinclair, or Jimmy Ross, as he was known to the community of Indian Head, was remembered as a precocious student and reader. He left high school in grade eleven to take a teller's position at the Union Bank of Canada in Abbey, Saskatchewan. The bank was taken over by the Royal Bank of Canada, and he was transferred to work at Royal Bank branches in the Saskatchewan towns of Lancer in 1928, and Arcola in 1929. He lived in Arcola with his mother for four years. It was in Arcola that he began writing short stories and probably started work on his novel *As For Me and My House*. (The fictional town of Horizon bears a certain resemblance to Arcola.) Here Jimmy Ross began music lessons, and during the early 1930s, travelled to Regina and enrolled for a term of study in the Conservatory of Music at Regina College. He became an accomplished pianist and organist, playing in the churches of various communities in which he lived.

In April 1933, Ross was transferred to a bank position in Winnipeg, and moved there with "Granny" Ross, as she was known in Arcola. He won third prize (of twenty pounds) in a major literary competition in London, England, the Nash's Short Story competition, with a short story called "No Other Way." It was published in the October 1934 issue of Nash's *Pall-Mall*. In the spring of 1935, his story "A Field of Wheat" was published in *Queen's Quarterly*, the first of a dozen Sinclair Ross stories to appear during the 1930s and early 1940s in the university quarterly. For many critics, this period marks Sinclair Ross's finest output as a creative writer, for it included his short stories "The Painted Door," "A Lamp at Noon," "Cornet at Night," and many other tales which have come to be recognized as features of Canadian literature. Now widely anthologized and translated to other languages abroad, they were barely noticed at the time.

When Ross completed his first novel, *As For Me and My House*, he sent it to the New York publishing house of Reynal and Hitchcock. It was published in 1941 to scant notice and unenthusiastic reviews. A psychological portrait of the wife of a small-town church minister, the novel also illustrated the relentless despair of life in a prairie community at the depth of the "dirty thirties." It was dismissed by a literary market looking for wartime escapism, and Ross himself perceived the novel as a failed venture.

Nevertheless, *As For Me and My House* eventually became recognized as one of the finest novels of modern Canadian literature, and is ranked by critics as one of the three or four most acclaimed literary works in Canada. Many writers, notably Margaret Laurence and Robert Kroetsch, have commented on its influence in their work. It takes the form of a diary composed by Mrs. Bentley, the otherwise unnamed wife of Philip Bentley, a failed artist and church minister. As the novel opens, the childless couple has taken up residence in the wind-blown town of Horizon, suffering through one of the late-Depression drought years. The Bentleys' marriage is in crisis, and in the course of a year's cycle of events, they go through a series of catastrophes and discoveries. Philip recovers his artistic integrity and ambition, and Mrs. Bentley adopts a child when a young woman in the town becomes pregnant (apparently by Philip) and dies in childbirth. At the end of the year the following spring, they depart from Horizon for a happier future elsewhere.

The novel is an unflattering portrait of life in a small prairie town, wherein the community's prejudices, hypocrisy, pettiness, and cruelty are observed in its relationship with the alienated Bentleys. The narrative technique shows good use of an unreliable narrator in determining the theme of artistic redemption. In the end, they depart from Horizon on cordial terms, and Mrs. Bentley seems surprised to discover that the townspeople actually like them. There is a farewell supper in the church, when the citizens sing the hymn "God Be With You Till We Meet Again."

Ross enlisted in the Canadian Army in 1942 and was sent overseas to serve with the Ordnance Corps. He was stationed in London, England, until 1946. He said in a later interview that he was grateful for the war, for it allowed him to live in cosmopolitan London for four years, taking in theatre, opera, music concerts, and art galleries for the first time in his life. In early 1946, Ross returned to Winnipeg, resuming his position with the Royal Bank. Later that year he was transferred to the bank's Montreal office, where he began working in the public relations division.

McClelland and Stewart republished *As For Me and My House* in 1957 in its New Canadian Library paperback series, and the novel soon began appearing in university literature classes across the country. Ross's literary reputation grew, and a second novel, *The Well*, was published in 1957, followed by the publication in 1968 of the New

SINCLAIR ROSS... ARCOLA, SASKATCHEWAN, CIRCA 1930.

Canadian Library paperback *The Lamp at Noon and Other Stories*, a collection of most of his stories which had appeared in magazines. This was the Canadian public's first awareness of Ross's 1930s stories, and generated much academic and literary interest in his work. A later novel, *Whir of Gold*, was published in 1970 to mixed reviews, and his final literary effort, *Sawbones Memorial*, appeared in 1974. The latter, a short novel of 138 pages, is an astonishing accomplishment by a veteran writer, a tour de force of narrative construction that examines the complex social relationships of an entire Saskatchewan town called Upward on one evening in 1948. The central character is Doctor "Sawbones" Hunter, a 75-year-old family doctor with a troubled history in the town, and the entire book takes place during the evening of his retirement and birthday party. It has a sense of humour and a warmth uncharacteristic of Ross's earlier work, and it went relatively unnoticed by the book-buying public.

Upon his retirement from the bank in 1968, Ross moved to Athens, Greece, to do his writing abroad as an expatriate. He had always been a private man, not to say reclusive, and he may have been disheartened by the Canadian response to his later work. He subsequently relocated to Spain, first in Barcelona, then to Malaga in 1973, just before the appearance of *Sawbones Memorial*. In ill health, he finally returned to Canada around 1980 to live in Vancouver, where he resided until his death.

KEN MITCHELL

About Writing... *If I have any claim to be considered a 'writer' it must be based on the stories in* The Lamp at Noon *and* As For Me and My House, *and that are, as you know, one hundred per cent Saskatchewan. I wrote them while in Winnipeg, but I was looking back, and drew on Manitoba not at all. If I had written them in London or Timbuctoo they would have come out exactly the same.*—SINCLAIR ROSS *[from "On Looking Back," Mosaic III Spring 1970].*

MARI-LOU ROWLEY was born in Edmonton, Alberta, on September 10, 1953, to Sadie (Bunee) Carswell and Vernon Placatko. Her father died tragically two months later. She and her mother moved back to her grandparent's home in Wyndotte, Saskatchewan (near Hanley), where her grandfather Walter Carswell taught grades one to twelve in a one-room rural school. She spent much of her first year with her grandparents, and visited them often as a child. There she developed a love of learning—and of the bleakly beautiful prairie landscape.

Two years later, her mother met Ken Rowley of North Battleford, and they married in the summer of 1955. Her adoptive grandparents lived and worked at the Saskatchewan Hospital, the psychiatric hospital in North Battleford, where her grandmother managed staff quarters and her grandfather was a stockman in the dairy barns. As a small child, she recalls wandering and exploring the expansive grounds and river valley with her grandfather's golden Lab.

Rowley's parents moved to Saskatoon, where she attended St. Edward's Elementary School and later E.D. Feehan High School. There her aptitude for the sciences and language became evident. Her grade twelve English teacher, Gerry Cooke, encouraged her writing; although he might not have had he known that she had stolen Leonard Cohen's *Flowers for Hitler* from the school library. "That was the book that inspired me to write poetry," she says. "One day I will return it."

In 1971, the year she graduated, Rowley

attended The Saskatchewan Summer School of the Arts at Fort San, where she worked with Ken Mitchell. The next year she joined Anne Szumigalski's writing group in Saskatoon. Some of her early poems are included in the group's 1973 anthology *Prairie*, published by Mendal Art Gallery and edited by Caroline Heath.

Rowley attended the University of Saskatchewan from 1972 to 1975, but found the experience less than inspiring. She remembers a chemistry lab instructor remarking "where is the little girl with the question," whenever she asked for clarification. And the professor of ancient Greek who didn't show up for the Christmas exam. "I thought, if this is academia, I want no part of it," she says.

Instead, she pursued a career in advertising and marketing, with stints as a waitress, sales clerk, court reporter, temp, and cook's helper on oil rigs along the way. In 1976, she became advertising supervisor for Eaton's in Saskatoon. Two years later she moved to Edmonton, where she worked in an advertising agency. In 1979, when she was 27, she became advertising manager for Eaton's, Alberta North, in charge of six stores and a $3.5 million budget.

In 1983, she moved to Toronto where she met—and was encouraged by—writers and poets Paul Dutton, Steven Smith, Anne Michaels, bp Nichol, Steve McCaffery, Chris Dewdney, and others. She also landed the high-stress job of marketing director for two high-profile complexes in the heart of Toronto—The Hudson's Bay Centre (Yonge and Bloor) and Renaissance Court and Plaza (Bloor and Avenue Road). She won national and international awards for her marketing programs, achieved double-digit sales increases, and burnt out. "Saved by restructuring and downsized with severance," she spent much of the summer of 1987 on the Toronto Islands, writing *a Knife a Rope a Book*, which was published by Underwhich Editions in 1990. That summer she also attended her first Writers/Artists colony at Emma Lake, where she began "CatoptRomancer," a long poem about the history and landscape of her childhood. She has found the Emma Lake and St. Peter's colonies to be the most productive writing times of her life. "The camaraderie and support I've received from everyone is remarkable."

In 1993, Rowley moved to Vancouver with her partner, artist Robert McNealy. In 1994, she was accepted into Simon Fraser University's Graduate Liberal Studies Program. As part of her M.A. studies, she organized a course in Prague to study Czech writers. In 1995, she also started her own corporate communications business, Pro-Textual Communications. She met her first client on the way to the bar after class, and soon found herself embroiled in the challenging task of gaining positive publicity for one of the most controversial redevelopments in the city's history—the old public library at Robson and Burrard. She involved local artists and writers and garnered corporate sponsorships for their work, which was a major factor in the turnaround of public opinion. Rowley co-authored Vancouver's controversial drug strategy document *A Framework for Action: A Four-Pillar Approach to the Drug Problem in Vancouver*, which has been distributed worldwide and translated into several languages.

PHOTO BY WENDY NIAMATH-KEELER
MARI-LOU ROWLEY

She also writes and edits science publications for UBC and other clients. "I have been privileged to interview many leading scientists in every field and the concepts in their work have filtered down into my poetry."

Rowley has read and performed her poetry across Canada, from Harbourfront to Hornby Island. She has been published in numerous literary magazines in Canada and the United States, and her chapbook *CatoptRomancer* was launched at the Walla Walla Poetry Party in Washington in 1997. Her work has been anthologized in *Pacific Northwest Spiritual Poetry* in the USA (1998), and *Listening with the Ear of the Heart: Writers at St. Peter's* (2003). In May 2003, she attended the Banff Writers Studio. Since then, she has published *Interference with the Hydrangea* (2003) and *Viral Suite* (2004). Rowley continues to live and work in Vancouver, and retreats to Saskatchewan whenever possible to visit friends and family, inhale the wind—and write poetry.

About Writing... *For me, the process of writing a poem is meditative and intuitive. Yes, there are ideas and perhaps even research, but the act of writing the poem—one that startles even the writer—becomes almost involuntary. A zone where meaning and sound and sensual experience (e)merge in language. Afterwards, there is a sense of stunned awareness. A different kind of brightness. For this, solitude is essential.*—MARI-LOU ROWLEY

JERRY RUSH (1937–1986) was born in Frontier and grew up near the Cypress Hills. For many years he taught in Canada's Eastern Arctic.

His first poetry collection, *Earth Dreams*, was published in 1982. His second book, *The Bones of Their Occasion*, came out in 1986. He was the editor of *Solitudes*, a collection of short stories and poetry by high school students across Canada.

A member of the Regina writing group, The Correction Line, which included Anne Campbell, Victor Jerrett Enns, Paul Wilson, Brenda Baker, Gerry Hill, and Bruce Rice, Jerry Rush was a promising and often brilliant poet. He passed away after a battle with cancer in late 1986. The Saskatchewan Writers Guild has established the Jerry Rush Memorial Scholarship, in his memory. The scholarship is provided to a poet attending Sage Hill Writing Experience.

NIK BURTON

ALLAN SAFARIK was born on September 27, 1948, in Vancouver, into a commercial fishing family. He was raised in North Burnaby and spent his childhood hanging out on the Vancouver waterfront at his grandfather's fish plant, Vancouver Shell Fish & Fish Company (at Campbell Avenue Fishermen's Wharf), or on his father's crab boat in Boundary Bay. During his childhood and teen years Safarik was obsessed by sports, particularly by soccer, and he had the opportunity of playing on North Burnaby Legion 148, winners of four BC provincial championships and Canadian junior champions in 1967.

Most of his life he has been interested in writing poems. It really started as a teenage preoccupation when he discovered in himself a contemplative side that could be tuned in to provide relief from dealing with the chaos of the real world and the repetitious cycles that dominate our daily habits. The dwelling of self contained a private room that soon became a sanctuary for the meditative pursuit of writing poetry.

Safarik's teachers thought he was taking

notes when really he was perfectly disguised working on something else. That something else grew steadily through the years, until an avocation turned into an obsession and finally became a half-assed occupation. Along the way he has been lucky enough to find continuous employment in the allied trades: the broader field of writing, editing, and publishing that fuel the book industry.

Safarik enrolled at Simon Fraser University in the fall of 1968 (graduating with a degree in English) and he was a student there during the turbulent years of the late sixties and early seventies. While students, Safarik and Brian Brett co-founded *Blackfish* magazine in 1971, a little magazine which eventually became a controversial irritant to the campus literary establishment which was dominated by a certain literary movement called Black Mountain. The group of professors who advocated this American-influenced style of writing (which owed much to Walt Whitman, Ezra Pound, and Charles Olson) had a community-based, almost cult-like, following amongst campus arty types.

Eventually, the magazine turned into *Blackfish Press*, a small literary press that published trade or limited edition books that included: Pat Lowther, Seymour Mayne, Dorothy Livesay, Al Purdy, F.R. Scott, John Glassco, Anita Lever, Albert Moritz, and Kenneth Rexroth. During the seventies and early eighties Safarik traveled constantly across the country putting books in stores and networking in the various literary scenes across the country.

For the past thirty years Safarik has published poetry in a wide variety of places in Canada and elsewhere, including appearances in most Canadian magazines. In addition, he has written widely in magazines and newspapers on books, literature, theatre, art, aboriginal affairs, and personal memoirs. He is the author of nine books of poetry including, *Advertisements For Paradise* (1986), *On The Way to Ethiopia* (1991), *All Night Highway* (1996), *How I Know The Sky Is A River* (1999), and *Bird Writer's Handbook* (2002). He is the editor of the acclaimed anthology *Vancouver Poetry* (1986), and the co-editor (along with Dolores Reimer) of four sports books on: Harold Ballard, Don Cherry, Wayne Gretzky and The Toronto Blue Jays.

Safarik has also produced a wide range of other materials including a best-selling cookbook and an aboriginal parenting manual. In the spring of 2004, his most recent collection of poetry, *Blood Of Angels*, will be published.

While holding down a number of positions related to the writing field, including teaching workshops (National Museum Program, Burnaby Arts Centre), organizing literary events (National Book Festival Co-ordinator, Canada Council, BC/Yukon, 1986–93), consulting (Consultant Intellectual Property, Wanuskewin Heritage Park, 1993–95), Director of Publishing (Timberholme Books 1997–99), he has continued to put out a steady stream of literary and commercial writing. In addition, he has read poetry at a variety of venues from coast to coast and participated in literary festivals in all of the regions of Canada.

From the late seventies until the early nineties Safarik lived in White Rock, British Columbia, in a ramshackle beach house (which has become known as the blue house) on the hill overlooking the pier and

ALLAN SAFARIK... AT THE CATHEDRAL ARTS FESTIVAL, 2003.

Semiahmoo Bay. During the past ten years he has lived in the ninety-six-year-old Jacoby house at 211 1st St. in Dundurn (population 500), Saskatchewan. He left the metropolis behind for the peace and tranquil existence of small town life in rural Saskatchewan so that he could have the absolute best conditions for a writer of his ilk—that is, total peace and quiet from the stress of wild traffic and outrageous urban sprawl. Here, he says, he has no excuses or distractions to keep him from his appointments with the muse.

Safarik was the writer-in-residence in Humboldt from 1999 to 2000 and in Estevan from 2001 to 2002. Three of his books have been nominated for the poetry award at the Saskatchewan Book Awards: *All Night Highway* in 1997, *How I Know The Sky Is A River* in 2000, and *Bird Writer's Handbook* in 2003. In 2003, *Notes From The Outside*, literary essays, won the John V. Hicks Manuscript Award. Safarik is married to writer Dolores Reimer, and they have three children: Jake, Emily, and Hank. Safarik also has two adult children, Jeremy Baisch and Jevon Greco, who he helped raise from an early age.

About Writing... *Poets, as well as other artists, are the mirrors of the people. They describe and illuminate in depth the passage of a people in their time and at their place on earth. Art is a part of the mystery that makes man the most complex, compelling creature. The artists of primitive people have provided a legacy for understanding the little we know of the past; just as the artists of today leave an impression for the future world. A culture that ridicules or ignores its artists is fighting against permanence.*—ALLAN SAFARIK

BARBARA SAPERGIA grew up in Moose Jaw, and now lives in Saskatoon with her husband, writer Geoffrey Ursell. In between, she's lived in Regina (twice), Winnipeg (three times), Victoria, and Vancouver in Canada, and London and Oxford in England. She earned her B.A. in 1964 at the University of Saskatchewan, and her M.A. in 1966 at the University of Manitoba. She completed a Pre-Master's program in Political Studies, also at University of Manitoba in 1973. Sapergia has taught English at the universities of Victoria, British Columbia, and Manitoba, and Creative Writing (briefly) at the University of Saskatchewan.

Sapergia had the good fortune to study with some of Canada's finest writers, including Robert Kroetsch and Jack Hodgins at the Saskatchewan School of the Arts (in the seventies) and the late Charles Israel at the Banff Screenwriters Workshop (1989). All were strong influences, Kroetsch for his powers of language and invention, Hodgins for his brilliant imagination and narrative rigour, Israel for his wealth of experience and love of good writing, all of them for their great generosity.

Sapergia writes fiction (novels and short stories) and drama (stage, radio, film, and television). Her fiction includes two novels, *Foreigners* (1984) and *Secrets in Water* (1999), and a short story collection, *South Hill Girls* (1992). All three reflect her childhood in Moose Jaw and the beautiful hill country near Old Wives Lake. They also reflect a heritage mixed between her mother's Romanian forebears and her father's Welsh-English roots.

Seven of her plays have been professionally produced—four for adults and three for children. *Matty & Rose* (Persephone Theatre, 1985) portrays the struggles of railway porters in the forties. *The Great Orlando* (Persephone, 1985) is a comic prairie fable. *Lokkinen* (25th Street Theatre, 1982) centred around the conflict between individualism and communal values in rural Saskatchewan, and

Roundup (also 25th Street, 1990) tried to deal with the effects of drought on farmers and ranchers. Her plays have won two Saskatchewan Writers Guild Major Awards for Drama. *Lokkinen* and *Roundup* have been published in book form, as has a poetry collection, *Dirt Hills Mirage* (1980).

Sapergia also has extensive dramatic productions in radio, including a five-part *Morningside* series about a reporter who finds out what it feels like to live on welfare, and a Stereo Theatre drama based on her story collection, also broadcast by the Australian Broadcasting Corporation.

One of three partners in Moose Jaw Light & Power Artistic Productions Ltd., Barbara is co-creator, with Geoffrey Ursell, of the preschool television series *Prairie Berry Pie*, currently airing on Global Television and the Aboriginal Peoples Television Network. She wrote or co-wrote five episodes in Season One and four in Season Two. Other television credits include a half-hour drama for CBC's *The Way We Are*; a CBC comedy pilot, *Midnight in Moose Jaw*, co-written with Geoffrey Ursell and Rod Coneybeare; and a one-hour drama for the MythQuest series produced by Mind's Eye Pictures. Sapergia has a television movie script, *And then the Sun*, in development with Mind's Eye, based on her novel *Foreigners*. She has also completed a screenplay based on her stage play *Matty & Rose* and is working to find a way to produce it.

Sapergia is a co-founder and current board member of Coteau Books (founded in 1975) where she has worked as acquisitions editor and also edited over twenty titles for young readers, including books by Judith Silverthorne, Dave Glaze, Betty Dorion, Mary Bishop, Mary Woodbury, Cheryl Foggo, Ruby Slipperjack, and Hiromi Goto. She coordinated Coteau's *In the Same Boat* millennium series of children's books celebrating authors from diverse cultural backgrounds.

Sapergia served as playwright-in-residence at Persephone Theatre in 1985. She has read at universities, libraries, and conferences throughout the west, as well as at Expo '86 in Vancouver, Harbourfront in Toronto, and at the Ontario Council of Teachers of English Annual Conference. She has been an active member of many writers' organizations and has served as treasurer of the Saskatchewan Writers Guild, president of the Saskatchewan Playwrights Centre, and western vice-chair of the Playwrights Union of Canada. Her work has been supported both by the Saskatchewan Arts Board and the Canada Council, support which has provided crucial spaces of time to devote to writing.

About Writing... *My writing has been driven by character, landscape, ethnicity, politics, and an attraction to Saskatchewan. I love fiction or screenwriting the most, depending on which I'm doing. Reading and editing books for kids has also been rewarding. I'm heartened by the Harry Potter books, because they're so lively and intelligent and so beautifully plotted, and because they show us that television and video games have not taken over world culture. These are books, and their success was created by readers.*—BARBARA SAPERGIA

CANDACE SAVAGE was very nearly born on the front seat of a pickup truck somewhere between Valhalla Centre (a cluster of frame houses at the intersection of two gravel roads in the Peace River Country of northern Alberta) and the Grande Prairie hospital. Her mother, Edna Sherk, had resigned her position as the primary teacher at the local two-room school a few months earlier to prepare for her first child, but her dad, Harry, had stayed on as principal and senior teacher. The trip to the hospital had been delayed until classes were dismissed for the day, and what with a bitter wind to slow their progress and rutted roads to hasten the birth, the baby came within minutes of being delivered en route.

In the event, of course, she was born to care and comfort (on December 2, 1949), and so her life continued. Her first word was "book"—or so her bookish parents said—and though the family didn't have much of a library, her mother always found something to read to her. After her two younger sisters were born, her mother read to them, too, so that Candace was able to extend the pleasures of bedtime stories almost into her teens. For several years, the family subscribed to a series of children's classics called Junior Deluxe Editions, hard-bound books with tan covers and pastel backs that arrived each month by mail. They bore titles like *Anne of Green Gables*, *The Jungle Book*, *Little Women*, and *The Adventures of Sherlock Holmes*. Cuddled up on the couch with her sisters, listening to their mother's voice, Candace soaked up the rhythms of written English. To this day, she still writes "by ear," listening to the beat of her sentences as she composes them.

Even though she often found school dead boring, she was good at passing tests and, in 1967, was admitted to the University of Alberta in Edmonton on a scholarship. She graduated four years later with an Honours Degree in English and was awarded the Governor-General's Gold Medal and the Rutherford Gold Medal in English for the year of her graduation. As part of her program, she completed an independent-study project on metaphor with Wilfred Watson, who was a poet, philosopher, and playwright as well as a professor. He encouraged her to develop a kind of intellectual "peripheral vision," so that, by looking at things from an angle instead of straight on, she could notice patterns and connections that were otherwise hidden.

By this time, Candace had been bopping around Alberta with her family for twenty-odd years, with stops in Beaverlodge, Vermilion, Pincher Creek, and Edmonton and a couple of brief forays into northern British Columbia. In 1970, she married Arthur Savage, a physics graduate whom she had met at the University of Alberta, and they moved to Saskatoon, where he found work as a lab instructor. What to do? For several years, she teased herself with the idea of doing graduate work in English or History or Biology or Medicine or Medieval Studies. But eventually she realized that (a) as a female, she could expect a rough ride in academia and (b) she could be more creative without the strictures of a narrow discipline. And so she started to write.

Her first books—*A Harvest Yet to Reap* (co-authored with three other women) and *Our Nell* (a biography of Nellie L. McClung)—explored the history of women in western Canada. Then, when Arthur decided that he wanted to write, too, she collaborated with him on a book about the

PHOTO BY KEITH BELL

CANDACE SAVAGE... AND HER FRIEND, STAR.

mammals of western Canada. These two themes—women's/cultural history and natural science—have persisted throughout her career and, between them, have so far found expression in 21 books. Her most recent work, *Wizards: An Amazing Journey Through the Last Great Age of Magic*, is a children's book that looks at the practice of magic in the seventeenth century and the transition from magic to science. Her next title will be a natural history of the Great Plains grasslands. By allowing herself to roam across the widest possible range of subjects, she keeps her mind on high alert and avoids the risk of becoming complacent or over-confident.

A daughter, Diana, was born in Saskatoon in 1979, and Arthur died about two years later. After moving to Edmonton and then to Yellowknife, Candace and Diana returned to Saskatoon in 1990, where Candace served for a term as writer-in-residence at the Public Library. In 1992, Candace had the good fortune to meet Keith Bell, an historian who teaches in the Department of Art and Art History at the University of Saskatchewan, with whom she fully intends to live happily ever after.

About Writing... *I love the concept of the "essay," with its connotations of exploration and experiment. How to capture in words the unfathomable strangeness of time and place and the world around us?*—CANDACE SAVAGE

GREGORY SCOFIELD can trace his ancestry back to the Red River Settlement near Winnipeg, Manitoba, although he was born in Maple Ridge, British Columbia, in 1966.

Scofield has lived in Whitehorse, Yukon, as well as in Prince Albert and Saskatoon.

He is the author of four books of poetry, *I*

GREGORY SCOFIELD

Knew Two Métis Women (2000), *Love Medicine and One Song* (1997), *Native Canadiana: Songs from the Urban Rez* (1996), and *The Gathering: Stones from the Medicine Wheel* (1993), and a book of memoirs, *Thunder Through My Veins: Memories of a Métis Childhood* (1999). His stories have been broadcast on CBC radio and anthologized in a variety of books internationally. He won the Dorothy Livesay Poetry Prize and the Canadian Authors Association Air Canada Award for the most promising writer in 1996. A former street youth outreach worker, he now lives and writes in Vancouver.

LEILAH NADIR

STEPHEN SCRIVER was born in Wolseley in 1947, the second son of Harry and Edith Scriver. His father had traveled east during the Depression where he met Edith in Toronto, served four years overseas during the war, and brought his eastern bride back to his hometown in 1946. He was a third-generation weekly newspaper editor, a stalwart supporter of the CCF/NDP, and a community booster. Edith was a teacher, a storyteller, and also a listener.

Stephen's early years found him working as the "printer's devil" for his father, casting printing plates, "dissing" (distributing) handset type back to the proper drawers, and wading in on press day as another edition of *The Wolseley News* "went to bed."

When he was eleven, Stephen's father made him obituaries editor, paying him ten cents a column inch to memorialize the passing of Wolseley's citizens. One of his early lessons was that the editor-in-chief was not interested in overly long writeups, which was as much an economic issue as one of good taste.

Stephen has always been an academic underachiever, scraping by in high school and university, eventually absconding with a professional teaching certificate. He has been much luckier in love, however, and took with him into his teaching career his wife, Barbara. They married in 1970 and had four children: Jason, Amy, Alia, and Luke. They lost Amy to leukemia when she was five years old. They now also have five grandchildren.

Scriver's teaching took his family to Rosetown, Grenfell, Nipawin, and Maidstone, and eventually to Edmonton, where he retired in 2002 after thirty-two years in the harness. Among the highlights of his teaching career were the 27 years he coached athletes, guiding provincial champions in football and track. Scriver received two nominations for excellence in teaching.

Early in his teaching career two things pushed Scriver further into the writing world. In 1974 he attended the Canadian English Teachers conference in Saskatoon where he attended a session on writing poetry led by Anne Szumigalski. He sat next to another rural English teacher, Lorna Crozier, who encouraged him to attend Fort San. About the same time he came across an article in a teaching magazine that mentioned the names of the

PHOTO BY BARBARA SCRIVER
STEPHEN SCRIVER... HIS LIKENESS.

two main influences in his formative writing days. These were Raymond Souster, who said that you could write about what moves you in your daily life, and Charles Bukowski, who said that you could express it any damned way you pleased. This was reinforced by his first two writing teachers at Fort San, Ken Mitchell and Robert Kroetsch. Mitchell asked him: "What's important to you?" and Kroetsch said, "Leave the language alone!"

This resulted in Scriver's winning of the W.O. Mitchell Bursary, which got him to Fort San again, and his first chapbook in 1977, *Between the Lines*. These hockey poems were widely anthologized and published in small magaziness, so it was two years before Scriver was to experience a rejection from a literary magazine. It also began a long association with *Morningside*, on which he guested four times. Scriver's winning of the poetry award of the Saskatchewan Writers Guild Literary Competition in 1980 was followed by more hockey poems in 1981 with the publishing of *All Star Poet!* It was a best seller, along with the sequel *More All Star Poet!* in 1989. One of Scriver's hockey poems was also published in Ken Dryden's book *Home Game*, initially without permission or payment. Scriver then changed subjects, honouring his father's war service with a book of poetry about RCAF ground crew, entitled *Under the Wings* in 1991.

The move to Alberta in 1990 brought Scriver into contact with Kenneth Brown, the hockey playwright. They collaborated on a play, *Letters in Wartime*, which they also produced at the 1995 Edmonton Fringe. The play won the Sterling Award for Best New

Fringe Work. At this time Scriver began his association with the Regina film company, Partners In Motion, by researching ten films for them and writing two. His script for *Missing On Way Back* (1997) won him a Regina Heritage Award and a nomination for Best Script from the Saskatchewan Motion Picture Association.

Scriver's work has been reviewed across Canada and he has been interviewed in most of the major media. Besides this, he was the Poet Laureate of Peter Gzowski's Golf Tournament for Literacy in Regina in 1993. He never lost his love of hockey, serving at different times as statistician of the SJHL Nipawin Hawks, Director of Operations for the University of Alberta Golden Bears, and Commissioner of Hockey for Western Canada Universities.

As Scriver moves into his retirement years, he has begun a novel, which encompasses his passions for the prairies and the effects of the air war on Canadians in World War II.

About Writing... *Throughout my life there were always obligations which came before my writing; the prospect of now having much more time to write is, frankly, frightening. There are no excuses. It's writing or macramé.*—STEPHEN SCRIVER

NANCY SENIOR was born in 1941 in Roseboro, North Carolina. She has lived in the United States and in Europe, and now lives in Saskatoon with her husband and son.

Senior teaches French at the University of Saskatchewan, with a specialty in eighteenth-century literature.

In 1980 and 1981, she organized a competition for university students writing in French and Spanish, and published the winning entries in *Les Moissons*.

Nancy Senior's poems have been broadcast on CBC's *Anthology* and have appeared in *Grain*, *Salt*, *Event*, *CVII*, and *Quarry*. Her book publications include *Poems* (1973), *I Never Wanted to be the Holy Ghost* (1977), *The Mushroom Jar* (1980), and *Les Moissons* (ed., 1980, 1981). Her poems have also been anthologized in *Number One Northern* (1977), *Aurora: New Canadian Poetry* (1979), and *The Best of Grain* (1980).

NIK BURTON

MAGGIE SIGGINS is a transplanted Torontonian who moved to Regina in 1983 to teach journalism and who now considers the west her home. Siggins had a Southam Fellowship from 1974 to 1975, and held the Max Bell Chair in Journalism at the University of Regina from 1983 to 1984.

A former magazine writer, political columnist, television producer, and journalism professor, Siggins now spends most of her time writing books.

She is the author of several award-winning books of non-fiction. *A Canadian Tragedy: Jo Ann and Colin Thatcher* (1985) received an Arthur Ellis Award (Crime Writers of Canada) in 1986, and was made into the CBC television mini-series *Love and Hate*. Siggins received the Governor General's Award for Non-fiction for *Revenge of the Land* (1991). Her biography of Louis Riel, entitled *Riel: a life of revolution*, won the City of Regina Best Book award in 1994, and *In Her Own Time, A Class Reunion Inspires a Cultural History of Women* (2000) was a co-winner of the City of Regina Best Book award in 2000. Siggins' other books include *Brian and the Boys: A Story of Gang Rape* (1984), and *Basset: A Biography* (1979).

HEATHER HODGSON

JUDITH SILVERTHORNE spent her early years living in the Glenavon area on a farm, moving to Regina with her family at age six. Her parents, Stan and Elaine (nee Assman) Iles, both came from Saskatchewan farming backgrounds. For many years her father worked as an electrician, and he later formed a company (Iles Electric) with Silverthorne's youngest brother. Her mother, a creative and efficient housewife, began her more than twenty-year stint working part-time at Sears while Silverthorne was a teenager cum writer.

With a strong desire to write, brought on by a feverish love of reading—mysteries, adventure, and practically anything she found at hand—Silverthorne dabbled with journalistic approaches as early as age 14. She explored other expressions, including poetry, but mostly felt a lack of support in her ambitions, or was too busy experiencing the life she would write about to find a way to pursue her strong inner aspirations.

Silverthorne found work in a variety of capacities with various library systems in the province for a few years. She also worked in bookstores, and restaurants as a waitress, cook, baker, and manager, as well as a photographic technician. In the early 1980s, she was employed with the Photographic Arts Department with the Saskatchewan government. In 1983 she moved with her journeyman carpenter and musician husband, Alan Silverthorne, to the Endeavour, Saskatchewan, area, where they embarked on a rustic adventure.

There, Silverthorne fully explored her compulsion to write, and she began freelancing human interest articles for newspapers and magazines, including many for Saskatchewan weekly newspapers. She also joined a local writing group that held their monthly meetings in the home of her mentor, Patricia Armstrong, in Sturgis.

While doing the research for one of her newspaper articles, she became enthralled with the subject matter, which resulted in her first published book, a biography, *Made in Saskatchewan: Peter Rupchan, Ukrainian Pioneer and Potter*. Prairie Lily Cooperative released the book in 1991, a year after her return move to the more populated and culturally stimulating environment of Regina.

By this time, she and her husband had a son, Aaron, and her writing and researching abilities brought her into contact with the television industry. She relished her brushes with a new medium and began assisting with research on the popular SCN regional show "One in a Million." With the major assistance of the producer of this show, the docu-drama *Rupchan: Spirit of a Prairie Potter* emerged in 1992. The show, based on her first published biography, was nominated for the Showcase Best Original Music Award (written and performed by her husband). The production was one of the first to be broadcast on CBC Saskatchewan and then CBC Canada, a high point when the Saskatchewan film and video industry was just burgeoning.

From then on Silverthorne was hooked with the medium, and she began some television projects of her own, while also continuing to make a living 'of sorts' in freelance writing about Saskatchewan people and issues for a variety of newspapers and magazines, including the *Western Producer/Western People*, the *Leader-Post*, *Uptown*, *Folklore*, and *Prairie Books Now*. Some 400 articles and columns later, she also began an extensive historical research and writing project about early Saskatchewan woodworkers and furniture makers (1870–1930).

Shortly after this time, Silverthorne became the owner/manager of Spiral Film Productions Inc. And in 1997, she produced a half-hour documentary, *Ingrained Legacy*, and *Splinters*, a series of ten vignettes, both based on her research material of the early Saskatchewan woodworkers. In that same year, she produced another series of vignettes about First Nations artists in Saskatchewan, called *First Visions*.

Silverthorne began sporadically taking some formal classes at the University of Regina in the Film and Video and English departments in the early 1990s. During this time, she also joined the Children's Writers Round Robin, a group of children's writers from around the province, and found herself inspired by such prolific and skilled writers as Alison Lohans, Jo Bannatyne-Cugnet, Dianne Young, and Gillian Richardson.

Silverthorne published her first children's novel, *The Secret of Sentinel Rock*, in 1996. It was based on her experiences growing up with the influences and stories of her two sets of farming grandparents from the Glenavon and Grenfell areas of Saskatchewan. That year, the book also won the Children's Literary Award at the Saskatchewan Book Awards Gala, and it also became an 'Our Choice' Award winner through the Children's Book Centre. As well, it was shortlisted for the Geoffrey Bilson Award for Historical Fiction for Young People, and the Saskatchewan Book Award for Publishing in Education.

In 1998, she produced *Roger Ing's Utopia*, a half-hour documentary on well-known Regina Chinese artist, Roger Ing and his Utopia Café. It was nominated for the Best Documentary Award at Showcase that year. In 2002, she changed her production company name to Spiral Communications Inc. and expanded from television productions to include other writing and communications under the new mandate.

Although producing television material was stimulating, Silverthorne found the financial rewards limited, especially while now functioning as a single parent. In the early summer of 1998, she secured a full-time position as the Executive Director of the Saskatchewan Library Association, where she remains currently, while still pursuing writing and producing initiatives.

JUDITH SILVERTHORNE...
WAITING FOR THE MUSE.

Throughout the years, Silverthorne has also done editing and critiquing of articles and books for publishers. She lectures, curates art shows, and is a promoter and publicist of cultural events, as well as a mentor to other aspiring writers. She has been on many boards and committees, including the Saskatchewan Motion Picture Association and the Saskatchewan Writers Guild. She has taught sessional classes at the SIAST Wascana Campus in the film and video industry, and has delved into the writing genre of screenplays.

Three of Silverthorne's books, *Made in Saskatchewan*, *The Secret of Sentinel Rock*, and *Dinosaur Hideout* have been listed in the Saskatchewan Education bibliographies, and are being used in Saskatchewan schools. Silverthorne is often a guest speaker at schools and libraries, especially with regards to her children's novels. *Dinosaur Hideout* won the Saskatchewan Book Award for Children's Literature in 2003, and was nominated for the 2004 Willow Awards.

Her newest children's novel, *Dinosaur*

Breakout, was published in the spring of 2004. The third book in this trilogy is to be released in 2005, followed by a sequel to *The Secret of Sentinel Rock*. Adult novels, including mysteries, are also in the works, along with some new children's books on various topics related to Saskatchewan.

About Writing... *One's writing inspirations come from the deep personal wellspring of creativity of your soul and which aligns with the divine. If you write from the heart, you are sure to tap into this powerful resource. Never write for your audience, but for yourself with all the depth of emotion and finesse that you can, and the rest will follow. Embrace the hard work, struggle, and effort that is part of this worthwhile pursuit and you will be successful.*—JUDITH SILVERTHORNE

REG SILVESTER is one of the many Saskatchewan writers who began careers in fiction and poetry at the Saskatchewan Summer School of the Arts in the mid-1970s. He studied with Ken Mitchell, Robert Kroetsch, and Jack Hodgins in the summers of 1974, 1975, and 1976, had his first short story published (in *Grain*, of course) in 1978, and then had his first book of fiction, *Fish-Hooks*, published in 1984.

Silvester remembers the summer school at Fort San with fondness. "I don't think I ever fit in anywhere, not in my whole life, before I went to Fort San. And then suddenly, down in that valley, in the midst of that huge stream of words and wonders and weirdness, I found friends who not only understood my madness but who were just as mad themselves."

Like many other Saskatchewan writers, Silvester was born in Moose Jaw. His first home was in an apartment above Thatcher's Hardware on River Street, that neighbourhood where people were known to gather for sinful purposes. It was right at the end of the Second World War, when housing was hard to find. His father was a travelling salesman for Gypsum Lime and Alabastine, and a Baptist, and his mother was an Anglican, a nurse who had quit her profession after her marriage. They took the apartment on River Street because, well, there wasn't any other room in the inn.

"If you think about reincarnation, you'd have to wonder what I'd done in a past life to deserve such nice, God-fearing parents living on a street where gambling and prostitution were rife. Maybe I had been a hard-drinking, hard-living, whoring soldier bound for hell, but who died heroically in the fight against Hitler and wound up reborn where I could aim for a loftier life, but where there would be prostitutes to walk with hand in hand to soften my confusion. But that's only if you think about reincarnation."

Silvester's family moved from Moose Jaw to Winnipeg, then Saskatoon, and then Lloydminster, where he started Grade One. His father opened Silvester Glass & Paint in North Battleford in 1953, a business which is still operating under the ownership of his brother Brian as Silvester Glass and Aluminum Products Ltd. His sisters, Myrl Barron and Linda Hebert, also remain in North Battleford and are engaged in businesses of their own.

After completing high school, Silvester joined the *North Battleford News-Optimist* as a reporter. He worked there for a year before going to Ottawa to study journalism at Carleton University. Upon graduation, he went to work for the *Victoria Times* as a reporter, then went back to Ottawa to work on an inner city newspaper called the *Centretown News*, a project started by then alderman Michael Cassidy, who later became leader of the Ontario NDP.

Financial difficulties at the *Centretown News* led Silvester to resign and find work at the Regina *Leader-Post* in 1973. It was while working at the *Leader-Post* that he decided to take a creative writing course at the Summer School of the Arts.

"Some people thought it was strange that I would take a vacation from my job, which was writing for a newspaper, to go take a writing course. But it's a huge step from journalism to fiction, and I wanted to take it. I couldn't have gone for a vacation in a more different world."

Silvester left Saskatchewan in 1978 with his first wife, Susan Sneath, who was an actress. He got a job with the *Edmonton Journal* and later worked as a freelance writer. In 1983 he joined a group of friends in the founding of *The Edmonton Bullet*, an arts and entertainment magazine that operated until it strangled in the tightened economy of 1993.

Silvester's two children, Matthew and Molly, were born in Edmonton in 1980 and 1983 and still live there. Their mother had a successful acting career through the 1980s, and was especially well known as the playwright's favourite actress in new plays. That marriage ended in 1997.

In 2002, Silvester returned to Saskatchewan with his second wife, Mary Walters, also a writer. They live in Rosthern where Mary writes novels and works as a freelancer and Silvester runs an antiques and collectibles store, sells junk on eBay, and continues to try to complete a comic novel with a central character named Starry Starry Knight. He's also struggling to get to the end of a collection of 72 golf poems, but so far he's only finished the first nine.

"The writer's first task, it seems, is to find ways to avoid writing, and I've been a champion at that. Starting a magazine, playing golf, starting an antique store, even teaching writing, are ways to avoid writing. If it weren't for the colonies program of the Saskatchewan Writers Guild, I might have quit writing by now. But while I was in Alberta I kept my Saskatchewan life and my writing life alive by attending colonies. Now I have my Saskatchewan life back full time and I hope that the writing life will continue and move further into the foreground."

Silvester's publications include two collections of short stories, *Fish-Hooks* (1984) and *Wishbone* (1991). He was also a collaborator in the collection of stories by Marijan Megla, called *Vajolin/The Violin* (1999). Megla writes in English in Yugoslavian phonetics, and Silvester provides an ordinary English parallel text for the book. Silvester has also had stories published in several literary magazines, and wrote an article about Saskatchewanians as immigrants to Alberta in the anthology called *The Road Home* (1992).

About Writing... *You have to have the courage to write badly. So many people who are interested in becoming writers seem to think that first they learn to write, then they come up with a plot, then they make their story, then they get published and become rich and famous. But no, you have to stride off half-cocked! You have to run without boots or mitts into the winter night because you heard a scream out there. You have to claim the right to be wrong. And you have to find out what's happening in the fiction by being in the middle of it yourself. You have to know that the correct order of things is: ready, fire, aim. In other words, write badly, read and understand it, then revise. Rich and famous don't matter.*—REG SILVESTER

LOIS SIMMIE. I was born in Edam, Saskatchewan, in June 1932. My father, Ed Binns, a tall, lanky Kentuckian, was the Pool elevator agent at Mervin; my mother Bessie was a wonderful cook, canner and pickle-maker, and was always painting or wallpapering something. I was embarrassed to have the only mother in town who smoked. She and my aunt both drove, and once when Aunt Annie was taking my two cousins and me to Turtleford to the dentist, Jeannie fell out the back window and the car made so much noise on the gravel road that my aunt didn't hear us yelling. Jeannie was in the ditch picking flowers when we went tearing back. I have one sister, Betty.

When I was eight, I got rheumatic fever and was confined to my parents' upstairs bedroom with a live-in nurse's bed beside mine. Every night she would undress in the closet, come out in a long white nightgown and curl her hair in paper strips. There was a streetlight just outside the window and she would stand there with her knobby little head outlined, then sigh deeply, get down on her knees between the two beds and pray out loud that I wouldn't die in the night. I got the impression it would be okay in the daytime. I wasn't allowed to read, and she would only read to me from the Bible which was scarier than she was, but not a lot. My dad couldn't stand her and she said, "your father has quite a vein of sarcasm" which set me wondering where that vein was located and if everybody had one. When my mother asked the teacher to send some books, she sent three: two were on manners, and the third I'd read at least four times. (She didn't have a lot of choice since our school library consisted of one half-empty shelf in the back of the room). I sometimes think that whole experience had something to do with my becoming a writer, and many years later wrote about it in the story, "Romantic Fever."

LOIS SIMMIE... SEVENTY GOING ON NINE.

I spent a lot of time down at my dad's elevator office, sitting at the desk drawing with indelible pencils and dashing out to the driveway every time a truck pulled in to watch it unload. He took me up on the lift to the top of the elevator, loud with birds. He was a great storyteller and told us outrageous lies about Kentucky, all of which I believed, telling all the kids about those hoop snakes that took their tails in their mouths and rolled around the country. I definitely got my love of story from him.

When I was eleven, we moved to Livelong, in the beautiful country just a few miles from Turtle Lake, with more than its quota of odd, interesting characters. In high school I wrote a few poems and old public school friends tell me I said I'd be a writer. If so, it took me long enough. By the time I started to write I was almost forty, with writers' magazines dating back fifteen years or so. I could never seem to read good books objectively, as they advised, but maybe I learned by osmosis.

University wasn't an option so I went to Success Business College in Saskatoon; not their star student, they changed the name to Saskatoon Business College when I left. (I did go to university as a mature student but, as writing full-time took over, not long enough to get a degree.) I had enough different jobs to make good book jacket copy. My best was copywriter at CJNB North Battleford, my worst a waitress for Sammy, the likeable drunk, who went across the street to the hotel as soon as the beer parlor opened—leaving me to try to cook for hungry farmers—and eventually blew up the café by leaving a pot of oil on the stove.

I married twice, raised four children, and now live a cliché'd but happy single life with my cat. I even like to knit.

Coteau published my first collection of stories, a chapbook, *Ghost House*, in 1976 and my newest adult novel *What I'm Trying to Say Is Goodbye* in 2003. (They were also the fourth publisher to bring out *They Shouldn't Make You Promise That*.) In between have been seven children's books, an adult novel, two books of short stories, and a non-fiction book. You know what they say about jacks of all trades. I likely would have been better off as a novelist but wouldn't change it, I've had too much fun writing for kids. Anne Szumigalski said we each have two ages, our chronological age and our real age, "and you're eight," she told me. She was four. I've read to kids in schools and libraries wherever, and been lost on more Saskatchewan roads than I can remember. I could write a book of stories called *You Can't Miss It*.

Editor's Note: Simmie has also published a short story collection, *Pictures* (1984), three collections of children's poems, *Auntie's Knitting a Baby* (1984), *An Armadillo Is Not a Pillow* (1986), and *Who Greased the Shoelaces?* (1989), a picture book, *What Holds Up the Moon* (1987), an early chapter book, *Oliver's Chickens* (1992), a children's play, *Auntie's Knitting a Baby* (1992), short stories, *Betty Lee Bonner Lives There* (1993), and *The Secret Lives of Sgt. John Wilson* (1995), which won the Crime Writers of Canada Arthur Ellis non-fiction prize. Her picture book, *Mister Got To Go* (1995), won the Saskatchewan Book Award for best children's book; the Alberta Book Award for best children's book, best illustrated book, and publishers prize;

short-listed for the Vancouver Book Prize, and won the British Picture Book Quarterly prize, winter 1995. Her picture book, *Mister Got To Go and Arnie* (2001) was short-listed for the Violet Downey Award and the Saskatchewan Book Award Saskatoon prize, and it won the Shining Willow Reader's Choice Award.

About Writing... *My thoughts on writing, or why I write? I think it's because I often think of the perfect repartee when it's too late and when you write, people think you're smarter and wittier than you really are. Ken Mitchell told us at my first writing class at Fort Qu'Appelle, that the first duty of writer is to entertain, and I've tried to do that. Some people say they'd write even if they knew they'd never be published and I think why would anybody put themselves through that unique torture for no reason? It's all about communication, isn't it? A painter can at least hang even a bad picture on a wall, but what can you do with a pile of paper? Oh yes, and someone wrote and asked me what qualities a writer had to have and I wrote back and said curiosity, empathy, and tenacity. I could have added, insanity. And that's enough from me.*—LOIS SIMMIE

ANNE SLADE ranches with her family south of Tompkins, in the east block of the Cypress Hills. She was born in Victoria, British Columbia, but has been a prairie girl since the age of seven.

Her poetry, prose, articles, and songs about rural life have been published in magazines, and in Canadian and American anthologies, and they have also been aired on radio and television.

Slade has co-authored, with Doris Bircham, several books of poetry for children. The authors particularly enjoy sharing their writing with students in Saskatchewan schools. Mediatalk Productions featured Anne and Doris in a video entitled *Cowboy Poetry:*

Words to Live By in 1997. *Prairie Women II* is a presentation of poetry, prose, and song by the two writers, which illustrates the lives of prairie women through the years.

Anne Slade was the recipient of the Saskatchewan Writers Guild Awards for Children's Literature, and for Poetry in 1988. The League of Canadian Poets selected her poem "Ghost Story" for inclusion in the 1997/1998 issue of *Vintage*.

ARTHUR GREGORY SLADE was born in Moose Jaw in 1967 and was raised on a ranch in the Cypress Hills. His parents (Robert Edmund Arthur Slade and Patricia Anne Shea) were raised in Moose Jaw, but moved to the ranch in the early 1960s. The ranch was owned by Robert's father (Arthur Hercules Slade) who also ran the Harwood Hotel in Moose Jaw. Arthur junior was the third of four boys (David, Kenneth, and Brett).

Slade attended grades one to nine in Tompkins and graduated from Gull Lake High School in 1985 (he was captain of the basketball team and an offensive end on the football team). He then attended the University of Saskatchewan, majoring in English. He rediscovered his love for mythology and storytelling and received an English Honours degree in 1989. He worked as a night auditor at a Saskatoon hotel for several months and then found gainful employment as a copywriter for a local radio station. After five years of writing ads about cars, stereos, and happy hours, Slade burned out and moved back to the ranch to write part-time and ranch part-time.

Slade's first story was published in the early 1990s, and he went on to publish several more in various magazines. To date he has only two poems published and no plans to write any more poetry (it's too hard). His main interest has been in novels. He wrote his first novel in grade eleven and twelve and continued to write another every couple of years. They ranged in topic from fantasy, to horror, to new age. The first six were never published, but his seventh novel *Draugr* was published in 1997 and was nominated for a Saskatchewan Book Award. It was the first book in the Northern Frights series and was followed by *The Haunting of Drang Island* (1998) and *The Loki Wolf* (2000). Slade then had his first foray into creative non-fiction with *John Diefenbaker: An Appointment with Destiny* (2001).

Slade next began work on *Dust*, a novel set during the depression near the Cypress Hills. It was his first book set solely in Saskatchewan. *Dust* was released in the fall of 2001 and received the Governor General's Award for Children's Literature, the Mr. Christie's Award and the Saskatchewan Book Award for Children's Literature. He then began another series called Canadian Chills, the first book titled: *Return of the Grudstone Ghosts* (2002). He also finished *Tribes* (2002), a novel set in Saskatoon in a high school in his neighborhood. He is currently working on *Megiddo's Shadow*, a novel that takes place in Palestine during World War One and is inspired by his grandfather's war experiences. Slade lives in Saskatoon with his wife Brenda Baker and their daughter Tori Lorranne.

ARTHUR SLADE BY ARTHUR SLADE.

About Writing... *It is not how many weeks or years you have been writing, it is how many hours. The absolutely most important pursuit for a writer is trying to somehow squeeze an extra hour or two out of the twenty-four we are given each day.*—ARTHUR SLADE

STEVEN ROSS SMITH was born in Toronto on June 25, 1945, to Ruth (McDonald) and Clarence Smith. He is married to J. Jill Robinson, fiction writer, and they have a son, Emmett H Robinson Smith.

He has published under Steven Smith, and Steven Ross Smith and is the author of the poetry books *blind zone* (1985), *Sleepwalkers* (with Richard Truhlar, 1987), *Transient Light* (1990), *Reading My Father's Book* (1995), *fluttertongue, Book 1: The Book of Games* (1998), and *fluttertongue, Book 2: The Book of Emmett* (1999). Smith is also the author of two collections of short fiction: *Ritual Murders* (1983) and *Lures* (1997).

Smith grew up in Toronto and graduated from Ryerson Polytechnical Institute with a diploma in Radio and Television Arts (1968). He then freelanced in various media capacities in Toronto until 1987, only to defect to Saskatoon to pursue his literary writing with vigour. Smith's work has been published in many periodicals and anthologies in Canada, the United States, England and Russia. He has also been interviewed and has performed his work for television and radio, including CBC National Radio, and CBC Radio Saskatchewan. He has also given readings across Canada, in England, Holland, and the United States, and has been writer-in-residence in Weyburn, Saskatoon, and Red Deer.

STEVEN ROSS SMITH... WONDERING IF THE PHOTOGRAPHER IS SHOOTING HIS BEST SIDE.

Smith is a founding editor with Underwhich Editions (since 1977), and is the executive director of the Sage Hill Writing Experience.

He has been performing sound poetry since 1975, and was a member of the sound/performance ensemble Owen Sound through its existence from 1975 to 1985, recording audiocassettes entitled *Beyond The Range* (1980) and *Sign Language* (1985). Smith also collaborated on other audio recordings: with British sound poets Bob Cobbing and Keith Musgrove on *Various Throats* (1983), and with Toronto sound poet/composer Richard Truhlar on *Sleepwalkers* (1987). From 1992 to 1999 he performed with DUCT, an improvisatory sound-text-music ensemble he founded. Their recordings are *DUCT TAPE* (1994), and the CD *galvanized* (1999). Smith is also a book reviewer and occasional literary essayist.

About Writing... *In writing poetry and fiction and composing and performing sound poems, I try to challenge myself to do what I haven't done before. Language is a material, and form is a projection of that material into a space—I try to stretch the material's formal and spatial possibilities.*—STEVEN ROSS SMITH

KAREN SOLIE was born in Moose Jaw in July 1966, the year, she has been told, of a record spring wheat harvest in southwest Saskatchewan. Her parents, Howard and Hilda Solie, were both born in Saskatchewan. Her paternal grandparents, Hans and Ingrid

Solie, emigrated from Norway to homestead near Richmound, Saskatchewan, in 1915, while her maternal grandparents, Aloysius and Johanna Lingnau, arrived from East Prussia in the 1930s to establish their farm near Pike Lake. Hilda, a teacher, met Howard after moving to teach high school (where she was younger than some of her students) in Richmound. They married in 1965. Howard taught at the Saskatchewan Technical Institute in Moose Jaw until Karen was two. The family then moved to Saskatoon, where Howard was employed as an instructor in the University of Saskatchewan's School of Agriculture and at Kelsey Institute. Karen's sister, Dianne, was born in 1969, and her brother, Craig, in 1974.

For several years, the family spent school terms in Saskatoon and summers farming the Solie place. They lived these summers in the once prosperous but even then defunct village of Horsham, in an old three-room teacherage that must have been, given the facts of small children and no bathroom, hell on her mother. Solie remembers it being okay, despite a few tetanus shots and one go-round of rabies vaccinations. Howard gave up teaching in the mid-1970s, and the Solies moved onto the homestead for good. Howard and Hilda, and recently, Craig, still farm that land.

After graduating from high school in 1984, Solie took a year of university transfer courses at Medicine Hat College, entertaining the idea of becoming a veterinarian. It didn't last. She's bad at math. In 1985, she moved to Lethbridge to attend Lethbridge Community College, and received her print journalism diploma in 1987, despite having failed music appreciation. The *Lethbridge Herald* took her on as a reporter/photographer the summer of that year, and she worked there until 1989. Depressed by covering court and traffic accidents, she enrolled at the University of Lethbridge, where, after lurching through sociology and linguistics courses, she found English and philosophy. Solie worked a number of jobs in these years—as a groundskeeper, a library assistant, and a barista in a downtown coffee bar and in a Second Cup in the Park Place Mall food court. She was hired by Sears but quit after one day. In 1992 she fled to Austin, Texas, and lived there for a few months playing in a friend's band, hanging out with musicians, and writing an independent study on William Blake. Having run out of money, she returned to Lethbridge, and completed her Bachelor of Arts in English in 1993.

Not sure what to do next, Solie started graduate school in Victoria in the fall of that year, and received her M.A. in English in 1995. By this time, she'd started writing poems. Two that she submitted while in Austin were accepted by a California literary magazine she had never heard of, nor has heard of since. Back in Victoria, she saw a call for submissions on the back of *BC Book World* for a new anthology—*Breathing Fire*, edited by Pat Lane and Lorna Crozier—and decided what the hell. They accepted three poems, and Solie began to think that this was maybe something she could do. And so, amidst English doctoral studies and teaching at University of Victoria, in between tutoring work, a research assistantship, and marking English term papers for Camosun College, she kept doing it. She

KAREN SOLIE... DRINKING WHISKEY WITH PHOTOGRAPHER J. MCLAUGHLIN AT SOLIE'S HOUSE IN VICTORIA.

published a chapbook, *Eating Dirt*, in 1998, and began to place poems in literary magazines in Canada and in the United States.

In 1999, Solie attended the Banff School for the Arts Writing Studio, where she worked with Don McKay. Don suggested that there might be a book in what she was working on. *Short Haul Engine* was published in 2001, and in the year following was shortlisted for the Griffin Poetry Prize, the Gerald Lampert Award, and the ReLit Prize, and won the BC Book Prize Dorothy Livesay Award for Poetry. Two newer poems received a National Magazine Awards Honourable Mention that year.

Solie moved to Toronto in 2002, and is, as of this writing, at work on a new manuscript of poetry, essays, and a collection of short stories. Her first story, "Onion Calendar," won *Other Voices'* 1999 short fiction contest, and was included in the *Journey Prize Anthology 12*. Another, "Gone to Vinyl," won *SubTerrain* magazine's 2001 fiction prize. She continues to review books for *The Globe and Mail*, and visits Saskatchewan whenever she can.

About Writing... *It's joy and solace. It's loneliness and fear. It's the way the street looks at 4 a.m. with vices arrayed around you. It's walking that same street on a gorgeous day with three perfect words in your pocket. It's the highway between Swift Current and Regina. Good writing entails risk. A willingness to be transported, and to be laid low. To never settle. And it means reading. Reading everything. It means keeping your eyes open. Writing, and reading, are reasons to get up in the morning. I can't remember the last time I've been bored.*—KAREN SOLIE

GLEN SORESTAD was born in Vancouver in 1937. His parents both grew up in Saskatchewan and in 1947 they moved back to live on a farm near Buchanan. Sorestad attended a one-roomed country school named after a famous Norwegian poet and playwright—though he was blissfully unaware of this at the time. He graduated from Sturgis Composite High School—seventeen and uncertain about his future. After a year working in several small town branches of the Canadian Bank of Commerce, he discovered his banking talents were negligible. By sheer chance, a few months after terminating his banking career he ended up, at 18, spending the 1955/56 school year as a "study-supervisor" in a one-roomed school near the Alberta border because qualified teachers were in such short supply. He enjoyed this experience enough that the following year he attended Teachers' College and in 1957 in Yorkton's Simpson School he launched what was to become a teaching career of over twenty years.

In 1960 Sorestad married Sonia Talpash and that year taught school in Brooks, Alberta, before entering the University of Saskatchewan. He graduated with his B.Ed (with honours) in 1963 and later earned his M.Ed in 1976. While attending the University of Saskatchewan he was greatly influenced by two of his English professors, Carlyle King and Edward McCourt, both of whom inspired and encouraged him as a teacher of literature and as a writer-to-be.

Sorestad taught in Yorkton from 1963 until 1967, then accepted a position at Alvin Buckwold School in Saskatoon. By this time he and Sonia had four children—three boys and a girl. In 1969 he joined the English Department of Evan Hardy Collegiate where he taught for twelve years. There he established the first high school Creative Writing program in the province. He was a key figure in spearheading at Evan Hardy the groundbreaking Prairie Writers' Workshop (1977), for which he was awarded a Hilroy Fellowship.

While at Evan Hardy, Sorestad was also responsible for bringing into the high school classrooms many notable Canadian writers. During this time at Evan Hardy, Sorestad began writing seriously and also became one of the co-founders of Thistledown Press in 1975.

In 1981 Sorestad decided to quit teaching in order to devote more time to his writing career which had, over the years, seen him establish a national reputation as a poet, fiction writer, editor, and publisher. From 1981 to 2000 he divided his time between his own writing pursuits and his role as president of the growing literary publishing house. In January 2000 the Sorestads retired from Thistledown Press after twenty-five years of publishing poets and fiction writers from Saskatchewan and across Canada, as well as several international poets. During their time with Thistledown the Sorestads saw the publishing house become one of the country's leading literary presses. Sorestad served on the executives of several publishing organizations and writers' organizations.

Sorestad continues to live and write in Saskatoon. He has written more than a dozen books of poetry, including *Icons of Flesh* (1998), *Today I Belong to Agnes* (2000), and *Leaving Holds Me Here* (2001), which won the Saskatoon Book Award. He is also the author of many short stories, personal essays, and articles. Sorestad's poems have appeared in over 40 anthologies and textbooks. His poems have been translated into French, Spanish, Norwegian, Finnish, and Slovene. His stories have appeared in literary magazines, anthologies, and on various CBC radio programs. One of his stories was filmed for television for Bravo TV.

Sorestad is a co-editor of many well known anthologies, including *Strawberries & Other Secrets*, *The Last Map is the Heart*, and *In the*

GLEN SORESTAD... READING AN ACHINGLY BEAUTIFUL PASSAGE ABOUT MINERS ("THE CLOSING DOWN OF SUMMER" IN ALISTAIR MACLEOD'S *ISLAND*) TO HIS NORWEGIAN FRIENDS IN OSLO, SUMMER SOLSTICE.

Clear. He has given well over 300 public readings of his poetry in every province of Canada, in 15 states of the United States, and in Europe. In 1998 the Canadian Ambassador in Oslo held a reception in his honour at which his reading was broadcast on Norway's public radio network. In 2001 he was one of a small number of poets invited to read at an international poetry reading in Lahti, Finland. In September of 2002 he gave a reading of his poetry in Ljubljana Castle as part of an international reading at Vilenica writers' festival in Slovenia before an audience that included the president of the country and the mayor of Ljubljana.

Sorestad has been active as a writer-in-residence, including a full year as the Saskatoon Public Library's writer-in-residence and numerous shorter term residencies in various libraries and school districts in places as far flung as Grande Prairie and the Annapolis Valley. He was artist-in-residence in 2001 at the Kenderdine Emma Lake Campus of the University of Saskatchewan.

Throughout his writing career he has served as a mentor for younger writers and has encouraged many young people to become writers themselves. Sorestad has been an active member of the Saskatchewan Writers Guild since it was formed and was given a Founders' Award by the Guild in 1990. Also a long-time member of the League of Canadian Poets, he was honoured with Life Member status in 1998 and remains very active in the League's activities. He has also been an ongoing member of the Writers Union of Canada for over 20 years.

In November of 2000 Sorestad was appointed the first Poet Laureate of Saskatchewan, becoming the very first provincially appointed poet laureate in the country. Glen Sorestad was awarded the Queen's Golden Jubilee Medal at Government House in February 2003.

About Writing... *All my life I have loved stories, whether as a listener, a reader, or a teller. All writing eventually boils down to story, one way or another; and I am a storyteller, first and foremost. In fact, I am a natural extension or continuation of the long tradition of poet as storyteller, a tradition that precedes books, that precedes novels and short stories and other written forms of storytelling that dominate our reading today. In my veins flows the blood of all the illustrious poet-storytellers—from Homer to Chaucer to Frost—that came before me; they nourish and sustain me.*—GLEN SORESTAD

WALLACE STEGNER (1909–1993) was born at Lake Mills, Iowa, on February 18, 1909, the son of Hilda (Paulson) and George H. Stegner.

Stegner's memoir, *Wolf Willow: A History, a Story and a Memory of the Last Plains Frontier*, was published in 1962. The book, which is about the six adolescent years Stegner spent in Eastend, Saskatchewan, is thought to have had an enormous impact on his subsequent life and work both as a writer and as a committed environmentalist.

After teaching at the University of Wisconsin and at Harvard, Stegner served for twenty-five years as the director of the writing program at Stanford University.

Wallace Stegner published some thirty books (including novels, non-fiction, short stories, and essays) over more than fifty years. These include *Remembering Laughter* (1937), *Mormon Country* (1942), *The Preacher and the Slave* (1950), *The Women on the Wall* (1950), *Beyond the Hundredth Meridian* (1954), *The City of the Living* (1956), *A Shooting Star* (1961), *Wolf Willow* (1962), *The Gathering of Zion* (1964), *All the Little Live Things* (1967), *The Sound of Mountain Water* (1969), *Angle of Repose* (1971), *The Spectator Bird* (1976), *Recapitulation* (1979), *Crossing to Safety* (1987), and *Where the Bluebird Sings to the Lemonade Springs* (1992).

Angle of Repose was awarded the Pulitzer Prize in 1972 and *The Spectator Bird* won the National Book Award. *Where the Bluebird Sings to the Lemonade Springs* was nominated for the National Book Critics Circle Award.

Wallace Stegner died in Santa Fe, New Mexico, on April 13, 1993.

HEATHER HODGSON

MARIE ELYSE ST. GEORGE and her stillborn twin brother were born at home on December 8, 1929, in Merritton (now part of St. Catharines), Ontario. Her father, Richard Edward (Ted) Yates from Chorely, Lancashire, England, came to Canada as a civil engineer to help build the Welland Ship Canal—precursor to the St. Lawrence Seaway, and worked in canal administration until retirement. St. George's mother, Marie Philomene Robertson, descended from Huguenots, who built the first stone farmhouse on the St. Lawrence.

She was also goddaughter to her grandmother Esther Papineau, who was the rebel Louis-Joseph Papineau's niece.

Until age seven, St. George was raised at Port Weller, Ontario, with her brother George Edward, her sister Evelyn Catherine, and sister Louise Auralie (Neff). In 1937 the family bought a fruit farm at Niagara-on-the-Lake where the children spent several isolated, bookreading, hardworking years until moving to St. Catharines. There St. George attended St. Catharines Collegiate and Vocational School. Her only claim to fame was a first prize in the yearbook for a melodramatic short story about her Huguenot ancestors' escape from France. The prize was somewhat eclipsed by St. George being reprimanded at full assembly for drawing a picture of Cleopatra on her barge on the wall of the girls' washroom.

St. George later worked for Bell Telephone as a switchboard operator, and then at City Hall on a billing machine, but this didn't last long (she is dyslectic in spelling and math). After taking painting lessons, she attended the Doon School in Doon, Ontario, and discovered something she was good at. She then studied in England at the College of The Fylde, Blackpool, Lancashire, circa 1948–1949, when her parents took her with them on a trip to England.

St. George later moved to London to work and study part-time. She applied at the Central School of Art but was told by a male professor that she was talented but since she was "not bad looking," she should go home and get married. Instead, she went to work at the Automobile Club offices in London, but that was no great success because she was faced with the dreaded billing again—this time with pounds, shillings, and pence! Finally, she took an eye-opening evening job as a waitress at the Criterion Restaurant, Piccadilly, so that she would be able to afford tickets to the theatre, opera, and various concerts she had discovered.

A bit burned out, St. George returned to Canada in 1952 and got a job as a filing clerk in the St. Catharines Land Titles office. In 1953 she became a commercial copy writer at CKTB radio in St. Catharines where she met her husband, an RCAF veteran and broadcaster, Leonard Bruce St. George. She and Bruce married in 1953 and had two sons: Leonard Kerry, born in 1959, and Hilary Sean, born in 1955. St. George and her husband also have a grandson, Liam Avison-St. George.

In the 1960s, St. George moved to the United States when her husband joined WENH public radio at the University of New Hampshire. There she studied painting and printmaking. St. George exhibited her work with the New Hampshire Art Association, and won the Weston Associates Prize at the Currier Gallery, Manchester, New Hampshire. In 1973 she moved to Saskatoon with her husband when he initially got a job at Kelsey Institute and later was employed at the University of Saskatchewan. St. George continued printmaking at the university in the 1970s and 1980s, and was a member of the Shoestring Gallery and the Group 5 Gallery. She was also art advisor for the Saskatchewan Writers Guild's colony committee.

An avid reader, St. George began writing with the encouragement of Lois Simmie and Bonnie Burnard (who used her paintings

MARIE ELYSE ST. GEORGE...
A TIME OF CHANGE.

for book jackets) and mentors Patrick Lane, David Carpenter, the late Anne Szumigalski, and her Connaught Group. In 1988 she participated in the Banff poetry writing studio. Her literary influences are Austen, Dickens, and Wilfred Owen, along with contemporary mentors Patrick Lane and Anne Szumigalski. For the last few years, St. George has been part of poet Elizabeth Brewster's group.

Her poetry, essays and art have appeared in many Canadian literary magazines such as *Grain*, *Prairie Fire*, and *NeWest Review*, and in several anthologies: *Heading Out* (1986), *Talking Peace* (1990), *Arc 25th Anniversary Edition* (1991), *Vintage 92*, *Vintage 93*, *Siolence* (1998), and *Sundog Highway* (2000). Her art appears on numerous book jackets, including: *It Never Pays to Laugh Too Much* (1984), *Pictures* (1984), *The Need of Wanting Always* (1985) *Women of Influence* (1988), *Voice* (1995), *Fear of Knives* (2000), *Imprint and Casualties* (2000), and *Ör* (2003). She has published catalogue text for art exhibitions, and she wrote commentary for two art exhibitions: "Do You Take This Seriously?" at the Glenbow Museum, Calgary, Alberta (1984) and "Women and Peace" at Mount Allison University, Nova Scotia (1985). Her poetry has been broadcast on CBC radio on *Ambience* (1990) and *Gallery* (2003), and she has participated in performance with the Saskatoon Moving Collective with *Known Species* (1984), *White are the Corners of my Room* (1985), and *Per Ovibos Ad Artica* (1987).

St. George has read her poetry for the League of Canadian Poets "Writes Of Spring" (1999 and 2004) and at "The Winnipeg Spring Literary Festival" in 1996. She has also read at the Vancouver Public Library (1996), and at the Eric Harvie Theatre in Banff in 1988, as well as at The Secret Theatre in Calgary (1987). St. George has produced readings with music, photos, and visual art.

In 1987 St. George's *White Lions In The Afternoon* was published. Her poetry also won first prize in both the League of Canadian Poets national competition and the Saskatchewan Writers Guild's poetry contest. St. George received the Jerry Rush scholarship to Sage Hill in 1990. In 1996, St. George received the YWCA Women Of Distinction Award for Arts and Culture. In 1995 she collaborated with Anne Szumigalski for an exhibition at the Mendel Gallery, Saskatoon, and the Susan Whitney Gallery, Regina, where she currently exhibits. This show exploring the imaginative interaction between text by Szumigalski and visual art by St. George was published in book form as *Voice*, which went on to win the Governor General's Award for Szumigalski's poetry in 1995.

St. George's work has been reviewed in the *Vancouver Sun*, *Midwest Book Review*, *Oregon WI*, *Poetry Toronto*, *Canadian Library Association*, *Halifax Chronicle Review*, *Small Press Review* (Paradise, California), and the *Globe and Mail*, and on CBC Radio.

She is currently a member of the Saskatchewan Writers Guild, the League of Canadian Poets, Pen, Canadian Artist's Representation, and was, in the past, part of the Saskatoon Moving Collective (multimedia performance, 1984–88), Shoestring Gallery, Saskatoon, 1974–80, and founding member of the Group 5 Collective Gallery, Saskatoon, 1980–83.

St. George's paintings, which recently have been about the civilian victims of war, (the old, young lovers, and children), often take six months to execute; writing has had to fight for equal time. The poetry manuscript she has been working on for several years was almost finished until, at a 2002 workshop, "Writing with Style," at Banff, it became plain that a different kind of book was bursting to be written. She is now completing this memoir manuscript of poetry, short stories, and essays incorporating relevant paintings, drawings, and family photographs, which will be published in 2006. It's a long process.

About Writing... *I write poetry when moved by certain ideas, stories, and experiences, and make visual art when moved by events and emotions but especially potent words and phrases. Before discovering poetry I was always trying to "WRITE" a painting, but now my paintings are much stronger because of their mystery—and stories are told in poetry or prose. I'll always be grateful to my fierce, dauntless mother who taught us "Stress Management" long before it became psycho-jargon, i.e., how to manage deadlines on our fruit farm; how to push yourself through weariness and tedium until you've accomplished your goal; how unpicked fruit rots quickly on the vine. So, hew your way through all those tangles that keep you from writing. Write first thing in the morning or whenever you've got an uninterrupted block of time. Wash that laundry at midnight if you've run out of clean underwear —but write first.*—MARIE ELYSE ST. GEORGE

GERTRUDE STORY was born in 1929 to Rheinhold and Matilda (Jabusch) Wudrick on a farm near the small CPR town of Sutherland, Saskatchewan, said town being later incorporated into the city of Saskatoon.

After high school she worked as a junior bank clerk thus preparing her to accede fairly readily to the blandishments of Joseph LeRoy Story, a country school teacher–hunter–trapper–fisherman. Their coal-oil-lamp–wood-stove–farming-country-teacherage lifestyle was to serve as fodder for the short stories and verse published in the likes of the *Western Producer* and for many of the stories and commentaries that appeared on CBC Radio beginning in 1962. The material was given a deliberately amusing slant often in direct contrast to the actual incidents (since humour sells better than "Oh, my God, not this!").

Widowed (and jobless) by 1973, she began a university career in 1976 with a class presented by the estimable and energetic David Carpenter who eventually became one of Saskatchewan's most famous writers. In 1980 she convocated from the University of Saskatchewan in Saskatoon as the most distinguished graduate and was awarded the Arts Prize as well as the President's Medal, thus demonstrating that a fifty-year tenure in the "School of Hard Knocks" provides a focused and energized incentive to succeed in the so-called halls of higher learning.

In the years following the publication of her first book, a collection of poems called *The book of Thirteen*, in 1981, she gradually became one of Saskatchewan's best-known storytellers and, thanks to Thistledown Press of Saskatoon, one of its temporarily acclaimed writers.

For nearly twenty years she was much in demand for readings and workshops, during which time her Saskatchewan Writers Guild-sponsored working visits to school classrooms teaching right brain creativity gave her particular satisfaction.

In due course she was a frequent participant in literary programs across the country. She credits P.A.W.S., the major writing group in Prince Albert and area at the time, as well as the spirited high-energy people of "Diefenbaker Country" as a whole, with the success of the Saskatchewan Writers Guild first artist-in-residence program that ran from 1983 to 1984. Story was its first literary resource person.

In addition to her initial book of poetry, her

PHOTO BY RUTH SMILLIE

GERTRUDE STORY...WRITER-IN-RESIDENCE AT THE FRANCES MORRISON PUBLIC LIBRARY IN SASKATOON; A FIRM SUPPORTER OF CANADIAN WRITING AND THE RESIDENCY PROGRAM.

career has been blessed (and somewhat sweetened with a widow's pension) with the publication of five works of fiction; namely, *The Way to Always Dance* (1983), *It Never Pays to Laugh too Much* (1984), *The Need of Wanting Always* (1985), *Black Swan* (1986), and *After Sixty: Going Home* (1991). She has also published two collections of reflections/reminiscences, namely, *The Last House on Main Street* (1988), a selection of her CBC Radio stories refashioned for print. The other collection is called *How to Saw Wood with an Angel* (1992), which gives glimpses of her spiritual journey over sixty years of enduring life on Planet Earth. *Counting Two*, published in 1993, is comprised of two "teaching tales" Story often used in her work of opening the creative minds of school children.

One of these teaching stories is from the "Story book" to which the author claims the closest ties and the deepest feeling, namely *Rowena, Rowena, Rowena*, which was published by Prairie Lily Co-operative in 1986. The book's chief character is a psychic child.

A *Globe and Mail* review of *The Way to Always Dance* touted Story, at the age of 54, as a new and unique prairie voice destined to be of significance. *Dandelion*, which at the time was Alberta's major literary magazine, called her "a great craftswoman and a major singer worth hearing." Meanwhile, *The Prairie Journal of Canadian Literature*, too, "spun her head," she says, by contending that she, "by sheer breadth of vision and technical virtuosity, has achieved a place among writers like William Faulkner and Virginia Woolf."

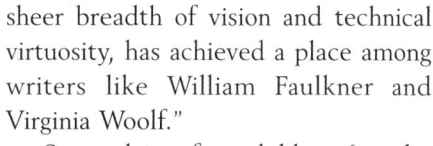

Story claims four children (two by birth and two by the birthlings' marriages) and two precious people earthlings called grandchildren.

About Writing... *A process equivalent to Joan of Arc's "voices" has produced all of my written work since a particularly arduous but enlightening Jungian "long dark night of the soul" that I was given to experience (and learn life lessons from) in 1979.*—GERTRUDE STORY

ALISON LEE STRAYER was born in Regina in 1958, and grew up in Saskatoon and Ottawa, Ontario. Her father, Barry Lee Strayer, was raised in Regina and Drinkwater; her mother, Eleanor Staton, was raised in Gray. They met at Luther College in Regina, courted while studying at the University of Saskatchewan, and lived in England for three years after they were married. Alison was born a year after the couple returned to Regina, followed by her brother Jonathan, then Colin, who was born the year the family lived in Cambridge, Mass.

Strayer completed grades one to five at Albert School in Saskatoon, studied ballet and piano, and was a devotee of the childrens' section at the new Main Library. She early developed the habit of reading her favourite books several times, sometimes back-to-back. Reading, she recalls, was a means of traveling to other worlds, of trying on the skin of another person or creature, of making discoveries—not always of a comforting variety. From the beginning, favourite books were the ones that kept her wondering, "How did that happen?

what happened next? what was the secret inside the secret? why was that character like that?" It was reading that compelled her to start writing her own stories.

At the age of nine, Strayer spent three months with her family in the countryside of West Quebec (Kingsmere), living—incidentally—in the house where Elizabeth Smart spent summers as a child. Writing took on a new kind of necessity, that of recording, preserving, completing the day. In her book *Jardin et prairie*, Strayer identifies that summer as a catalyst for her writing: a first experience travelling, a meeting of west with east, of contrasting landscapes, of English and French. The theme of "West and East"—essential, indissociable from one another, and by no means free of conflict—are ongoing preoccupations in her work.

In 1968, the family moved to Ottawa for a year that extended into a second year, and after that, the temporary relocation to the East became permanent. In Ottawa, Strayer finished elementary school and attended high school. Studying French for the first time, she was an enthusiastic but floundering pupil for many semesters. While in high school, for class assignments and on her own, she continued to write stories that were grimly futuristic, and were inspired by works of Kurt Vonnegut, Ursula Le Guin, and John Wyndham. She was encouraged by her mother to read Canadian writers, including Margaret Atwood, Alice Munro, and Margaret Laurence.

Taking a part-time job at a second-hand bookstore, Strayer first read the works and journals of Virginia Woolf and Katherine Mansfield, to which she would return on many occasions over the years. At the age of seventeen, when Strayer discovered—and read in one evening—Hubert Aquin's 'Prochain episode,' captivated by the book's incandescent spirit and style, she decided that Quebec was where she wanted to live and pursue her studies of French and literature.

Strayer attended the Université Laval, Glendon College (Toronto) and McGill University in Montreal, graduating in 1979 with an Honours B.A. in French and Québécois Literature. Montreal would be her home base for the next 30 years, between travels (Italy, Hungary, Greece) and sojourns of various durations in Toronto, Ottawa, and Regina.

After completing her diploma in French and working for two years in a Montreal café, Strayer completed a Certificate in Applied Linguistics. After finishing her teacher's training, she taught English as a Second Language and tutored French for ten years in private language schools, as well as in adult education programmes at Carleton (Ottawa), Concordia (Montreal), and the University of Regina. During these years, she worked on numerous stories and novels in English, all of which were consigned, unfinished, to a bottom drawer. She published short essays and translations in French, including an article on the works of Jane Bowles (1988) and two short translations from works of Edna Alford and Sharon Butala (1992). In the mid-eighties, Strayer returned to McGill to do a diploma in Russian language and literature, but completed only one year. She remains an avid reader of

PHOTO BY PIERRE FILION, LEMÉAC EDITEUR

ALISON STRAYER... MONTREAL, QUEBEC.

Dostoevksy, Chekhov, and Anna Akhmatova (to name a few), and retains from the same period a special interest in other languages and literatures of Eastern Europe.

Strayer started doing freelance translation in the late 1980s, primarily in the film and public relations sector, and also worked as a scriptreader and advisor. With the novelist Yvon Rivard, she worked on a number of scripts for various Montreal feature and documentary productions. Starting in 1989, over a six-year period, she frequently traveled to Regina. Those years, notably the time she spent with her grandmother, constitute one of the main subjects of *Jardin et prairie*, published in 1999 in Montreal. Written in French, the book was shortlisted for a number of awards, including the Governor General's Award for fiction, the City of Montreal literary award, and the Prix France-Quebec Philippe-Roussillon.

In 1998, Strayer made her first visit to France. In 2001, she moved to Paris, where she now lives with her husband, Jean-Philippe Cresceri. She continues to work as a freelance translator, and submits occasional articles to a variety of publications. Recent texts include an essay on reading and writing after 9-11 ("Ecrire sous le choc," 2002), another on Virginia Woolf's "On Being Ill" ("Le froissement du rideau," 2003), both for the Montreal quarterly *l'Inconvénient*, and a piece entitled "The Way of Imperfection," for *Writing Addictions: Towards a Poetics of Desire and Its Others* (edited by Béla Szabados and Kenneth Probert). She is in the process of completing her second book, a novel set in Paris.

About Writing... *Writing has been, for as long as I can remember (or almost), a way of being, of participating, of mediating between what happens inside with what happens outside. I tend to do most of my thinking on paper—thinking of any kind. Once I write something down, I'm not as likely to carry it around in my head; that can be a good thing, but isn't always. Writing has been many things for me and fulfilled many purposes in my life. It is a way of living more fully and a means of creating order when all else is upheaval and chaos. It is sometimes sheer heady pleasure, sometimes a conundrum, sometimes itself a source of chaos. For various reasons—practical and otherwise—writing is not something I've managed to do in moderation, day in-day out—anyway, not for long. However, as time goes by, the idea of writing in that way becomes more appealing and more feasible.—*
ALISON STRAYER

ANDY SUKNASKI was born on a small homestead near Wood Mountain in 1942 to a Ukrainian father and Polish mother. His father had settled the homestead in 1914. His first prolonged exposure to English was when he attended Wood Mountain's Ambassador School. His parents separated when he was seven, and he moved into the village of Wood Mountain with his mother and five brothers and sisters. He left home at seventeen and from then on was seldom in one place for long. Indeed, in time, he began to conceive of himself as a solitary gypsy figure. He attended the L.V. Rogers School in Nelson, British Columbia, and went on to the Kootenay School of Art, also in Nelson, the University of Victoria, the School of Art and Design at the Montréal School of Fine Arts, and Simon Fraser University—all part of his restless aesthetic quest in the areas of visual arts and literature. He also read widely in spirituality, mythology, and history.

In 1973, influenced by histories of the prairie West and Sinclair Ross's *As For Me and My House*, he returned to live in Wood Mountain and began to write about the region and its people. In Wood Mountain he was looking to centre himself. There, his writing became less derivative as he developed his own voice. Early in the 1980s he travelled to eastern Europe to explore his roots. Previously, he travelled to Australia and the Northwest Territories. He put in a stint as writer-in-residence at Saint John's College of the University of Manitoba in 1977 and later moved to Regina. He worked on an occasional basis at a variety of jobs from farmhand to night watchman, listing his occupation as "migrant worker" in 1976. After surgery for colitis in the mid-1980s, Suknaski fell prey to psychiatric problems that required a brief hospitalization. He eventually moved to Moose Jaw and not long after the age of fifty was no longer active as a writer or artist.

Earl Birney's "David" is the poem Suknaski credits for first awakenimg his interest in poetry. Later, while attending Simon Fraser and hanging around Vancouver he met Birney in person and got to know him. Other influences he credits are bill bissett, Patrick Lane, Joe Rosenblatt, Al Purdy, and John Newlove. He makes special mention of Barry McKinnon's book-length poem *I Wanted to Say Something* (1975) for showing him the documentary potential of regional poetry that he applied to his most popular work, *Wood Mountain Poems* (1976), which was edited and introduced by Purdy. Influences outside Canada that Suknaski has acknowledged include Charles Olson, William Carlos Williams, André Vosnezenky, and Yevgeny Yevtushenko.

Prior to the advent of small literary presses on the prairies in the later 1970s, Suknaski played a key role in introducing the work of several new prairie writers, among them Sid Marty, Charles Noble, Glen Sorestad, and Gary Hyland. He printed his own early efforts as well and adorned all these publications with his distinctive visual art. During sojourns in Vancouver, Calgary, Lake Louise, and Wood Mountain, he operated this one-man publishing house, releasing chapbooks under the imprints Elfin Plot, Sundog, Anak Press, Three-Legged Coyote, and Deodar Shadow Press. His specialty was the handmade limited edition mailed to a select list of friends and supporters.

Suknaski's poetry achieved early recognition in Al Purdy's anthology *Storm Warning* (1971) and in broadsheets, pamphlets, and chapbooks, many issued by himself, in the early 1970s.

By his early thirties, some attention as a conceptual artist and experimental poet landed him in publications alongside Earl Birney, bill bissett and Judith Copithorne. These early works were frequently concrete poems allied with drawings. Later, he composed variations of vernacular poetry using longer lines and anecdotal structures, especially in writing about First Nations people, his own family and acquaintances, and the immigrants to the Wood Mountain district. In writing of the generations in the Wood Mountain region Suknaski goes beyond historical accuracy, creating a kind of local mythology. One can see the influence of the beer parlour raconteurs once common in small prairie towns. Dramatic monologue, in which his subjects speak in broken English laced with foreign phrases, is a frequent technique. His renderings of migrant speech patterns are energetic and vivid. Some of Suknaski's poems from this period are effectively presented in the NFB film by Harvey Spak, *Wood Mountain Poems*. In the thirty-minute film, Suknaski also talks about his part of the world, its multicultural background, its Indian heritage, and the customs and stories of its different ethnic groups.

Suknaski's work shows a sensitivity to several cultures—First Nations, Polish, Ukrainian, Roumanian, Chinese, Dene, and Métis. His goal, as he once said in an interview, was to "document the West," particularly the people's myths and spiritual beliefs. The *Globe and Mail* said, "If Canada ever needed an argument for the regional artist, Andrew Suknaski is it." In 1979, Suknaski won the Canadian Authors Association Poetry Award for *The Ghosts Call You Poor* (1978).

Into the 1980s Suknaski's writing became increasingly ambitious. Influenced by Robert Kroetsch, he pursued the long poem. He was working continually on a project he called "Celestial Mechanics," a series of explorations of what he considered to be the fundamental themes of human experience. Part one of Mechanics was *Montage for an Interstellar Cry* (1982); part two was to be called "Divining West," a long poem that was never completed, although excerpts were published in various small literary magazines. Part three was *Silk Trail* (1985); part four was to deal with "the experiences of Chinese coolies working on different continents" and was to be called *Ussuri Line*. It, too, was never completed.

In *Plainspeaking* (1988) Suknaski described being overwhelmed by the immensity and complexity of his vision for the "Celestial Mechanics" while working on *Montage for an Interstellar Cry*: "... what I was trying to do there was such a grandiose, free-wheeling, all-encompassing thing that it was mind-boggling." He took the manuscript through several drafts before it was distilled into its published form by Dave Arnason and David Carr. He also began a history of the Roumanians on the prairies entitled *In Search of Parinti* that never reached fruition.

In 1987, depressed and tired of hauling his personal papers from one short-term abode to the other, Suknaski burned many of his personal papers. Much of what remained—papers, photographs, tapes and other materials—were sold to the archives of the University of Manitoba. This collection includes drafts of many of his published works as well as correspondence with literary figures like Eli Mandel, John Newlove, Robert Kroetsch, and Kristjana Gunnars, many unpublished poems and several drafts of the films that Suknaski worked on for the National Film Board and CBC. Perhaps the most valuable portion of the collection are the unpublished manuscripts that Suknaski worked on during the 1980s, including "Divining the West," *Ussuri Line* and *In Search of Parinti/History of the Roumanians in Western Canada*.

GARY HYLAND

KATE SUTHERLAND was born in Dundee, Scotland, in 1966. Her family tree is full of Scottish ancestors. In addition to the expected coalminers, steelworkers, blacksmiths, shepherds, and factory girls, recent genealogical forays have uncovered one great-great-great grandfather who was an Orkney schoolmaster, and another who was a Glasgow phrenologist.

Kate's parents (Ron Sutherland and Betty Eaddy) met at a Glasgow dance hall. They courted in St. Andrews, where Ron earned his Ph.D. in Chemistry and Betty worked as a schoolteacher. After they married, they did a bit of globetrotting and Kate's brother Ian was born in California. They returned to Scotland in time for Kate to be born next to the North Sea.

Two years later, the family moved to Canada when Ron took a job as a professor at the University of Saskatchewan. Kate grew up in Saskatoon, spending some of her happiest hours selecting a weekly allotment of ten books each Saturday at the Frances Morrison Library. She particularly enjoyed stories about aspiring writers, and checked out Maud Hart Lovelace's Betsy-Tacy books and L.M. Montgomery's Emily books over and over again.

The Sutherlands returned to Scotland nearly every summer, and Kate enjoyed having a foot in both worlds. She regards prairie skies and Scottish seas as flipsides of the same thing; a glimpse of either evokes an immediate sense of home.

Kate had the good fortune to attend high school at Evan Hardy Collegiate in Saskatoon. She took English classes from Glen Sorestad, Allan Forrie, and Paddy O'Rourke, each of whom gave contemporary Canadian writing a central place in the curriculum. This made for good reading of course, but also provided inspiration for writing. From the outset it was clear that Saskatchewan was a place where good writing happened.

Kate entered the University of Saskatchewan in the fall of 1983, where she eventually earned a B.A. (1986) and an LL.B. (1989). During those years, she wrote for *The Sheaf* (the University of Saskatchewan student newspaper) and served as editor of its literary supplement. In 1989, Kate moved to Regina to take a job as law clerk to the Chief Justice of the Saskatchewan Court of Appeal. That was the year she switched her focus from poetry to fiction and her writing really took off. She often turned up at work on Monday mornings with a new story in hand which the judges' secretaries and the court librarian subjected to uncompromising critique.

PHOTO BY ERIC BRIDENBAKER

KATE SUTHERLAND... ON THE WEST SANDS OF ST. ANDREWS, SCOTLAND.

For the next few years Kate zigzagged across the country, clerking for the Chief Justice of the Supreme Court of Canada in Ottawa, serving as acting director of the Centre for Constitutional Studies in Edmonton, and getting her first taste of teaching back at her *alma mater* in Saskatoon. She signed up for creative writing classes in each new city, and her fiction flourished under the guidance of Brenda Riches, Lorna Crozier, and Gerald Lynch. Her first publication was a story that appeared in *Grain* in 1992. Subsequent work was published in magazines like *Prairie Fire, New Quarterly*, and *Queen Street Quarterly*.

In 1993, Kate moved to Cambridge, Massachusetts, to undertake an LL.M. (1994) and later a doctorate (2002) at Harvard Law School. She hooked up with an international group of writers there, including Larissa Behrendt, Jud Tussing, and fellow-Saskatchewanian, Harold Johnson. They met every second week at Charlie's Kitchen in Harvard Square to share whatever they were working on over cheap beer and cheeseburgers.

Kate's first collection of short stories, titled *Summer Reading*, was published in the fall of 1995. It won the Brenda Macdonald Riches First Book Award in the Saskatchewan Book Awards that year. Kate felt particularly honoured to win a prize named for one of her first writing teachers.

In 1998, she accepted a teaching position at Osgoode Hall Law School. She arrived in Toronto with a big prairie chip on her shoulder and so was astonished by how quickly she became enamoured of the city. She felt particularly energized by the whirlwind of chapbooks and little magazines and reading series generated by the small press community. She has become friends with and takes inspiration from Toronto writers like Jennifer LoveGrove, Alexandra Leggat, and Jonathan Bennett.

Kate continues to return to Saskatchewan for regular visits. She has attended the Sage Hill Writing Experience four times in recent years. Her work has benefited greatly from these sojourns, thanks in particular to the feedback she received from fiction workshop leaders Ven Begamudré and Bonnie Burnard.

Kate has recently completed the manuscript for her second collection of short stories. She is currently dividing her writing time between two new projects. The first is a novel set in 1970s Saskatoon. The second is a book about Scotland which is part travelogue and part family history.

About Writing... *People often conceive of my double life as a lawyer and a writer as some sort of right brain–left brain fight to the death. Certainly the two pursuits compete for my time. But apart from that, law and fiction are entirely compatible. Telling a good story is at the centre of both.* —KATE SUTHERLAND

BÉLA SZABADOS was born in 1942, in the city of Kolozsvár, in the disputed territory of Transylvania, which at the time belonged to Hungary. This city was also the birthplace of the poet Endre Ady and home to the inventor of non-Euclidean geometry János Bolyai. The Count Dracula was not a cultural icon, nor was he part of the cultural folklore. The first Act of Religious Tolerance was introduced there, assuring the right of religious worship for the many ethnicities and plurality of faiths. His father, the original Béla Szabados, was an architect; his mother, Rosa Niedermeier, a striking beauty and a master of the fine art of caring for children.

Szabados finished elementary school in a devastated and desolate post-war Hungary. His main interests were playing soccer, swimming, reading (the books his sisters Éva and Edit brought home) and writing, activities which somewhat allayed an acute sense of being stifled and of the pain of the loss of a father at an early age. He escaped from Hungary with his mother and sisters after the defeated Hungarian revolution of 1956 and arrived in Montreal in 1957, where he attended Daniel O'Connell High School. On graduation he entered Sir George Williams University, where the study of chemistry and laboratories depressed him so badly that he chose to read philosophy for a degree. Afterwards he did graduate work at the University of Toronto and the University of Calgary, where he got his Ph.D. in 1972. An academic gypsy for three years, he held visiting appointments first at Lethbridge, then at Simon Fraser, then at Calgary, eventually finding a tenure-tracked position at the University of Regina in 1975.

He started writing in the fifth grade, amidst the spiritual desert of a stifling milieu, having sensed the possibilities of emotional and ideational expression and freedom in writing. In his first year university English composition class, he wrote about the desire for enlivening color, while working in a rather gray paint factory as a quality control technician. Although for a decade or so in his teaching career he wrote for philosophical journals, he has not made a rigid distinction between his philosophical and literary writings. The topics he tackled and tried to shed light on were related to literature: the issues of sincerity, self-deception, hypocrisy, embarrassment, and eros seen as endless striving. His influences were the novelists Proust, Camus, Sartre, Steven Vizinczey, and the poets Endre Ady, Ted Hughes, George Faludy, and Kristjana Gunnars.

Then came a period of literary activity as conventionally understood—writing an autobiographical account of his boyhood in Hungary and his experiences as a young immigrant and student in Montreal. This was intended as a way of introducing his son, Imre, to his father as boy and young adult, as well as capturing a beehive of memories that cried out for telling waking him up at nights. He wanted to recreate a Hungarian childhood for his son, whom he tragically lost to a car accident in 1990, the same year that the book *In Light of Chaos* was published. This was followed by the publication of a brief story which received honourary mention in *Grain*'s "short-shorts" competition, as well as by the appearance of a cluster of poems in *Prairie Fire* and *Dandelion*.

After this he turned to reflection on the nature and neglected role of the autobiographical voice in philosophical writing, bringing literary genre closer to philosophy and vice versa. It is through this lens that in his many essays he looked at aspects of Ludwig Wittgenstein as a philosopher of culture. Szabados's books include: *In Light of Chaos* (1990), *On the Track of Reason* (co-edited, 1992), *Hypocrisy: Ethical Investigations* (co-authored, 2004), *Wittgenstein Reads Weininger* (co-edited, 2004). A collection of essays entitled *Writing Addiction: Towards a Poetics of Desire and Its Others* (coedited) is forthcoming. He is working on a sequel to his autobiographical novel *In Light of Chaos*, as well as on a little book tentatively titled *Wittgenstein Listens to Music*.

From 2001 to 2003, Szabados was anglophone president for the Canadian Society for Aesthetics, a bilingual and interdisciplinary society. From 1967 to 1984 Szabados was married to Sonia de Grandmaison, the mother of his son Imre. In the late 1980s, Kristjana Gunnars and he were partners. In 1995, he married Heather Hodgson; they live in Regina.

PHOTO BY HEATHER HODGSON

BÉLA SZABADOS... IN TOFINO, BRITISH COLUMBIA, WITH FRIEND, DOUG FIR, 1997.

About Writing... *For me, like for Montaigne before, writing is a window to otherness—in myself and others. It is liberatory from an emotionally stifled, repressed condition, from a kind of emotional imprisonment that somehow I find myself in. It involves a primitive urge to say something I cannot yet say, to become what I am not yet. The impulse is a kind of longing to belong to a larger community, of those in the now, of those who went before and of those who are yet to come. As I write I struggle with and against language to find words or a style for an inchoate, instinctive set of ideas anxious to burst forth with primitive force.*—BÉLA SZABADOS

ANNE SZUMIGALSKI (1922–1999). One of Canada's most accomplished writers, Saskatoon's Anne Szumigalski was a master of transitions—from London to the remote Canadian prairie, from rural to urban, from student to teacher, genre to genre, mentor to friend. She welcomed into her home and worked with writers of all ages, dispensing advice, support, and inspiration with her tea. Born in London, England, in 1922, Szumigalski immigrated to Saskatoon in 1951. In addition to editing and writing poetry, prose and drama, Szumigalski taught creative writing.

Her skills as a writer, mentor and teacher are legendary. She won accolades from the province and the nation for her achievements as an arts volunteer and writer—the Saskatchewan Order of Merit, the Saskatchewan Arts Board Lifetime Achievement Award for Excellence in the Arts, life membership in the League of Canadian Poets, and the Governor-General's Award for poetry, among others. Rita Dove, while Poet Laureate of the United States, praised Szumigalski's achievements in a *Washington Post* column.

A risk-taker who refused to repeat herself and who bloomed in the vastness of the plains, Szumigalski wrote twelve books characterized by passionate engagement, exciting innovation, and mythic probes. More and more, her work approached the pure horizons of the imagination and embodied an impressive range of form and thought. She liked to refer to herself as a "Blakian" and Blake remained her most pure literary influence for all of her life.

As Anne's brother John has said, "She seemed to come into the world as she was—she knew who she was and what she wanted." As a young woman of twenty-three, Anne became involved in the Second World War, working with the British Red Cross Civilian Relief as medical auxiliary, interpreter, and welfare officer. It was during this time that Anne encountered the crucible of war-torn Europe, and was involved in assisting civilians who had been liberated from concentration camps. This was an experience that would stay with her for the rest of her life. As a writer she held the experience for fifty years until she wrote the play *Z: A Meditation on Oppression, Desire and Freedom*, which was produced in 1994 by 25th Street Theatre in Saskatoon.

During the war she met Jan Szumigalski, a Polish army officer. In 1946 they were married and the couple lived in North Wales before immigrating to Canada in 1951. Her short time in Wales would have a striking impact on Anne Szumigalski as a writer. From the distance of Canada her Welsh experiences would form the basis of many of her early poems.

It might seem that Anne Szumigalski had great patience as a writer, since she didn't publisher her first book, *Woman Reading in Bath* until she was 52 (in 1974). Yet she often said that it wasn't until she arrived in Canada that she began to take her writing seriously. By the time she and her family moved to Saskatoon in 1956, it was clear that she was "devoted to her craft." It also has to be remembered that Anne was the mother of four children: Katherine and Elizabeth who were born in England in 1946 and 1947, and Tony and Mark who were born in Saskatoon in 1961 and 1963.

In the eighteen years between her arrival in Saskatoon and the publication of her first book the Saskatchewan writing scene made a remarkable transformation and Anne was at the centre of it. She established the first writers' group in the province, and in 1969 she was one of the founding members of the Saskatchewan Writers Guild. She was also an instructor at the Summer School of the Arts at Fort San where she taught for ten years.

Szumagalski was a prime mover in the founding of the

ANNE SZUMIGALSKI

Saskatchewan Writers and Artists Colony, and the literary magazine *Grain*. She was perhaps the most visible and galvanizing figure in a writing community that was bursting at the seams. In 1981 and 1982 she was appointed the first writer-in-residence at the Frances Morrison Library in Saskatoon.

Throughout the rapid growth of the writing community in this province, Anne Szumigalski flourished as a poet. The 1980s were her most prolific time. During that decade she published her second collection, *A Game of Angels*, and other projects followed in quick succession. In 1983, her long poem *Risks* was published as well as her collection *Doctrine of Signatures*. In 1984 the performance piece *Litany of the Bagladies* was performed and in 1985 *Instar*, a collection of poetry and prose, came out. In 1986 *Dogstones*, a collection of poems new and selected, was released, and in 1988 *Journey/Journee* poems was produced in collaboration with Terrence Heath. Although the 1980s were a time of great growth for Szumagalski, 1985 also marked the passing of her husband Jan. During the 1990s Anne continued to produce outstanding work and her reputation as a poet reached national and international proportions.

Her books from the 1990s are *The Word, The Voice, The Text*; *Rapture of the Deep*; and *Voice*, which won the Governor General's Award for poetry in 1995; "Z" won the Saskatchewan Book of the Year award in 1995. In 1997 Coteau Books published *On Glassy Wings*, a major retrospective of Anne's work, deftly edited by Don Kerr.

As her reputation grew, Anne could have moved her work toward national poetry presses. Yet in the late 1990s she saw a new need in her beloved Saskatchewan writing community. She saw the need for a new literary press that would publish the work of writers who took a "spiritual" approach to writing. With Anne's encouragement, John Clark and Don Ward established Hagios Press and Anne provided them with their first book *Sermons on Stones: Words and Images*. The book featured Anne's prose and her idiosyncratic drawings. In 1997 the book won the Non-Fiction Award at the Saskatchewan Book Awards and helped launch Hagios. In 2000 Hagios published the posthumous collection *Fear of Knives: A Book of Fables*, illustrated by Marie Elyse St. George, who had collaborated so successfully with Anne on *Voice*.

Anne Szumigalski died in 1999; her work remains and will no doubt continue to astound and delight readers of poetry.

PAUL WILSON

About Writing... *How, in fact, did we come to write anything: what's behind our passion for narrative, our devotion to words: must we always be unsatisfied with what we write, what we imagine, what we express? It's these questions and many like them that occupy my mind when I am not actually writing myself. Digging in the garden, soaking in the bathtub, eating my solitary supper, my mind returns always to these speculations and arguments. They are as much a part of my being as poetry itself.*—ANNE SZUMIGALSKI *[The Word, The Voice, The Text: The Life of a Writer (Fifth House, 1990)].*

LEONA THEIS was born in eastern Saskatchewan in 1955. She grew up in the town of Bredenbury and attended Yorkton Regional High School. Theis moved to Saskatoon in 1973.

After working for a year, she enrolled at a technical college and completed a certificate in library technology. She worked for a number of years in school libraries. While still working for the school board, she enrolled as a part-time student at the University of Saskatchewan, majoring in sociology.

In 1979 she became librarian at the Co-operative College of Canada in Saskatoon. She stayed with the institution for ten years, eventually leaving the library position and becoming a researcher and adult education program developer. In the fall of 1989 her employer, which had been re-named the Canadian Co-operative Association, moved its head office to Ottawa. Leona, who had by then begun coursework at the University of Saskatchewan for a master's degree in adult education, stayed in Saskatoon. She gave birth to a son, Michael Fulton, in 1990, and earned her M.Ed. degree in 1991.

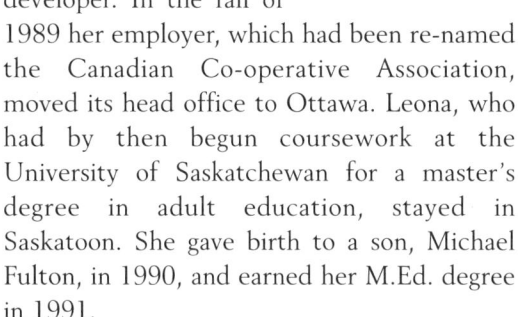

A few days after she defended her thesis, Leona and her family moved to Australia for a year. Having no job and no arrangements for daycare, she began to look for ways to spend her time creatively and still be on call for her son. It was during this year in Australia that she began to write fiction.

When she returned to Saskatchewan, she spent several years working a variety of freelance research and consulting projects. She also took advantage of the opportunities Saskatchewan affords new writers to improve their craft: the Sage Hill Writing Experience, a creative writing class offered through the University of Saskatchewan, and consultations with writers-in-residence at the Saskatoon Public Library. Her mentors included Dave Margoshes, Guy Vanderhaeghe, and Sandra Birdsell.

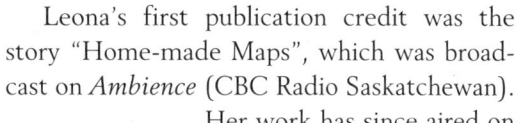

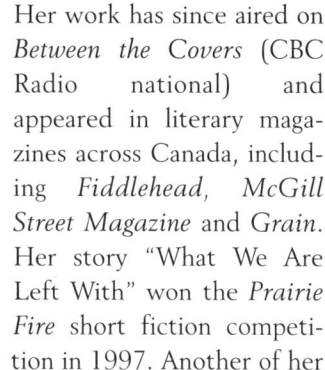

PHOTO BY MURRAY FULTON
LEONA THEIS... OFF THE COAST OF SANTORINI.

Leona's first publication credit was the story "Home-made Maps", which was broadcast on *Ambience* (CBC Radio Saskatchewan). Her work has since aired on *Between the Covers* (CBC Radio national) and appeared in literary magazines across Canada, including *Fiddlehead*, *McGill Street Magazine* and *Grain*. Her story "What We Are Left With" won the *Prairie Fire* short fiction competition in 1997. Another of her stories, "Roadside Attractions" was a finalist in the short prose competition for developing writers sponsored by the Writers' Union of Canada. In 1998 three of her stories appeared in the well-regarded annual anthology *Coming Attractions*.

Leona Theis's first book, a collection of thirteen interlocking short stories entitled *Sightlines*, was published by Coteau Books in 2000. That year it won two Saskatchewan Book Awards: the Fiction Award and the Saskatoon Book Award.

Leona lives in Saskatoon with her husband Murray Fulton and their son Michael. Although Saskatoon is home, they have been fortunate to live for short periods of time in Australia, Vancouver, Denmark, and France. Leona's two main professional activities are now the writing of fiction and freelance editing, in that order. She is at work on her first novel, *Temperance Street*, which will be set in Saskatoon.

About Writing... *Be curious about your characters, their lives, their actions, their emotions. Remember that most writers have occasions when they'd like to give up. The books were written by the ones who didn't give up.* —LEONA THEIS

LUETTA TREHAS was born at Tompkins in 1917. She attended school at Anzac, Tompkins, and Moose Jaw, and she went to university in Saskatoon. As well as her writing, she has an interest in music, playing the drums and the fiddle.

Trehas worked on the family farm, in post offices, a factory, and also as a schoolteacher. In 1950 she married John Trehas, whom she met at a poetry club. They made their home in Regina.

Trehas began writing poetry at the age of 20. She won awards from Alberta Poetry Yearbook, Credit Union Central and others, and her work has been published in a number of literary magazines including *Fiddlehead*, *Salt*, *Elfin Plot*, and *Poets of Canada*, and well as in *Number One Northern* (1977).

Trehas published *Buffalo Bean Stories* in 1980.

NIK BURTON

GEOFFREY URSELL. Born in Moose Jaw on March 14, 1943, Geoffrey Ursell has Scottish, Italian, and English ancestors. He went to public school in Regina and Saskatoon, then attended Nutana Collegiate in Saskatoon. When his family moved to Winnipeg, Geoffrey obtained his B.A. (Hons) and M.A. from the University of Manitoba. During university, he worked for two summers at Chateau Lake Louise. Inspired by the folk song movement, he taught himself guitar. He met his wife, Barbara Sapergia, who was also born in Moose Jaw, at university, and they married in 1967.

In 1966, an IODE War Memorial Scholarship enabled him to go to England to study at University College, London. He became a graduate student of the new Head of the English Department, the famous critic and scholar, (now Sir) Frank Kermode, and did research on Joseph Conrad. While doing this research, Geoffrey discovered an unknown event in Conrad's life, and wrote an article that appeared in the *Times Literary Supplement*. This discovery also made the front page of *The Times* itself.

Returning to Canada in 1969, Geoffrey worked on his thesis and began to write fiction, while Barbara taught English at the University of British Columbia. In 1971, they moved back to Winnipeg. His first one-act play, *The Park*, won a Performing Arts in Canada award in 1972, and some poems were published the same year. In 1973, the year he received his Ph.D., he sent a song called "Moose Jaw Meetin'" to *Morningside*, which resulted in his first interview with Peter Gzowski and the recording of two songs. He also wrote and hosted a *Country Canada* program about the state of farming in Saskatchewan.

Wanting to return to the province of their birth, Geoffrey and Barbara moved back to Regina in the summer of 1974. There they met Robert Currie and Gary Hyland, and together founded Coteau Books in 1975. Geoffrey continued to write songs about Saskatchewan, and produced an album of five Saskatchewan songwriters (including Connie Kaldor's first recording appearance) in 1976, called *Prairie Grass, Prairie Sky*. CBC recorded a number of songs, and Geoffrey was interviewed by Barbara Frum on *As It Happens*. He wrote songs for National Film Board and CBC documentaries,

PHOTO BY A.K. PHOTOS
GEOFFREY URSELL

and had songs published in *The Canadian Folk Bulletin*.

After two years of research and writing, Geoffrey created a full-length play, *The Running of the Deer*, set in Newfoundland in 1768, which won a national playwriting award in 1977 and was produced by the University of Alberta in Edmonton the following year. And he began an association as a songwriter with Globe Theatre and fellow writer Rex Deverell, which led to Geoffrey's writing songs for *Superwheel*, a play for high school students about cars, in 1976; *Number One Hard*, a 1979 play about the grain industry, for which a cast recording was done; and *Black Powder: Estevan, 1931*, on the fiftieth anniversary of the miners' strike. In 1982, a CBC special, "The Songs of Geoffrey Ursell," was filmed at Fort San.

Geoffrey's second full-length play, the musical comedy *Saskatoon Pie!*, set in Regina in 1906, won Persephone Theatre's national playwriting competition in 1981. Produced the following year, the play was a great hit, and went on to several professional and many amateur productions in Saskatchewan. He also wrote his first novel, *Perdue: Or How the West Was Lost* (1984), a fantasy based on prairie history, and winner of the Books in Canada Best First Novel Award.

His stories and poems continued to appear in many magazines and anthologies, including *Saturday Night*, *Grain*, *Quarry*, *Canadian Fiction Magazine*, *Border Crossings*, and *This Magazine*. His first book of poetry, *Trap Lines*, appeared in 1983, and a second book, *The Look-Out Tower*, appeared in 1989. In the same year, a book of stories, *Way Out West*, was published.

Over the years, Geoffrey continued to write plays for stage, both for adults and children, in collaboration with others and on his own. These include *The Tenth Negative Pig* (about tuberculosis), *The Willow Bunch Giant* (about Edouard Beaupré), and *Midnight in Moose Jaw* (about River Street in the 1920s)—all with Barbara Sapergia—and *Is There Anybody Here From Moose Jaw?* (a celebration of Moose Jaw's first one hundred years of history)—with Sapergia and Ken Mitchell. He's written ten radio plays, including *The Auction*, *The Rum-Runners of Rainbow Ravine* (a series), and *I Love Food*, all produced for CBC. In 1985, he wrote *Distant Battles*, a CBC television docudrama about the conflict at Batoche in 1885.

Geoffrey is one of three partners in Moose Jaw Light & Power Artistic Productions Ltd. (founded in 1982). Beginning in 1993, he and Barbara developed a preschool television series, *Prairie Berry Pie*. Geoffrey wrote or co-wrote five of thirteen episodes for the first season, three episodes for the second season, and co-produced both seasons with Mind's Eye Pictures. The show is broadcast on the Saskatchewan Communications Network, Global Television, and the Aboriginal Peoples Television Network.

Over the years, Geoffrey also put in countless volunteer hours with Coteau Books, helping it become a major Canadian press, winner of two Governor General's Awards, for poetry in 1995 and for fiction in 2003, among many other awards. Geoffrey is now Publisher and President of the press. He has edited several anthologies for Coteau, as well as many award-winning, single-author titles. He is himself a winner of the Vicky Metcalfe editor's award for his work on the children's anthology *Jumbo Gumbo*. In 2000, he created the children's series *In The Same Boat* for Coteau, with the support of the Canada Council Millennium Fund, and edited two of the first five titles in that series.

Geoffrey has taught creative writing at the University of Regina, was editor-in-chief of *Grain Magazine* from 1990 to 1994, and twice served as writer-in-residence at public libraries in Saskatoon and Winnipeg. He is a member of the Writers Guild, the Writers Union, the Playwrights Guild, PEN, the Saskatchewan Writers Guild, and the Saskatchewan Playwrights Centre. His work has been supported both by the Saskatchewan Arts Board and the Canada Council.

A full-time writer, producer, and publisher, Geoffrey is working on two new novels, one set in Regency England and the other in contemporary Canada, as well as an opera (score by Rob Bryanton). His new musical, *Gold on Ice: A Celebration of the Sandra Schmirler Curling Team*, was produced by Dancing Sky Theatre in 2003, with runs at Meacham, Moose Jaw, and Biggar.

About Writing... *Every form of writing has its own pleasures, and I'm fortunate enough to work in many of them. I've had great joy in seeing and hearing actors and musicians perform my words and music, and also the joy of holding books I've written in my hands. My writing ranges from the absurdly comic to the completely serious, and includes novels for adults and television shows for children, yet it all seems linked to me. One of those central links is an exploration of the prairie—its history, landscape, and people.*—GEOFFREY URSELL

PHOTO COURTESY OF MCCLELLAND & STEWART
PHOTO BY MARGARET VANDERHAEGHE

GUY VANDERHAEGHE

GUY VANDERHAEGHE was born in Esterhazy in 1951, where he received his elementary and secondary education. His pursuit of an interest in Western Canadian history instilled in him by his grandmother through her stories of her father's arrival before the Riel Rebellion, is clearly reflected in his education. Vanderhaeghe received a Bachelor of Arts degree in history in 1972, and a Master of Arts in 1975, both from the University of Regina. These were followed by a Bachelor of Education degree in 1978 from the University of Saskatchewan. Although Vanderhaeghe thought about continuing his academic education, he chose to be a writer and does not regret that decision. He was awarded an honourary D. Litt. from the University of Saskatchewan.

Vanderhaeghe is the author of three collections of short stories, *Man Descending* (1982), *The Trouble with Heroes* (1983), and *Things as They Are?* (1992); four novels, *My Present Age* (1984), *Homesick* (1989), *The Englishman's Boy* (1996), and *The Last Crossing* (1996); and two plays, *I Had a Job I Liked. Once* (1992) and *Dancock's Dance* (1996).

Vanderhaeghe has consistently produced award-winning work. His short story collection *Man Descending* won the Governor General's Award for English fiction and the Geoffrey Faber Memorial Prize in Great Britain. His novel *Homesick* was a co-winner of the City of Toronto Book Award. In 1985, he was named one of the ten best young fiction writers in Canada in the 45 Below Competition sponsored by the CBIC. *I Had a Job I Liked. Once* won the Canadian Authors Association Award for Drama. *The*

Englishman's Boy won the Governor General's Award and "Book of the Year" at the Saskatchewan Book Awards, as well as being shortlisted for the Giller Prize (Vanderhaeghe has been working on a film adaptation of the book). *The Last Crossing* received the Libris Award for fiction of the year and swept the Saskatchewan Book Awards with four awards including "Book of the Year."

Influenced by prairie writers such as Sinclair Ross, Margaret Laurence, and Robert Kroetsch, Vanderhaeghe's fiction is a part of this tradition. His protagonists struggle with the hardships and the loneliness of the landscape, but the stories are not without humour. The themes in his works are affirmative in their celebration of the undying quality of the human spirit. He also admires short story writers Alice Munro, Flannery O'Connor, Evelyn Waugh, John Cheever, and John Updike.

Vanderhaeghe has worked as a teacher, an archivist, and a researcher, but now turns his full attention to his writing. He has been Visiting Professor of English at St. Thomas More College, University of Saskatchewan, since 1993, and he and his wife, who is a painter, live in Saskatoon. Although he enjoys a success that is international in scope, Vanderhaeghe remains in Saskatchewan, saying that he likes the "solitude of Saskatoon" and claims that "the universal grows out of the particular." Blending genres of history and fiction, he dedicates *The Last Crossing* to "all those local historians who keep the particulars of our past alive."

CINDY MACKENZIE

About writing... *The guiding principle to fiction writing is the notion of cause and effect. Stories are built in sequences. Writing is one good sentence, then another good sentence, then another good sentence....* — GUY VANDERHAEGHE

SEÁN VIRGO was born in Mtarfa, Malta. He lives in southwest Saskatchewan.

In between he had to learn four national anthems, three of them bilingual.

His sister, Máire, was born too early to have his luck and advantages. It's not fair. She's smarter than he is and most of what he abidingly learned as a child was her doing.

He's much too private a person to offer a very forthcoming biography. Other people seem to enjoy doing that for him and, as with their character assessments, they get it all wrong. That has its advantages.

His earliest reading, apart from Rudyard Kipling, was Charles G.D. Roberts and Grey Owl, and they, without doubt, are why he became a Canadian.

When he came to Canada, and discovered the great stone age cultures of the West Coast, his life was changed forever. Another tumble along the road to Damascus had been the work of William Faulkner. He reads *The Horse's Mouth* every year, and thinks *Citizen Kane* and *Casablanca* are the most overrated films in the world. He wishes he had written *The Twa Corbies*. He also wishes he had been a painter instead. And that he had been born 1200 years ago (perhaps he will be, next time around).

His last published biography said, "He has

PHOTO BY YVONNE ADALIAN

SEÁN VIRGO...

"HOUSMAN SAID THAT THE TEST OF A TRUE POEM WAS THAT IF YOU RECITED IT WHILE SHAVING, YOUR HAIRS WOULD STAND UP."

taught, logged, blasted, dug graves, witched wells, shepherded, smuggled and edited." Whoever wrote that got it more or less right, actually, as far as it goes.

About Writing... *Stop reading your contemporaries, except for relaxation. It's too late to learn anything from them. It's never too late to learn from the great ones. Honour the language.*—SEÁN VIRGO

FRED WAH. *When I was eight my aunty Lil took me to a hockey game between the Nelson Maple Leafs and the Trail Smoke Eaters and on the way to the game she turned around to me holding her just-lit lipsticked cigarette between her long painted fingernails and after blowing a cloud of smoke up to the ceiling of the car said If you want to be a Smoke Eater when you grow up don't ever let me catch you smoking.*

Like so many other Saskatchewan families after WWII, Wah's family moved west for a greener life. He grew up in the West Kootenays of B.C. playing hockey and trumpet.

When I was eight my dad took me to the Crown Point after a hockey game and we had potatoes lyonnaise which he said was a foreign language but the cook was Chinese.

Wah learned to love Salisbury steak, borscht, egg foo yung, tofu and other highlights of western Canadian cuisine and he didn't know "You mucka high" was Chinook jargon and not just the cooks swearing at him in Chinese.

After the war the universal became part of my identity as if I was penetrated by a constitutive lack though who would have wanted to be different certainly not the Chinese or even the Italians up the Gulch.

Wah grew up in Chinese-Canadian cafes of the 1940s and 1950s and you can read all about that in his biofiction, *Diamond Grill* (1996) which, according to the dust-jacket blurb, "serves up the story of a hyphenated identity.... Fred Wah's father was a Canadian-born Chinese-Scots-Irishman raised in China; his mother is a Swedish-born Canadian from Swift Current. Wah senior ran [cafes in Swift Current, Trail, and Nelson] where Fred... grew up, white enough to "pass," yet marked for life by a foreign name and a taste for foong cheng and lo bok."

When I was eight who would have thought that the sheer material factualness of my body would be borrowed to lend the world I was being constructed inside of the aura of "realness" and "certainty" but then who was organizing their thinking around the disruption of difference certainly not famous people far away like Mackenzie King or Just Mary.

He can remember, as a toddler in Swift Current, listening to *Just Mary* on the radio. *Jake and the Kid* was the big one. Language lurked problematically, the master's tongue seeming distant yet tyrannical. By the time he attended UBC in the early 1960s he had learned, from necessity, how to "fake it" through playing jazz improv and watching his father negotiate the racialization underlying multi-culti in small-town, Canada. The poetics of these social and cultural convergences are outlined in *Faking It: Poetics and Hybridity* (2000).

Writing would have a lot to do with "place," the spiritual

PHOTO BY PAULINE BUTLING

FRED WAH... STOMACH KNOWS ALL THE MAPS.

and spatial localities of the writer. I see things from where I am, my view point, and I measure and imagine a world from there. Who I am. Am I? Oaxaca, Vancouver, the Kootenay River a thousand years ago or today, my father's father's birthplace, become "local" to me and compound to make up a picture of a world I am native of. Writing sometimes remembers this image, and sometimes it has to make it up… The towns become predictable (thus memorably comfortable) in their activities and appearances. Castlegar and Prince George, though specifically themselves, share certain aspects of distance, colour and taste. One feels at home nearly anywhere there are rivers, pulp mills, trucks, the mysterious gravel roads further inward, and similar "local" inhabitants. Down and out there the exterior becomes more. Vancouver leads to other cities and countries. But all of it, out there, is measured from in here. In the particularity of a place the writer finds revealed the correspondences of a whole ~~world~~. *And then holes in that wor()d.*

But geography implicates class. Writing alongside some of those others from the small towns of the interior in the early 1960s was a "class" act. So he became interested in the implicit friction dynamically situated between language, the social, and the world. He left the graduate programme at the State University of Buffalo in 1967 for a job at Selkirk College in Castlegar, B.C. In the late 1970s he helped develop the writing programme at David Thompson University Centre in Nelson and then taught creative writing and poetics at the University of Calgary from 1989 to 2003. He's also been a writer-in-residence at the University of Manitoba and the University of Alberta and has taught poetry workshops at Fort Qu'Appelle, Red Deer, and Sage Hill.

In grade two I fell in love with a blonde named Elizabeth who lived in Sunningdale near Sandy Beach where I was lying on my towel on the grass drying off when she and her friends from that part of town walked by with ice cream cones.

Many of his early books (*Lardeau, Among, Tree, Pictograms from the Interior of B.C.*) are attempts to locate place as an interpolation of identity. So, when our cultural attention shifted to the politics of identity in the early 1980s, he was ready with a disjunctive poetics he called "drunken tai chi" (*Music at the Heart of Thinking, Alley Alley Home Free, So Far*) that has helped support a 20-year biotextual probe into self and art with books like *Breathin' My Name With a Sigh, Waiting for Saskatchewan, Diamond Grill*, and *Faking It* and collaborations with performance artists, painters, and photographers.

At eight the social formation of my gender didn't know biology as discourse and it was only within the post-war bourgeois capitalist order that my sexuality emerged as a separate discursive reality and I became interested in girls.

Pauline Butling (*Seeing In the Dark: The Poetry of Phyllis Webb*) and Fred have two daughters, Jenefer and Erika, and two granddaughters, Elena and Claudia, living in Vancouver where, after a 14-year stint in Calgary, they will spend their winters.

When you were eight you picked up a broken bottle and as you were walking along accidentally gouged your right thigh where you now have a phantom scar that expresses nostalgia for your body's prior unity and wholeness just as it etches a kind of "soul" or interiority but could also identify your body should it be found.

When I was eight there was no question I would smoke.

[FROM "STRANGLE 6" IN *FAKING IT: POETICS AND HYBRIDITY* (2000)].

About Writing... *I never knew writing was this easy. All I have to do is do what I'm doing right now, like writing "I never knew writing was this easy"—just writing it. Just writing!*—FRED WAH

DONALD WARD is a writer, editor, designer, and publisher who has been involved in the creation of over eighty books. He has also been the managing editor and art director of a monthly magazine, associate editor of a weekly paper, publications director for a liberal arts college, and copyeditor, typesetter, and designer for a philosophical academic journal. His first book-length work of fiction, *Nobody Goes to Earth Any More*, was published in 2003, and received the Saskatchewan Book of the Year award. He also published a biography of Stanley Knowles in 2003.

Ward is the co-author of *The World Is Our Witness: The Historic Journey of the Nisga'a into Canada* (2000), and author of *The People: A Historical Guide to the First Nations of Manitoba, Saskatchewan, and Alberta* (1996).

He lists among his interests the hobbies of winemaking and blacksmithing. Donald Ward lives with his family at Muenster, within earshot of the bells of St. Peter's Abbey.

NIK BURTON

BETSY WARLAND was born in Fort Dodge, Iowa, in 1946, and now lives in Saskatoon. She is a poet, lyric prose writer, essayist, teacher and editor.

Warland obtained her B.A. in Art and Education at Luther College, Decorah, Iowa, in 1970. She emigrated to Canada in 1973, and became a Canadian citizen in 1980. She is regarded as one of Canada's leading feminist and experimental writers.

Warland is the coordinator of The Writer's Studio (in which she has also taught and mentored) at Simon Fraser University's Writing and Publishing Program in Vancouver. In addition, she has taught Poetry at the Sage Hill Writing Experience in Saskatchewan (2001–2003) and at Booming Ground, University of British Columbia (2004).

Warland has published nine books of poetry and prose that include, *A Gathering Instinct* (1981), *open is broken* (1984), *serpent (w)rite* (1987), *Double Negative*, Daphne Marlatt co-author (1988), *Proper Deafinitions* (1990), *The Bat Had Blue Eyes* (1993), *Two Women in a Birth*, Daphne Marlatt co-author (1994), *What Holds Us Here* (1998), and *Bloodroot—Tracing the Untelling of Motherloss* (2000). She has published numerous criticial essays for art catalogues.

Warland has also edited various collections, including *Inversions: Writing by Dykes, Queers and Lesbians* (1991) and *Telling It: Women and Language across Cultures*, Sky Lee, Lee Maracle, Daphne Marlatt, Betsy Warland, editors (1990).

Betsy Warland served as a juror for the national poetry award, The Governor General's Award, in 1996. She is a member of The Writers' Union of Canada.

HEATHER HODGSON

About Writing... *When, as writers, we commit ourselves to writing a poem or prose piece, we rappel down the cliff of our verbal vertigo. Hand over hand, we make our way toward a narrative ground we have only sensed. Word after word, we come closer to this untried ground we want footing on.*—BETSY WARLAND *(from the unpublished manuscript,* Breathing the Page*).*

DIANNE WARREN was born in Ottawa in 1950, but Saskatchewan is the place of her roots, her upbringing, and her imagination. Her mother, Helen Taylor, grew up on a homestead farm near Beechy, Saskatchewan. When Taylor completed high school, her parents arranged for her to live with relatives in the east and attend business school. While working in Ottawa after the war she met and married Ray Warren. On a trip to Saskatchewan to meet his new in-laws, Ray fell in love with the west and in 1955 the family moved to North Battleford.

DIANNE WARREN... ON HER HORSE, SHADOW.

In 1965 the family moved to Swift Current where Dianne graduated from high school. She attended the University of Regina and completed a Bachelor of Fine Arts degree in Visual Art. Dianne thinks of Swift Current as her home town, and the Beechy area and the family stories as the sources of her interest in place and narrative. Now living in Regina, Dianne and her husband (artist Bruce Anderson) have two sons.

Warren began writing poems and stories as a child. The North Battleford library (now the Allen Sapp Gallery) was within walking distance of her house and she read every horse, dog, and Hardy Boy book it had to offer. She remembers her mother once suggesting she attend a creative writing class, but she declined because she thought creative writing was what she later came to know as calligraphy. The first "adult" book that Dianne remembers reading (besides her father's Zane Gray novels) was *Catcher in the Rye*, which had a huge impact on her. For years she didn't know why, but now she knows it was the voice, the depth of character in the book, and the author's scrutiny of the society in which the novel is situated. She remembers feeling mysteriously unsettled and the experience changed her expectations for books.

Perhaps she would have studied creative writing at university had there been a writing major in the Fine Arts faculty. However, she has no regrets about studying Visual Art and believes it provided a good education for a writer. Her interest in visual images manifests itself in her writing, and a visual image is often what captures her attention and sparks a narrative. At the age of 30 she decided she was a better writer than she was a visual artist, and she began to focus exclusively on writing. She published her first story in the Coteau Books anthology *Saskatchewan Gold*, and soon after became a member of a Regina writing group known as the Bombay Bicycle Club. Her first book of fiction, *The Wednesday Flower Man*, was published in 1987, and in 1993 her second collection, *Bad Luck Dog*, was published. It won three awards in the inaugural year of the Saskatchewan Book Awards. In 2002, Warren's third collection, *A Reckless Moon*, was published.

Warren has won the Western Magazine Award for fiction twice for stories published in *Grain Magazine*, and in 1995 she won the National Magazine Gold Award for fiction for another story published in *Grain*. She finds it impossible to answer the question, What are your favourite books? The following is a quotation she likes from Charles Frazier's place-specific novel *Cold Mountain*: "What was required to speak that language was a picture held in the mind of the land one occupied.... General to particular. Everything had a name.

To live fully in a place all your life, you kept aiming smaller and smaller in attention to detail." She's currently enjoying several Australian writers whose stories are intrinsically linked to their settings.

Warren remembers being fascinated by a production of *Antigone* on television when she was a child and thinks her interest in playwriting probably goes back to that. In addition, at the University of Regina during the 1970s, the Visual Art and Drama Departments shared the old Normal School Building on the corner of Broad and College, and she would often attend drama student performances, where she would think about the possibilities offered by an empty stage. In the early 1980s she took a script writing class at the University of Regina and one of the assignments was to write a full-length play. That one remains in a drawer, but since then she has written three plays that premiered at Twenty-fifth Street Theatre in Saskatoon: *Serpent in the Night Sky* (1989), *Club Chernobyl* (1995), and *The Last Journey of Captain Harte* (1999). *Serpent in the Night Sky* was short-listed for the Governor General's Award for Drama in 1992. Its most recent production was at Pandora's Box Theatre Company in Buffalo, New York. She credits the Saskatchewan Playwrights Centre and its artist-run workshop programs with providing an opportunity for her to develop her plays even though the possibilities for production of new plays are so limited.

Warren is now working on a rambling narrative set in southern Saskatchewan, near Swift Current. It might be a novel.

She is grateful to the Saskatchewan Arts Board, the Canada Council for the Arts and the City of Regina for their support in the form of writing awards over the years. She can't thank enough her writing friends, in particular Marlis Wesseler and Connie Gault.

About Writing... *Dianne likens the writing of a first draft to the construction of a game with characters and words and images as the game pieces. In the rewriting she moves them around, moulds the playing surface, adds and subtracts images and scenes until a structure emerges that is satisfying. The pay may not be great, but a writer is lucky enough to have the ability to live in the worlds of her imagination. Dianne is thankful for this and for the fact that her parents, especially her mother who recently confessed that she'd wanted to be a writer when she was young, didn't try to steer her in a more practical direction.*—DIANNE WARREN

LARRY WARWARUK was born and raised in Glenavon, a village halfway between Regina and Kenosee Lake. His childhood and teen years took place during the booming 1950s, when he played on the front street, and worked in his parents' general store and meat market. This was experience for his stories, some published, some read on radio, and some to be possibly the meat of a future novel or two.

Warwaruk married a lovely young woman of Finnish-Canadian extraction, a genre one must probe deeply and carefully to understand. A book resulted in 1984, *Red Finns on the Coteau*, followed up with a novel on the same mysteries, *Rope of Time*, in 1991. During this decade of writing, he attended Writers Guild summer workshops and colonies to further learn and hone his craft.

After *Rope of Time*, Warwaruk searched his own ethnic background to arrive at *The Ukrainian Wedding*, winner of the 1998 Saskatchewan Book Award for Fiction. He then wrote *Andrei and the Snow Walker* in 2002. It too was about ethnicity, but this time with a recognition of a people here long before the immigrants.

Warwaruk spent years with drama students

LARRY WARWARUK...
HOLDING THE TSYMBALI
WHICH INSPIRED *THE
UKRAINIAN WEDDING*.

at Beechy High School developing Collective Creations, fifteen of which have been staged for Saskatchewan High School Drama Festivals. He worked twelve years with Beechy's Snakebite Players, culminating with 'Railroaded,' a Collective Creation on rural Saskatchewan which played to the 1998 SARM Convention in Saskatoon.

Warwaruk saw something new developing in our literature. Trevor Herriot's *River in a Dry Land* and Sharon Butala's work have sensed this change. Just at a time when we want to hurry up and capture the stories of our homesteaders before it is too late, the paradigm shifts. There is more now than a society built around agricultural enterprise. Those of us who are the children of immigrants find our cultural base to be but a short century's span slotted into a long history of this place, and it is a base not necessarily permanent. This question prevails in Warwaruk's novel in progress, *Bone Coulee*.

About Writing... *I carry a notebook in my shirt pocket, to capture creativity when the urge hits. This can happen when sitting alone in a donut shop, or when attending important meetings. Free up the child within. Let your delicate right-brain daydream surface and write it down. Find the places and times, the writing sanctuaries for these fragments of stories to flower in safety, undisturbed.*

Something that works for me is to try and write my story from start to finish before I revise. This draft may be grammatically horrendous, and dramatically flat, but that is all right. At least it is down on paper. Now enjoy the work. Expand from within. Insert passages here, there, and everywhere. My first draft of 'Andrei and the Snow Walker' was 70 pages. The final draft was 200.

And grow with time. I was once told that it takes ten years for a writer to develop. For me it has been many years and I'm still developing, and not in isolation. For at least 15 years I've worked with 'The Revisionists,' a writers' group in Beechy. We critique each other's work. So if someone out there takes exception to something I might write, blame 'The Revisionists.' —LARRY WARWARUK

MARLIS WESSELER was born in 1952 in Kinistino. Her parents, Elliot and Clara Nordin, farmed in the Haggstrom School District, where she grew up with two younger brothers and attended grades one and two in a one-room country schoolhouse. After finishing her secondary education in Kinistino, she attended university in Saskatoon. She took a year or so off to travel to Mexico with a friend, artist Joanne Shannon (who is still a good friend living in Regina) and to work in Edmonton, then returned to the University of Saskatchewan, earning a teaching certificate in 1973. She taught school in isolated villages in northern Saskatchewan, eventually taking more time off to travel to Europe where she met her husband, Lutz Wesseler.

They moved to Regina in 1978 to attend university there. Encouraged by writer and professor Joan Givner, Wesseler began to write short stories. The first story she wrote, "Victor," was accepted by Wayne Schmalz for CBC Radio's *Ambience*, and from then on she was addicted to writing (though it took some

MARLIS WESSELER... SIGHTSEEING IN BERLIN, 1998.

years before she published a second story). At university, she met another writer, Connie Gault, and they began to meet regularly to critique each other's work. At one of many lunches with Givner, they met Dianne Warren, and the three of them began a long tradition of getting together to discuss their writing (among other things). They joined the Saskatchewan Writers Guild and, together with Bonnie Burnard, Chris Fisher, and Ven Begamudré, formed a writing group, the Bombay Bicycle Club, which met once a month. Several other members came and went over time, but the core group continued meeting for about seven years. Since 1986, Wesseler and Gault have been walking around Wascana Lake on weekdays, ostensibly for exercise, but also discussing (again among other things) their work. The influence of Wesseler's literary friends on her writing has been immeasurable.

Her background, the Saskatchewan landscape, her family, her experiences teaching in the North and travelling, all have influenced her work. But from the time she discovered reading as a child, books have been the foundation of her development as a writer. Her mother, who was an avid reader and an astute judge of good literature, was a great influence. Her university studies focused on the Victorians, but her favourite authors have ranged in style and era from Austen and the Brontës to Dostoevsky; William Faulkner to Barbara Pym; Margaret Laurence and Alice Munro to Manuel Puig and Richard Ford. She fondly recalls the first book she borrowed from the Kinistino Library when she was five or six, Sid Hoff's *Danny the Dinosaur*, and her favourite book in grade two, E.B. White's *Charlotte's Web*.

Studying English at the University of Regina while working part-time, receiving the Lucy Murray Scholarship, Wesseler earned an Honours Degree in 1984. After teaching adult education for the Saskatchewan Indian Community College, in 1985 she was contracted to write teachers' guides and other educational material for Saskatchewan's Department of Education. Eventually she returned to the University of Regina to take classes towards her Masters degree in English, which she was happy to have interrupted by the arrival of her son, Evan, in 1988.

During the 1980s and 1990s, her fiction appeared in anthologies and literary magazines, and several of her stories and plays were broadcast on CBC Radio. Two of her monologues were winners in Twenty-Fifth Street Theatre's short play writing contest.

She has published a novel, *Elvis Unplugged* (1998) and two short story collections, *Life Skills* (1992) and *Imitating Art* (1994), to positive reviews. *Life Skills* and *Elvis Unplugged* were both finalists in all categories of The Saskatchewan Book Awards for which they were eligible. During her writing career, Wesseler has been awarded several Saskatchewan Arts Board grants, has participated in juries and committees for the writing community, has worked for Coteau Books, and has been the fiction editor of *Grain Magazine*.

She still lives and works in Regina. Her new novel, *South of the Border*, which is about two young Canadians travelling in Mexico, has been submitted to a publisher. She is working on her fifth book, another novel, about a group of senior citizens in rural Saskatchewan, tentatively titled *The Man Haters of Pleasant Manor*.

About Writing... *I have a quote from Hagar attached to my fridge. It's not from the Bible's Hagar, nor from Laurence's character in* The Stone Angel *(though come to think of it, it could be), but from a cartoon. A preacher is telling Hagar the Horrible that it's better to light one little candle than to curse the darkness. As the preacher walks away, Hagar looks at us, blankly, and says, "But I enjoy cursing the darkness." This, I think, sums up much of the joy writers derive from their art. It's one of the reasons I write. I've never had much use for the creations of candle lighters.* —MARLIS WESSELER

JOANNA M. WESTON was born on January 20, 1938, in England. She immigrated to Canada in 1960, and lived near Hamilton, Ontario, before moving to British Columbia.

Weston worked in advertising, libraries, and cancer research. She received a Bachelor of Arts in 1967 and a Master of Arts in 1969 from the University of British Columbia, majoring in children's literature. Her thesis was about Walter de la Mare.

She married her husband Robert in 1967. They have three sons, one daughter-in-law, three grandchildren, a green thumb, and an enlarging garden. They moved to Saskatchewan in 1997.

Weston has had more than 1,000 poems published in magazines across Canada, internationally, in numerous anthologies, and broadcast on CBC radio. She has published four chapbooks: *One of These Little One* (1987), *Cuernavaca Diary* (1990), *Seasons* (1993), and *All Seasons* (1996, 1997). Weston has led numerous workshops and given readings. She also won the Enid M. Pickel Memorial Contest in 1998 and 1999. Her book *The Willow-Tree Girl* was published in July 2003. Weston now lives at Shawnigan Lake, British Columbia.

HEATHER HODGSON

RUDY HENRY WIEBE was born in Speedwell, Saskatchewan, on October 4, 1934. His parents were among the many thousands of Mennonites who fled from the Soviet Union in the late 1920s and 1930s. Wiebe grew up in a polyglot rural environment in Western Canada, speaking Friesian-Prussian Low German at home, High German in church, and English at school. His family were members of an insular Bible-centred Mennonite Brethren Church community similar to that depicted in Wiebe's first novel, *Peace Shall Destroy Many* (1962).

Wiebe's first attempts at creative writing were made during his undergraduate years at the University of Alberta (1953–56). He studied abroad in West Germany at the University of Tübingen in 1957–58, after which he completed an M.A. in Creative Writing at the University of Alberta in 1960, and was appointed editor of the *Mennonite Brethren Herald* in 1962. Throughout his career, he has worked in a range of genres including short stories, religious journalism, travel writing, editorials, a historical documentary, and drama. His reputation rests, however, on his novels and, more recently, on his biographical work, *Stolen Life: The Journey of a Cree Woman* (1998).

Wiebe's abiding moral and spiritual themes are explored in stories about Mennonite, First Nations, and Métis history and politics. His first novel, *Peace Shall Destroy Many* (1962), explores what happens in a small, isolated

Mennonite community when larger secular historical forces break into their previously closed world. The novel was written while Wiebe was editor of the Mennonite Brethren Herald, but it caused such controversy in the Mennonite community that he resigned his editorship of the newspaper, and moved to the United States where he took up a teaching post at Goshen College, Indiana, in 1964.

Two years later, he published his second novel, *First and Vital Candle* (1966), and the following year was appointed to a position in the English Department of the University of Alberta. In 1970 Wiebe published *The Blue Mountains of China*, the first novel about the Mennonite diaspora, the people who fled their farms in the Ukraine to seek a life free from religious persecution in Canada and South America. In *The Blue Mountains of China*, Wiebe brought the rhythms, diction, and syntax of Low German into the English language fiction.

Wiebe's fourth novel, *The Temptations of Big Bear* (1973), traced the story of the great Cree spiritual leader, Big Bear, who refused to sign a treaty and refused to give away the land—gift of the great Spirit. Set in the years between 1876 and 1888, when the federal government was "opening up" the West by enclosing the Indigenous population on reserves, *The Temptations of Big Bear* highlights Big Bear's spiritual leadership. In response to mainstream historical accounts that characterise Big Bear as a troublemaker and an impediment to progress, Wiebe presents Big Bear as a hero, a leader whose authority is based on the strength of his spiritual beliefs. *The Temptations of Big Bear* contains sections of archival documents, and imaginative reconstructions (in English) of indigenous oratory and other spoken forms. The multitude of narrative perspectives in the novel highlights the fact that the past is never directly or objectively knowable, but is always partial, always a construct, and always textually mediated.

The Temptations of Big Bear was followed four years later by *The Scorched-Wood People* (1977), which focuses on the relatively well-known story of Métis leader Louis Riel and the so-called rebellions at Red River in 1869–70 and in Saskatchewan in 1885. Wiebe presents Riel as a morally ambivalent figure. He is at once a prophetic hero fighting for the rights of his people against the oppressive alien power of the Ottawa government and a deluded religious fanatic who falls into the same traps as some of the early leaders of the Anabaptist churches in Reformation Europe. Wiebe presents Riel's story as an oral tale told by Métis bard Pierre Falcon.

Wiebe's sixth novel, *My Lovely Enemy* (1983), explores the relationship between sexual passion, spiritual love, and Western Canadian history. The boundaries of James Dyck's nuclear family break open when Gillian Overton invades his body-space in a manner analagous, in certain regards, to the invasion of the territory of the Cree chief Maskepetoon. Canadian history is again central in *A Discovery of Strangers*, which won the 1994 Governor General's Award for Fiction. This book recounts the story of explorer John Franklin during his 1820 expedition through the territory of the Tetsot'ine (Yellowknife) Indians to Canada's Arctic coast. Wiebe has published several collections of short stories, the most recent being *River of Stone* (1995). He has also published a play, *As Far as the Eye Can See* (1977), and a number of non-fiction works, including *War in the West: Voices of the 1885 Rebellion* (1985, with Bob Beale), and *Playing Dead* (1989), a collection of essays about the Arctic.

Wiebe has won critical acclaim for his

technical virtuosity and his epic historical and spiritual vision. His early works attracted criticism, however, because they moved too far in the direction of religious rhetoric. In his middle and later works, Wiebe developed various modes of indirect address, dispersing and refracting his authorial voice in sometimes complex ways through the voices and texts of others. These indirect modes of address permit readers to make sense of Wiebe's texts in different ways, and to engage with Wiebe not as passive recipients of a pre-packaged message, but as active co-creators of the meanings they "find" in Wiebe's writings.

Wiebe's practice of refracting his views through the voices of others has introduced a new political problem—the problem of appropriating or ventriloquising other people's voices to articulate his own beliefs and values. This is especially a concern in *Stolen Life: The Journey of a Cree Woman* (1998), a biographical/autobiographical account of the life of Big Bear's great-great granddaughter, Yvonne Johnson, who co-authored the book with Wiebe. While serving life imprisonment for murder, Yvonne Johnson read *The Temptations of Big Bear* and invited Wiebe to help her write her life-story. The collaboration of Wiebe and Johnson has produced an extraordinarily powerful and disturbing book. In September 2003, Wiebe and illustrator Michael Lonechild published their book *Hidden Buffalo*.

Wiebe was named an Officer of the Order of Canada in 2001.

PENNY VAN TOORN

EDWARD WILLETT was born July 20, 1959, in Silver City, New Mexico, the youngest of three brothers. His father, James Willett, was a schoolteacher and a preacher for the Church of Christ.

When Willett was two years old, his family moved to Lubbock, Texas, where his father taught at Lubbock Christian High School and his mother, Nina, worked as a secretary. When he was five, he started kindergarten, where his teacher introduced the alphabet and the sounds associated with each letter. Putting two and two together, Willett soon knew how to read and write.

When he was six years old, Willett's family moved to Tulia, Texas, where his father taught in the public high school and his mother worked as a secretary for the county judge. He started grade one, but was quickly skipped ahead to grade two when it was discovered he could already read and write.

When Willett was eight, his family moved due north a thousand miles to Saskatchewan, where his father began teaching at Western Christian College, then located in the old Commonwealth Air Training Command buildings at the Weyburn airport. He graduated from high school at Western Christian College in 1976.

Both of Willett's older brothers read science fiction, and so his first short story, written as a rainy-day activity when he was about eleven, bore the memorable title *Kastra Glazz: Hypership Test Pilot*. In high school, Willett's teachers encouraged his passion for writing, a passion shared by his best friend, John Smith. They would meet in an empty classroom after school, writing and reading their writing to each other, alternating one sentence from Willett's story with one sentence from Smith's story. Since Smith was writing a historical drama, and Willett was writing science fiction, the results were interesting.

Willett wrote three short novels in high school, all science fiction or fantasy. Typed and bound in red paper covers, they were widely circulated among his classmates.

Willett then went on to Harding University in Searcy, Arkansas, a smallish college affiliated with the Churches of Christ where his parents had met. He majored in journalism, with a minor in art, and returned to Weyburn in 1980 with a shiny new B.A. He was promptly hired by the *Weyburn Review* as a reporter/photographer, and was soon writing a regular column; he even began drawing the weekly editorial cartoon. In 1984 Willett was promoted to news editor.

Willett sold his first short story, about two youngsters caught in a blizzard, to *Western People* in 1982. Over the next few years he sold a handful of young adult science fiction short stories to various magazines.

He was very involved with Weyburn's community theatre group, Crocus 80 Theatre, eventually serving as its president.

In 1988 Willett moved to Regina as communications officer for the Saskatchewan Science Centre, then under construction. He wrote most of the text for the original exhibits (and continues to write text for new exhibits), and also began writing a weekly science column for CBC Radio's "Afternoon Edition" and the Regina *Leader-Post*, a column that continues today.

In 1993, Willett quit the Science Centre to become a full-time freelance writer, and by writing everything from magazine articles to TV scripts to "advertorial" copy for newspapers, managed to avoid starvation. His first book, published in 1995, was *Using Microsoft Publisher for Windows 95*. Willett has written many more computer books since then, first for Que, then for IDG Books (which became Hungry Minds, and is now John Wiley and Sons) and America Online.

Willett is also the author of numerous children's non-fiction books for educational publishers, on topics ranging from hemophilia and Ebola to skateboarding, careers in outer space, the Iran-Iraq War and the Ayatollah Khomeini. He recently wrote a children's biography of J.R.R. Tolkien and is currently working on a biography of author Orson Scott Card.

Willett's first novel, the young adult fantasy *Soulworm* (set mainly in Weyburn) appeared in 1997, and was shortlisted for the Brenda Macdonald Riches Award for Best First Book at the 1997 Saskatchewan Book Awards. His second young adult fantasy, *The Dark Unicorn*, came out late in 1998, and was shortlisted for best children's book at the 1999 Saskatchewan Book Awards. Willett's third novel, *Andy Nebula: Interstellar Rock Star*, appeared in 1999; it was a finalist in the Manitoba Young Readers Choice Award.

Willett's most recent novel, the young adult fantasy *Spirit Singer*, published as an electronic book and in print, won the City of Regina Award at the 2002 Saskatchewan Book Awards. It has also won an EPPIE Award for best electronically published young adult novel and a Dream Realm Award for best electronically published young adult science

EDWARD WILLETT... STANDING OUTSIDE THE BIRTHPLACE OF ROBERT A. HEINLEIN IN BUTLER, MISSOURI, HOPING TO SOAK UP SOME OF WHATEVER IT WAS THAT MADE HEINLEIN THE "DEAN OF SCIENCE FICTION WRITERS."

fiction, fantasy, or horror novel.

Willett is currently working on the first book for a new young adult fantasy series set in Saskatchewan (but with Arthurian elements).

Besides writing, Willett continues to be very involved in theatre. He has performed professionally with Globe Theatre, Persephone Theatre, Prairie Opera, Opera Saskatchewan, Souris Valley Theatre, and the Station Arts Centre in Rosthern, and non-professionally with all of Regina's community theatre groups, especially Regina Lyric Light Opera (on whose executive he has served for many years).

In 1997, Willett married Margaret Anne Hodges, an engineer with SaskTel. They have one daughter, Alice.

About Writing... *Forget trying to write great literature. Forget deathless prose. Writing is a response to the ancient cry around the primeval campfires to "tell us a story." Heed that cry. Tell a story. Make us care about what happens to your characters. And above all, forget that stale old adage to "write what you know." We live in an infinite universe of wonders, and can imagine universes more wonderful yet. Dare to imagine them!*—EDWARD WILLETT

GARRETT WILSON's earliest memories are of the grasshoppers that filled the sky and formed concentric circles of light around the mid-day sun. No wonder. Born in 1932 and raised in the small town of Limerick, smack in the middle of the Saskatchewan dustbowl, the Dirty Thirties were his boyhood years. He claims, with only modest exaggeration, that he was twelve years old when he met his first tree.

His father was Charles Wilson, an Irish immigrant from Wicklow, the Garden County south of Dublin, who came ashore in Montreal in July 1905 to read in his first Canadian newspaper of the founding of the new provinces of Saskatchewan and Alberta. "Irish Charlie" came west as a homesteader but in 1912 he sold his land and followed the steel to the new town of Limerick for a career as a financial and insurance agent. That same year Florence Sproule, a school teacher, also of Irish background, journeyed west with her brothers, sisters, and sixty-year-old parents trekking from their worn-out Nova Scotia farm to establish a homestead in the West. Florence became the first teacher in two of the one-room country schools that sprouted south of LaFleche. In 1916 Charlie and Florence were married in her parents' sod home in the Harwood school district.

As a boy, Wilson accompanied his father on his business trips to the Wood Mountain country and drank in stories of Sitting Bull, Jean Louis Legare and the North-West Mounted Police. They were great stories. Irish Charlie had travelled that historic region by horse and buggy for fifteen years before the railroad arrived. He knew all the first settlers and had been a guest at the Wood Mountain NWMP post, still operational in those early days.

While studying law at the University of Saskatchewan, Wilson discovered an interest in writing. Editor of the student newspaper, *The Sheaf*, during his final year, he won three national awards in journalism in competition with all other Canadian campus papers. Ignoring that message, Wilson took up the practice of law in Regina. Early in his career, he served as Regina City Prosecutor and became closely associated with Regina Police, a relationship that would later return him to writing.

An avid hunter and fisher, Wilson was drawn to the sports tourism industry. A 1958 trip by freighter canoe down the Saskatchewan River to The Pas introduced him to the historic communities of Cumberland House and Sturgeon Landing. There he participated in one of the area's earliest sports outfitting operations. Later enterprises took him to the far north and much of the North American outdoors. Wilson has travelled the fabled South Nahanni River in a McKenzie River scow. He has fished for Arctic char in Lake Hazen, the most northerly lake in the world, lake trout in Dubawnt and Henik Lakes of the Barren Lands, Arctic grayling in the Fond du Lac and Black Birch Rivers, as well as cutthroat trout in the South Fork Flathead River of Montana, Atlantic salmon in the Miramichi River of New Brunswick, and bonefish off the Florida Keys. Since the early 1960s he has maintained a picturesque fishing camp at Namew Lake, on the old voyageur fur trade route to the Churchill and Athabaska Rivers, where the Wilson family spent many summer vacations. But Wilson's first delight remains migratory and upland bird hunting, always accompanied by a setter or a spaniel, with some deer hunting later in the season.

A lifelong interest in aviation carried Wilson to a reserve commission in the RCAF and years of flying (and numerous adventures) as a private pilot, mostly throughout northern Saskatchewan.

Saskatchewan is agriculture and Wilson succumbed to the siren call of grain farming and purebred cattle breeding, a multi-year experiment that provided painful understanding of the agony of helplessly watching hard-won land equity bleed into the banks.

Active in politics and government, he held

GARRETT WILSON... AT BUENA VISTA.

executive positions in both provincial and municipal governments—a stint as chair of the Saskatchewan Public Service Commission and several years as chair of the Regina Rail Relocation Committee. He also served in senior positions with the Liberal Party, both provincially and federally. This close acquaintance with the province's political passions and undercurrents, and the denizens in the backrooms, led to Wilson's first novel.

In 1984 Colin Thatcher was arrested and tried for the murder of his ex-wife, Joann Wilson. It was the story of a lifetime and it brought the lawyer back to writing. Drawing on his close association with the Regina Police, and assisted by his daughter Lesley, Wilson produced *Deny, Deny, Deny* (1985), the definitive and best-selling account of the murder investigation and trial.

Deny's success led straight to another non-fiction work, *Diefenbaker For The Defence* (1988), a biography of the colourful legal career of the former prime minister. This time the research was provided by Wilson's lawyer son Kevin, who dug through trial transcripts in musty courthouse basements and archives.

Wilson's first work of fiction was inspired by the political excesses Saskatchewan experienced in the 1980s. *Guilty Addictions* (1999), nominally a political mystery, is a thinly-disguised account of the intrigue and drama of backrooms inhabited by those desperate for power and personal gain. *Guilty Addictions* was nominated for both the 1999 Saskatchewan Book Awards and the prestigious Arthur Ellis Awards.

In 2000 Colin Thatcher returned to the courtroom in an attempt to secure eligibility for early parole, prompting Wilson to produce an up-dated second edition of *Deny, Deny, Deny* (2000), nominated that year to the Saskatchewan Book Awards.

Garrett is presently at work upon a non-fiction historical account of the first decade of the prairies as part of Canada, the 1870s.

About Writing... *A writer should be courageously humble. Don't fear to expose your puerile thoughts to a cynical world; they're not as bad as you might think they are. But, also, avoid becoming overly fond of your creation; perhaps it's not quite a classic.—*
GARRETT WILSON

PAUL WILSON was born in Lacombe, Alberta, in 1954, the son of John Robert Wilson (deceased) and Gladys (Hortie). His father was wounded in action on May 23, 1944. Due to the seriousness of his wounds John spent four years in the hospital. In 1948 John married Gladys Hortie in Edmonton. Paul's parents lived in Hayer, Alberta, for two years and then moved to Edmonton where John joined the postal service. They moved to a farm near Lacombe and then in 1955 to a farm near Mirror, Alberta. In 1962 the Wilson family moved into Mirror and John became the postmaster for the town and served until his retirement in 1986. John Robert Wilson died of cancer in January of 1990. Wilson's mother Gladys grew up in the Peace River country and Edmonton; she was very active for many years in the Royal Canadian Legion; she currently lives in Ponoka, Alberta where she is married to Jim Davenport.

Wilson grew up in the central Alberta community of Mirror. He graduated from MAC (Mirror, Alix, Clive) Central High School in 1971. In high school he discovered the poetry of Ginsberg and Ferlingetti but had still not met a living, breathing writer. Knowing that he wanted to pursue some form of writing, Wilson enrolled in Communications with the focus on radio at the Lethbridge Community College. Graduating from LCC in 1974 Wilson pursued a career in radio and over a period of seven years worked at radio stations in Grande Prairie, Red Deer, and finally Regina, Saskatchewan. In Regina at CKCK Wilson met fellow writer and poet Joan Crate. Although neither knew the other was writing poetry they have remained friends. Slowly Wilson began to make connections within the Regina writing community. In 1980 he joined the Saskatchewan Writers Guild and in 1981 was asked to give his first reading by the late Jerry Rush who was coordinating the Warm Poets for Cold Nights Series. Wilson left his radio work to spend more time writing. He took a job as a bartender at night so he could write during the day. In the fall of 1981 Nik Burton, the Executive Director of the Arts Board of that time, offered him a position at the SWG as an administrative assistant.

Wilson's development as a writer paralleled to some degree his career as an arts administrator. In the mid- and late-1980s he was bolstered as a writer by the creative writing program at The Saskatchewan School of the Arts at Fort San. He worked with writers who would remain important to him as a poet. These writers included Anne Szumigalski, Joe Rosenblatt, Gary Geddes,

PAUL WILSON... AT THE DEDICATION OF THE ANNE SZUMIGALSKI LIBRARY, ST. PETER'S COLLEGE, MUENSTER, SASKATCHEWAN, 2003.

Patrick Lane, and Lorna Crozier. He published his first book of poems, *The Fire Garden*, in 1987 with Coteau Books. Wilson joined the League of Canadian Poets in 1987 and has been active within the LCP since. He is currently the Saskatchewan representative on the LCP National Council. Wilson's association with the Poet's Combine, a writing group he has been involved in since the 1980s has been important to his development as a poet. Members of that group have been Byrna Barclay, Robert Currie, Gary Hyland, Judith Krause, and Bruce Rice.

Following the death of his father in 1990 Wilson found himself blocked creatively. It was only when he turned his craft to the subject of his father's death that he was able to write again. Those poems were published in *Dreaming My Father's Body* in 1994, which was nominated for the City of Regina Book award.

Wilson was program director of the SWG in the 1980s which was a time of expansion of programming within the organization. Through the 1980s and 1990s Wilson was involved in establishing new programming for the SWG including festivals and conferences, a manuscript evaluation service, a mentorship program for emerging writers, and many, many author reading series. He is also a founder of such programs as The Saskatchewan Book Awards and the Saskatchewan Poet Laureate Program. From November of 1999 to October 2001 Wilson was the Executive Director of the SWG. Wilson has worked as a policy consultant for the Saskatchewan government and is currently employed as Member Services Manager with Nature Saskatchewan.

Wilson's poetry has been published in numerous literary publications across the country as well as in a number of anthologies including, *Toward 2000: Poetry for the Future, Garden Varieties, Lodestone: Stories By Regina Writers, Compañeros: Writings About Latin America, 200% Cracked Wheat* and *Heading Out: The New Saskatchewan Poets*. In 1997, he won the Sterling Writing Awards prize for poetry. His poetry has also been broadcast on CBC Radio.

In the spring of 1999 Wilson published his third book and one week later, the Saskatchewan writing community lost one of its giants, the poet Anne Szumigalski. Wilson lost a long-time mentor and friend. His third book, *The Long Landscape*, which was edited by Gary Hyland, was nominated for three Saskatchewan Book Awards including Book of the Year. *The Long Landscape* was awarded the City of Regina Book Award.

In May 2002 Wilson became a co-publisher in Hagios Press, a literary press that publishes poetry, fiction, and creative non-fiction. Wilson's duties with the press include administration and editorial work. He edited a new collection of poems by Lorna Crozier entitled *Bones in Their Wings: Ghazals*, which was published in the fall of 2003.

Since 1979 Wilson has lived and worked in Regina. In 1983 he met his life-partner Elizabeth George. They have made their home in the Cathedral Village area of Regina where they live with their two daughters, Emily and Sarah. Wilson is hard at work on his fourth collection of poetry, entitled *Turning Mountain*.

About Writing...

As a poet I connect with the human, with the struggle within our/selves, and the gaps that breath alone cannot bridge. I hope for too much from poetry and I pray I always will. Stanley Kunitz has said, "Poetry is the most difficult, the most solitary, and the most life-enhancing thing that one can do in the world." I somehow cannot expect less from my choice to write poems. —PAUL WILSON

— Appendix A —

CONTRIBUTORS

MARION BECK wrote the biography for the late Norma Dillon. Originally from England, Beck has lived in Regina since 1966. Beck, whose own biography is contained in this volume, became friends with Dillon through poetry.

JANE BILLINGHURST wrote the biography for Grey Owl. She has lived in Saskatoon, Saskatchewan, since the early 1980s and has spent many summer weekends in Prince Albert National Park, Grey Owl's home during his last years. Billinghurst has been an editor for twenty years and in 1999 she published *Grey Owl: The Many Faces of Archie Belaney*.

NIK BURTON wrote the biographies for Liz Allen, Veronica Eddy Brock, Catherine Buckaway, William Conklin, Violet Copeland, Archie Crail, Jean Marie de Moissac, Betty Dorion, Chris Fisher, Thelma Foster, Louise Bernice Halfe, Mary Harelkin Bishop, Jim McLean, S. Padmanab, Jerry Rush, Nancy Senior, Luetta Trehas, and Donald Ward. Burton is the managing editor of Coteau Books, and has worked in the Saskatchewan literary community for most of the last 27 years.

JUDY CHAPMAN, who co-edited the collection of Eli Mandel's poetry with Andrew Stubbs, was born out of a place called Estevan. She wandered around the world to find the world in her own neighborhood. She works at the University of Regina doing what she can to ensure that others have the same opportunity to learn the lessons she did from Saskatchewan. She lives with her daughters and parents and celebrates life in Lumsden, a wonderfully artistic community.

KEITH COMSTOCK wrote the biography for his mother, the late Eileen Comstock. He lives in Regina and works for the Government of Saskatchewan as a policy manager. In addition to helping out on the family farm as much as possible, Keith enjoys golf, photography and spending time poolside with family and friends.

PAUL DENHAM wrote the biographies for Sarah Binks and Edward McCourt. He teaches English at the University of Saskatchewan and is married to Margaret Gail Osachoff; they have two adopted children and a grandson. In his other life, he is a painter, with a particular interest in the Saskatchewan landscape. He served on the editorial board of *NeWest Review* for many years.

JOSEPH HEATH, who wrote the biography for his late mother, Caroline Heath, is associate professor in the Department of Philosophy at the University of Toronto.

TERRENCE HEATH wrote the biography for the late Richard E. Rashley. Heath, whose own biography is included in this volume, was a student and friend of Rashley.

HEATHER HODGSON is an interdisciplinary instructor at the First Nations University of Canada and the editor of the biographies in this volume. She wrote the biographies for Edna Alford, Greg Button, Maria Campbell, Ken Carriere, Harry Dillow, Joanne Gerber, Beth Goobie, Dennis Gruending, Lee Henderson, John V. Hicks, Lewis Horne, Sherry Johnson, Joann McCaig, Farley Mowat, John Newlove, Suzanne North, Maggie Siggins, Wallace Stegner, Betsy Warland, and Joanne Weston.

GARY HYLAND wrote the biography for Andy Suknaski. Hyland, whose own biography is included in this volume, is an arts activist and writer living in Moose Jaw.

CINDY MACKENZIE wrote the biography for Guy Vanderhaeghe. She teaches English at the University of Regina and wrote her M.A. thesis and doctoral dissertation on Emily Dickinson. Editor of the *Concordance to the Letters of Emily Dickinson* (2000), her articles appear in the *Emily Dickinson Bulletin* and the *Emily Dickinson Journal*. Mackenzie is on the Board of the Emily Dickinson International Society and is chair of the Saskatchewan chapter.

DAVE MARGOSHES, a Regina poet and fiction writer whose own biography appears in this book, wrote the biography of Donna Caruso, who had bigger fish to fry that day. The two have collaborated on several literary and video projects.

KEN MITCHELL wrote the biography for Sinclair Ross. Mitchell is a writer of many forms and genres, the most recent being cowboy poetry. He is currently working as a professor of English at the University of Regina.

ORMOND AND BARBARA MITCHELL wrote the biography for W.O. Mitchell, Ormond's father.

LEILAH NADIR wrote the biography for Gregory Scofield. Nadir lives in Vancouver, British Columbia, and works as a publicist for Raincoast Books.

STEFAN RICHES is the son of the late Brenda Riches. He is the author of *Moving Forward, Looking Back: Saskatchewan Rowing in the 20th Century*. He is currently living in Taiwan, where he is teaching English, working on a novel, and coaching hockey.

NICHOLAS RUDDICK, who wrote the biography for Ross King, is a professor of English, President's Scholar 2002–04, and director of the Humanities Research Institute at the University of Regina.

BERNARD SELINGER wrote the biography for Gail Bowen. Selinger teaches in the English Department of the First Nations University of Canada (formerly Saskatchewan Indian Federated College) in Regina.

MICHELE SEREDA wrote the biography for Kay Parley. Sereda is the artistic director of Curtain Razors, a company that focuses on the development of new Canadian theatre through various media to discover new ways of telling stories. An accomplished performer and director in theatre, film, radio, and TV, she also conducts workshops for schools, organizations, and universities.

ANDREW STUBBS, who co-wrote the biography of Eli Mandel, teaches writing and rhetoric in the English Department at the University of Regina.

PENNY VAN TOORN, who wrote the biography of Rudy Wiebe, teaches in the English Department at the University of Sydney, Australia. She is the author of *Rudy Wiebe and the Historicity of the Word* (1995).

PATRICIA WHITNEY wrote the biography for Joan Givner. Whitney, formerly co-ordinator of Women's Studies at the University of Prince Edward Island, now devotes her time to writing and lecturing at the Institute of Women's Studies at the University of Ottawa.

PAUL WILSON wrote the biographies for Hilary Clark, Mildred Rose, and Anne Szumigalski. Wilson is a poet, publisher and arts administrator who lives in Regina with his wife Elizabeth George and their two daughters Emily and Sarah. He knew Anne Szumigalski for nearly twenty years.

— Appendix B —

INSTRUCTORS WHO FOSTERED WRITING IN SASKATCHEWAN

Edna Alford, Liz Allen, David Arnason, Ven Begamudré, Warren Bennett, Steven Michael Berzensky, Sandra Birdsell, Clark Blaise, Di Brandt, Bonnie Burnard, Phil Campagna, Warren Cariou, David Carpenter, Dennis Cooley, Lorna Crozier, Robert Currie, Marilyn Dumont, Floyd Favel, Brian Fawcett, Gary Geddes, Dave Glaze, Douglas Glover, Beth Goobie, Lee Gowan, Susan Goyette, Susan Andrews Grace, Regine Haensel, Phil Hall, Robert Harlow, Paul Hiebert, Gerry Hill, Jack Hodgins, Hugh Hood, Gary Hyland, Paulette Jiles, Treena Kortje Carson, Janice Kulyk Keefer, Myrna Kostash, Judith Krause, Pat Krause, Robert Kroetsch, Lydia Kwa, Patrick Lane, Shelley Leedahl, Tim Lilburn, Gordon Lish, Alison Lohans, Kevin Major, Eli Mandel, Dave Margoshes, Daphne Marlatt, Don McKay, Ken Mitchell, W.O. Mitchell, Frank Moher, Daniel David Moses, Erin Mouré, John Murrell, John Newlove, Rosemary Nixon, Kit Pearson, Elizabeth Philips, Sharon Pollock, William Robertson, Leon Rooke, Joe Rosenblatt, Allan Safarik, Andreas Schroeder, Gregory Scofield, Carol Shields, Gerry Shikatani, Reg Silvester, Lois Simmie, Robin Skelton, Arthur Slade, Fred Stenson, Gertrude Story, Rosemary Sullivan, Anne Szumigalski, Sharon Thesen, Jane Urquhart, Seán Virgo, Fred Wah, Betsy Warland, Dianne Warren, Rudy Wiebe, David Williamson, and others....